UP FROM THE DEPTHS

UP FROM THE DEPTHS

HERMAN MELVILLE, LEWIS MUMFORD,
AND REDISCOVERY IN DARK TIMES

AARON SACHS

PRINCETON UNIVERSITY PRESS

PRINCETON AND OXFORD

Published by Princeton University Press
41 William Street, Princeton, New Jersey 08540
99 Banbury Road, Oxford OX2 6JX

press.princeton.edu

All Rights Reserved

Library of Congress Control Number: 2022933337
ISBN 978-0-691-21541-9
ISBN (e-book) 978-0-691-23694-0

British Library Cataloging-in-Publication Data is available

Editorial: Eric Crahan and Barbara Shi
Production Editorial: Jill Harris
Text Design: Karl Spurzem
Jacket Design: Bárbara Abbês
Production: Danielle Amatucci
Publicity: Maria Whelan and Kate Farquhar-Thomson

Jacket image by channarongsds / Adobe Stock

This book has been composed in Arno Pro

Printed on acid-free paper. ∞

Printed in the United States of America

10 9 8 7 6 5 4 3 2 1

For Christine—again, always.

Yea, foolish mortals, Noah's flood is not yet subsided. . . . Panting and snorting like a mad battle steed that has lost its rider, the masterless ocean overruns the globe.

—HERMAN MELVILLE, 1851

What has happened in history before, may happen again: after disintegration, renewal.

—LEWIS MUMFORD, 1951

CONTENTS

ILLUSTRATIONS

PREFACE

Melville, Mumford, Modernity

This is a story of two modern wanderers, convinced of their aloneness but still looking for connection. Lewis Mumford, born in New York a few years after Herman Melville died there, had the chance to look backward and find a kindred spirit: as of the mid-1920s, only one biography of Melville had been published, and Mumford decided to write the second, helping to bolster the so-called Melville Revival.[1] That kind of rediscovery can be a saving grace. But it takes work.

Modernity, after all, has been full of discontinuity and disorientation. The pace of change—the slippage of time—leaves people unmoored in space. Neighborhoods are razed—neighbors move away—the world is remade. In modern cities, there is the exhilaration of possibility, of fluid identity, of new experiences—the buzz of constant encounter. There is also the reality of crowding, pollution, poverty, injustice, mechanization, alienation. "To be modern," as the philosopher Marshall Berman put it, "is to find ourselves in an environment that promises us adventure, power, joy, growth, transformation of ourselves and the world—and, at the same time, that threatens to destroy everything we have, everything we know, everything we are." To be modern is sometimes to feel in touch, tapped in, attuned; it is also to feel lonely, inward, nervous, overwhelmed. Modernity has delivered movies, rockets, computers, cell phones, and vaccines, which politicians and business leaders tout as clear evidence of Progress—in part to distract people from other modern realities, like nuclear bombs, toxic chemicals, factory farms, sweatshops, and global warming.[2]

Some traumas are more acute than others, but it may make sense to think of modern times as generally traumatic.[3] We repeat many of the same, doomed experiments. And we often fail to notice the repetition. In certain dark times, when change comes fast and our challenges seem brand-new, it can feel as though we have been completely cut off from the wisdom of history.[4]

Melville understood modern trauma, which is partly why we know him as America's great nineteenth-century tragedian.[5] Just over a hundred years ago, though, almost no one had heard of him. Talk about discontinuity: in 1850, he was one of the best-known writers in the western world, but by 1900 he was utterly forgotten. It was only between 1919 (the centennial of his birth) and 1951 (the centennial of Moby-Dick) that Melville was rediscovered and ultimately canonized. Apparently, American culture in the 1920s, 30s, and 40s had need of a forebear with a dark vision. Publishers put out new editions of even Melville's most difficult and obscure works; scholars produced several more biographies and critical studies; and college students started to read Melville as often as they read Walt Whitman, who had, let's say, a rosier view of America's accomplishments and prospects. The Melville Revival was part of a broad push toward revisionism, toward a fuller, more honest reckoning with the past—which, in turn, helped Americans reckon with the wars and economic panics and technological upheavals and vicious social divisions of their present.[6]

These were also the decades when Lewis Mumford made his reputation, not only as a Melville biographer but also as an urban theorist, cultural critic, and historian of technology. Though Mumford's is no longer a household name, back in 1951—the year he published the final installment of his unique four-volume masterwork, The Renewal of Life—he was one of the foremost public intellectuals in the United States. And his influence endured for three more active decades. Your attitude toward ecology, modern architecture, and even social media has probably been shaped by Mumford's eerily prescient writings.[7] Today, in what many people are experiencing as a new dark age, full of foreboding over disease outbreaks, climate change, economic inequality, racial and religious bigotry, technological overload, refugee crises, neo-fascism, and near-constant warfare, it is time for a Mumford Revival. History provides perspective; perspective can help us work toward renewal. True hope, as the historian Christopher Lasch noted, "rests on confidence not so much in the future as in the past": history shows that better times have generally been achieved through the open-eyed efforts of those who push on despite the number of times they have already failed.[8]

Mumford is relevant today precisely because his writings confronted one of the bleakest eras in American history, spanning the anxious aftermath of World War I; the Great Depression; World War II, in which his son was killed; the invention of the atomic bomb; and the narrow viciousness of McCarthyism. Modernity was not looking particularly attractive, and Mumford analyzed its traumatic tendencies with an eloquent frankness, hoping ultimately to redirect it into more humane formulations, like Garden Cities. And, perhaps counterintuitively, it was Melville, more than any other intellectual or artistic ancestor, who helped him cope with his own overwhelmedness and then develop his alternative vision. The work Mumford did on Melville nearly killed him: he had a yearlong nervous breakdown after finishing his biography in 1929, and he placed the blame squarely on Melville's desolate outlook. Yet he remained obsessed with and inspired by Melville for the rest of his life, referring to him constantly in both his public and private writings.[9]

One of the key reasons Melville's legacy turned out to be so generative for Mumford is that he recognized his predecessor's demons as being not just personal but political. Rather than a melancholy, old-fashioned man left behind by the fast-moving world, Melville was a writer keenly engaged with the concerns of his day. In chapter 1 of *Moby-Dick*, "Loomings," our narrator, who famously tells us to call him Ishmael, goes to sea specifically because he can't stand modern life in New York City, where everyone is "tied to counters, nailed to benches, clinched to desks."[10] Twenty-first-century readers encountering Melville tend to see his novels as timeless and metaphysical (with Ishmael standing in for any outcast since the Bible), but for Mumford they were anchored in the mid-nineteenth century—in the rise of a stultifying new labor regime, for instance—and so they helped him think about what had changed and what hadn't between Melville's time and his own. Often, the resonances were surprising. The modern art of rediscovery requires frequent pauses and head-turnings, a willingness to flash back and forth in time, an openness to the uncanny.[11]

Certainly, a book like *Moby-Dick* plumbed universal questions of fate and evil and the indifference of nature, but it was also about Ishmael's peculiarly modern kind of ennui, his feeling of alienation from the environment and disconnection from the past. To Mumford, *Moby-Dick* succeeded not because of its evocation of grand tragedy but because it captured the tension between "the two dissevered halves of the modern world and the modern self—its positive, practical, scientific, externalized self, bent on conquest and knowledge, and its imaginative, ideal half, bent on the transposition of conflict into art, and power into humanity."[12]

Ishmael, an archetypal modern hero, is torn apart and tormented by modernity, but survives to swim in its currents, buoyed by modernity's own quirky opportunities for solidarity. Aboard the *Pequod*, named for a "celebrated" but supposedly "extinct" tribe of Indians, he feels a deep bond with all his diverse, worldly "co-laborers," despite his pained awareness that modern history has drawn stark lines between them, has labeled some of them conquerors and others conquered. The injustice and helplessness are overwhelming—all the more so because Americans were supposed to be enjoying a land and an era of equal opportunity—but at least the whale hunters, enmeshed in modern commercial networks spanning the globe, are joined together in their "fatal goal" and thus "welded into oneness."[13] They know they'll all go down together; at sea, a sense of doom provides some common ground, however watery.

For many years, I associated my own sense of cultural trauma with global warming and the dawning of the digital age, two seemingly new trends that I became acutely aware of in 1992, when I graduated from college. Two decades later, though, as I dug deeper into Mumford's life and work, I started seeing eerie continuities between my peer group (aimless Gen-Xers) and Mumford's (the Lost Generation). "One further effect of our closer time co-ordination and our instantaneous communication," Mumford wrote—*in 1934*—"must be noted here: broken time and broken attention."[14] How much had really changed between the 1930s and the twenty-first century, between, say, the Great Depression of Mumford's prime and the Great Recession of 2008? Could the internet have been any more jarring than electricity, telephones, and petroleum-powered airplanes? Didn't modernity always seem to have a kind of unjust and catastrophic logic, with constant motion and relentless acceleration leading to ever more crashes and clashes, to destruction on an incomprehensible scale?[15]

And then I came to understand that Mumford's investigation of the past had caused him to ask similar questions about modernity's continuity amid discontinuity—that the trauma of World War I had not made sense to him until he studied the trauma of the Civil War—that he could see his own era clearly only after he had trained himself to look through Melville's eyes. We are still living with the consequences of the changes that Melville started to notice: the shift to industrialism and fossil fuels, the rise of unfathomable financial systems, the disintegration of local communities and ecological relationships. So this book, though grounded in Mumford's career in the 1920s, 30s, and 40s, when he was working on *The Renewal of Life*, takes regular trips back to Melville's life and times, during which Melville himself also regularly looked backward. And this book's design is also meant to help us look ahead to the new/old crises of our present day and to the visions of the future that the past might help us generate.[16] The alternating Melville and Mumford chapters, the jump cuts between the nineteenth century and the twentieth, are meant especially to capture the continuity that persists in the face of undeniable change, to provide the visceral experience of suddenly hearing history's uncanny echoes.[17]

Over the last two hundred years, continuity has gotten harder and harder to discern. Historians will never agree about exactly when the modern period began in the West, but there's a fairly clear consensus that perceptions of time started to shift drastically in the Revolutionary period of the late eighteenth century. Before that, a certain amount of continuity was simply assumed: people largely experienced time in cyclical terms, through the turning of the seasons, through holiday festivals and rites of passage, through planting and harvesting and letting land lie fallow, through weeks of labor and sabbath days of rest. There was a comfort to these cycles, especially during dark times. Everyone figured that the wheel would eventually come around again, that at least some of the dominant trends of the past would be restored. But the leaders of the Enlightenment shifted people's gaze away from the past and toward the future, insisting on the notion of steady, linear Progress. And by the time Melville was born, in the wake of the American and French revolutions, Progress had come to mean not the extension of a continuum but a series of great, disjunctive leaps. In fact, the idea of revolutionary shifts seemed to define the new era; change was so constant and rapid that history felt potentially irretrievable and, in any case, largely irrelevant.[18]

Since then, the pace of change has only accelerated. Western society is more disconnected from the past than ever before. The Covid-19 pandemic was certainly a shock, but only an ahistorical culture could refer to it so relentlessly as "unprecedented." Both Melville and Mumford would have scoffed at the word, because they both came to understand that, despite the seeming dominance of change, the past is always interwoven with the present. Some of our current challenges—climate change, perhaps most importantly—have novel elements, but it's helpful to remember that past societies and individuals have confronted parallel threats. When Covid-19 started to dominate our reality in the spring of 2020, many historians wondered why we didn't just move our activities outside, as people tended to do, with good success, during the flu pandemic of 1918–19 (which Mumford lived through). Much had changed in the intervening century, and the pandemics were not exactly the same, but in both cases the simple strategies of mask-wearing and physical distancing made a huge difference—at least, in communities where leaders encouraged a willingness to sacrifice for the common good.[19]

This book insists on a dialectical relationship between change and continuity. Both Mumford and Melville have their own chronological arc, showing their development as thinkers and writers and husbands and fathers. But the juxtaposed resonances between their lives matter just as much. Taking a cue from modernists like Virginia Woolf, who was one of Mumford's favorite writers and who experimented with time and nonlinear narration in nearly all of her novels, I want to emphasize the persistent significance of the past without denying the reality of dizzying shifts.[20] And like Melville and Mumford themselves, I want to critique modernity on its own terms, without romanticizing simpler times, when men were men and stories had a predictable form.[21] The deepest experiences of rediscovery are simultaneously bolstering and unsettling.

Mumford did not turn to Woolf as often as he turned to Melville, but he did note his enduring appreciation for Woolf's 1927 novel *To the Lighthouse*.[22] The three-part story is seemingly dominated by its first and last sections, each one quite long, yet each covering just one day. The middle section, entitled "Time Passes," uses only a few pages to cover ten years. During that decade, World War I comes and goes, a few key characters die (in parenthetical asides), and the islanded house where most of the action takes place gradually degenerates, despite the noble efforts of an elderly woman who scrubs the floors and brushes away the cobwebs. Time passes; entropy rules. Everything, it seems, has changed. Yet when the remaining characters reconvene at the house, it is their shared past that dominates their consciousness. All around them, as Mumford put it, they see "layer upon layer" of history, bursting with a "sense of time" that somehow includes both erosion and accretion, both unpredictability and steadiness. Woolf reminds us that although the beam of the lighthouse flashes and flickers in patterns that can be hard to interpret, it is in fact revolving at a regular rate. "There is a coherence in things," thinks one character, who will soon be dead, "a stability; something, she meant, is immune from change, and shines out (she glanced at the window with its ripple effect of reflected lights) in the face of the flowing, the fleeting, the spectral, like a ruby; so that again tonight she had the feeling she had had once today, already, of peace, of rest. Of such moments, she thought, the thing is made that endures."[23] Yet: they are only moments; they themselves are fleeting. They will need to be rediscovered.

The seizing of such moments is especially precious in a culture that fetishizes Progress and innovation and an orientation toward the future. Modernity feels traumatic to many people precisely because one of the hallmarks of trauma is a sense of temporal rupture: you face a horror, and from now on everything will be different. Those who study trauma suggest that it's counterproductive to imagine a full recovery: you can never be the person you were before. Rather, the goal is to dwell with the horror as calmly as possible. But the process of working through your trauma may well involve rediscovering older parts of yourself, which, after all, are never completely erased. There is often solace in that rediscovery, even if it's only temporary. And that holds for societies as well as for individuals.[24]

Both Melville and Mumford, in their obsession with seeing the past in the present, remind us of the communal obligation to endure. My hope is to rediscover their capacity for realism, connection, and orientation, amid modernity's ongoing traumas.[25]

UP FROM THE DEPTHS

CHAPTER 1

Loomings (1927–29)

Do you know any optimistic historians? There aren't many. Spend almost any length of time studying the past, and the rosiest conclusion you'll come to is that our record is, well, mixed. Every time we take a hundred steps forward, we take ninety-nine back, and it's unclear where the next one is going to land.

For every scholar willing to claim that, say, the 1950s were a "great" era in American history, when the income gap closed and opportunity knocked at everyone's door, a hundred others will remind you that not everyone had a door, that there was a war in Korea, that some veterans were drinking too much and beating their wives, that women were kept from the workforce, that African Americans were kept from voting, that children grew up with air-raid drills, that artists were blacklisted and intellectuals jailed for controversial opinions, that synagogues were bombed, that radiation and toxic chemicals were seeping into everyone's bodies.

But pessimism does not exclude the possibility of hope—because history teaches that things do shift. The most dour among us will argue that all change just represents entropy, the inevitable drift toward further chaos. But then why didn't Nature reclaim our cities centuries ago? Yes, we are part of the chaos, but we also sometimes struggle against it: we create culture, make meaning, insist on ideals like liberty, equality, and solidarity, sometimes with startling, unpredictable success.

Lewis Mumford's first book, published in 1922, just before he turned twenty-seven, was *The Story of Utopias*. It was, of course, a story of failure, because Utopia is an impossible dream. But the point was the value of the dreaming, the restless striving toward collective thriving, the determined envisioning of alternatives to hierarchy and domination. If there was no such thing as a perfect place, there could at least be a "good place," which Mumford sometimes referred to as "*eu*topia," drawing on the Greek root in words like eulogy and euphonious. And he argued that our collective "will-to-eutopia" was in fact the only thing preventing society's disintegration. Predictably, for the rest of his life, Mumford would have to fend off the label of dreamy Utopian, and that drove him crazy. In his 1940 book, *Faith for Living*, he included an entire chapter called "Life Is Better than Utopia," and when he issued a new edition of *The Story of Utopias* in 1962 he cantankerously reminded his readers that "my utopia is actual life." What he always returned to was the need, in any half-decent society, to protect people's ability to protest and resist, to contest dominant values, which so often serve merely to keep the powerful in power: "Unlike utopian writers, I must find a place in any proposed scheme for challenge and opposition and conflict."[1]

In short, to be a eutopian meant to believe in the constant, open renegotiation of what the good society should be, in the face of stiffening conventions and constraints—meant embracing hope, despite ever-looming "Ordeals of Reality." That's another chapter title, from the very last book Mumford published, just before the onset of dementia; it referred to the period when he was writing his Melville biography, from 1927 to 1929.

He had started work on the Melville project under congenial circumstances: summer, Martha's Vineyard, with his wife, Sophia, and their two-year-old son, in "a shabby little shack" they had rented, "on a lonely heath." The sea was their "constant companion," washing against the cliffs, "whispering or roaring, soothing or threatening, advancing or retreating"; nearby was an ancient, tree-lined farm worked by two elderly women. Mumford delighted in the flow and ebb, the stimulation and repose of the landscape: "a ridge of sandy cliffs, skirting the shores for a couple of miles until they sank into dunes, marked the abrupt end of the land, and at the bottom of these cliffs we sunned ourselves and bathed."[2]

It was a refuge, a retreat: many members of the Lost Generation escaped the trauma of the Great War by immersing themselves in nature and seeking inspiration from the past. Up to this point, Mumford had been ensconced in New York City, and he still lived there in the fall,

FIGURE 1. Lewis and Geddes Mumford in 1926 or 1927.

winter, and spring, but in his writing, throughout the 1920s, he had already begun to search historical landscapes for ways of transcending his life amid skyscrapers and offsetting his society's fixation on power and conquest. Unlike most 1920s intellectuals, though, who generally looked to Europe for alternatives to the conservatism dominating the United States, Mumford dove ever deeper into American cultural history.[3]

After *The Story of Utopias* he published *Sticks and Stones: A Study of American Architecture and Civilization* (1924), in which he proposed the classic Massachusetts village as the embodiment of a highly "intelligent partnership between the earth and man."[4] Then, in his breakthrough book, *The Golden Day: A Study in American Literature and Culture* (1926), Mumford wrote even more yearningly of old New England, celebrating the efflorescence of imagination in the 1840s and 1850s, noting the outdoor energy of antebellum poetry and prose, the embrace of both science and art, modernity and timelessness. *The Golden Day* established writers like Emerson, Thoreau, Whitman, Hawthorne, Poe, and Melville as the archetypal American geniuses, sparking a new scholarly movement to appreciate what we now call "The American Renaissance."[5] The clear heroes of that book were Emerson and Whitman, and either could easily have served as the subject of a new biography. But Mumford chose Melville.

Perhaps he wanted to embrace tragedy as openly as possible, to shake off the public's perception that he was primarily a nostalgic utopian. Perhaps he truly craved a dose of darkness, found it exhilarating to follow Melville in a "flight . . . over an unconquered and perhaps an unconquerable abyss." Or perhaps he wanted to redeem Melville: "his perplexities, his defiances, his torments, his questions, even his failures, all have a meaning for us."[6]

Certainly, he wished to contribute to the revival that had been initiated by Raymond Weaver's book of 1921, *Herman Melville: Mariner and Mystic.* Mumford agreed with Weaver that Melville was "distinctly modern" and that his tragic sensibility was deeply relevant to the post–Great War world.[7] But he was also eager to revise Weaver's accounting of the second half of Melville's life.

To Weaver, the great author's final four decades, from 1851 (after *Moby-Dick* was published in November) until his death in 1891, seemed an utter waste—years of bitter withdrawal, disillusioned sterility, perhaps even mental illness. Yes, he wrote a few poems, but, as Weaver put it, "his signal literary achievement was done. The rest, if not silence, was whisper." After devoting 350 pages to that early achievement, Weaver tacked on one final chapter, called "The Long Quietus," to cover Melville's whispering defeat, even referring to *The Confidence-Man*, published in 1857, as "a posthumous work."[8]

Mumford read Weaver's book in the fall of 1927, and paused in his research notes to record his outrage: "Weaver, to support his melodramatic thesis, puts forty years into forty pages."[9] When Mumford's biography of Melville came out, it gave three times as much space to those final four decades, and the last chapter of the book was called, pointedly, "The Flowering Aloe."[10] Indeed, Mumford insisted not only that Melville had written some beautiful, poignant poetry in his later years but also that he had stumbled onto a kind of "peace": especially during the 1870s and 1880s, "Melville found life, not good or bad, malicious or forbearing, true or false. Something more important had happened: he found it livable."[11]

Mumford had been through his own crucible from about 1915 until 1925, when he was in his twenties, struggling with his marriage, with vague but debilitating illnesses, with his conviction that he was destined to write plays and poetry, with a tangled relationship to his overbearing intellectual mentor, Patrick Geddes. But once he started work on *The Golden Day* and once Sophia gave birth to their first child (named Geddes) in July 1925, Mumford came into a new confidence. He saw Melville as the ultimate challenge. Until that point, Mumford believed, "I had never pushed myself to my limits," but by confronting Melville's "dark life story," he thought he could convey "the lesson of a noble defiance."[12] On Martha's Vineyard, in the summer of 1927, islanded, surrounded by the sounds of the sea, he took great pleasure in getting "a drenching in the nakedness of natural scenes, natural forces, natural acts."[13] He seemed to assume that his "sanguine disposition," his "naturally buoyant temperament," would help him resurface after he went plunging after Melville into "those cold black depths, the depths of the sunless ocean."[14]

But the writing process is fickle, unpredictable: "I could not guess then that Melville's tragic exploration of his depths would in time unbare parts of my own life which I had never been ready to face."[15] By the fall of 1928, as Mumford was finishing the biography, he found himself grappling with "problems, pressures, bafflements, and emotional crosscurrents of my own similar to those I was probing in Melville."[16] Apparently there was a "deeper parallel" than he had realized: he had found a "brother spirit."[17] And this sudden identification would evolve into his lifelong obsession not only with Melville but with the darkness of his own soul, and of human history.

As both the year and his book drew to a close, Mumford found that his "energies were badly depleted," and he began hoping he would fall ill, just so he would have an excuse to rest.[18] "In a verse I addressed to Melville . . . , I pictured my relation to him, 'a sick man,' as that of a nurse, watching by his bedside, tending him through the fever that brought him almost to death. In that office, I poured my sunlight upon him, only to find myself being swallowed up by his blackness, falling with him into chasms no light of mine could ever penetrate. Before that vigil was over, I wrote, 'the weakened nurse became the patient: I watched the fever take possession of my bones.'"[19] Even his marriage began to falter again, as Sophia suffered a miscarriage and expressed jealousy over Lewis's attentions to their neighbor Helen Ascher, a "dark, sensuous" woman (Lewis's words) who lived nearby both in New York and on Martha's Vineyard and who was married but known for having many lovers.[20] And then, as Mumford put it, "with a kind of Melvillian fatality both Sophia and I from November on went through the most desolate year of our whole lifetime until our son's death in 1944."[21] As Mumford paced along New York avenues, he sometimes "composed obituaries, nice ones, written in the New Republic style, about myself."[22] It was, as Ishmael would say, "a damp, drizzly November" in his soul.[23]

By May 1929, Mumford should have been celebrating his book's publication, but instead, at the age of thirty-three, he was reading Dante and imagining himself lost in the darkest of forests—in a purgatory. His son had been in the hospital for months after barely surviving surgery for a double mastoid, which had come close to infecting his brain, and Lewis would be haunted by the boy's feverish wails for the rest of his life. He felt he had experienced "one of the deepest torments a human being can know: his utter helplessness, as in a nightmare, to save the person he loves from mortal injury."[24] Now he was actively considering an affair with Helen, and he suspected that Sophia was already seeing another man: "we felt inwardly estranged, with nothing in common except our distance from each other." By July, the adjective "Melvillian" had entered his lexicon to stay (though with two different spellings). "The inner me has never been worse," he wrote, in his private notes. "For the last few days I have been conscious of a bleak, Melvillean feeling of despair: vast, blank, senseless, but unaccountably desperate. His image is bad medicine; and when I am feeling down I begin to regret that I had anything to do with him."[25]

Melville, it turned out, was Mumford's white whale. But did that make him Ishmael or Ahab?

The biography did reasonably well at first, and was selected for the Literary Guild's new paperback series. That provided a nice windfall. But sales dried up a few months later. On October 19, Mumford turned thirty-four. On October 29, the stock market collapsed, launching what would become the Great Depression. No one cared about white whales after Black Tuesday.

CHAPTER 2

The Whiteness of the Page
(1856–65)

In early 1857, still alive, Melville published *The Confidence-Man: His Masquerade*, a work of darkly tangled prose. It came out on April Fool's Day, also the day on which all of the novel's action takes place—but no one seemed to get the joke. A frank, gentlemanly swindler aboard the Mississippi steamboat *Fidèle* (Faithful) offers various passengers their heart's desire—offers, essentially, to save their lives—for a small fee or a temporary loan. The reading public wasn't buying. Reviewers suggested that it was Melville himself who was the con artist.[1]

Late that summer, Melville's publisher, surprised by what came to be known as the Panic of 1857, went bankrupt—along with a number of other book and magazine publishers. It looked like the national economy might need years to recover. Melville's net profit from *The Confidence-Man* was zero.[2]

Financial troubles had been vexing Melville throughout the 1850s. He wrote furiously, to keep pace with his debts. But the utter failure of *The Confidence-Man*, combined with the general weakness of the publishing industry, spurred him to a painful acknowledgment: he could no longer pretend that he was making a living as a writer. His masquerade was over.

Between 1846 and 1857, Melville had published ten books: *Typee: A Peep at Polynesian Life* (1846); *Omoo: A Narrative of Adventures in the South Seas* (1847); *Mardi: And a Voyage Thither* (1849); *Redburn, His First Voyage* (1849); *White-Jacket; or, The World in a Man-of-War* (1850);

Moby-Dick; or, The Whale (1851); *Pierre; or, The Ambiguities* (1852); *Israel Potter: His Fifty Years of Exile* (1855); *The Piazza Tales* (1856); and *The Confidence-Man* (1857).

Between 1858 and 1865, Melville published: nothing.

In the famous chapter of *Moby-Dick* called "The Whiteness of the Whale," Melville wrote with horror of the "dumb blankness, full of meaning, in a wide landscape of snows—a colorless, all-color atheism from which we shrink."[3] I picture him shrinking at the farmhouse he and his family owned in the Berkshires from 1850 until 1863, staring out at the fields and forests and mountains during the long New England winter. Sometime during that span of years, Melville crossed the narrow line between faith and doubt. A blanketing of fresh snow can soften a landscape, can seem clean and calming; or it can drain away living color, so that the countryside becomes dull, pale, sickly. It depends on your perspective.

Mumford would be the first to insist that Melville "did not surrender; for he kept on writing to the end of his days."[4] But *The Confidence-Man* clearly represented a crisis of confidence. The book itself, Mumford thought, revealed that "sweetness and morality had become for Melville the greatest of frauds."[5] Later, in a letter to a friend, Mumford called the novel a "product of [Melville's] madness . . . , written with only sand and thirst for inspiration."[6] Mumford believed that "by 1858 Melville had regained possession of himself," but for a long time afterward he would be prone to depression and violent mood swings, which tormented his family.[7]

Melville's wife, Elizabeth, usually called Lizzie, had grown deeply concerned about Herman by the summer of 1856, when she wrote to her father, Lemuel Shaw, the chief justice of the Massachusetts Supreme Court, for help. Shaw responded with money for Herman to go on a long trip and an invitation for Lizzie and the kids to move in with him in Boston. In truth, Justice Shaw already knew about Herman's tendencies: "When he is deeply engaged in one of his literary works, he confines him to hard study many hours in the day—with little or no exercise, & this especially in winter for a great many days together. He probably thus overworks himself & brings on severe nervous affections."[8]

Melville had been filling pages obsessively for eleven years, and that had taken a toll. For some time already there had been eye trouble and chronic back pain; various family members had witnessed his "ugly attacks," and he often seemed "dispirited and ill."[9]

We have all these testimonials, and yet we know hardly anything precise about what Melville was feeling or how he interacted with his family. Was he becoming unhinged in 1856? He himself had no comment—at least none that has survived. But he was certainly bitter about his finances and the reception of his books. Desperate to repay a substantial loan that spring, he had started to auction off precious parcels of the land surrounding his house. For a man accustomed to daily circumambulations of his estate, during which he could be seen "patting" various trees "upon the back," such an act of liquidation might easily intensify the scorn he harbored for the money economy, and also for himself.[10] That scorn is at the heart of *The Confidence-Man*: the novel dissects a society in which every interaction is an attempt at extortion or exploitation, in which consumers and investors are more likely to support new products like the Omni-Balsamic Reinvigorator or the Protean Easy Chair than to engage with deep meditations on faith. If only, as the novelist Jonathan Franzen once wrote, Melville had been able "to say to himself, when he was struggling to support Lizzie and their kids: Hey, if worse comes to worst, I can always teach writing."[11]

What he could do, thanks to his father-in-law, was sail for Europe and then the Holy Land. Did he actually want to go? I find it impossible to tell. Did he enjoy himself? His travel journal is, well, mixed. The years 1856 and 1857 seem to have been particularly trying for Melville. But the bulk of the evidence we have about his adult life suggests that for at least a couple of decades he quite regularly swung back and forth between boisterous affability and bleak, despairing withdrawal. Did he suffer from what we might recognize today as some form of bipolar disorder? Possibly, but if so, it was not severe, for he worked his entire life and stayed married for forty-four years.

In early October 1856, having delivered the manuscript of *The Confidence-Man*, Melville prowled around New York City for a few days before boarding the steamship *Glasgow*, and he seems to have relished the break in his writing routine. His friend Evert Duyckinck described him as "right hearty" and "charged to the muzzle with his sailor metaphysics and jargon of things unknowable"; the two passed more than one "good stirring evening" together, during which Melville appeared to be "warming like an old sailor over the supper."[12]

Once he arrived overseas, though, and renewed his friendship with Nathaniel Hawthorne, who was serving as a diplomat in England, Melville seemed, in Hawthorne's words, "much overshadowed," as though he "did not anticipate much pleasure in his rambles, for that spirit of adventure is gone out of him."[13]

Pleasures did come, eventually: "Beautiful morning. Blue sea & sky. Warm as May. Spanish coast in sight. Mountains, snow capped, always so Captain says. Mate comes out with straw hat. Shirt sleeves. Threw open my coat.—Such weather as one might have in Paridise. Pacific."[14]

But, reading through Melville's journal, one might be tempted to say that such pleasures were, in the end, overshadowed: "I am emphatically alone, & begin to feel like Jonah. . . . Ride over mouldy plain to Dead Sea. . . . Foam on beach & pebbles like slaver of mad dog—smarting bitter of the water,—carried the bitter in my mouth all day—bitterness of life—thought of all bitter things—Bitter is it to be poor & bitter, to be reviled. . . . Whitish mildew pervading whole tracts of landscape—bleached—leprosy—encrustation of curses—old cheese—bones of rocks,—crunched, knawed, & mumbled. . . . The unleavened nakedness of desolation—whitish ashes."[15]

Hawthorne had peered into his friend's soul. On one of the days they spent together, they had taken a long walk along the Irish Sea; eventually, as Hawthorne noted, they "sat down in a hollow among the sand hills (sheltering ourselves from the high, cool wind) and smoked a cigar." It was November. Melville summed up: "Sands & grass. Wild & desolate. . . . Good talk." Hawthorne was more expansive: "Melville, as he always does, began to reason of Providence and futurity, and of everything that lies beyond human ken, and informed me that he had 'pretty much made up his mind to be annihilated'; but still he does not seem to rest in that anticipation; and, I think, will never rest until he gets hold of a definite belief. It is strange how he persists—and has persisted ever since I knew him, and probably long before—in wandering to-and-fro over these deserts, as dismal and monotonous as the sand hills amid which we were sitting. He can neither believe, nor be comfortable in his unbelief; and he is too honest and courageous not to try to do one or the other. If he were a religious man, he would be one of the most truly religious and reverential; he has a very high and noble nature, and better worth immortality than the rest of us."[16]

When Melville returned home, he took up residence again with his family in the Berkshires. But instead of trying to compose and sell more obscure novels, he decided to go on the speaker circuit—in part because domestic life had always been so fraught for him. Each winter (the lecture season), between November 1857 and February 1860, he gave dozens of talks, throughout the Northeast and as far west as Milwaukee, on topics ranging from "Ancient Statuary" to "The South Sea." One reporter noted in awe that the audience showed a "continuous merriment" in response to Melville's "facetious tone"; indeed, in his role as a "humorist," Melville had even managed to get his listeners to applaud his scathing criticism of the U.S. government for the atrocities it had committed against Native peoples. A different reviewer called his style "nervous and vigorous, yet easily flowing, and falling constantly into the most melodious cadences." Yet most of the people who recorded their reactions to Melville's lectures complained that he was a hopeless mumbler: "his delivery was . . . monotonous and indistinct"; "the words came through his moustache about as loud and with as much force as the creaking of a field mouse through a thick hedge."[17] It was not a sustainable career.

When his old creative urges came back to him, during these years, he turned to poetry, and by 1860 he had finished enough poems to make a short volume—which no publisher would touch.

That spring, he transferred ownership of the Berkshire estate to Judge Shaw. In March 1861, when President Lincoln took office, Melville went to Washington to try to get some sort of government appointment, perhaps the type of consulship that had served Hawthorne so well in his middle age. He shook Lincoln's hand but came away with no job. In November 1862, he suffered traumatic injuries when his horse came

FIGURE 2. Melville in 1860.

unhitched from his wagon, and he "fell with his back in the hollow of the frozen road."[18] A year later, he and his family moved to New York City, to stay.

The Civil War had started the month after Melville met Lincoln, and the pain he felt from that vicious conflict, on top of his many personal struggles, nearly broke him. Strangely, though, it also broke him out of his silence. In 1866, the year after the fighting ended, as the so-called Era of Reconstruction got under way, Melville published *Battle-Pieces, and Aspects of the War*, a brand-new collection of poetry.

And then, once again, he retreated. The next book he published came out a decade later: *Clarel: A Poem and Pilgrimage in the Holy Land*. It revisited the bitterness and doubt of his trip abroad in 1856–57, his confrontation with Jerusalem's "blanched hills" and "blank, blank towers."[19]

Throughout his career, Lewis Mumford cited a particular passage from Melville's novel *White-Jacket*—in reference to Melville's life, in reference to his own life, even as a kind of universal truth. "But, sailor or landsman," Melville had written, "there is some sort of a Cape Horn for all. Boys! beware of it; prepare for it in time. Gray-beards! thank God it is passed. And ye lucky livers, to whom, by some rare fatality, your Cape Horns are placid as Lake Lemans, flatter not yourselves that good luck is judgment and discretion; for all the yolk in your eggs, you might have foundered and gone down, had the Spirit of the Cape said the word."[20]

Both Mumford and Melville had more than one Cape Horn.

CHAPTER 3

Bitter Morning (1918-19)

Looking backward, Mumford claimed that he did not lose his naiveté until the late 1920s: it was only his study of Melville, he said, and the pain it caused him, that had opened his eyes to "the underlying realities of human experience," and ultimately allowed him to mount a useful challenge to the "current faiths of my generation"—"our glib futurism, our pious belief in the progressive solubility of all human problems through science and technology."[1] But I think his constructive disillusionment began a full decade earlier, and at first, it was just disillusionment.

Mumford acknowledged his "fatal resignation" in the immediate aftermath of the Great War, and he was not alone in that feeling.[2] It was clear to almost everyone that the reformist spirit of Progressivism, which dominated the first years of the twentieth century, was in abeyance. That spirit would surge again in the 1930s, when Franklin D. Roosevelt launched the New Deal, with all its idealistic government programs dedicated explicitly to social welfare. But in 1919 many American intellectuals and activists were experiencing an "oozing deflation," which quickly became a boozing deflation, as Prohibition, ironically, ushered in a period known for alcoholism.[3] Shell shock was more than a military phenomenon.

Mumford served in the navy for ten months, from April 1918 until February 1919, at a time when people were dying of influenza by the tens of thousands. Though he did not see direct action, he knew he had been shaped by the war's violence, and he resented the crushing tedium of his service, despised the military's dependence on hierarchy and

FIGURE 3. "Self-Portrait (in Navy Costume)," 1918.

authority. He railed against the navy's addiction to "inspection and drudgery," its "laziness, its bluntness, its obtuseness, and its magnificent triviality."[4] And in 1919 he saw that the "bleak training camps, the humiliating routines, the blind obedience" were all spilling over into civilian life, that the war had brought an "ultimate massive arrest of civilization," that in fact the "archetypal mode of military-bureaucratic organization" was what defined modernity: "grilling and drilling" and complicity in violence were now what all Americans had in common.[5]

At the same time, there was certainly a measure of relief that the war was over, and Mumford was delighted to have secured a job at *The Dial*, a literary and political journal whose typesetter was a young Jewish woman named Sophia Wittenberg. *The Dial* claimed direct descent from the Transcendentalist magazine of the same name, founded in 1840 by Emerson and Margaret Fuller and their circle of friends. But the New England Transcendentalists were never dragged to "inquisitorial State hearings" during a Red Scare the way Mumford's editorial colleagues were in the summer of 1919, while Attorney General A. Mitchell Palmer "kept on with that series of vindictive violations of civil liberties" known as the Palmer Raids.[6] Starting in 1917, with the passage of the Espionage Act, partly in response to the Russian Revolution, and continuing with the Sedition Act and the Alien Act in 1918, the federal government had gradually created a new surveillance regime that targeted almost all forms of dissent. Not just possible abettors of the German enemy but virtually any groups or publications that expressed sympathy for communism or anarchism or even labor activism were now subject to a kind of sanctioned terror. Federal agents pulled newspapers and magazines from the mails, confiscated files from raided offices, and arrested, jailed, and sometimes even deported any leftist "radicals" whom they could charge with having "revolutionary intent."[7]

One result was generational despondency. Mumford felt that "millions of young people" had been "dragged along in the same powerful currents, sharing the sense of desolation, feeling bitter and scornful over the betrayal of our hopes by the politicians, the businessmen, the military leaders." The thought came to one of his friends: "Perhaps we are at the beginning of a new Dark Age." Loomings, indeed. To Mumford himself, 1919 seemed like "the year when the Age of Confidence visibly collapsed."[8]

But it was also the centennial of Melville's birth—as a few critics and scholars noticed. Eventually, Mumford came to see 1919 as the start of the Melville Revival, and that helped him understand the country's crisis of confidence in more nuanced terms. His generation had been forced "to face the black side of human experience," just as Melville had in the era of slavery and the Civil War. And that kind of confrontation, while often overwhelming, could spur a determination to create a more realistic and resilient culture. To make progress that mattered, Mumford realized, his cohort had to dispense with "our very belief" in progress's "inevitability."

When he wrote an editorial proclaiming "The Collapse of Tomorrow" in 1921, he was recognizing the possibility that young people might be tempted to gravitate toward "immediate enjoyment and satisfaction."[9] But, in the face of a compromised future, he was hoping that his generation, instead of living purely in the present, might turn toward the claims of the past. "What right had we to be so disheartened?"—especially given the horrors that their forebears had faced. Didn't they owe something to those who had offered up their lives in previous struggles, including the recent unpleasantness? "Unless we who survived were prepared to take over, and make sacrifices as great as the dead had made doing their duty, their efforts would become meaningless."[10] This was the impulse that led him first to study past Utopianisms and then to explore Melville's "cosmic defiance." By the time he wrote his Melville biography, he was ready to insist "that the effort of culture, the effort to make Life significant and durable, to conquer in ourselves that formidable confusion which threatens from without to overwhelm us—this effort must begin again." And it had to begin again not with technological optimism but with "spiritual hardihood" and "surrender" and "vital relationships."[11]

Ultimately, Mumford even reinterpreted his stint in the navy as necessary experience: here were "the raw realities of everyday existence" and also "essential insights into the miscarriages of life," which he explicitly connected to the kinds of insights he gained by reading Melville. Indeed, he came to suspect that it was precisely his military service that had allowed him "to get under Herman Melville's skin." Being in the navy meant facing the flaws in human institutions, the abuses of power, the structural inequalities. But it also meant earning a new kind of solidarity, gaining a more "vivid sense of my whole American background. My shipmates, coming from all parts of the country, from many different trades and callings, taught me far more about my own country than I could have discovered in a similar period of travel."[12] In other words, Mumford's shipmates were much like Ishmael's, those individualistic "isolatoes" who hailed from all over and represented a wide range of classes, races, ethnicities, and religions but were now "federated along one keel"—from Tashtego the "unmixed Indian" of Martha's Vineyard, to Daggoo the "imperial negro," to the mates Starbuck, Stubb, and Flask, to Ishmael's bedfellow, Queequeg, the "soothing savage" who had the appearance of "George Washington cannibalistically developed."[13] They were engaged in systematic violence, and they were subject to their commander's whims, but they learned to work together.

Mumford titled the first chapter of his Melville biography "Bitter Morning" because he thought that his subject's early years had been marked by deprivation and humiliation. When Melville was twelve, his father went bankrupt and died, and almost immediately Herman faced what would turn out to be a lifelong struggle to earn a living in a brutally industrial age. Yet Mumford also noted Herman's vigor, for "in Melville's youth even a city lad could sail a boat, tramp into the country, shoot game, experience the active, outdoor life."[14] No matter how bitter, all mornings hold promise.

The understanding that trauma is unavoidable may be the difference between naive optimism and determined hope. In dark times, individuals and societies yearn for the restoration of some kind of health or golden age, ache desperately for recovery. But loss and bitterness are constants in human experience; health and happiness are always partial and fleeting. As Thoreau once noted, "no man is quite well or healthy. . . . Disease is, in fact, the *rule* of our terrestrial life."[15] Once you've plunged into the blackness of that truth, not only will you have an easier time appreciating any moments of peace or excitement, but you might also start to see trauma in a deeper context. Herman Melville's life had not been easy or simple before his father died, and American society had not been progressing steadily in the glorious Progressive Era. The shock of the Great War was not entirely shocking, given existing trends in western society. Dark times will always spur retrospection, but we need to look backward not simply to track either progress or decline but rather to open our eyes wider to the crosscurrents, contradictions, and eerie resonances of history.

In 1919 the Great War was over, but America still seemed to be at war with itself. It was a year of mail bombs, constant labor strife, weekly lynchings, and race riots in twenty-six cities. Mumford didn't know what to do with himself. "The rest is blankness," he wrote, "the thought of the futile year that is gone and the unwritten year that approaches."[16]

There is no evidence to suggest that he noticed when Raymond Weaver published an article in *The Nation* on August 2, marking Melville's centennial. Melville had been lost; Weaver was engaged in a project of

recovery. But he found this obscure writer to be essentially unrecover-
able. "Melville eludes summary classification," he observed, and *Moby-
Dick* "reads like a great opium dream." Melville and his family had destroyed many of his private writings in ceremonial bonfires, and in his
published work he rarely opened a window onto his inner life. Mumford, on the other hand, is overdocumented: he kept meticulous records, noted every passing thought, left detailed instructions for future
archivists. For Melville we have only scraps—and his opium-dream
novels and poems. "The world to him was a darkly figured hieroglyph,"
Weaver wrote; "and if he ever deciphered the cabalistic sign, the meaning he found was too terrible, or else too wonderful, to tell." Still, in a
troubled age, it seemed worthwhile to engage with a wracked soul who
had an "abiding craving to achieve some total and undivined possession
of the very heart of reality."[17]

Some people welcomed such engagement, and some turned away. In
November 1919, Mumford's beloved magazine, *The Dial*, "changed hands
almost overnight," and the "politically radical fortnightly" became an
"esthetically oriented monthly." All the editors were fired—all except
Sophia, who was retained for her typesetting skills. The old publisher
moved to Hollywood and went into the movie business. Mumford had
met the woman he would marry, and she supported him for a while,
since, professionally, he was suddenly at sea: "a baffling period of exploration began, when, to avoid the financial uncertainties of journalism, I
hovered on the outskirts of a subacademic literary career"—a characterization in which I can't help but hear Melville's evocation of a "sub-
sub-librarian" at the beginning of *Moby-Dick*. Money was scant, for
Mumford, and irregular. "Economically the bottom dropped out of my
life," he explained many years later, and "some of the uncertainties and
tensions" of this time would haunt him for decades. Even when the financial situation picked up, he and Sophia struggled with the question
of whether she ought to keep working, and Sophia would ultimately
harbor a tinge of resentment that her career wound up getting cut
short.[18] The drift of Lewis's career, meanwhile, despite occasional hints
of the fair winds and favorable currents ahead, was looking, for the moment, distinctly Melvillean.

CHAPTER 4

Fragments of War and Peace (1865–67)

How does a nation recover, after it has blown itself to pieces?

It doesn't. It has to acknowledge the trauma. You can hope that the bad dreams and visions become less vivid and less frequent, but even if they stay away for a while, you can never trust that they've disappeared. It's more about learning to live with your wounds. The "phantom" pain in an amputee's stump may get less severe, but it will always be more real than any phantom. "A dismasted man," says Melville, of Ahab, whose leg was bitten off by Moby Dick, "never entirely loses the feeling of his old spar, but it will be still pricking him at times."[1] What matters is how the crippled veteran, of war or of whaling, responds to the reality of that pricking.

———

Battle-Pieces and Aspects of the War: after nine blank years without a published book, Melville probably took his time choosing this title. It's an appeal both to the senses and to the intellect; he was asking his readers to step back and take a long look. The phrase "battle-pieces" most often referred to grand-scale paintings, though it was also applied to certain musical works that attempted to develop martial themes more indirectly or abstractly.[2] In the actual battles of the Civil War, there were some old-fashioned "set-pieces," in which soldiers lined up in formation and marched at each other across open fields. But there were also scattered, fragmentary struggles in the wilderness.

Many Civil War soldiers wound up with shrapnel, grapeshot, canister balls, or pieces of shells lodged in their bodies.

And soldiers sometimes referred to their guns as "pieces."

But "piece" is also a homophone, and what ultimately spurred Melville to write this book was his preoccupation with what the postbellum peace would look like. His "battle-pieces" are almost never snapshots; rather, they look backward and forward simultaneously. They are memorials, inscriptions, requiems, eulogies, elegies, epitaphs—but also pleas, warnings, meditations on providence, dreams of reconstruction.

———

Lincoln also looked backward and forward, ceaselessly. At Gettysburg, in November 1863, he invoked the Declaration of Independence (1776) to transfigure his nation's flawed Constitution (1789) and thus to envision "a new birth of freedom." There had been death, carnage, mayhem, in the town's fields; the local and national communities were reaping the bitter harvest of long-standing divisions, exclusions, injustices. But now there could be a fresh growth. Reunification after the war would entail not just reinscribing "government of the people, for the people, by the people" but actually living up to that ideal for the first time: the United States would finally become its true self. Lincoln sought new fulfillments of old destinies.[3]

In April 1865, he rejoiced that the war had ended but admitted uncertainty as to the future. He hoped for "a Union of hearts and hands as well as of States." But he knew that many Americans were incapable of imagining such a Union; certainly, it had never existed before. After hearing General Grant's testimony about the final confrontation at Appomattox, Lincoln recounted a recent dream: he was aboard a ship out on the ocean, and it was "moving with great rapidity towards an indefinite shore."[4]

———

The first four poems of *Battle-Pieces*, all set before the outbreak of war (the book proceeds chronologically), are called: "The Portent"; "Misgivings"; "The Conflict of Convictions"; and "Apathy and Enthusiasm." The first line of "Apathy and Enthusiasm" is "O the clammy cold November": the period between 1859 and 1861 was another dark, damp season in Melville's soul, and in the nation's—another season of Loomings.[5]

But those four poems applied equally to the season right after Lincoln's assassination.

In fact, they were probably written after the war, not before: Melville insisted that "with few exceptions, the Pieces in this volume originated in an impulse imparted by the fall of Richmond," which happened on April 3, 1865. Lincoln was shot on the fourteenth. For a week and a half, Melville may have felt a kindling of hope, especially because he trusted Lincoln, as the president put it in his Second Inaugural Address, "to bind up the nation's wounds" and secure "a just, and a lasting peace," in a spirit of magnanimity rather than retribution, "with malice toward none; with charity for all."[6] Once Lincoln was dead, Melville started to fear that the trauma might be too deep, that healing, recovery, Reconstruction, might be impossible.

The whole volume is full of fragments, broken meters, ponderous rhymes, suspended lines—full of portentous images and failed commemorations, pale phantoms and blank monuments. The aftermath of the war, for Melville, was a bleak new age of futility and discontinuity. In "The Stone Fleet: An Old Sailor's Lament," he evoked the sad scene at the mouth of Charleston Harbor, where the federals had scuttled sixteen whaling ships weighed down with granite to create a permanent blockade. "And all for naught. The waters pass—/ Currents will have their way; / Nature is nobody's ally." Melville's sympathy lay entirely with the "old whalers" themselves, rendered obsolete when oil was discovered in Pennsylvania in 1859: "I have a feeling for those ships, / Each worn and ancient one, / With great bluff bows, and broad in the beam: / Ay, it was unkindly done."[7]

One of the book's later poems is called "Commemorative of a Naval Victory"; unsurprisingly, the nominal victory seems empty. There is not even any direct reference to a specific marine conquest. The poem, instead, dives deep into the general experience of realizing, "in years that follow victory won," how quickly all success and confidence can fade. "But seldom the laurel wreath is seen / Unmixed with pensive pansies dark; / There's a light and a shadow on every man / . . . Elate he can never be / . . . The shark / Glides white through the phosphorous sea."[8]

———

Nathaniel Hawthorne never expected anything from the war—except maybe a permanent separation from the hated South. The violence, the killing, canceled out the values he lived for. "Life, which seems such a priceless blessing, is made a jest, emptiness, delusion, a flout, a farce, by this inopportune Death."[9] His own death came in 1864, from a strange, wasting illness. Many people considered him another casualty of the war, whose "disturbing influences," he said, left him "mentally and physically languid" and often unable to write.[10]

While Lincoln and Melville sometimes allowed themselves to dream of a new, stronger, more inclusive democracy, Hawthorne anticipated only further convulsions, and he cursed all those who blessed the fighting: "I sympathize with nobody and approve of nothing." When pressed, he wished the North "military success," but he also admitted that he did not "quite understand what we are fighting for." Indeed, immediately after Secession, he had found it something of a relief "that the old Union is smashed. We never were one people, and never really had a country since the Constitution was formed." Rather than restoration, then, he dreamed of amputation. End the misery, he entreated his fellow northerners, and focus on "selecting the point where our diseased members shall be lopt off."[11]

———

Melville could be as alienated and ornery as Hawthorne; Mumford thought he had a "perpetual feeling of being an Ishmael," an outsider, a misfit. But perhaps that sense of isolation made him yearn all the more for community, fraternity, solidarity, Union—for the "comradeship" he had tasted in risking his life with other sailors: "The whaleman's joy," as Mumford put it: "the soldier's joy: the joy of hard living and easy dying!"[12]

Looking back over his Battle-Pieces before publishing them, Melville made a remarkable decision: he added a long essay at the end, a prose "Supplement," intended to soften his poems' "bitterness." He wanted his readers to remember that war could be ennobling—on both sides. In the wake of a "terrible historic tragedy," he wanted northerners, in particular, to take a long view, to recognize that future generations would condemn not only the defeated slaveholders but their conquerors, too, if they attempted "to pervert the national victory into oppression for the vanquished." Melville wanted all Americans to work toward some sort of "Re-establishment."[13]

The "Supplement" is perhaps the most directly earnest piece of writing Melville ever published. It is dominated by idealistic nouns: not just Re-establishment and Reconstruction but common sense and Christian charity, patriotic passion, moderation, generosity of sentiment, benevolence, kindliness, freedom, sympathies, solicitude, amity, reciprocal respect, decency, peace, sincerity, faith, democracy.[14] Superficially, it is the sort of essay I could imagine Melville himself dismissing as hopelessly naive. But in fact it is tightly argued.

Again and again, Melville acknowledged that America had never been Great, that the Revolution had produced not a promising democratic republic but rather "an Anglo-American empire based upon the systematic degradation of man." (In one of the poems, he lamented that "the world's fairest hope" had been "linked with man's foulest crime.") And he emphasized that "those of us who always abhorred slavery as an atheistical iniquity, gladly we join the exulting chorus of humanity over its downfall." The problem was that some exultant northerners seemed to take their victory as a sign of moral perfection. To Melville, the fight against slavery was a righteous one, but it was "superior resources and crushing numbers," rather than righteousness, that determined the outcome. Indeed, northerners had been complicit in the slave system from the beginning, both morally and economically. And how could northerners ultimately blame southerners for upholding the traditions of their ancestors? The conquered slaveholders were "a people who, though, indeed, they sought to perpetuate the curse of slavery, and even extend it, were not the authors of it, but (less fortunate, not less righteous than we) were the fated inheritors." It takes unusual strength of character to repudiate inherited assumptions.

Toward the end of the "Supplement," Melville's argument became more recognizably Melvillean, as he fell back on humility in the face of an inscrutable universe: "Let us revere that sacred uncertainty which forever impends over men and nations." The northern and southern roles could easily have been reversed. Moreover, the weathering of a terrible squall does not guarantee smooth sailing afterward. The outcome of the war, Melville realized, had only intensified the scorn and suspicion between whites and blacks in the South, so if white northerners were to heap additional scorn and suspicion on white southerners, then black southerners would probably pay the dearest price. "Benevolence and policy—" Melville wrote, "Christianity and Machiavelli—dissuade from penal severities toward the subdued. Abstinence here is as obligatory as considerate care for our unfortunate fellow-men late in bonds."[15]

We all depend on each other. To lop off the South like a bad limb, pierced by shrapnel and disease, would be to sacrifice the possibility of a true peace. Northerners, Melville thought, would always be forced to "turn our eyes toward the South, as the Neapolitan, months after the eruption, turns his toward Vesuvius."[16] There was no choice but Union. "It's a mutual, joint-stock world, in all meridians," Ishmael imagines Queequeg saying at one point in *Moby-Dick*. "We cannibals must help these Christians."[17]

———

The United States did not fulfill its highest destiny in 1866, and Melville's book of poems sold poorly. Most people wanted to forget about the war rather than ponder its meaning. But at least Melville had become a published poet. "Battle can heroes and bards restore," he wrote, in one of the Pieces.[18]

Poetry was something of a rediscovery for Melville. There were some poems, in the form of songs, in his long 1849 novel *Mardi*, and then there was the whole volume of poetry that he'd hoped to publish in 1860. But from the beginning he had been engaged with poetry as a reader: studies of Melville's library suggest that though we might imagine him surrounded by whaling manuals, his most sustained inclination was to reach for books written in verse.[19]

Like many of his contemporaries, Melville had grown up memorizing and reciting poems, and his interest in the English poetic tradition deepened as he grew older. Poetry helped keep him anchored during the long voyages he took as a young man; when he encountered another sailor who knew the same lines, by Shakespeare or Milton or Butler or Goldsmith, he immediately felt like less of an Ishmael. And once he became a writer, he casually sprinkled well-known verses into his novels, hoping both to create common ground with his readers and to elevate his narrative via "beautiful archaisms, scattered remnants of our language"—in the phrase of an author Melville admired.[20]

Poetry, for Melville, usually evoked earlier eras—it carried the weight of antiquity, as opposed to the aptly named "novel"—but in the best verses that sense of history translated into a kind of transcendent timelessness. He was after not musicality but an intense crystallization of complex thought, writing that would slow people down and make them more philosophical citizens, driven to ask unanswerable questions about the human condition. In the introduction to a new translation of *The Iliad*, Melville made vigorous markings next to the writer's assertions about "the subtle influence of poetry upon the rising spirits of the age." Carefully wrought poems, he hoped, could help create "a finer order of human beings."[21]

Melville wrote poetry for the last quarter century of his life—during those infamous years of retreat and withdrawal.[22] It seems that he still dreamed of having a subtle influence. He may even have assumed that a volume like *Battle-Pieces* would remain significant much longer than a book like *Moby-Dick*. The Civil War, after all, would define America for decades to come, and he had tried to capture both its age-old conflicts and its peculiarly modern traumas.

In December 1866, Melville finally got a steady job, as deputy inspector at the New York Custom House. Perhaps he was relieved to have the reliable income he had sought for so long, or perhaps he felt he was giving up. He had always envied Hawthorne's government jobs, but he also surely approved of his friend's satirical treatment of the typical custom house in the opening section of *The Scarlet Letter* (1850). Here was a space where commercial excess met government bureaucracy, with the result that anyone who worked there got buried alive "under a bulk of incommodities."[23] Melville himself, as Mumford pointed out in his biography, had described the work of customs inspectors in *Redburn* (1849) as "worse than driving geese to water."[24]

Mumford desperately wanted to believe that Melville finally felt settled, that, in fact, "from this time on a sweetness and serenity began to spread over the man."[25] And the regularity of the new work did help— but not in the immediate term. As of May 1867, Lizzie had told her minister and her relatives that she could not imagine remaining with Herman: after years of difficulties, she had finally decided, as her brother put it, "that her husband is insane."[26] No one knows exactly what happened. Some family stories paint Melville as an abusive alcoholic; certainly, he was known to be brusque and impatient within the domestic sphere. Yet, in mid-March, Melville's cousin Kate had reported that his custom house job, requiring significantly more "intercourse with his fellow creatures," seemed to have had "a beneficial effect" on all his relationships: "he is less of a misanthrope." And surviving letters show that he was capable of acting as a sweet, affectionate father, and also as a solid, faithful husband who shared secrets with his wife about his writing and trusted her as a copier and proofreader of his manuscripts. All we can say for sure is that, by the late spring of 1867, tensions were rending the Melville household.[27]

Then, one day in September, Herman and Lizzie found themselves pounding on the locked door of their eldest son's upstairs bedroom. Malcolm, eighteen years old, had returned to the house at 3 in the morning after a night on the town and then had never gotten up. He was dead, from a self-inflicted gunshot. The coroner's report called it suicide. A few days later, though, there was an official correction: Malcolm had died by his own hand, yes, but the act was not "by premeditation or consciously done, no motive for it having appeared during the inquest or after it." Indeed, by all accounts he was "an upright and amiable young man." It must have been an accident. Malcolm had recently joined a postwar volunteer regiment and had been issued a pistol, which he kept under his pillow; it must have been discharged as he rolled over while asleep, or as he reached for it upon waking. Not suicide, his parents always insisted. An accident.[28]

Lizzie stayed in her marriage. Herman stayed at the custom house—for nineteen years. They learned to live with their wounds. They set about rebuilding their household.

CHAPTER 5

Reconstruction (1930–31)

Melville had worried that a too-radical Reconstruction might alienate the South forever, creating an unbridgeable fissure in the Union. But the bitterness of white southerners surely would have festered no matter what the federal government did. In any case, Reconstruction turned out to be a fairly conservative affair: slavery was abolished, but racism wasn't, and many antebellum trends simply reasserted themselves, as northern leaders deepened their investments in industrialism, mobility, and power. If the radicals had won out, then the truly significant development, regardless of how ex-Confederates were treated, would have been the offering of more benefits to African Americans, not just nominal rights but material reparations: forty acres and a mule, to help them move toward a more equal footing in society. Then it might have become an era of Renovation. Instead, the Era of Reconstruction quietly faded into the Gilded Age, a period that Melville found not terribly different from what had come before. "There seems to be no calamity overtaking man," he had written in 1849, "that can not be rendered merchantable."[1]

"Reconstruction" resurfaced as a cultural touchstone several decades later, in Mumford's era, immediately after the Great War. In the "shattered areas of Europe," as Mumford explained, it usually meant "restoring the blasted factories and flooded mines with which the defeated German armies had vengefully punctuated their retreat." But in the United States, it held "a far broader significance. . . . Reconstruction here carried the hopeful notion that the war had given each country such a jolt that every institution, shaken off its ancient base, would be searchingly re-examined and reshaped on a more humane pattern." Mumford and his circle, at least, were radical Reconstructionists. In 1919, at the editorial offices of *The Dial*, "Reconstruction was our watchword"—though "it was not till a decade later, with Franklin D. Roosevelt's New Deal, that many of the major proposals of Reconstruction were at last carried through."[2]

It also took until the early 1930s for Mumford to dedicate himself fully to the project of radical cultural Reconstruction, in the sense of true renewal. He arrived at that dedication through a complex process of rediscovery.

When a culture comes to an agreement that dark times have fallen, it's most often based on a common experience of shock: bombs get dropped, or the market collapses, and suddenly everything feels different. These crises then become the major markers of History (it's much harder to pinpoint the arrival of an era of thriving)—which has contributed to the defining of History as, most importantly, Change over Time: a series of disjunctures. But Mumford, by the early 1930s, having been through the crucible of his Melville biography, started thinking of History more as the entanglement of change and continuity. That revelation was in a sense the foundation of his mature worldview. To be deeply, constructively, engaged with the past, he thought, was to recognize that there will always be white whales. The spirit of Moby Dick was unkillable. At the same time, though, white whales might hold very different meanings in different eras. Mumford decided, therefore, that a human being's deepest responsibility was to contribute actively to the construction of such meanings. There is a long human tradition of hunting white whales, and that can be a noble pursuit under certain circumstances; then again, the sole survivor of *Moby-Dick* is the character who focuses on a different, though equally difficult, task: *interpreting* white whales. The key to Ishmael's interpretation is his willingness to see Moby Dick as both the expression of a timeless malignancy and a reflection of antebellum America's most pressing problems.

In the early 1930s, the task confronting people like Mumford was to interpret another of the darkest times in U.S. history: the Great Depression.

It was a clear disjuncture: the country had gone from Boom to Bust almost instantaneously on Black Tuesday, and now millions of people were suffering. American culture sagged under the weight of mass distress and gradually turned the ashen color of Hoovervilles and desiccated fields.[3] Instead of the hardy pioneer or the self-made magnate, it was the unemployed laborer huddling in a bread line who was now the archetypal national figure. Mumford's awareness of this shift and this suffering spurred him to favor immediate, large-scale, humane responses. So, though he considered himself to the left of FDR, he ultimately embraced the grand, reconstructive vision of the New Deal, whose best job programs "gave discouraged unemployed people of widely different social classes and vocations the hope of economic survival without losing their self-respect."[4]

At the same time, though, Mumford's increasing historical sophistication led him to pause and recognize that the trauma of the Depression was neither entirely new nor entirely unpredictable. Many of the shared feelings dominating American culture in the early 1930s actually had their origins in the early 1920s. To Mumford, looking backward in 1930, it became obvious that "the deflation of the War and the deflation of our recent 'prosperity' were not altogether dissimilar events: each left behind a sinister aftermath of hunger, terrorism, disillusionment."[5] He kept flashing back to the shell shock, the labor strife, the desperation in the face of a confrontational, militaristic government.

Moreover, the famous Boom of the 1920s had by no means been shared equally. In March 1929, seven months before the Crash, Mumford reviewed a book called *The Rediscovery of America* by his friend Waldo Frank; the two men agreed that the nation's Progress had been vastly overestimated, that in fact the rush to economic growth represented a dangerous flight from America's basic democratic heritage. "After one has read the lyrical ballads that are composed about the benefits of mass production and the reign of universal prosperity," Mumford wrote, "it is a little discouraging to walk half a mile from the heart of any large city and come upon a sordid environment whose physical destitution contrasts oddly with the happy ejaculations of the economists."[6]

It is tempting, even for historians—perhaps especially for historians—to slice the past into discrete periods, to sum up the dominant ethos of, say, a decade, in a snappy, easy-to-remember phrase. And so we still learn about the Roaring Twenties. But what Mumford realized in the early 1930s was that recognizing the downside of a Boom might make it easier, in turn, to see the upside of a Bust.

What should we remember about the 1920s? Some scholars of course still draw a stark Boom/Bust line, but others have followed Mumford in noting certain continuities between the 1920s and 1930s and in emphasizing that the Roar of the 1920s might have drowned out crucial expressions of discontent and resistance. Many Americans, in these years, enjoyed contact with more people, from more diverse backgrounds, but had less of a sense of intimate community. They marveled at grand buildings that led their eyes upward and raised the question of whether there was any height that human ingenuity could not attain—but many of them had fewer opportunities to gaze at the horizon, to experience wide-open expanses, and to breathe fresh, freely circulating air. They came to have less of a sense of place, because the places they inhabited were so overwhelmingly large and changed so quickly, and because they were now so integrated into elaborate networks, so entangled in large, complex institutions, so implicated in international affairs. It was exhilarating to many Americans to be able to escape their hometown, to drive a car, to speak on a telephone, to use electrical appliances, to see a motion picture show, to understand themselves as consumers. But their new work spaces were increasingly marked by standardization, routinization, regimentation, abstraction, and hierarchy—and by an acid stink and the clank of metal. On the one hand, the Great Migration brought tens of thousands of African Americans up to Harlem, where they launched a cultural Renaissance; on the other hand, membership soared across the country in the newly revived Ku Klux Klan, originally founded as a terrorist organization in 1866, at the dawn of Reconstruction. Over the course of the 1920s, many Americans, white and black, male and female, in their freeing modern clothes, at their roaring jazz clubs, with their machines that promised to deliver them from hard labor, complained of being lost, choked, constrained, Prohibited.[7]

As Mumford pondered these contradictions of modernity, trying to track the continuity and change in his own lifetime, he was also pursuing another historical project, analyzing American culture during the *first* Era of Reconstruction. Published in 1931, *The Brown Decades: A Study of the Arts in America, 1865–1895*, started from the premise that Reconstruction had been quite literally a dark time, especially in art and architecture: by the end of the Civil War, Mumford asserted, "browns had spread everywhere: mediocre drabs, dingy chocolate browns, sooty browns that merged into black. Autumn had come." In fact, all of society, in Mumford's view, seemed covered in coal dust, or perhaps even charred: "the laval flow of industrialism after the war had swept over all the cities of the spirit." Americans were traumatized; the only real changes they were able to make—for instance, "the substitution of petroleum for whale oil"—just contributed to the darkening of the landscape and the transformation of adventurous laborers in the open air to cramped toilers in blackened factories. Everyone seemed "sadder, soberer"; it was a time of "renounced ambitions, defeated hopes."[8]

At first blush, then, *The Brown Decades* seemed a natural follow-up to Mumford's 1926 book *The Golden Day*, in which he had posited that the Civil War put a stop to the burgeoning of the arts embodied by antebellum writers like Emerson, Thoreau, and Fuller. The point remains a compelling one. Most writers and artists, like Hawthorne—like most Americans—were completely flummoxed by the war.[9]

By the summer of 1930, though, Mumford was beginning to work through his own Melvillean trauma, and in a new spirit of generative self-criticism, he had become eager to test his assumptions about the nineteenth century more rigorously. Among other things, he was thinking of *Battle-Pieces*, which he believed should have earned Melville, "if nothing else did, a wide hearing from his countrymen."[10] And weren't the Brown Decades also the years of Emily Dickinson's poems, and Whitman's *Democratic Vistas*, and Mark Twain's satires, and Frederick Law Olmsted's park systems? Couldn't moments of raging conflagration offer opportunities for germination? It was in the midst of the Civil War, after all, that George Perkins Marsh had published his world-changing manifesto, *Man and Nature*, announcing that "Man" must cease operating everywhere as a "disturbing agent" and instead, in Mumford's words, "become a moral agent: to build where he had destroyed, to replace where he had stolen—in short, to stop befouling and bedeviling the earth."[11]

Once Mumford sat down to write *The Brown Decades*, he had significantly amended his premise. Now he insisted that "one must not forget the measure of intellectual hope" that had been sustained by postbellum artists and critics fighting to make American modernity more endurable and just. The period could just as easily be called "The Buried Renaissance," he realized.[12] It wasn't that he didn't know about these cultural accomplishments before; it's just that he had to rediscover them. He had to see beyond the obvious trauma of the Civil War—just as he had considered the promise of utopianism even in the brutal aftermath of World War I—just as he would insist that the 1930s must not be defined solely by Depression. His deep engagements with present and past were starting to intertwine, as in the modernist novels of Virginia Woolf that he so admired.

"It is impossible to see one's own period in perspective," Mumford wrote, in *The Brown Decades*; "but on the surface, the points of resemblance between our own post-war difficulties and those which followed the Civil War are so numerous that in going through the records and memoirs of the earlier period, one has the sense of following our own history, told in a slightly foreign language."[13] Mumford found this kind of research and writing eerie, uncanny, and full of pitfalls, since he was keenly aware of his subjectivity, of the ways in which his own desire could skew his understanding. But this work also made him feel deeply connected and even hopeful: as he reached back through the years, he rediscovered his conviction that grappling with the past was the first step toward taking responsibility for the future.

In a letter from late June 1930, Mumford expressed his hope that his new book would be "very clear and insistent and well-woven" but also his fear that it might turn out rather "dusty," in keeping with its title. The whole thing felt rather workmanlike: "never am I carried along, as on a tide, as happened when I was writing the Melville [biography]—a fact which accounts for all its Melvillian virtues and defects."[14] But it was just such a manageable, straightforward project that he needed to knock him out of his doldrums. In the end, he recaptured the enthusiasm he had felt back when he was writing *The Golden Day*—when he first felt the thrill of rediscovering a relevant, usable cultural heritage—when he first started trying to convince his fellow Americans of "the notion by which every real culture lives and flourishes—that the past is a state to conserve, that it is a reservoir from which we can replenish our own emptiness, that, so far from being the ever-vanishing moment, it is the abiding heritage in a community's life. Establishing its own special relations with its past, each generation creates anew what lies behind it, as well as what looms in front; and instead of being victimized by those forces which are uppermost at the moment, it gains the ability to select the qualities which it values, and by exercising them it rectifies its own infirmities and weaknesses."[15]

Living in one dark time, and looking back to another, Mumford was bolstered by the example of those creative people who had acknowledged the darkness and nevertheless struggled to kindle and diffuse new light. Perhaps he could claim that some measure of Reconstruction had in fact been achieved; perhaps this reframing of the past represented his best chance to shape his society's future.

It would take a considerable effort: he had to contend with both societal and personal desolation. In the spring of 1930, still feeling alienated and somewhat desperate, he blamed "the gods" for "a series of delicate thrusts" that had put him in an even more "advanced stage of debilitation. . . . The wretches: no wonder they drove Captain Ahab mad!"[16] And in that spiritual state he started the first of a series of intermittent but passionate affairs that would nearly undermine his marriage, again and again, over the course of the following decade. Somehow, though, the unsettledness of this time brought with it a new commitment to "tragic defiance" and radical reconsideration. "The conclusion that I drew for myself was that the situation demanded, not specific attacks on specific evils and specific points of danger, but a wholesale re-thinking of the basis of modern life and thought, for the purpose of eventually giving a new orientation to all our institutions."[17] Like George Perkins Marsh, Mumford had decided to confront humanity's destructive energies head-on and try to transfigure them, to effect a revolution in morals and mores, to lay out plans for a more resilient and sustainable society.

By the fall of 1930, having finished *The Brown Decades* (one of his shorter books), Mumford launched the expansive project that would dominate the next twenty years of his life: a study of technology, cities, the environment, social organization, politics, psychology, religious values, and relationships. At first he thought he could cram all these subjects into one book, with the "outstretching comprehensiveness of sweep" that Melville had claimed for *Moby-Dick*. Mumford would "include the whole circle of the sciences," as Melville put it, "and all the generations of whales, and men, and mastodons, past, present, and to come, with all the revolving panoramas of empire on earth, and throughout the whole universe, not excluding its suburbs."[18]

Eventually, there would be four volumes, forming a series, *The Renewal of Life*—suburbs included. The third and fourth tomes, *The Condition of Man* and *The Conduct of Life*, appeared in 1944 and 1951, having caused Mumford a great deal of grief. But the first two books, *Technics and Civilization* and *The Culture of Cities*, poured right out of him and made huge splashes, in 1934 and 1938. As he began some preliminary scribbling, in November 1930, he recorded his new, somewhat delusional, frame of mind: "I begin over again, married once more to my work and to Sophie, a sounder and wiser man."[19]

CHAPTER 6

The Golden Day (1846-50)

For a few years, living in the heart of New York City, Herman Melville was a successful writer. All five of the novels he published between 1846 and 1850—*Typee, Omoo, Mardi, Redburn,* and *White-Jacket*—were ocean-going affairs, offering an insider's perspective on the contrast between a rapidly modernizing America and life on various ships and islands. Of course, modernity leaked into even the tightest vessels, in the form of rigid routines and industrial-grade boilers, but Melville understood the appeal of an affable exoticism. He wrote of typhoons and tropical lagoons and naked cannibals, cruel captains and poetic foretopmen. These were adventures, yes, but they unspooled at a tranquil, premodern pace, allowing readers a respite from the Go-Aheadism of the day.[1] Sales, for the most part, were brisk.

Did Melville relish these years? As usual, the hieroglyphs he left behind are hard to interpret. And, needless to say, there were numerous challenges along with the triumphs. His first book, *Typee,* made him something of a literary sensation, but a year after it was published he traveled down to Washington, D.C., to beg (unsuccessfully) for a government position with a regular income.[2] He and Lizzie were engaged at this point, but everyone knew that it was virtually impossible to earn a living as a writer, and Lizzie's well-established Boston family had some concerns. Give Melville credit: he had dedicated *Typee* to Justice Shaw, well in advance of his engagement. Perhaps what stands out most in this period is Melville's energy and commitment, his willingness to do whatever was necessary to make a place for himself in a society where he would never feel entirely at home.

I might even say that, despite hints of Melville's ever-present dark side, his writings of these years reveal an irrepressible good humor. In *White-Jacket*, which exposes the banality of abuse in the navy, you'll nevertheless find chapters called "The Pursuit of Poetry under Difficulties," "Sea-faring Persons peculiarly subject to being under the Weather," "The great Massacre of the Beards," and "A Dish of Dunderfunk." Melville had gone to sea at age twenty-one and traveled the world for almost four years because his previously prominent family was in decline and he had no desire to work in an office or a factory. But now, in his late twenties, he could look back on his youthful escapades and literally make something of them: "his roaming, wasted life," as Mumford put it, "was all to the good: its idlest moments could be salvaged."[3] Indeed, *Typee* is largely about idleness and the shirking of "duty," and Melville's readers seemed to enjoy his casual contrasting of his own "feverish civilization" with the indolent paradise he found in the South Seas, where it was "altogether unknown" for a healthy young man to find himself "digging and delving for a livelihood." So what if the Natives had "not advanced one step in the career of improvement"? Melville had eventually returned to his nation of relentless improvers, because he got tired of bananas and bread-fruit, but he retained within his soul that experience of being utterly "removed from harassing cares."[4]

Back in what he sometimes called "snivelization," Melville continued to encounter his share of harassment, but he met it with a remarkable resilience, and often with determined labor.[5] Though *Typee* and *Omoo* made Melville's reputation, they also produced some controversies (Melville was accused of being untrustworthy, depraved, heretical), so in his third book, *Mardi: And a Voyage Thither*, he completely abandoned the goal of pleasing his readers and cooked up a roiling stew of romantic fantasy, political satire, and poetic philosophy. His readers, predictably, were not pleased. One reviewer referred to the prose in *Mardi* as "equally intolerable for its affectation and its obscurity."[6] Plus, the book was more than twice as long as either of Melville's previous works. A different critic found it "not only tedious but unreadable."[7] The

consensus was that Melville should either go back to the straightforward adventures of his first two books or give up writing altogether. But
he pressed on. In less than a year he completed both *Redburn* and *White-
Jacket*, and neither one contained any titillating capers in the South Seas.

Looking back on *Mardi*, after most of the reviews had come out, he
referred to it wryly as "a plant, which . . . may possibly—by some miracle,
that is—flower like the aloe, a hundred years hence—or not flower at all,
which is more likely by far, for some aloes never flower."[8] One is tempted
to read bitterness into all of Melville's musings about his failed books,
but in these years I think he had enough "individual vitality" to do as
Ishmael suggests in *Moby-Dick* and take the self-regulation of whales as
inspiration: "Do thou, too, remain warm among ice. Do thou, too, live in
this world without being of it. Be cool at the equator; keep thy blood
fluid at the Pole. . . . Retain, O man! in all seasons a temperature of thine
own."[9] Early in 1850, having inscribed a copy of *Mardi* to a friend, Melville
joked that "political republics should be the asylum for the persecuted
of all nations; so, if 'Mardi' be admitted to your shelves, your bibliograph-
ical Republic of Letters may find some contentment in the thought that
it has afforded refuge to a book which almost everywhere else has been
driven forth like a wild mystic Mormon into shelterless exile."[10]

These years had seen not only the Mormon exodus to Utah Territory
but also the Mexican-American War, increasing tension over slavery,
and revolutionary upheavals in Europe—all of which Melville followed
closely, even while maintaining his own internal calm. It turns out that
each of the five books he wrote during this time is full of politics and
social criticism, from *Typee*'s condemnation of the "unprovoked atrocities" committed against Native peoples to *White-Jacket*'s condemnation
of military flogging, which also stands in for slavery.[11] In other words,
Melville was a full participant in the sharp-edged cultural burgeoning
that saw Emerson and Thoreau attacking industrialism and Margaret
Fuller launching American feminism and Nathaniel Hawthorne exposing the sins of Puritanism. Indeed, Mumford thought of *Typee* as "Melville's *Walden*," a contemporaneous thought experiment through which
Melville came to understand, like Thoreau, "what it meant to throw off
the impedimenta of civilization."[12] And American civilization in the late

1840s was heavy with new baggage, not least the all-encompassing market revolution that seemed to offer endless economic opportunities and yet simultaneously rendered all opportunists vulnerable to forces beyond their control.[13]

In part because *Redburn* and *White-Jacket* did wind up selling so much better than the more ambitious *Mardi*, Melville tended to denigrate them. "They are two *jobs*," he explained to Justice Shaw, "which I have done for money—being forced to it, as other men are to sawing wood." His most "earnest desire," as a Thoreauvian individualist, was precisely "to write those sort of books which are said to 'fail.'" All in good time: *Mardi* would later be joined on the shelves of exile by several other persecuted asylum-seekers. Meanwhile, though, Melville could at least say that "in writing [*Redburn* and *White-Jacket*], I have not repressed myself much . . . , but have spoken pretty much as I feel."[14] And though neither book attracts many readers today, they are both compelling, heartfelt works.

Redburn tells the story of Melville's first voyage, from New York to Liverpool and back, on a merchant ship, during the summer he turned twenty. It captures a young man's initial exposure to "the real sights of this world," which leave him disillusioned, but also enlarged in his sympathies: "surrounded as we are by the wants and woes of our fellow-men, and yet given to follow our own pleasures, regardless of their pains, are we not like people sitting up with a corpse, and making merry in the house of the dead?" While the narrative is straightforward, the narrator is less so, and by the end, this sensitive "son-of-a-gentleman," though still without prospects and swindled out of his wages, is able to forget his own grief and turn his thoughts toward the immigrants entering New York harbor, many of whom were likely to be turned away. "Let us waive that agitated national topic, as to whether such multitudes of foreign poor should be landed on our American shores; let us waive it, with the one only thought, that if they can get here, they have God's right to come. . . . For the whole world is the patrimony of the whole world."[15]

In *White-Jacket*, Melville decided not to bother with plot at all: the novel, closely resembling a work of nonfiction, is essentially a portrait of culture and society aboard a frigate, based on Melville's own experience on the navy ship that brought him home from Honolulu to Boston between August 1843 and October 1844. But, like the ship itself, the book is "full of all manner of characters—full of strange contradictions"; its prose, in Mumford's words, "has a richness of texture, a variety of rhythm, a decisiveness of phrase that [Melville's] earlier work had only promised"; and, in the end, it vividly reveals "the sham republicanism of a country" that is supposed to uphold democracy through "checks and balances" but instead imposes a modern "system of cruel cogs and wheels, systematically grinding up in one common hopper all that might minister to the moral well-being" of those people not lucky enough to hold positions of power.[16] Of course, there's also the important incident involving dunderfunk (a sailor's treat "made of hard biscuit, hashed and pounded, mixed with beef fat, molasses, and water"), not to mention the "heartless massacre of hair" in which all the sailors were forced by the captain to become barbers to each other and shave off their whiskers—"I swear, it was barbarous!"[17]

Melville grew his beard, during these years, and walked the New York streets, and lived in the world without being of it. To Mumford, Melville fit the mold of what he called the Golden Day in American literature precisely because he absorbed the excitement of modern times while nevertheless maintaining a critical distance: "An old provincial culture, closely bound to the land, was being overthrown by a new order based upon trade and imperialistic enterprise and military expeditions in support of the prestige of the state; and, at this moment of dissolution, the spirit fulfilled itself in a sudden outburst which expressed, in a new form, all that was valuable in the old culture, with an additional energy, derived partly from the seething activities of the new life that was inimical to it and already threatened it."[18] The best literature, Mumford thought, forged new possibilities for the future by interrogating the relationship between past and present. In the late 1840s, the worlds Melville created in his novels felt both reassuringly old and refreshingly new.

Herman and Lizzie had gotten married in the summer of 1847, and though Lizzie wasn't thrilled about moving to Manhattan, she insisted, in September, that "with Herman with me always, I can be happy and contented anywhere."[19]

FIGURE 4. Elizabeth Shaw Melville, c. 1847.

In February 1849, their first child was born—Malcolm. Herman, in a letter to his brother, referred to him as "the phenomenon. . . . We desire to have him weighed, but it was thought that no hay scales in town were strong enough. It takes three nurses to dress him; and he is as robust as Julius Caesar. . . . I think of calling him Barbarossa—Adolphus—Ferdinand—Otho—Grandissimo Hercules—Sampson—Bonaparte."[20] I'll wager that Herman didn't change many of the little emperor's diapers, because 1849 was the year in which he wrote both *Redburn* and *White-Jacket*.

In the summer of 1850, Melville took his family on vacation to a place that had been dear to him since childhood: his uncle's farm in the Berkshires. A visiting friend attested that Herman knew "every stone & tree

& will probably make a book of its features."[21] On the first of August, Melville celebrated his thirty-first birthday at the grand old farmhouse, and then, on the fifth, he found himself climbing a mountain with Nathaniel Hawthorne, who was living in a cottage nearby, and who seemed to be in excellent shape, despite being fifteen years older than Melville. By mid-September, to everyone's surprise, Melville had purchased his own Berkshire estate, which he named Arrowhead, for a price surpassing the combined earnings of his five novels. It helped to have a wealthy father-in-law.[22]

Melville moved to the country for quiet, for mountains, for connections to the past, and for Hawthorne. An intimacy developed quickly between the two writers, both known for their reclusion. According to Nathaniel's wife, Sophia, Herman testified that Hawthorne's "great but hospitable silence drew him out—that it was astonishing how *sociable* his silence was. . . . He said sometimes they would walk along without talking on either side, but that even then they seemed to be very social."[23] Within days of their first meeting, Melville had picked up Hawthorne's *Mosses from an Old Manse*, and within a few more days, he had written a long, admiring essay called "Hawthorne and His Mosses," the first half of which appeared in a New York literary magazine on August 17.[24]

"For spite of all the Indian-summer sunlight on the hither side of Hawthorne's soul," Melville wrote, "the other side—like the dark half of the physical sphere—is shrouded in blackness, ten times black." He had seen how haunted Hawthorne was by the ghosts of grim New England Puritans, witch-hunting purveyors of fire and brimstone who had created a culture of guilt and paranoia. That spring, working at his usual breakneck pace, Melville had almost completed the book that would become *Moby-Dick*, but now his thinking about the manuscript took a dark, Shakespearean turn that caused him a long but intensely stimulating delay. He wallowed in Hawthorne's blackness, his "probings at the very axis of reality," and wondered how far tragedy ought to go. "Now, it is that blackness in Hawthorne of which I have spoken that so fixes and fascinates me. It may be, nevertheless, that it is too largely developed in him. Perhaps he does not give us a ray of light for every shade of his dark. But however this may be, this blackness it is that furnishes the infinite obscure of his background."[25] What constituted a healthy confrontation with the most troubling realities? How much blackness could American readers be expected to handle? How much blackness could Melville himself handle?

He finally released Moby Dick into the open water, in all his blazing whiteness, in the damp November of the following year, 1851. The book was dedicated, "in token of my admiration for his genius," to Nathaniel Hawthorne.

CHAPTER 7

Retrospective (1956–82)

Reconstruction is also what historians do. Autobiographers, too. And the question always arises: How much reality should they include? What balance should their narrative strike between darkness and light? It's never a matter of simply "telling the truth." No narrative can accomplish that—just as no map can accurately represent physical geography. What human being could account for all the biases of memory, personality, identity, culture? You'll even find your own opinion of the past changing over time, as you examine it at different moments in your life. Sometimes you'll see the shadows intensify; sometimes you'll be blinded by brightness. "All this to explain," as Melville put it, "would be to dive deeper than Ishmael can go. The subterranean miner that works in us all, how can one tell whither leads his shaft by the ever shifting, muffled sound of his pick?"[1]

Mumford started to look back at his past more purposefully after he had completed the *Renewal of Life* series, and after he had come through some serious health problems, in the early to mid-1950s, as he approached his sixtieth birthday. By the end of 1956, at age sixty-one, he had a draft of an autobiography—which he did not publish until 1982.[2] He never stopped agonizing over his life and legacy, and when he finally released *Sketches from Life*, he had given up on the idea of creating a coherent, comprehensive narrative. The book takes 460 pages to get to 1930; then it spends 30 more pages touching on the next few years; and then it abruptly ends. Though beautifully written, it is even more skewed than Raymond Weaver's biography of Herman Melville.

A curious reader can find a few of the later years and missing topics in two choppy, episodic memoirs that Mumford published in the 1970s: *Findings and Keepings: Analects for an Autobiography* (1975) and *My Works and Days: A Personal Chronicle* (1979). If you put all three books together, then you will learn the secret of his scandalous parentage, which his mother did not reveal to him until he was forty-seven; you will catch hints of the pain he felt when certain friends broke with him over his fierce, interventionist antifascism, and then when his son died actually fighting fascists; and you will hear a bit about one of his extra-marital affairs. But there were other women, with whom he had deep, serious relationships; and he never wrote a public word about his troubled relationship with his daughter; and he never found a way of coming to grips with the whole second half of his life. In his private writings, he confronted most of his life's realities with a relentless meticulousness. His biographer called him "the most deeply honest person I have ever met."[3] His published works, though, are full of evasions and omissions. In the end, he could not figure out a constructive way of sharing the full range of his personal suffering: the blackness might have overwhelmed his quest for Renewal.

His doubts had started as early as January 1957, right after he finished the first draft of the autobiography. In his private notebook, he explained that as he moved through the events of his life, he'd had a buoyant sense of his story's usefulness—"until I came to deal with the years since 1935: public years of anxiety and economic depression, preparation for the war, the war itself, with all its bleak duties and empty fulfillments, and finally the period after the war. The memories of this period I found deeply disturbing; the tensions they created then and still create were almost unbearable. I am sure that the record itself is historically valuable, and I am not sorry to have put down all that I have actually put down; but it is not something I want to go back to, to correct, to elaborate, to reflect on further." In fact, he excised almost all of it. I don't think he wanted to; his goal, ultimately, was to redeem his struggles, just as he had redeemed Melville's later years. Yes, it had been torturous to write about World War II; but "on the other hand, now that I have brought the crude ore to the surface, I can see many rich veins, opened by this first effort, which I haven't even begun to explore. . . ."[4] With Sophia's help, he did produce an entire book about his son, Geddes, aiming to create some sort of meaning from his short life, to make up for all the years that would never be. But *Green Memories*, published in 1947, was received in the same way as Melville's *Battle-Pieces*, and that left Mumford even more bitter. As he grew older, it became harder to express hope in the face of humanity's record of brutality. By the time of the war in Vietnam, he had lost a great deal of faith in democracy's capacity to check the violence of capitalism.

In his published writings, Mumford perhaps valued balance above all else. That's what truly stands out in *Sketches from Life*, which wound up being his final book. You can see it even in the first sentence: "I was a child of the city, and for the first thirty years of my life I knew the country only as a visitor, though the occasional summers I spent on a Vermont farm before 1910 had first and last an influence on me that offset my long incarceration in what Melville called 'the Babylonish brick-kiln' of New York."[5]

It's a brilliantly maddening opener, traveling in opposed directions, forcing us to pause and ask ourselves whether we ought to expect any resolution. Has Mumford's retrospective posture left him feeling constructive, or cynical? Though he was best known as an urbanist in 1982, he seems to imply here a contrarian move from city to country, a long-awaited liberation, an abandonment of smoke and other modern corruptions for Green Mountain pastures. But the first clause—"I was a child of the city"—is pure romance, and its cloud of enchantment hovers over the entire sentence, even mellowing Melville's bitter condemnation of urban life.

Indeed, on the very next page of *Sketches from Life*, Mumford acknowledges having spent his entire career "wandering about cities, studying cities, working in cities," and having been "stirred by all their activities."[6] And then, in a direct echo of the "offsetting" image of his first sentence—an image that conjures up modern printing techniques and their dependence on the repulsion of oil and water to separate the printing area from the non-printing area[7]—he goes on to explain that his main task has been to understand how urban civilization's "enormous gains in controlling the physical environment and raising the ceiling of human achievement in the arts and sciences were offset by an obsession with power as an end in itself."[8] These words are a clear echo of a sentence about *Moby-Dick* that Mumford had written in his biography of Melville and that I quoted in this book's preface: the novel, Mumford believed, balanced "the two dissevered halves of the modern world"—the half "bent on conquest" and the half "bent on the transposition of conflict into art, and power into humanity."[9]

Is it significant that in his 1929 sentence construction a humane culture seemed to transfigure our will to conquer, while in 1982 the obsession with power seemed to trump the arts and sciences? Perhaps. Though Mumford fought gamely against despair until the end of his life, the struggle did become more challenging. But the crucial point about offsetting forces is that they are both necessary, as death gives life meaning, and the whiteness of the page allows the black words to become legible. Melville made the point explicitly in *Moby-Dick*: "Oh grassy glades! oh, ever vernal endless landscapes in the soul. . . . Would to God these blessed calms would last. But the mingled, mingling threads of life are woven by warp and woof: calms crossed by storms, a storm for every calm."[10]

I think Mumford was grateful to Melville for having noted New York's drawbacks in the century before he himself did. And both writers clearly understood that their sense of imprisonment in the city could be counteracted. Of course, if you had the means, you could simply move to the countryside, as Melville did in 1850 and Mumford did in 1936. And they imprinted on very similar landscapes, in the rolling hills, known as the Taconics, that line New York's eastern border with Connecticut, Massachusetts, and Vermont. I was able to drive between their two houses, through snow flurries and pine forests, in just over an hour.

It's especially strange that Mumford pointed to 1935 as a marker for when the more difficult period of his life began, since the home that he and Sophia made for themselves in the secluded valley of Amenia, New York, starting in 1936, was his single greatest source of contentment. Indeed, *Sketches from Life* ends with a glowing invocation of their "fourteen acres that stretch back to the Webutuck River," comprising "a

FIGURE 5. "Our House on the Other Side of the Road," 1944.

woodlot, a swath of cleared meadow, a vegetable garden," and "a minia-
ture woodland walk."

Even once they had moved to Amenia, though, Mumford tended to
spend a couple of days a week down in Manhattan: "at no point, I must
emphasize, did we ever lose contact with the city." He always retained
his determination to "make the best of both worlds and discover
through experience how each was necessary and complementary to the
other."[11]

Mumford was acutely aware that many people did not share his ability to shuttle between different landscapes, and so what he ultimately
aimed for was to make the city more like the country, to make it incorporate its own offsetting force, or "saving opposite."[12] That couldn't be
taken for granted in the modern world, as he discovered at a young age:
"the fresh west winds that blew across the Hudson also blew the fumes
and smoke from noisome factories on the Jersey shore." But balance
might still be achievable, through careful design and cultural stubborn-
ness. Nature could persist in all kinds of enclaves. Looking back on his
New York childhood, Mumford found his environmental memories to

be "mostly bleak and stuffy." But they would have been even worse "had not Central Park and Riverside Park always been there to gladden my eyes and to beckon my legs to a ramble."[13] Even in an increasingly blighted city, one could cultivate the modern art of rediscovering the country.

Needless to say, those cherished parks and neighborhoods were also enclaves of history. Bits and pieces of the past could help offset the rush of the present. Mumford delighted in stumbling upon older, more humane districts in the city—for instance, rows of red-brick houses that had stood firm against the swirling "current of enterprize" and now remained as "relics" to remind people that "here at one time a tradition had flourisht, which had not altogether been trampled under in a (crudely) utilitarian age."[14] Indeed, even as modern forces seemed to remake the entire material and cultural landscape, seemed to open a permanent rupture between present and past, Mumford's forays into both urban geography and environmental history consistently managed "to uncover potentialities that the existing institutions either ignored or buried . . . , 'remnants' and 'persistents' that have been deposited by every previous generation and that add unimaginably to the richness of human life, and indeed, like language itself, are essential to human survival."[15]

Ultimately, Mumford's cautious, balanced method of retrospection led to the conclusion that culture is always many-sided and contested, that one is always wrong to make sweeping generalizations about particular periods, that there are always "strange eddies and countercurrents." Of course, adopting a different metaphor, he acknowledged that there may be "dominant" and "recessive" traits of a given age: the desire to see balance can also be misleading. But it is never wrong to concern yourself with "survivals and mutations": "Mutations arise in human communities from unexpected sources: the social heritage makes society much less of a unity than we are compelled to conceive it, by the nature of language, when we interrupt the complex stream of actual life in order to take account of it in thought. Out of these mutations, a new social dominant may arrive: veritably a saving remnant."[16]

Saving opposites, saving remnants. Especially in dark times and dark places, one must never give up the search for offsetting forces. Thanks to the dedicated labor of our most persevering forebears—activists and planners and stewards and scholars and artists, some famous and some anonymous—countless surprising potentialities have persisted. It's our permanent responsibility to find, embrace, and develop them. If the tragedy of Melville's career, as Mumford saw it, was his conflict with "the ideology dominant in his time," that is also why his work remains valuable to us.[17]

Despite fond memories of his own early career, Mumford never would have characterized his life before 1935 as a "Golden Day": he was too keenly aware of how he had suffered in the aftermath of the Great War and in the year after he wrote his Melville biography. And, in parallel fashion, I'm sure he could recognize, at times, that the second half of his life had been just as full of joys, successes, and fertile ideas as the first half. There were moments when he was able to celebrate his later works, like *The City in History* (1961), which won the National Book Award, and he certainly cherished his life in Amenia and his amazingly resilient marriage and the steadfast friends with whom he exchanged hundreds of letters. His engagement with history, in particular, gave him constant stimulation and deep inner resources. He always knew those resources were there. It just became harder, in old age, to rediscover them.

CHAPTER 8

A Bosom Friend (1850-51)

Pittsfield. June 29th, 1851.

To Hawthorne.

The 'Whale' is only half through the press; for, wearied with the long delay of the printers, and disgusted with the heat and dust of the Babylonish brick-kiln of New York, I came back to the country to feel the grass—and end the book reclining on it, if I may. . . . Come and spend a day here, if you can and want to; if not, stay in Lenox, and God give you long life. When I am quite free of my present engagements, I am going to treat myself to a ride and a visit to you. Have ready a bottle of brandy, because I always feel like drinking that heroic drink when we talk ontological heroics together. This is rather a crazy letter in some respects, I apprehend. If so, ascribe it to the intoxicating effects of the latter end of June operating upon a very susceptible and peradventure febrile temperament.[1]

Melville sounds happy, in his letters to Hawthorne. There is a kind of infatuation here, both with his new friend and with his own sense of opening and sprouting. The older writer had "dropped germinous seeds into my soul."[2] Melville deferred to Hawthorne, even apologized for his manic keenness—but did not censor himself. He wrote with the intimacy of someone who had joined the shy, retiring Hawthorne in reclining on the grass. It was late June, a time for picnics and long walks; the planting was done, and now came the season of growth. Hawthorne would understand Melville's frustration with his publisher and the heated rush of the industrial city, would recognize the mixed anxiety and excitement of nearing the end of a long writing project. "Shall I send you a fin of the *Whale* by way of a specimen mouthful? The tail is not yet cooked—though the hell-fire in which the whole book is broiled might not unreasonably have cooked it all ere this."[3]

———

Pittsfield. Wednesday morning (April 16th?), 1851.

To Hawthorne.

There is a certain tragic phase of humanity which, in our opinion, was never more powerfully embodied than by Hawthorne. We mean the tragicalness of human thought in its own unbiassed, native, and profounder workings. We think that into no recorded mind has the intense feeling of the visable truth ever entered more deeply than into this man's. By visable truth, we mean the apprehension of the absolute condition of present things as they strike the eye of the man who fears them not, though they do their worst to him,—the man who, like Russia or the British Empire, declares himself a sovereign nature (in himself) amid the powers of heaven, hell, and earth.[4]

Melville was training himself to stare into the abyss, the pit of hell-fire. From Emerson, he had adopted a radical self-reliance, an intellectual individualism that gave him his sea legs on his first few writing adventures. But he did not find Emerson transcendent: nature seemed too gentle in landlocked Concord, too accommodating. Hawthorne was from Salem, on the coast; his great-great-grandfather had been a judge in the witch trials; his father, captain of a brig called the *Nabby*, had died at sea when Nathaniel was four years old. From Hawthorne, Melville took the acknowledgment of both oceanic chaos and "Innate Depravity."[5] Radical individualism faltered in the face of radical interdependence, and radical uncertainty, and radical perversity. Melville, in his essay about his new Berkshire neighbor, made a point of quoting from a story called "Fire-Worship," in which Hawthorne lamented the replacement of the wild, open hearth by the modern, "cheerless" stove. For both writers, it seems, the appeal of visible, devouring Fire was that its reassuring light was balanced by latent darkness. Fire was a complicated character, simultaneously divine and satanic: "Nor did it lessen the charm of his soft, familiar courtesy and helpfulness, that the mighty spirit, were opportunity offered him, would run riot through the peaceful house, wrap its inmates in his terrible embrace, and leave nothing of them save their whitened bones."[6]

Hawthorne's vivid willingness to acknowledge the fascination of the abyss reminded Melville of Shakespeare, who "through the mouths of the dark characters . . . craftily says, or sometimes insinuates the things, which we feel to be so terrifically true, that it were all but madness for any good man, in his own proper character, to utter, or even hint of them. Tormented into desperation, Lear the frantic King tears off the mask, and speaks the sane madness of vital truth."[7]

Ahab: "All visible objects . . . are but as pasteboard masks. . . . If man will strike, strike through the mask!"[8]

There is no true sovereignty, no self-possession, no agency, without recognition of the "inscrutable malice" in the world—and in your own soul.[9] For Melville, the archetypal abyss would always be the mirroring ocean. In his earlier novels, though, he felt that he had only gazed at the "gently awful stirrings" on the surface of the serene Pacific. Now he would plunge to the hell below, baptize himself in the name of the devil, confront the restless undead, the "millions of mixed shades and shadows" who roiled the deeper water and disavowed any ultimate peace.[10]

_____

Pittsfield. June 1st? 1851.

To Hawthorne.

If ever, my dear Hawthorne, in the eternal times that are
to come, you and I shall sit down in Paradise, in some little
shady corner by ourselves; and if we shall by any means
be able to smuggle a basket of champagne there (I won't
believe in a Temperance Heaven), and if we shall then
cross our celestial legs in the celestial grass that is forever
tropical, and strike our glasses and our heads together, till
both musically ring in concert,—then, O my dear fellow-
mortal, how shall we pleasantly discourse of all the things
manifold which now so distress us.[11]

How did Hawthorne react to all these intimate musings on Heaven and
Hell? We have ten letters from Herman to Nathaniel between 1851 and
1852, but only one from Nathaniel to Herman, and it's all business. "The
next time you go to Pittsfield (and I believe you to go every day) will
you be kind enough to inquire at the railroad depot, or express-office,
for a large box, directed to me?"[12] It's tempting to conclude, with Mumford, that the friendship was rather one-sided, that Hawthorne's long
silences allowed Melville to project his own blend of darkness and light
as if onto a mirror: "his descriptions of Hawthorne's powers, Hawthorne's achievements, are nearer to his own than to Hawthorne's."[13]
    Melville refers to other missives, though, now lost, which may have
come closer to requital: "I thank you for your easy-flowing long letter
(received yesterday) which flowed through me, and refreshed all my
meadows, as the Housatonic—opposite me—does in reality."[14] The
two men did spend long nights with each other, drinking brandy and
gin and champagne and sherry and port and lord knows what else, and
smoking cigars, even in the "sacred precincts of the sitting-room" at the
Hawthornes' house, where Sophia normally prohibited tobacco. By all
accounts, it was virtually impossible to get Hawthorne to make social
calls, so Melville must have charmed him, because there were also bouts
of drinking at Arrowhead, and Hawthorne even testified as to "how

snug and comfortable Melville makes himself and friends." On the night of the taboo cigars, which was Melville's thirty-second birthday, Hawthorne affirmed that they "had a talk about time and eternity, things of this world and of the next, and books, and publishers, and all possible and impossible matters."[15] During the months Melville was finishing *Moby-Dick*, the two men seemed to think of each other as soul mates.

There is a chapter in the final version of the novel called "A Bosom Friend," in which Ishmael comes to admire the way that Queequeg always seems "entirely at his ease; preserving the utmost serenity; content with his own companionship; always equal to himself." The two sailors had already shared a bed, though, and now they recognized their shared sense of sovereignty—and soon they were sharing a peace pipe—and then Queequeg "pressed his forehead against mine, clasped me round the waist, and said that henceforth we were married."[16]

————

Pittsfield. Monday afternoon. November 17th? 1851.

To Hawthorne.

Your letter [about *Moby-Dick*] was handed me last night on the road going to Mr. Moorewood's, and I read it there. . . . I felt pantheistic then—your heart beat in my ribs and mine in yours, and both in God's. A sense of unspeakable security is in me this moment, on account of your having understood the book. . . . Whence come you, Hawthorne? By what right do you drink from my flagon of life? And when I put it to my lips—lo, they are yours and not mine. I feel that the Godhead is broken up like the bread at the Supper, and that we are the pieces. Hence this infinite fraternity of feeling.[17]

Hawthorne had helped Melville confront irrationality, evil, inscrutability, hauntedness, but he had also helped him rediscover the sense of connection and solidarity that he had sometimes experienced at sea.

The two writers read each other's books, and recognized a kinship, and suddenly it was as if they were standing together on deck with the rest of their crewmates, squeezing globules of spermaceti into liquid, and squeezing each other's hands, "as much to say,—Oh! my dear fellow beings, why should we longer cherish any social acerbities, or know the slightest ill-humor or envy! Come; let us squeeze hands all round; nay, let us all squeeze ourselves into each other; let us squeeze ourselves universally into the very milk and sperm of kindness."[18]

Especially for a loner, an Ishmael, such feelings of electric connection might be as vital as a fire in winter. In 1850 and 1851, Melville was struggling not to be swallowed by "The Whale," struggling to pay his debts, struggling to keep the domestic peace. Lizzie later attested that Herman "wrote White Whale or Moby Dick under unfavorable circumstances— would sit at his desk all day not eating any thing till four or five o'clock—then ride to the village after dark—would be up early and out walking before breakfast."[19] But Hawthorne, who had been paid all of $75 for *Mosses from an Old Manse*, understood what Melville was contending with. "Dollars damn me," Melville wrote to him, freely, anticipating empathy; "and the malicious Devil is forever grinning in upon me, holding the door ajar. . . . What I feel most moved to write, that is banned,—it will not pay. Yet, altogether, write the *other* way I cannot. So the product is a final hash, and all my books are botches."[20] The two penurious authors were like whaling ships encountering each other on the open ocean: "not only would they meet with all the sympathies of sailors," as Ishmael put it, "but likewise with all the peculiar congenialities arising from a common pursuit and mutually shared privations and perils."[21]

Sometimes, in the Berkshires, especially in June, when "the bloom of these mountains is beyond expression delightful" and "the beauty of every thing around you populates the loneliness of your way," Melville felt he was part of an oceanic cosmos, pulsing with interconnection.[22] And in June 1851, he wrote to Hawthorne of his sense that their mutual understanding might put them in touch with a whole universe of sensation, might help them do as the poet Goethe had recommended and "'*Live in the all*.' That is to say, your separate identity is but a wretched one,—good; but get out of yourself, spread and expand yourself, and bring to yourself the tinglings of life that are felt in the flowers and the woods, that are felt in the planets Saturn and Venus, and the Fixed Stars. . . . You must often have felt it, lying on the grass on a warm summer's day. Your legs seem to send out shoots into the earth. Your hair feels like leaves upon your head."[23] It might be only a fleeting experience, and it might be rare—you will know wretched separateness more than transcendent blending—but this truth, too, lay below the surface.

Melville's gratitude, in November, when Hawthorne raved to him about *Moby-Dick*, was boundless. But Hawthorne had also told him that he and his family had decided to leave Berkshire County and move to a house in West Newton, a Boston suburb—where, as it happens, I grew up (unknowingly, I walked by the Hawthornes' home site every day on my way to elementary school). Melville's glowing reply, then, was also a poignant goodbye. "Truth is ever incoherent," he wrote, "and when the big hearts strike together, the concussion is a little stunning. Farewell." Of course, his goodbye took a few additional paragraphs beyond that first "farewell," and there were two postscripts, and he made sure to undercut himself with jokes and "gibberish." The dominant tone, though, was sweet and sentimental: "Ah! it's a long stage, and no inn in sight, and night coming, and the body cold. But with you for a passenger, I am content and can be happy. I shall leave the world, I feel, with more satisfaction for having come to know you."[24] It's the sole letter we know of, besides those written to family members, that he signed with only his first name.[25]

———

Pittsfield. June 1st? 1851.

To Hawthorne.

I am told, my fellow-man, that there is an aristocracy of the brain. . . . So, when you see or hear of my ruthless democracy on all sides, you may possibly feel a touch of a shrink, or something of that sort. It is but nature to be shy

of a mortal who boldly declares that a thief in jail is as
honorable a personage as Gen. George Washington. This is
ludicrous. But Truth is the silliest thing under the sun. Try
to get a living by the Truth—and go to the Soup Societies. . . .
It seems an inconsistency to assert unconditional democracy
in all things, and yet confess a dislike to all mankind—in
the mass. But not so.[26]

Despite the intense identification, the infatuation, the love, Melville
suspected all along that he and Hawthorne harbored deep differences,
and especially that his own sympathetic range was significantly broader
than the older man's. The two of them shared an acute awareness of
humanity's dark side, which led them to distrust virtually everyone. But
Melville's self-criticism was so disciplined that he would never dismiss
even those he scorned, for he knew that he was as corrupt as they were.
To Hawthorne, southern slaveholders were beyond hope, and he refused to care what became of them: Dixie could go whistle its way to
Mexico. Melville, though, wanted everyone to be redeemed.

While the older man churned away at his New England novels, exploring an inward, provincial culture still haunted by its Puritan roots,
Melville created a shipboard society that was ruthlessly cosmopolitan,
reflecting his own worldly experience. The politics of diversity are at the
heart of *Moby-Dick*: the *Pequod*'s democracy has been hijacked by a
monomaniacal tyrant, but there is still a sense of possibility among the
multicolored crewmen, as they learn to cooperate in an expansive, collective endeavor, despite differing opinions of what it is they're meant
to be doing (making money, proving their manhood, progressing spiritually, conquering nature, exploring the universe, blowing off steam,
gathering material for a story). Hawthorne's characters find it impossible to escape their history and geography; Melville's characters sail into
the future to see how their society will develop on the frontier—to see,
especially, if old racial hierarchies will hold.

In October 1850, Melville's friend Evert Duyckinck had written from
New York to make sure Melville knew that the U.S. Navy had just abolished flogging, a few months after the publication of Melville's stern

attack against the practice in *White-Jacket*.[27] The spectacle of an officer violently humiliating an underling, on the command of the captain, in order to maintain discipline and reinforce a brutal power dynamic—to Melville, it was the spectacle of the plantation transposed to a frigate, a betrayal of democracy precisely parallel to the slave system. And so, as he wrote *Moby-Dick*, he rejoiced that the military was becoming more humane—but gritted his teeth over the Compromise of 1850 and the new Fugitive Slave Law, which his father-in-law, Justice Shaw, upheld in the Massachusetts Supreme Court. In one infamous case, which sent both Thoreau and Emerson into spasms of righteous rage, Shaw delivered Thomas Sims back to Georgia, where he almost died during his ritual punishment—a public flogging.[28]

Aboard the *Pequod*, the African American cabin boy Pip becomes something of a fugitive slave when he jumps overboard to escape the terrors of the whale hunt. And he barely survives. Melville worried about democracy—understood the danger of demagogues—did not imagine that the new territories of the West would vote to exclude slavery—could not see a way to abolish slavery in the South—did not anticipate that the different races and religions would ever be able to commingle peacefully. Yet the *Pequod* was an unconditionally democratic experiment, and on its decks and in its rigging were ligatures of understanding that crossed great gaps of difference.

Though Ishmael and Queequeg found much in common eventually, they were at first consumed by mutual suspicion. To Ishmael, his bedmate appeared as a bald, purple, heathen cannibal—in short, "some abominable savage"—from whom one might want to flee. Queequeg, for his part, immediately threatened to kill Ishmael—then, turning "cool as an icicle," treated him with the utmost indifference. When they finally did embrace and become "a cosy, loving pair," Ishmael wrote an entire sermon about what they had accomplished—sampling each other's exotic religions, sharing their life stories and their savings, recognizing each other's humanity, cheering each other up. Difference itself, Ishmael realized, while huddling with Queequeg under the covers in a room with neither stove nor hearth, was the key to everything: "truly to enjoy bodily warmth, some small part of you must be cold, for there is no quality in this world that is not what it is merely by contrast."[29]

Melville's ultimate coupling with Hawthorne had a similarly halting start—partly because the older man, as Ishmael says of Queequeg, "appeared to have no desire to enlarge the circle of his acquaintances," and Melville took that as another sign of Hawthorne's "overawing" darkness.[30] In February 1851, he wrote to Duyckinck that he had paid Hawthorne a visit recently and found him, "of course, buried in snow"—perhaps figuratively as well as literally. "There is something lacking—a good deal lacking—to the plump sphericity of the man."[31] Hawthorne seemed almost wraithlike sometimes, like one of his New England ghosts—cold, reserved, blank. By summer, the two writers had thoroughly warmed to each other, but their differences remained as significant as their commonalities.

Sophia loved to witness their conversations. The Hawthornes were somewhat notorious as a couple—for being almost exclusively preoccupied with each other—but Sophia watched Melville carefully, drawn to his "free, brave, & manly" bearing, his "fresh, sincere, glowing mind," his "fluid consciousness." It was remarkable, she thought, to hear him reveal "his innermost about GOD, the Devil, & Life if so be he can get at the Truth. . . . Nothing pleases me better than to sit & hear this growing man dash his tumultuous waves of thought up against Mr Hawthorne's great, genial, comprehending silences—out of the profound of which a wonderful smile, or one powerful word sends back the foam & fury into a peaceful booming, calm—or perchance, not into a calm—but a murmuring expostulation."[32] The agitated surf beating against the steady headland: offsetting forces in near-perfect equilibrium.

CHAPTER 9

Amor Threatening (1930-35)

Some biographers and literary critics have thought that Melville was in love with Hawthorne. Some have thought that he was in love with Jack Chase, the gallant captain of the main-top with whom he sailed in 1843 (Chase steals some scenes in *White-Jacket*, and *Billy Budd* is dedicated to him). Throughout Melville's writing, you can find tantalizing suggestions of his erotic experience and imagination, from his dalliance with the alluring Fayaway in *Typee*, to his strangely loyal friendship with the gay hustler Harry Bolton in *Redburn*, to the impossible love triangle in *Pierre*, to Ishmael's cozy cuddles with Queequeg. And there are many more, not only in the novels and poems but also in the letters. In 2016, the "forensic journalist" Michael Shelden published a book arguing that Melville had carried on a secret affair with Sarah Moorewood (Melville would surely insert a joke here about her name), one of his closest neighbors in the Berkshires. It was Mrs. Moorewood, Shelden insisted, not Hawthorne, who was the true "muse of *Moby-Dick*."[1] Countless Melvilleans have enjoyed imagining that Melville had quite a lot of sex.

Mumford, who came of age when Freud was the most important intellectual in the western world, thought that Melville was repressed. That perspective is certainly defensible; of course, it may also have been a projection of the repression that Mumford perceived—and condemned—in himself. Men of Mumford's generation tended to believe that all human beings, but especially males, were driven by a powerful physiological need for sex and that it was unhealthy for them not to act on their urges.[2]

When Mumford laid out his argument about Melville's sexuality, both in his biography and in subsequent writings, he grounded it in *Pierre* (whose subtitle is *The Ambiguities*—about which more later) and in a crucial poem called "After the Pleasure Party," published in 1891 in the collection *Timoleon, Etc.*[3] The poem seems to begin with an epigraph (though no one has ever found a source for it, so Melville probably composed it himself), which has its own title: "LINES TRACED UNDER AN IMAGE OF AMOR THREATENING." We're meant to conjure up a picture of an angry Cupid, perhaps sharpening his arrows or already taking aim at someone who has scorned him. And then comes the epigraph/prologue itself, a six-line stanza, comprising Cupid's threat, spoken in his own voice: "Fear me, virgin whosoever / Taking pride from love exempt, / Fear me, slighted. Never, never / Brave me, nor my fury tempt: / Downy wings, but wroth they beat / Tempest even in reason's seat." To Mumford, the meaning was clear: Melville had opportunities to embrace passion, but instead he remained faithful to his pleasureless marriage, and the blocking of his sexuality eventually blocked his writing. Mumford was determined to give his own libido more room to expand. Feed the fire: the more wood, the better.[4]

"After the Pleasure Party" is a tangled poem, and Mumford did not free all of its strands. He saw it as entirely about Melville, but in fact the main character is a woman, an accomplished astronomer called Urania, who has dedicated her life to celestial visions and higher thoughts and has thus remained precisely the kind of proud virgin whom Cupid disdains. Now, suddenly, at the end of a lovely day of picnics on the grass amid the grapevines, she finds herself battling a "sensuous strife," a "winged blaze that sweeps my soul / Like prairie fires that spurn control." She is furious that her Reason is being unseated by a mysterious, unsummoned desire for another person to complete her. "Why hast thou made us but in halves—/ Co-relatives? This makes us slaves. / If these co-relatives never meet / Selfhood itself seems incomplete. / And such the dicing of blind fate / Few matching halves here meet and mate." In the end, she is tempted to join a cloister, and thus to remove herself from the temptation of "softened glances" from athletic young men. But instead she prays to stern, mighty Athena: "O self-reliant, strong and free, / Thou in whom power and peace unite, / Transcender! Raise me up to thee, / Raise me and arm me!" To me, it seems more like a prayer to Emerson or Margaret Fuller—a prayer that wouldn't ever be answered in any poem of Melville's, for Melville knew that passion, whether acted on or not, would always make people slaves, and selfhood would always feel incomplete, and transcendent peace was out of reach.

Urania, then, is left struggling to forget the party, to "live down the strain / Of turbulent heart and rebel brain."[5] Melville seemed to sympathize with her. "Who ain't a slave?" he had asked in *Moby-Dick*. It seemed to him that our inevitable perversity would always lead us to betray ourselves and each other—that everyone is "served in much the same way—either in a physical or metaphysical point of view, that is; and so the universal thump is passed round, and all hands should rub each other's shoulder blades, and be content."[6] Sometimes a physical touch that is only suggestive—a hand squeeze, a shoulder rub—can be more comforting, more affirming of community and solidarity, than a sexual touch. But Mumford, a cynical Freudian, took on the simplifying perspective of Cupid and proposed, rather condescendingly, that both Melville and Urania could have improved their lots by first admitting that "sex is deep and central in every life" and then doing whatever they had to do to get some.[7]

Mumford did what he had to do. In March 1930, he was still recovering from his Melville biography and struggling with his alienation from his wife: "these are hateful days," he wrote, and he yearned "to get a hard tight grip" on his new work. "The last year and a half, since the finish of Melville, [have] been too broken and inconsecutive." At first he prescribed for himself heavy doses of "silence: poise: meditation."[8] But then, suddenly, he decided that he needed a clean break from the past. He set out to shatter the "cramped and restricted mold" of his first thirty-five years, "to seize and embrace with open arms life's unexpected blessings, whatever the risk—even though these departures more than once threatened the stable structure of my marriage and broke the smooth life-curve I had so far actually followed."[9] In April, he took the opportunity to sleep with an impressive young woman named Catherine Bauer and thus entered a new phase of life, in which he would constantly swing back and forth between ardent commitments until the start of World War II. Somehow, he and Sophia stayed together through it all.

In his eagerness to avoid what he saw as Melville's tragedy, Mumford became increasingly selfish and self-indulgent, though of course he rationalized this development as a kind of "maturation" that was necessary for the grand-scale books he intended to write. To develop a mature plan for cultural and societal Renewal, he needed to be renewed himself, completed, by an offsetting force. "Catherine and I were opposites," he remarked decades later, exaggerating for literary effect—"almost enemies. But our erotic intimacy enabled both of us to profit by this polarity; and this, I can see now, broke through some of the limitations in my own character and experience, and helped release energies needed for the work I was at last ready to do."[10]

Mumford's sense of male privilege is hard to stomach. All that seemed to matter was his stimulation, the full development of his powers. At times, his honesty can be disarming: he told Sophia everything, right away; he recognized the pain he was causing; he knew he was a "scoundrel," guilty of "error and vice," not to mention "miscalculation, self-deception, and blackguardism."[11] But he also found it relatively easy to excuse himself, in both senses, sometimes abandoning Sophia and Geddes for days at a time to lounge in a hotel room with Catherine. In the summer of 1932, he even traveled with Catherine through Germany and France, where she helped him with his research on the history of cities, architecture, and technology.

If Melville was repressed, then repression might be preferable to arrogant entitlement. It was not sexual frustration that ended Melville's writing career—nor was it sexual liberation that launched Mumford's *Renewal of Life*. Mumford did explicitly spurn Melville's "tormented chastity and self-renouncing loyalty," but at the same time he was trying to embrace Melville's "open-eyed participation in the Divine Comedy of human existence," his "wide-awake return to the common earth, where heaven and hell and all that lies between are, in varied measure, everyone's daily portion from cradle to grave."[12] In the end, both Catherine and Sophia helped him with this effort—not through sex but through their insistence that he confront the messiness of his self-justifications.

Sophia started calling him out almost immediately, in writing, in May 1930, having realized that when Lewis had asked her to give him a few months to figure things out, what he had really meant was that he intended to sleep with Catherine until she left on a planned summer trip to Germany—and then he wished to be welcomed back into his marriage bed. "It seems to me, my dear," Sophia wrote, "that I should be kept in complete ignorance, or else that I should know how things stand. This in between state is ghastly." Moreover, she argued, it was both unkind and unfair of him to rave about Catherine's intellect and the insights she contributed to his work, since those insights arose from the career she was pursuing, and Lewis had squashed Sophia's professional aspirations in the early 1920s: "I am left with no proper place of my own. I'm a hanger-on to you." This was a reality that they never fully confronted and that would occasionally come back to torment them. Perhaps most immediately, though, Sophia knew that her inclination to persevere through this marital tempest—Geddes was not yet five years old—would tempt Lewis to pass her off in his "airy and witty" way as being a game modern woman, a "good sport," a fellow Freudian realist. "If you can't see that I am a human being in distress," she wrote, "I am lost."[13]

In fact, Sophia and Lewis almost lost each other that year. "Catherine satisfies every part of me," Lewis exclaimed, in his private notes, right after their first sexual encounter—"spirit, mind, body. . . . She is Sophie's first real rival and if I were free to choose between them the odds—dare I say it?—would be against Sophie."[14] Looking back years later, he affirmed that in the winter and spring of 1930 his marriage had been "at lowest ebb; we were wracked and frayed, and for the first time the possibility of marrying someone else had become real. I was 34; Sophy 30: not too late for either of us to make a new start if we could face the break for Geddes."[15] Of course, retrospection has its limits. Given the heat of this new flame, it does seem likely that Mumford considered divorce in 1930. At the same time, though, he clearly enjoyed being intimate with *both* Catherine and Sophia, and he immediately wondered if maybe a long-term affair might be best for all concerned. "This is the hardest paradox of love: my love at all events," he wrote, very early in his relationship with Catherine. "When I am opened by anyone else, I am doubly opened by Sophia: she feels it and responds fully: we enjoy days of harmony. Whereas all the weeks I was forced to stay away from Catherine, I hated Sophie, too: pounced upon and magnified every carelessness." And as usual, when pondering paradoxes, Mumford thought of Melville: "Here is one of Pierre's Ambiguities with a vengeance: it is in opposition to all I had ever thought, believed, or for that matter felt before. I must force this out and come to some conclusion."[16]

The conclusion he came to was that he quite liked ambiguous love triangles. In later tellings, it was an affair Catherine had that summer in Germany that made him realize he did not want to leave the ever-loyal Sophia. But Catherine had probably already recognized that Lewis was never going to make any sacrifices in this situation, regardless of her behavior. There were times, like in September 1930, when he shared fantasies with her and implied that he lived for their intellectual exchanges; and then there were times, like in November, when he rededicated himself to his work and his marriage. Both Catherine and Sophia ultimately decided to ride out Lewis's waves of lust and angst and focus on their own pleasure and stimulation, and, off and on, the three of them counterbalanced one another tolerantly and effectively— sometimes even lovingly, for Sophia actually grew fond of Catherine[17]— until the fall of 1934, when Sophia became pregnant with the Mumfords' second child, after years of trying and hoping.

Lewis would have nurtured the triangle indefinitely, but Catherine had started to gain confidence and lose patience. "The girl does not exist, could not exist," she wrote to him in July 1933, "who would not make you feel that she had failed you."[18] By this time, she had started sleeping with the architect Oskar Stonorov, and, just as important, she had started writing her own book, *Modern Housing*, which would come out in late 1934, just months after Mumford's *Technics and Civilization*, the first volume in his *Renewal of Life* series. Indeed, in a very short time, Bauer had become a leading voice on housing and labor issues, working with Mumford's Regional Planning Association of America but also with organizations in Philadelphia pushing for community architecture and federally funded low-income housing. After her split with Mumford, she dove into the New Deal, advising President Roosevelt on housing and launching her career as a planner, professor, and social activist. But even before she and Mumford went their separate ways, she was urging him to embrace a more bottom-up approach to planning, reminding him that housing developments whose design was "perfect" might still fail unless managed and governed from within: the goal was "a real gain in understanding, power, and responsibility for the people who live in them."

What Catherine consistently communicated to Lewis in the last year and a half of their relationship was that he had been consistently selfish and controlling. They had always met when it made sense in *his* schedule—when, for instance, he could spend the afternoon with her in Manhattan and then get back to Sophia and Geddes for dinner at Sunnyside Gardens in Queens. Well, she asked, what if she wanted to have some of her own "temporary relationships" on the side, "situations which I dominate, which I start and stop . . . and in which I call the tempo"? He seemed incapable of acknowledging her independence, of seeing beyond the narrow world he had so carefully constructed for himself. As Lewis got deeper into *Technics and Civilization*, Catherine saw him retreating into himself, becoming an aloof writer again, with no sense of social context. In that role, she argued, as an "isolated intellectual," he could not "expect to provide *direct* leadership, straight-line influence on policy and action," for true leaders had to "win their spurs thru organizational activity of one sort or another." Her jabs about his thinking and his career, though, were also jabs about the way he conducted his personal relationships. She knew he would never leave Sophia, and that meant that the two of them were trapped in an endless, artificial present. His grand task was to dive back into the past in search of ways of renewing the present and creating a more just, humane, sustainable future. But, Catherine pointed out, "we have no Future."[19]

Both *Technics and Civilization* and *Modern Housing* were extremely well received, as salvos in the moral struggle against Depression. With the New Deal taking off, 1934 brought surges of hope: it was a moment of great solidarity among striking workers across the nation, and American intellectuals began turning their attention away from Europe to reengage with homegrown radicalism. Mumford and Bauer, joining cultural figures like Woody Guthrie, Archibald MacLeish, and Langston Hughes, became prominent participants in a long-term effort to reimagine American society along more democratic, communalist, egalitarian lines.[20]

But Mumford felt stuck. "This has been [another] broken period, the last six months," he wrote in his private notes, in the fall of 1934. Sophia almost had a miscarriage, and Geddes suffered a disconcerting eye injury. "So here I am, tired, dismal, ratty, miserable."[21] He missed Catherine. In a letter to her, he said that he felt as though he had woken up "on a battlefield," and there was "a corpse hooked over a fence and half an arm with a clenched fist is lying next to one's coat. . . . One's throat is sore, too, and so probably one shouted a great deal during the battle, and one can scarcely move one's right leg."[22] Alas, she no longer felt sorry for him—though they did exchange letters, off and on, until her death thirty years later.

Mumford's affair with Catherine Bauer was the only one he ever wrote about. It's explained toward the end of *Sketches from Life*, and it takes up most of a chapter in *My Works and Days* called "Amor Threatening," which is immediately preceded by a chapter called "Melvilliana." From Lewis's perspective, he had faced his white whale and survived to tell the tale. What mattered most was that he had produced *Technics and Civilization*, a more ambitious work than anything he had previously attempted—and he had preserved his marriage. At the end of "Amor Threatening," enlisting Sophia's help in confirming that this had been a time of renewal, he quoted a letter she wrote to him much later, in the 1970s: "Looking back on our life, I'd have nothing changed. . . . I could accept your having been in love with other women. I don't believe a blameless life is a good life."[23]

By early 1935, Mumford had started writing the second volume of *The Renewal of Life*, to be called *The Culture of Cities*, a book with Catherine

Bauer's political fingerprints all over it. And he had also started a secret, devastating affair with Catherine's close friend Alice Decker. In April, Sophia gave birth to a healthy girl, Alison. "Life," Mumford wrote, that summer, "if one attempts to describe it, is a steady process of butchery and torture, that can only lead one to a black Melvillean pessimism: but so long as one faces it silently one can live through it, assimilate it, and grow with it."[24]

CHAPTER 10

Cetology (1851–52)

Most readers of *Moby-Dick* did not understand it the way Hawthorne had. Though the occasional notice, between November 1851 and February 1852, hailed the novel as a brilliantly original masterpiece, the majority of the reviews bestowed on it such labels as "tiresome," or "shockingly irreverent," or just "strange."[1] To Melville, it must have felt like butchery and torture.

The most influential reviewers condemned the book as "an ill-compounded mixture of romance and fact," its storyline constantly interrupted by "ravings and scraps of useful knowledge flung together salad-wise."[2] The simple tale of a wild, wayward whale hunt could have made for a successful novel. Or, alternatively, the author could have produced a definitive, comprehensive handbook about whales and whaling, leaving aside the "phantasmal" plot and utterly unbelievable characters, the "attempted description of what is impossible in nature and without probability in art."[3] What could not be tolerated, in the era of clear-cut, modern Progress, was any sort of hash or hedging, any monstrous hybridity, any confusion or ambiguity. It made no sense to interweave a weird, extravagant whaling narrative with a semester's worth of cetology.

But that interweaving was at the heart of Melville's purpose. *Moby-Dick* thrums with images of looms, with the offsetting forces of warp and woof. The book threads together not just fiction and fact, not just past and present, not just storms and calms, but fate and free will, submission and defiance, culture and nature, doubt and faith, "civilization" and "savagery," grief and good cheer, chaos and order, land and sea, darkness and light (amid all these binaries, the tension between male and female is conspicuously absent). Sometimes the weaving is the kind that human beings have been doing for millennia, as in the chapter called "The Mat-Maker," which shows Ishmael and Queequeg silently working together, not spinning yarns but threading them together, in rhythm with the gently lapping waves, as an "incantation of revery" seemed to hover over the ship. At other times, Melville invoked the modern looms he had seen in northeastern textile mills, where all "spoken words" became "inaudible among the flying spindles." Regardless, the weaving together of opposites took on thick, hempen meanings: "There lay the fixed threads of the warp subject to but one single, ever returning, unchanging vibration, and that vibration merely enough to admit of the crosswise interblending of other threads with its own. This warp seemed necessity; and here, thought I, with my own hand I ply my own shuttle and weave my own destiny into these unalterable threads."[4] Was this warp-and-woof construction a reflection of how Melville thought the world worked, or just an oversimplified conceit suggesting the limitations of human perception? Neither, and both. One point of all of Melville's binaries is that, whenever you get caught up in a one-sided assumption—whenever you feel utterly constrained by fate or utterly sure of your free will—you'll soon be shown the power of the opposite perspective. Offsetting forces are humbling.

Melville must have known that the unusual structure of his book would rattle his readers. Clearly, his contemporaries had little use for his defiance of expectations and conventions, for his questioning of categories, for his constant impulse to tack and jibe between genres. They would not have taken kindly to the chapters written as if they were scenes in a Shakespearean drama, nor the soliloquies that Ishmael could not possibly have overheard, nor the abstruse facts of natural history he could not possibly have known. So Melville must have been deeply committed to his chosen technique—as he hints, perhaps, in the Sunday sermon that the old whaleman Father Mapple delivers before the *Pequod* has left her port. "Woe to him who seeks to please rather than to appal," says the preacher, condemning Jonah for being unwilling to utter "unwelcome truths in the ears of a wicked Nineveh." On the other hand, "Delight is to him—a far, far upward, and inward delight—who against the proud gods and commodores of this earth, ever stands forth his own inexorable self."[5]

One of the reasons *Moby-Dick* seems so modern in comparison to, say, Hawthorne's novels is that its unpredictable swerves appear to offer a glimpse of the ever-shifting contradictions inside Melville's inexorable mind. For a time, perhaps, he saw the Whale purely in symbolic terms, as embodying fate, or power, or evil, or the world's indifference to humanity. But almost instantaneously the thought came to him that the Whale was also meaningful as a living being with certain physical characteristics and habits and relationships. Then he realized that the Whale also lit the world's drawing rooms, and influenced the arts, and spurred adventures. Do you want to understand the world? No single narrative or perspective will ever steer you right.

Yet each new perspective could add something to the others. Modern science mattered as much to Melville as poetry. How could you write about whales without consulting the most recent volumes of natural history? When it came time to draft the chapter called "Cetology," though, Melville realized that science was not quite as clear-cut as he had imagined, for the natural historians, having learned that whales possessed warm blood and lungs, were not even sure anymore "whether a whale be a fish." Indeed, the proliferation of facts, based on empirical observation; the increasingly narrow specialization of experts; the commitment to systematized knowledge—all these modern developments had seemingly made it harder, not easier, to tear away the "impenetrable veil covering our knowledge of the cetacea."

Melville did his winking best to provide a thorough classification schema, based on the one used by book publishers to distinguish the different sizes of their volumes: thus, Folio whales, Octavo whales, and Duodecimo whales. He also kept apologizing, though, for his "endless subdivisions based upon the most inconclusive differences," which made for a "repellingly intricate" system, and which perhaps lent his chapter a dangerous aura of comprehensiveness: "any human thing supposed to be complete, must for that very reason infallibly be faulty." The whole chapter is, in truth, a testament to his scientific inclinations, his desire to dissect reality. But Melville felt ambivalent about almost all of his inclinations. After a dozen pages, he threw up his hands: "God keep me from ever completing anything. This whole book is but a draught—nay, but the draught of a draught. Oh, Time, Strength, Cash, and Patience!"[6]

Science returns again and again in *Moby-Dick*, usually in the guise of modern progress, and usually serving to stall the actual progress of the narrative. Melville luxuriated in the undulation he was creating between drama and tranquility, motion and stillness, as he shifted between his increasingly desperate story and his research-based meditations on that story: "fact and fancy, half-way meeting, interpenetrate, and form one seamless whole."[7] In a sense, Melville had latched onto the radical, Romantic conception of science popularized by the great naturalist Alexander von Humboldt, whose magnum opus, *Cosmos*, was enthralling the western world in the late 1840s. For Humboldt and his followers—who included not just natural historians but also such poets as Emerson, Thoreau, and Whitman—the pursuit of scientific truths, in Mumford's words, "no longer [meant] a restriction, a dried-up quality, an incompleteness; it no longer [deified] the empirical and the practical at the expense of the ideal and the aesthetic: on the contrary, these qualities [were] now completely fused together, as an expression of life's integrated totality."[8] Or, as Humboldt himself explained, the holistic depiction of Nature must balance rigorous observation with wild imagining: "In the first place, I have endeavored to present her in the pure objectiveness of external phenomena; and, secondly, as the reflection of the image impressed by the senses upon the inner man, that is, upon his ideas and feelings."[9]

That balancing, that interweaving, that aspiration to capture a unified whole, mattered much more to Melville than moving his plot forward. His critics' attachment to straightforward narrative reflected an assumption that their countrymen would continue to march through time confidently, successfully, as pioneers, conquerors, masters. But Humboldtian science could have a critical, political edge, juxtaposing the humility of interconnection with the hubris of colonial advance. "Progress" always doubles back on itself; the future is interwoven with the past.[10]

Melville wanted his readers to feel as though Moby Dick had always been lurking in the depths, and always would be. Upon seeing the great skeletons of ancient leviathans, Melville himself was, "by a flood, borne back to that wondrous period . . . [when] the whole world was the whale's. . . . I am horror-struck at this antemosaic, unsourced existence of the unspeakable terrors of the whale, which, having been before all time, must needs exist after all humane ages are over." Today, in the age of climate change, scientists have started to suspect that warming oceans will pose a serious threat to many whales, especially the northernmost species. But Melville, whose apocalyptic imagination could keep pace with that of any twenty-first-century environmentalist, insisted that the cetaceans could never be overcome: "if ever the world is to be again flooded, like the Netherlands, to kill off its rats, then the eternal whale will still survive, and rearing upon the topmost crest of the equatorial flood, spout his frothed defiance to the skies."[11]

Ahab's defiance, which drives all the action of the novel, may seem as timeless as the whale's, but it is also meant to offset one specific malevolent act, the central trauma of his own personal past. Moby Dick took his leg; he must take Moby Dick's life.

What forces can offset trauma? Perhaps the old rituals of community— the solidarity of shared risk—a squeeze of the hand all around. Perhaps the embrace of difference—the transcendence of our inclination toward endless subdivision. Perhaps a breath of salt air, bright sun, the rolling of the ocean, the curve of a welcoming bay. Perhaps the recognition that we are all inevitably intertwined, each with the other, all with the world. Perhaps the adjustment of our "conceit of attainable felicity," so that it's not about recovery but rather "the heart, the bed, the table, the saddle, the fire-side, the country."[12]

Captain Ahab, though, could no longer believe in the concrete joys of human existence. There could be no compensation, for him, but revenge. "Oh! how immaterial are all materials! What things real are there, but imponderable thoughts? . . . So far gone am I in the dark side of the earth, that its other side, the theoretic bright one, seems but uncertain twilight to me."[13]

Still, as Mumford understood, more deeply than many of his contemporaries, Ahab was not just a tragic figure. His defiance was also heroic, for we are all traumatized to some extent, and not to fight back against "the mystery of evil and the accidental malice of the universe" is to risk becoming the universe's pawn. "Ahab is the spirit of man," Mumford wrote, "small and feeble, but purposive, that pits its puniness . . . and its purpose against the black senselessness of power." We humans may go humbly about our business—we may seek a simple life—"a happy marriage, livelihood, offspring, social companionship, and cheer"—and yet, regardless of our worthiness, we will eventually meet with "illness, accident, treachery, jealousy, vengefulness, dull frustration." To Mumford, *Moby-Dick* belonged at the heart of the western canon, because ultimately all of western history, "in mind and action, in the philosophy and art of the Greeks, in the organization and technique of the Romans, in the precise skills and unceasing spiritual quests of the modern man, is a tale of this effort to combat the whale—to ward off his blows, to counteract his aimless thrusts, to create a purpose that will offset the empty malice of Moby-Dick."

We offset meaninglessness through the construction of meaning. Ishmael may have been more skilled at interpretation than Ahab, but Ahab, an accomplished cetologist himself, who knew all there was to know about whales and simultaneously recognized their inscrutability, made a lasting contribution. Even as he lost faith in everything, he kept up his pursuit. "Without the belief in such a purpose," as Mumford put it, "life is neither bearable nor significant: unless one is polarized by these central human energies and aims, one tends to become absorbed in Moby-Dick himself, and becoming part of his being, can only maim, slay, butcher."[14]

The problem with Ahab's approach was that he armed himself "with power instead of love."[15] Against the brute force of Moby Dick, he consolidated the forces of modernity, turning his men into machinery, his ship into a steaming engine of vengeance—"as if from the open field a brick-kiln were transported to her planks."

Ahab merely provided the instigating motion. "'Twas not so hard a task," he muses. "I thought to find one stubborn, at the least; but my one cogged circle fits into all their various wheels, and they revolve." He is satisfied, and yet also a little disappointed. "D'ye feel brave men, brave?" he asks, once they've finally found Moby Dick.

"'As fearless fire,' cried Stubb.

"'And as mechanical,' muttered Ahab."[16]

It's as if, in Mumford's words, Ahab recognized his own complicity in transforming whaling "from a brutal but glorious battle into a methodical, slightly banal industry."[17] His men have become mere tools, to him; he can't maintain his respect for them once they have coupled themselves to his locomotive. "The permanent constitutional condition of the manufactured man, thought Ahab, is sordidness." Even his own passion could be understood as mechanical: "the path to my fixed purpose is laid with iron rails, whereon my soul is grooved to run." By the story's climax, Ahab has acquired so much momentum that he himself resembles "the mighty iron Leviathan of the modern railway," and he seems to negate all the old, traditional offsetting forces of the world: "Alike, joy and sorrow, hope and fear, seemed ground to finest dust, and powdered, for the time, in the clamped mortar of Ahab's iron soul. Like machines, [the crew] dumbly moved about the deck, ever conscious that the old man's despot eye was on them."[18]

Ahab's purpose was higher than that of the Pequod's owners, who believed only in profit and comfort and "sluggish routine," but his turn toward modernity, his exclusive embrace of the future, was also his death wish.[19] Moby-Dick is a tragedy—in part, the tragedy of American society as a runaway train. Ahab dies when his own harpoon line catches him around the neck as it's being violently unspooled, with a sound like "the manifold whizzings of a steam-engine in full play."[20]

Yet Melville had found a new, compelling form for his tragic tale, one that balanced modern fluidity with ancient steadfastness. The mere survival of a lone sailor, Ishmael, spinner and interweaver of yarns, offered a measure of redemption. Through the act of storytelling, as Mumford argued, Melville had "conquered the white whale in his own consciousness: instead of blankness there was significance, instead of aimless energy there was purpose, and instead of random living there was Life. The universe is inscrutable, unfathomable, malicious, so—like the white whale and his element. Art in the broad sense of all humanizing effort is man's answer to this condition: for it is the means by which he circumvents or postpones his doom, and bravely meets his tragic destiny. Not tame and gentle bliss, but disaster, heroically encountered, is man's true happy ending."[21]

Melville never faltered in the belief that in confronting his white whale he had pushed his art as far as it could go—and so he struggled in confronting his scornful reviewers. As usual, his emotional condition in early 1852 is almost impossible to determine, but there are signs of dismay, and Mumford posited that he must have been "exhausted and overwrought." Regardless of the reviews, Mumford thought, the effort of writing *Moby-Dick* would have left the author in a state of "irritation, debility, impotence."[22] Of course, it's again possible that Mumford was projecting: surely Melville's experience composing his magnum opus must have run parallel to his own experience composing his Melville biography. Here was a Cape Horn in Melville's life, Mumford insisted, a "crisis" that "almost unseated him," as he "first became aware of the riled depths of his unconscious."[23] Certainly, the accomplishment had been supreme: "a new integration of thought, a widening of the fringe of consciousness, a deepening of insight, through which the modern vision of life will finally be embodied."[24] But the price had been steep, and few readers appreciated his long, drawn-out plunge into the depths.

Mumford, at least, would always be grateful. *Moby-Dick*, for him, was a fully modernist questioning of modernity. It looked both backward and forward; it embraced science but also critiqued science; it told a classic adventure story but interrupted itself to take stock of the writer's inner world.

In 1952, after completing the final volume in *The Renewal of Life*, Mumford was musing on the style he had developed for the series, and his mind immediately jumped back to Melville. His approach in all four books, he said, was modeled on a "new kind of writing that grew up first in the nineteenth century: a species represented by 'Moby-Dick' and by William James's Psychology, in which the imaginative and the subjective part is counterbalanced by an equal interest in the objective, the external, the scientifically apprehended." He thought his prose was marked by a strong inner voice, but what he ultimately strove for was a "combination of personality and individuality with impersonality and collective research."[25]

Everyone needs to be checked and balanced, in a modern democracy, or else the captains, like master sprockets, might wield too much power. "Cursed be that mortal inter-indebtedness," Ahab exclaims.[26] But the power of the interdependent collective was one of the key lessons of Melvillean cetology. Moby Dick, it's true, swam forth his own inexorable self; perhaps he was immortal, indestructible. The survival of cetaceans, though, especially in the age of empire, depended on their banding together in great armadas, "as if numerous nations of them had sworn solemn league and covenant for mutual assistance and protection."[27] Mortal inter-indebtedness was timeless; what modernity demanded was a new, deliberate interweaving.

CHAPTER 11

Neotechnics (1932-34)

Mumford thought that *Moby-Dick* had frustrated Melville's contemporaries, in part, because its composite form, though springing from radical nineteenth-century sources, was ultimately too far ahead of its time. The novel "presupposes, for its acceptance, a more integrated life and consciousness than we have known or experienced, for the most part, these last three centuries."[1] But perhaps the depths of the Great Depression—during which the renewed interest in Melville continued to grow—could offer an opportunity for fresh beginnings, for just the right kind of integration. Mumford imagined himself crafting models for an interwoven society whose modernity did not rely on the mechanized, exploitative factory system.

A deep, historically sophisticated critique of that system lies at the heart of *Technics and Civilization*, but Mumford insisted that this first volume of the *Renewal of Life* series also had to be forward-looking, like *Moby-Dick*. In his previous work, he had posited the Great War as having launched a new kind of dark modernity, marked by its unprecedented destructive power and its fetishization of surveillance and control. One key innovation in *Technics* was the suggestion that the war might be seen more properly as the *end* of an era, the culmination of a devastating epoch in which far too many human beings had signed over their agency and spirit to machines and captains of industry. Now the task was to usher in the dawning "Neotechnic" era, an age of distributed energy, lighter materials, social cooperation, and environmental balance. Modern ecological science served as Mumford's cetology: it ultimately provided more questions than answers, but its central, inexorable premise was universal interconnection.[2]

It wasn't that this sense of interconnection had never existed before; the problem was that the previous several centuries had buried it under a mass of specialized technical developments. Now, "amid the host of stimuli to which people are subjected, it becomes more and more difficult to absorb and cope with any one part of the environment, to say nothing of dealing with it as a whole."[3] Back in the 1920s, Mumford had taken from his mentor, Patrick Geddes, the idea that in order to launch the Neotechnic age, the western world would first have to renounce the "Paleotechnic," which came into full power around 1850 in the United States, with the consolidation of industrial capitalism. It could also be called the "Carboniferous" period: Mumford associated it most explicitly with the "fever of exploitation" that marked the mining of fossil fuels. The layers of soot and ash and dust and grime, he thought, had not only covered all the walls but seeped into everyone's lungs and minds, creating a new psychological profile, with easily recognized traits: "the lowered morale, the expectation of getting something for nothing, the disregard for a balanced mode of production and consumption, the habituation to wreckage and debris as part of the normal human environment."[4] Paleotechnic people, for better or worse, were driven by a narrow embrace of limitless wants and endless growth.

As Mumford had explained in *The Story of Utopias* (1922), it seemed to him that most of his compatriots had simply accepted life in Megalopolis, while the unluckiest were stuck in Coketown, and the lucky few occasionally escaped to a Country House, where they tried to deny the existence of those whose labor made their escape possible. It was precisely the "Country House standards of consumption" that were "responsible for our Acquisitive Society."[5] The old, aristocratic ideal of being able to enjoy any commodity without worrying about how it was produced or delivered had become the model of the Good Life for everyone, such that work was no longer a decent way of living, of connecting with one's surroundings and producing one's own essentials, but rather a mere means to possessing and consuming as many goods as possible.[6]

The sad denizens of Coketown, though, rarely attained any significant purchasing power, bent as they were to the degraded task of "providing the rest of the world with necessities, comforts, luxuries, and nullities." Coketown's layout, determined entirely by the factory owner, was in the pattern of the classic gridiron, and the school and the jail and the hospital and the city hall all looked like the factory, and "what remains is obscured by smoke."

Meanwhile, the bureaucrats inhabiting Megalopolis purposely closed their eyes to "the palpable earth, with its mantle of vegetation and its tent of clouds," spending their days attempting "to conduct the whole of human life and intercourse through the medium of paper." What was Megalopolis, after all, but "a paper purgatory," a series of intermediary institutions, exchanges, custom houses, where everything could be tallied at a safe remove?[7]

In *Technics*, Mumford went beyond the description of this seemingly unaccountable transition to modernity and started probing its strangeness, started unpacking the psychology of paleotechnic personhood. It was true, he noted, that certain critics of the American scene, starting in Melville's time, had tried to highlight the poverty, degradation, and demoralization that accompanied technical development. But the myth of Progress as constant and unstoppable became so powerful in the Gilded Age that most Americans were literally blinded to hard realities. Astoundingly, in the midst of squalor and despair, it was simply understood that the modern city was cleaner and more pleasant than the premodern city, that the quality of life was now higher, because, while the world might spin in circles, the directionality of modern society was perfectly linear. If some people were suffering, maybe it was their own fault for not keeping up. In any case, they weren't worth thinking about. "The new environment," Mumford wrote, "did not lend itself to first hand exploration and reception. To take it at second hand, to put at least a psychological distance between the observer and the horrors and deformities observed, was really to make the best of it. . . . A certain dullness and irresponsiveness, in short, a state of partial anesthesia, became a condition of survival." Everyone was traumatized, then, but of course a few managed to profit from the trauma, while most felt trapped: "If the landlords and other monopolists enjoyed an unearned increment from the massing of population and the collective efficiency of the machine, the net result for society at large might be characterized as the unearned excrement." One of Mumford's personal conditions of survival was a dark sense of humor.[8]

Technics and Civilization was Mumford's most explicit account yet of the ways in which basic human experiences had been reduced and degraded in modern times, and it was meant to shock people out of their mechanical militarism. He acknowledged the "vast gains in energy and in the production of goods"; yet he thought that they came with a commensurate "impoverishment of life," at least for most people. Sometimes, predictably, apologists for modernity challenged him by asking if we would be better off living amid the filth and ignorance and violence of medieval times. Mumford had a trump card ready: World War I. "If one compared the amount of destruction caused by a hundred years of the most murderous warfare in the Middle Ages with what took place in four short years during the World War, precisely because of such great instruments of technological progress as modern artillery, steel tanks, poison gas, bombs and flame throwers, picric acid and T.N.T., the result was a step backward."[9]

Most often, though, Mumford's arguments in *Technics* focused less on machines and more on mindsets—especially on rediscovering the much longer history of the mental transition to modernity. Previously, following Geddes, Mumford had thought of the Paleotechnic as relatively new, delimited most notably by the invention of the steam engine in 1712, for the specific purpose of pumping water out of a mine. In *Technics*, though, he resolutely attacked that perception of machines' determinative power, railing against "the careless habit of attributing to mechanical improvements a direct role as instruments of culture and civilization." His new emphasis was on the way in which technics always reflected certain "human choices and aptitudes and strivings, deliberate as well as unconscious, often irrational when apparently they are most objective and scientific."

After his 1932 trip to Europe with Catherine Bauer, during which he read some crucial scholarship in German and French, Mumford began to think that the key choices leading to modernity had been made back in the Middle Ages. The era of the machine, he insisted on the first page of *Technics*, had been "developing steadily for at least seven centuries" before the so-called "industrial revolution." Alas, "men had become mechanical before they perfected complicated machines to express their new bent and interest; and the will-to-order had appeared . . . in the monastery and the army and the counting-house before it finally manifested itself in the factory."[10] Sometimes rediscovery is just about recognizing that the mess we're in isn't as new as we'd thought.

It wasn't the steam engine that launched the western world's "unflinching assault" on Nature; it was a gradual cultural shift that had started much earlier, when Europeans were struggling with Plagues and Wars and Famines, and they started to dream of controlling the "erratic fluctuations and pulsations" of the world. In a climate of doubt and chaotic uncertainty, they put less stock in patient cultivation and eventually developed a "will to dominate the environment," linked to their broader desire to achieve a new order and discipline in everyday life. They were tired of pinning the success of their crops on prayers for better weather. Like Ahab, they wanted a better grip on their lives: "I like to feel something in this slippery world that can hold."[11]

Ultimately, Mumford imagined modernity unfolding from the rigid, regimented routines of the forty thousand Benedictine monasteries that sustained culture through the Dark Ages—where the "canonical hours" were rung seven times a day. The Benedictine bells, functioning as a clock (until actual mechanical clocks were invented in the thirteenth century), gave "human enterprise the regular collective beat and rhythm of the machine; for the clock is not merely a means of keeping track of the hours, but of synchronizing the actions of men." Even monks, in other words, were focusing less on eternity and faith; from now on, they would nurture a new "belief in an independent world of mathematically measurable sequences." And whatever could be measured could also be mastered.[12]

The modern mindset quite purposefully repudiated common, organic experience. Previously, people had accepted that days and nights were of uneven duration; that time was cyclical and cumulative as well as linear; that the qualitative, the emotional, the mystical, were at the heart of the human condition. But when the Royal Society was founded in England in 1660, "the humanities were deliberately excluded." Now, all that mattered in the world were the things that lent themselves "to accurate factual observation and to generalized statements." Why did Linear Progress become the all-important goal in the West? In part, because "uniform motion in a straight line" was the easiest kind to map in the new "system of spatial and temporal coordinates." Organic experience was messy, unpredictable. Better to devalue context and extract whatever could be extracted from the world, in neat, regular units, to be "weighed, measured, or counted" and ultimately controlled.

Though we think of ecology as arising in the nineteenth century, Mumford pointed out that critics of extractive industries noticed environmental interconnections hundreds of years earlier. As the sixteenth-century German writer known as Agricola explained, "when the woods and groves are felled, there are exterminate the beasts and birds, very many of which furnish pleasant and agreeable food for man. Further, when the ores are washed, the water which has been used poisons the brooks and streams, and either destroys the fish or drives them away." You can't escape context. Yet Agricola went on to defend both timber-mining and metals-mining, because he could not imagine going against the new definition of success, which was based explicitly on "the methods and ideals" of extraction. There would be collateral damage, yes. But the pattern, as Mumford put it, had been set: "blast: dump: crush: extract: exhaust." That way, at least, you'd have something concrete to show for your efforts; you wouldn't have to depend on a capricious climate and other unfathomable forces.[13]

Still, it was important to recognize that there had always been resistance to the modernization of mindsets. The other key rediscovery in *Technics and Civilization* is the wealth of promising ideas and practices dating to the early modern period—which Geddes had never really explored in depth and which Mumford now dubbed the "Eotechnic." Historical change is never straightforward. Though Mumford placed the roots of the Paleotechnic era in the Dark Ages, he saw enough alternative trends arising simultaneously to justify a complex, overlapping

periodization in which "Eo" and "Paleo" developments were in competition for several centuries, with the Eotechnic achieving a slight
dominance until the eighteenth century and the age of carboniferous
capitalism.[14] (In the 1950s and 1960s, when Mumford revisited the history of technics, eventually publishing a two-volume work called *The
Myth of the Machine,* he dismissed this periodization as misleading.
What mattered to him in the end was the constant clash of ideals and
values rather than a determination of which ones may have dominated
in any given era.)

Mumford's Eotechnic world was in many ways a dreamscape, a shorthand for some of the guiding practices we might revive in the coming
Neotechnic era. In its ideal form, the Eotechnic was a time and place
where life was slower, where artists like Rembrandt helped usher in a
modern kind of introspective autobiography, "not as a means of edifica-
tion but as a picture of the self, its depths, its mysteries, its inner dimensions." The Eotechnic was characterized by limits on growth, by a "balance between agriculture and industry," as embodied by the small town
with a sawmill or a gristmill at its center—where the standard of living
might be expressed less often in terms of money and power than in
terms of "an adequate diet, proper facilities for hygiene, decent dwell-
ings . . . , and opportunities for education and recreation"—not to mention "sunlight and open spaces . . . , leisure, and health, and biological
activity, and esthetic pleasure, and . . . environmental improvements
that lie outside of machine production."[15] Clearly, Mumford's Eotechnic
fantasy elided politics and many social inequalities and injustices, as
Catherine Bauer had noted: for instance, like *Moby-Dick, Technics and
Civilization* essentially left out women. And the mill towns of America
had been made possible by extermination campaigns against Indians.

At the same time, though, it seems worth acknowledging Mumford's
point that during the Renaissance, "thanks to the menial services of
wind and water," Europeans had enough energy to create "great works
of art and scholarship and science and engineering," all "without recourse to slavery." Indeed, for at least a brief time in the fifteenth century,
Mumford thought, certain great minds—Michelangelo and Leonardo
da Vinci, for instance—had achieved a "balance between the sensuous

and the intellectual, between image and sound, between the concrete and the abstract," before the era of print inevitably biased people toward abstraction. Even the larger towns of this period, gradually turning into great cities like Venice and Amsterdam, seemed relatively relaxed and social, seemed "solidly built and commodiously arranged," seemed to foster "a greater intensification of life" and to nurture, "alike for rich and poor, the spirit of play"—such that "in every department of activity, there was equilibrium between the static and the dynamic, between the rural and the urban, between the vital and the mechanical." Who wouldn't choose the Eotechnic over "the contraction and starvation of the senses which had characterized the religious codes that preceded it" or, alternatively, "the phases of mechanical civilization that followed it"?[16]

What the western world needed in the 1930s was to rediscover the glory of the ideal Eotechnic while also incorporating certain carefully selected aspects of modernity. This would not be a simple reversion to simpler times. Perhaps most importantly, the Neotechnic era would move toward what Mumford was already calling in *The Brown Decades* "a more biotechnic economy."[17] The new technical regime would replace coal and oil with solar and wind and water power, but also with electricity; and there would be plenty of new ecologically sensitive alloys and synthetics. Generally, Americans would "return to Nature" and embrace humanity's "dynamic interpenetration" with the environment and organic processes. Buildings would be made from local materials, adapted to the land, woven into the local ecology. "Instead of simplifying the organic," Mumford explained, "to make it intelligibly mechanical ... , we have begun to complicate the mechanical, in order to make it more organic: therefore more effective, more harmonious with our living environment."[18]

At the same time, the Machine would also receive credit for having "disclosed new esthetic spectacles, new worlds." Mumford celebrated photography, for instance, as a democratic art, "capable of coping with and adequately presenting the complicated, inter-related aspects of our modern environment," allowing any citizen to relearn "Whitman's lesson and behold with a new respect the miracle of our finger joints or the reality of a blade of grass." He also admired new kinds of scientific gardening that "respected the natural ecological partnerships." And he thought that communally funded institutions like modern fire departments and "schools, libraries, hospitals, universities, museums, baths, lodging houses, gymnasia," as well as certain kinds of "roads, canals, bridges, parks, playgrounds, and . . . ferry services," could all serve as basic models of the kind of development that could bolster people's sense of place and integration. FDR's New Deal, in other words, with its public arts and infrastructure projects, would turn out to be a fulfillment of many aspects of Mumford's vision. Ultimately, Mumford hoped, the Neotechnic approach, through its balancing of science and art and of individual and collective development, might "produce a state in which creation will be a common fact in all experience: in which no group will be denied, by reason of toil or deficient education, their share in the cultural life of the community."[19]

Of course, full Renewal would also require some hard mental labor: even the most elegantly designed Neotechnic community would founder if its inhabitants were unwilling to shift their mindsets. "The gains in technics," Mumford wrote, nodding to Catherine Bauer, "are never registered automatically in society: they require equally adroit inventions and adaptations in politics." In a culture infatuated with its own modernity, people were likely to embrace innovation for its own sake rather than to ensure robust debate about each significant technical development. Not all kinds of creation were created equal. Mumford knew that in many previous eras, "invention had become a duty, and the desire to use the new marvels of technics, like a child's delighted bewilderment over new toys, was not in the main guided by critical discernment: people agreed that inventions were good, whether or not they actually provided benefits."[20]

How could a society guard against the allure of sparkling, new devices created explicitly to get users addicted to particular types of stimulation and satisfaction? Mumford thought the key might be to sustain arguments about the purpose of life—to insist that some of the best human experiences could not be measured or counted or even firmly grasped—to remind people, as Melville liked to do, "that life may be most intense and significant in its moments of pain and anguish, that it may be most savorless in its moments of repletion." In a period like the Great Depression, people would be tempted to focus on producing more goods to meet the basic, concrete needs of consumers. But it is precisely in such moments, Mumford insisted, that we must remember how hard it is to define basic needs. Material fulfillment goes only so far. "The sure click and movement of machines" may create an illusion of control and certainty, may tempt us to reduce life to the production of countable supplies for the satisfaction of clear demands. But some human needs can't be met mechanically; some "might in fact be vague, complex, undefinable, perpetually a little obscure and shifty."[21] Neo-technics would always have to retain an Eotechnic sense of mystery.

CHAPTER 12

The Ambiguities (1852)

I first learned of Melville's novel *Pierre; or, The Ambiguities* in college: according to the course catalogue, a well-known literature professor was offering an upper-level seminar devoted to just that one book. My immediate assumption was that the novel had to be twice as long and complicated as *Moby-Dick*. And since I knew from reading Joseph Conrad that "The Doldrums" referred to an actual part of the ocean, infamous for its dead calms, I guessed that "The Ambiguities" might also be a place named by mariners—perhaps something like the Bermuda Triangle of the Pacific.

I was wrong on all counts. *Typee, Omoo, Mardi, Redburn, White-Jacket, Moby-Dick*: over five years and six novels, Melville had spun nothing but sailors' yarns. And he had fairly consistently spurned women. Then, in the frenzy of finishing *Moby-Dick*, he decided to overturn every readerly expectation he could imagine and create something of "unquestionable novelty":[1] this new book would move inland and inward, toward Hawthorne's territory, to explore the tragic entanglements of the sexes in the domestic corners of middle-class New England. *Pierre* turned out to be significantly less expansive than *Moby-Dick*. And "ambiguity," in the mid-nineteenth century, referred to navigational difficulties not on the open sea but in the closed spaces of the mind: if you came across as "ambiguous," you might be going crazy. Once the book was published, though, the main question in reviewers' minds was who might be crazier: Pierre or his creator.

Fundamentally, the book is about an ambiguous love triangle—or, perhaps, pentagram. Pierre is a young man surrounded by women, as

Melville often was (wife, mother, sisters, sisters-in-law, aunts, cousins). At the start of the story, Pierre lives with his widowed mother on an idyllic Berkshire estate; they share meals, call each other "brother" and "sister," and engage in playful banter. Several chapters later, Pierre winds up in an apartment in New York City, with a "fallen" woman whom he is committed to helping; with his loyal ex-fiancée from the Berkshires; and with his long-lost half sister (probably), whom he has pretended to marry so as to help her recover some share of their family's wealth—and with whom he seems to be infatuated.

It's a crazy book—made even crazier by the revelation, only after Pierre has arrived in New York City, that in fact he is a writer, struggling to balance the demands of his conscience and the market. Melville seems to have added all the parts about Pierre's literary career after spending some time in New York himself in January 1852, where he read the most recent reviews of *Moby-Dick* and argued with his publisher over his advance for the new manuscript, which was already tragic but which would become significantly more bitter over the next few weeks.

Lewis Mumford found *Pierre* endlessly provocative, but he worried that maybe it could have used a stronger dose of ambiguity: the final version seemed to him "like a living man with his entrails exposed."[2]

It is hard not to read *Pierre* as Melville's desperate cry of disillusionment. All the motion in the novel takes us from sentimental, idealistic innocence to hard, dark experience. "Round and round does the world lie as in sharp-shooter's ambush, to pick off the beautiful illusions of youth, by the pitiless cracking rifles of the realities of age."[3] Pierre worshipped his father, who died when he was twelve (Herman's age when his own father died); now it turns out that this gentle Christian had (probably) sired an illegitimate daughter, whom he permitted to be raised in poverty. Both of Pierre's grandfathers (like both of Melville's) had been heroes in the Revolution, conquerors of the British, and of the Indians who had previously ruled "those noble woods and plains" of the Berkshires to which Pierre's family, the Glendinnings, now held the deed. Pierre grew up perfectly secure in these ancestral accomplishments— "little recking of that mature and larger interior development, which should forever deprive these things of their full power of pride in his soul . . . , thoughtless of that period of remorseless insight, when all these delicate warmths should seem frigid to him."[4]

Many thoughtful Americans of Melville's generation were starting to reckon with the gap between Revolutionary ideals and early republic realities, with the vast inequalities in their democracy, and especially with the inhumanity of the slave system on southern plantations. But Melville was somewhat unusual in condemning the landed estates of the North—those "mighty lordships in the heart of a republic"—as reeking of aristocratic privilege, as well as genocide and theft. The Glendinnings even had tenant farmers working their lands and paying them tribute, so that they themselves could focus on enjoying life's finer pleasures. Pierre had grown up in the archetypal Country House, never seeing—as Melville put it—"that darker, though truer aspect of things, which an entire residence in the city from the earliest period of life, almost inevitably engraves upon the mind of any keenly observant and reflective youth of Pierre's present years." Melville had grown up (partly) in New York, and at nineteen (Pierre's age) he had sailed to Liverpool: during that trip he began to understand, viscerally, how the idle ease of the wealthy rested on the grueling labor of the poor, the worst-off of whom he saw dying in the gutter. So Melville moved Pierre to the city, to join other "social castaways" in anonymous misery. Indeed, Pierre winds up "feeling entirely lonesome, and orphan-like": he has been "driven out an infant Ishmael into the desert."[5]

Pierre also becomes an Ahab, though. Once he gains a certain amount of experience, he starts to burn for glimpses of darker truths, starts to attack all the world's masks, starts to believe that injustice and trauma and revenge are the only Realities. "Welcome then," he says, "be Ugliness and Poverty and Infamy, and all ye other crafty ministers of Truth." Disowned by his mother, he can barely stand to think about his prior inheritance: "how disdainfully now he eyed the sumptuousness of his hereditary halls—the hangings, and the pictures, and the bragging historical armorials and the banners of the Glendinning renown." His forebears had been perfect Christian gentlemen—in other words, hypocrites. "Christianity calls upon all men to renounce this world," Pierre noted, "yet by all odds the most Mammonish part of this world—Europe and

America—are owned by none but professed Christian nations, who glory in the owning." His compatriots, meanwhile, liked to speak of how Society as a whole was constantly progressing, but Pierre knew that "only some of its individuals do, and by advancing, leave the rest behind." Indeed, though few people would acknowledge the utter unfairness of America's false meritocracy, Pierre saw clearly that the "operative" principle in northeastern capitalism was the further enrichment of the rich and the further impoverishment of the poor: "he who is already fully provided with what is necessary for him, that man shall have more, while he who is deplorably destitute of the same, he shall have taken away from him even that which he hath."[6]

Pierre's purported half sister, Isabel, had been abandoned to deplorable destitution, with neither family nor friends, while Pierre had luxuriated in the "preservative and beautifying influences of unfluctuating rank, health, and wealth." So the climax of the novel comes when Isabel confronts Pierre with her story, and he decides that he must help her, no matter what the consequences to himself. Isabel, in other words, comes to symbolize every kind of absolute truth and ideal. Society had discarded her; Pierre would embrace her. Society prized respectability, convention, legitimacy, progress, placidity, superficiality; Pierre would sacrifice all his comforts and advantages, would brave scandal and disgrace and scorn and isolation, for the sake of true Christian charity, for loyalty, for the protection of the helpless, for "the highest heaven of uncorrupted Love."[7]

In addition to ethical purity, though, as Mumford was quick to note, Isabel also represented Melville's aesthetic ideal. Isabel was Melville's defiant determination to write *Moby-Dick*, to sail through storms, to blend genres and flout expectations. (Pierre's fiancée, Lucy, at least at the start of the book, represented the temptations of the market: she was air and light, "all symmetry and radiance," utterly conventional, safe, fun, pleasing—she was *Typee* and *Omoo*.) In breaking off his engagement and linking himself with Isabel, Pierre was upholding tragedy, affirming again "that not to know Gloom and Grief is not to know aught that an heroic man should learn"—for he recognized from the start that his plan would surely fail. Instead of raising his sister to a more privileged status he would in fact be lowering himself to her level, that of the outcast, struggling just to be admitted to the circle of the common laborer. Pierre's story would be tragic, like Ahab's, because all the greatest stories were tragic. "The truest of all men," Melville had written in *Moby-Dick*, "was the Man of Sorrows, and the truest of all books is Solomon's, and Ecclesiastes is the fine hammered steel of woe. 'All is vanity.' ALL."[8]

Isabel is Truth, then. But Melville doubted Truth as much as he doubted everything else. Yes, he had been swept up in the fever of *Moby-Dick*, had felt the power of its dark realism while he was working on it. Once he had finished writing, though—well, how could he be sure that he was right and the critics were wrong? In *Pierre*, it is not even clear how much actual truth there is in the tale Isabel tells of her parentage. She has no definitive evidence; she isn't sure herself that she's a Glendinning. The whole novel hinges on moments of uncanny recognition, on phantasmagoric suggestions, on "swift but mystical corroborations": Pierre has seen Isabel's face before in strange visions, and she looks eerily like a portrait of Pierre's father as a young man with a mischievous glint in his eye, a portrait his mother unaccountably hates. Thus: Pierre has rediscovered his sister! That fact is "intuitively certain" but "literally unproven," and Pierre, though choosing to believe from the start, is also wracked with doubt, trapped in an "endless chain of wondering." He feels "bewitched" and "enchanted," as though "all the world, and every misconceivedly common prosaic thing in it, was steeped a million fathoms in . . . haziness." Isabel's ultimate Truth is ultimately a mystery.[9]

Pierre is a novel of fractured selves and impossible relationships. No one knows what to think about what is happening; no one knows where to turn for comfort and communion. This time, no one will survive. Pierre himself recognizes that even his love and generosity and idealism are impure. What if this lost sister had been "a humped, and crippled, and hideous girl"? He has to admit that his desire to help Isabel is partly based on other desires, sparked by her graceful face, "so bewilderingly alluring, speaking of a mournfulness infinitely sweeter and more attractive than all mirthfulness, that face of glorious suffering, that face of touching loveliness." Hints of forbidden yearnings arise at the very start of the book, when we learn that the "reverential and devoted" Pierre "seemed lover enough" for his lonely mother. Indeed, mother and son show an "inexpressible tenderness and attentiveness" toward each other, as if engaged in "courtship"—but, of course, there is no future for them. And then Pierre chooses to pair himself with his sister, whom he seems to adore even more—but that relationship also can't go anywhere, and, moreover, it precludes any other possible romantic connection. He has become a celibate monk, sharing quarters with three beautiful, young women. By the middle of the book, Pierre can look neither backward nor forward; he can live only in the present. Burning his father's portrait, and all his family letters, he stares at the fire and proclaims that "Pierre hath no paternity, and no past. . . . Twice-disinherited Pierre stands untrammeledly his ever-present self."[10]

Even worse, in a way, is the simple fact that Pierre's act of self-sacrificing charity is not only tainted and ineffectual but also essentially private. No one else actually knows the nature of his relationship with Isabel—a circumstance that somehow seems to cut to the heart of Melville's own torment. Almost every thoughtful reader of *Pierre* has come away with the sense that Melville must have been harboring some dark, anguished secret.

Was he gay? Well, it's an anachronistic label, but there are many passionate descriptions of male bodies in Melville's writings. In the nineteenth century, it was common for young men to have intense relationships with each other: countless male-male love letters have survived. Some of those relationships were homosexual; most were just Romantic, youthful preparations for more mature courtships. On sailing ships, such relationships tended to be, let's say, expedient.[11] Pierre never went to sea, but his mother, who perfumed his wardrobe, indulging his "little femininenesses," admitted to a fear that out in the world he might prove to be too "sweetly docile": "is this baton but a distaff then?" In his earlier years, Pierre had formed a deep bond with his cousin Glen—the sort of "empyrean of a love which only comes short, by one degree, of the sweetest sentiment entertained between the sexes."[12] Then, in the action of the novel, after Pierre abandons his fiancée, Lucy, Glen steps in to earn her love by defending her honor; when Glen calls Pierre a liar and a villain and slaps him in the face on a crowded New York street, Pierre kills him with two pistol shots. It seems as much a lovers' quarrel as anything else. Melville and Hawthorne, though, as far as we know, never pulled their guns on each other.

Mumford was satisfied with the conclusion that Melville must have been stuck in a mostly sexless marriage, tempted by other possible dalliances but ultimately committed to "the bleak waste land" of cold fidelity to his wife. *Pierre* was Melville's complaint about his own private limbo, but Mumford found it a mostly sterile book, not suggesting any path out of the desert. He treated it as "a warning," a cautionary tale that "spurred me to follow another way."[13]

But Mumford's fundamental sense of the novel as revealing that "Melville's emotional and sexual development" was probably "in a starved and stunted state" may ultimately stem from too literal a reading.[14] I prefer his somewhat tangential suggestion that Melville's true secret was simply that he considered himself better than his reviewers, that he was becoming more and more bitter as he adhered to his private understanding of what true literature ought to aim for, while American readers continued to crave banal entertainments. "I will gospelize the world anew," says Pierre, "and show them deeper secrets than the Apocalypse!" But at the end of the novel Pierre's dark, ambitious book gets rejected by his publishers as a "blasphemous rhapsody"; they proclaim him a swindler and sue him for the return of his cash advance. Pierre remains disgusted with his "bantering, barren, and prosaic, heartless age," but he has also become disgusted with himself—with his ambition—with his inability to bear down and earn a living—with his dreams and doubts and deceptions. He is disgusted even with his own pointless disgust.[15]

Pierre does contain hints of hope, though—glimpses of the life still left in Melville's writing career. In New York City, Pierre and his female companions confront a fair share of squalor and vice, but they also manage to find living space in an old, repurposed church, among "artists of various sorts, painters, or sculptors, or indigent students, or teachers of languages, or poets, or fugitive French politicians, or German philosophers"—in short, among "glorious paupers," who teach Pierre "the profoundest mysteries of things." Melville gently mocked these mid-nineteenth-century hipsters, but it's clear that he also enjoyed the way they peddled their "heterodoxical tenets" and admired how they "began to come together out of their various dens, in more social communion, attracted toward each other by a title common to all." The culture of The Apostles, as the former church was known, seems almost to prefigure the communalism Mumford and some of his friends fostered at Sunnyside Gardens, in Queens, in the 1920s. Both Melville and Mumford had a keen fondness for old buildings, which "sweetly and sadly remind the present man of the wonderful procession that preceded him in his new generation." The "tide of change and progress" had brought new offices and warehouses to the neighborhood, but The Apostles held its ground, standing for some combination of continuity and flexibility. Though Pierre slowly sank into his final gloom while living in the old church, he nevertheless drew inspiration from its "gray and grand old tower, emblem to Pierre of an unshakable fortitude, which, deep-rooted in the heart of the earth, defied all the howls of the air." Melville himself strove to become such a tower, grounded in hard realities but pointed toward heavenly ideals. Despite this latest novel's moments of dead-end despair, it still embodied Melville's aspiration to engage with the great mysteries of everyday living: "the profounder emanations of the human mind, intended to illustrate all that can be humanly known of human life, these never unravel their own intricacies, and have no proper endings."[16]

Alas, Melville's reviewers wanted the mysteries cleared up. "What the book means, we know not"—though maybe its senselessness indicated that Melville had given up the very project of meaning-making. "To save it from almost utter worthlessness, it must be called a prose poem, and even then, it might be supposed to emanate from a lunatic hospital rather than from the quiet retreats of Berkshire." If *Moby-Dick* was a botch, a hash, a chaotic intermixing of fact and fiction, *Pierre* was even more of a "crazy rigmarole," an "incoherent hodge-podge" of social satire, gothic romance, domestic sentimentalism, and obscure philosophy. It was "muddy, foul, and corrupt." The main characters cared not a whit for morality or decency, and any of their discernible "motives . . . are such as would consign the best of them to the madhouse. . . . Were there no mad doctors in that part of the country where they lived? Were the asylums all full?" One dismayed newspaperman claimed to have heard a rumor that Melville, whether he had been sane at the time of writing or not, had actually become "deranged" once the reviews started coming out, and that "his friends were taking measures to place him under treatment." Well, that was understandable, the newspaperman thought. And then, dropping any pretense of sympathy, he declared his earnest hope that if Melville did wind up in a hospital, "one of the earliest precautions will be to keep him stringently secluded from pen and ink."[17]

Melville managed to stay clear of the asylum, but he surely seethed at these reviews. The public's desire for clarity and sanity and certainty signaled their own diseased thinking. What could anyone know for sure? "I comprehend nothing, Pierre," Isabel says, mirroring back her brother's relentless doubts. "There is nothing these eyes have ever looked upon, Pierre, that this soul comprehended. Ever, as now, do I go all a-grope amid the wide mysteriousness of things."[18]

CHAPTER 13

Spiritual Freedom (1935-38)

Mumford's audience must have been confused, at first, as they listened to his commencement address at Oberlin College in June 1935. The talk's title was "The Recovery of the American Heritage," but it opened with a broad condemnation of the entire modern history of what Melville had called "the all-grasping western world": "The industrial exploitation of the new enterpriser, regimenting the new factory workers, was matched by the equally savage treatment of the subject peoples that came under the heels of the new national states; for these states represented the capitalist ego writ large. Within our own country the spoliation of natural resources went hand in hand with an equally corrupt exploitation of the Indian, the Negro, the poorer native whites, and, finally, the new immigrants who built our railroads and paved our cities."[1] Mumford's message would not be out of place at a twenty-first-century environmental justice rally, but, despite the enduring truth that it captures, it has never had a broad appeal in the United States, because it seems to preclude any pride in American history: Mumford was explicitly contradicting our national narrative of Progress. Who wants to recover a heritage based on exploitation, regimentation, and spoliation? But confusing your audience can be an effective way of calling its assumptions into question.

In any case, Mumford never rested his case with a critique. Ever since the Great War, that culmination of the West's gradual buildup of destructive power, he had doggedly searched for evidence from the past that reconstruction could be worthwhile. The whiggish whitewashers who glorified every stage of U.S. history were clearly deluded—but so were the naysayers who saw nothing but rigid selfishness and oppression. The point, ultimately, was that "the American heritage" should never be fixed or reducible: one of our central civic duties has always been to foster a perpetual debate about the potential meanings of that heritage. And Mumford could find something constructive in even the most tainted past.

Now, in the midst of the Great Depression, having wrestled with Melville and the rise of Technics, he felt prepared to fight for a transvaluation of one of the most cherished American symbols: The Frontier—the Open Range—the lonely spaces of the West, where cowboys and mountain men and homesteaders had supposedly pioneered a new form of rugged democracy. No longer, Mumford argued, could the Frontier legitimately represent equal opportunities for all—but neither should it be dismissed as merely a site of violence and dispossession. Perhaps, instead, the remembered experience of "a vigorous, many-sided frontier life," with its Eotechnic resonance, "with its social insurgence and its physical derring do—may offer something of decisive importance toward the humanization of the machine." And, in the specific context of the rise of European fascism in the 1930s, perhaps the myth of the Frontier could help nurture a particularly American espousal of "spiritual freedom—freedom of opinion—freedom of expression—freedom to follow the truth wherever it leads—freedom to alter our manner of life and our institutions. . . . Such freedom, so far from being essentially antagonistic to cooperative effort and discipline, is the very condition of their success."[2] A bit more intellectual independence might even have helped unite the *Pequod*'s crew against Ahab's tyranny.

Mumford's own spiritual freedom, though, which did lead him to alter his manner of life, sometimes seemed to be antagonistic to the cooperative institution of marriage. By August 1935, Sophia was starting to believe that her husband might be addicted to having affairs: "If only I knew whether Lewis was going to go on finding one woman or girl after another unique and desirable."[3] She was nursing her four-month-old daughter, chasing her ten-year-old son, and running the household in Sunnyside Gardens, while Lewis worked on the second volume of *The Renewal of Life* and arranged romantic getaways with Catherine Bauer's friend Alice Decker, an unhappily married sculptor and social worker. Once again, the Mumfords flirted with divorce. It was common for married men in their circle to have affairs, but even though they both acknowledged that reality, they also both struggled to decide whether their marriage ought to bow to it. From the start, they had fully embraced the new, modern ideal of a companionate union in which each partner was to be stimulated and satisfied by the other.[4]

Lewis had claimed that he did not want any further entanglements after Catherine left him for good—but, he said, he simply could not resist Alice. As he was falling in love with her, early in 1935, he told a friend that his mind was stuck on a particular passage from *Pierre*: "For in tremendous extremities human souls are like drowning men, well enough they know they are in peril, well enough they know the causes of that peril;—nevertheless, the sea is the sea, and these drowning men do drown."[5] Mumford was so drawn to freedom that he embraced it even when he knew it would leave him trapped; perhaps the sense of entrapment was a perverse confirmation of his freedom. He wanted to experience everything, all at once.

What had he experienced when his daughter, Alison, was born, in April, and both Catherine and Alice came to visit Sophia in the hospital, offering her some flowers and honorary membership in their "League Against War, Fascism, and Lewis Mumford"? Sophia accepted, only because she did not yet know that Lewis was sleeping with Alice. Once he made his guilty/not-guilty confession, hoping that Alice could simply slide into the slot Catherine had filled for so long, without disturbing his marriage, Sophia realized that she would have to rethink everything, and she began to withdraw. "I find it bitter," she confessed, in June, "to face his feeling for Alice when my own baby's name is a constant reminder of her."[6] Lewis, meanwhile, continued to go back and forth between the two women, wanting to be with both of them, even as Alice's husband grew increasingly menacing and Alice herself threatened suicide if Lewis refused to leave Sophia. Amazingly, though the intensity almost never abated, this ambiguous triangle endured for two and a half years. Alice wound up divorced; Lewis and Sophia stayed together. At one point, Alice burned all of Lewis's letters; a week later, he burned all of hers, in retaliation. This relationship caused much deeper scars than had Lewis's relationship with Catherine: he essentially erased Alice from the record of his life, and Sophia was furious that his biographer, Donald Miller, found enough traces to tell the story.[7]

While the affair was happening, though, and immediately afterward, Lewis and Sophia both wrote about it with their usual analytical remove: they were partners in facing the most difficult truths and somehow muddling through. "What I really want," Sophia noted, "is a sympathetic soul to whom I can say all the grievances I have against life and Lewis. Someone who will listen to them all, and know that no word is to be said against Lewis, because he is not to blame." She recognized that Lewis truly did love these other women, and she supposed he couldn't help it; he continued to love her, too, and sometimes his passion seemed redoubled. These were the confusing facts she had to live with. "If only Lewis hadn't thought to make matters clearer by explaining that . . . Alice . . . reacted in a way so akin to his that he could predict her reactions, and so felt mirrored in her and therefore close. The poor dumb-squitch. Does he think it makes me feel happier to know that some other woman is in such close harmony with him?"[8]

She knew he didn't think that. He was just acknowledging the truth of her perennial observation that he was a "divided man," and they both understood that he always would be, and that no relationship would ever be as important to him as his work. He actually finished writing The Culture of Cities late in 1937, as his relationship with Alice was finally ending. "Alice and I have been deeply in love," he wrote that December; "still are deeply in love; always will be, in a certain way that neither of us has ever shared with anyone else. But our love is tragic in its very nature."[9] He probably knew all along that, forced to choose, he would choose Sophia. In April 1936, around Alison's first birthday, he found himself writing about his wife's "quiet heroism" during the life they had built together, hailing "her ungrudging assumption of all its physical difficulties, her strong sense of truth, her sanity and balance—her tender warnings over my weaknesses in dealing with people and events.

How much of what is good in me and my life is Sophy's—must always remain Sophy's. *Compared with her no other girl has even touched my life.* And I have a sense of the poverty of my own gifts, compared with what she has given me."[10]

It was Sophia's strength that Lewis drew on when he tried to confront the Melvillean realities of the world in the mid-1930s. Fascism—the Machine Age—Depression—Neo-Utilitarianism: by 1935, Mumford was writing about "The Menace of Totalitarian Absolutism," and he meant not just Hitler in Germany but also the "prevailing anti-social doctrines" in the United States, the "gangster principles" in politics as well as the actual gangsters, not to mention the "one-sided capitalistic and mechanistic culture" that often seemed dominant despite the idealism of the New Deal.[11] At Oberlin, trying to reclaim the rough-and-tumble individualism of the Frontier in the service of cooperative, communalist goals, Mumford urged his audience to face the damage wrought by the theft of Native land and by the system of "private property and private rights"—and then to determinedly "recapture our physical heritage." Americans needed both to redistribute land "for the benefit of the whole community" and to "conserve the primeval environment as a resource for living." He explicitly brought them back to the time of Melville and Audubon and Crockett and Whitman and Thoreau and Lincoln, the kinds of "whole" men who insisted that everyone deserved a "fresh start," who relished freedom in the manner of the sailor or "the pioneer, capable of facing life at every point that it offered." And even though Mumford consciously invoked the assumed vigor of heroic white men, he also insisted on "the acceptance of variety and diversity as elements of strength, rather than weakness, in the constitution of our country. Whatever the United States may be, it is not a Totalitarian State. From the beginning no one race, no one religion, no one national group has been in possession of America; and to our original diversity one must add the effect of the immense variety of landscapes and soils and modes of working and living that now characterize our continent."[12]

Mumford himself made a commitment to work the land in 1936, when he and his family left Sunnyside Gardens for good and moved

upstate to Amenia, where they had much more space for their gardening projects (their farmhouse was technically in a "town" called Leedsville, but there was no actual town there; Amenia, three miles away, had
the Toll Gate Inn Restaurant for special occasions).[13] The Mumfords
had always lived in the city, though they had been coming to Amenia
for parts of the summer since 1926, and they bought their house there
as a warm-weather retreat in 1931. Now they would invest fully in country living, and Lewis found a new, precious freedom in dropping germinous seeds into the soil, and picking apples and peaches from the
orchards, and making strawberry jam in June, and choosing a lone fir
from the forest at Christmas, and playing with his children in the grassy
fields. If he thought of his life, and the world, as increasingly troubled
after 1935, then his arcadian frontier at least offset some of the turbu-
lence. Here was peace, balance, a chance to work without distraction,
to interweave nature and culture, to find the countermodern ground-
edness that people like Liberty Hyde Bailey had been touting for two
decades as part of The Country Life movement.[14] In November 1936,
Mumford made a vow in his private notes to "live more austerely," to
renew his dedication to *The Renewal of Life*, to infuse his writing with
all "the richness and fullness of living, the tenderness, the passion, the
intensity of feeling." At times the countryside even seemed to have a
healing effect on his marriage: he and Sophia would go on quiet walks
together, just to take in "the passing clouds, the setting sun, or the rising mist."[15]

Mumford still made frequent trips to the city, though: he was serving
on the New York City Board of Higher Education and writing columns
on art and architecture for the *New Yorker*, which required him to wander regularly through Manhattan's ever-changing streets and galleries.
Since 1919, when he had impressed the editor of the *Journal of the American Institute of Architects* with a piece of criticism he submitted, Mumford had thought of himself as an urbane, sophisticated aesthete, and no
matter how attached he got to his garden in Amenia, he never relin-
quished that identity as a "sidewalk critic."[16] Besides, his main project
in the mid-1930s was *The Culture of Cities*. And, through the end of 1937,
he insisted on making time in New York for trysts with Alice.

Then, just days after their final break, in December, once Alice had checked herself into "a sanatorium, to try to achieve, in a fortnight, a little strength with which to face the nothingness," Mumford got embroiled in yet another affair. This time his partner was Josephine Strongin, a poet whom he had first met twelve years before, when she was only sixteen. Now she was married, but miserable, and she wanted Lewis to acknowledge their long-standing mutual attraction. She wrote to him of "the power of your voice instantly to press upon my senses, your words to make the blood stand up and sink in my veins." He was flattered—and interested—but wary. As usual. Jo pressed him: "Ask Sophy to let me have one night. . . . It would harm Sophy but she is generous. You are wrong about its hurting us. It would be my life." So Lewis took the proposal to Sophia, and one can almost hear her sighing. Lewis transcribed her response: "If I thought you really could part after being together, I would not stand in your way. But I know you too well. . . . I'd have to face another couple of years of widowhood, and at the moment that is more than I can bear. I find myself writing two sorts of letters to Josephine: one claiming you completely, the other giving you up."

At first, Lewis clung to his bemused, intellectual perplexity: "Is that tragedy or comedy or just the mixed Shakespearean facts of life?" Then he decided to sleep with Jo, in April, when he went down to New York to work on a documentary film called *The City*, for which he wrote the voice-over narration. And at this point he stopped telling Sophia anything about the affair, which lasted for at least another year, though it's possible that he and Jo went to bed together only twice, and his performances seem to have left a lot to be desired.[17] Sophia, meanwhile, had learned to enjoy her husband's attention when she received it and to do without him when he was distracted. "In one way you are the most exasperating man," she said to him, in October 1938—"because you are so sweet and so good—and so absolutely ruthless."[18]

Mumford did not excise Jo from the story of his life, but he never told Sophia the whole truth about what happened. There were some realities about her marriage that she did not confront until Lewis was suffering from dementia and Donald Miller went through all their private papers while working on Lewis's biography. This was a particularly lonely kind of pain, though she fought it with her usual fortitude, and she also shared it with Jo's daughter Jill, who was "up in arms against" Miller for "bringing her mother into his story."[19] There is always collateral damage in the work we scholars do, no matter how careful and discreet we fancy ourselves to be. I hope that I've kept the harm in check.

When Mumford wrote of his affair with Jo, he framed it as a friendship, though he admitted to falling in love with her mind. Back in 1927, upon receiving some of her poems that he had agreed to help publish, he immediately expressed his ravishment: "I salute you, as Emerson did Whitman, at the beginning of a great career." And he told her that "occasionally I find some strange, oblique glimpse of you in Melville: in Pierre's sister, and in Yillah, the creature in *Mardi* that the stranded seamen wander from island to island seeking to capture. Yillah is, I think, your right name: not that I know who she is, or what she means in Melville's parable: but you are she." Mumford included an entire chapter in *My Works and Days* called "Letters to Yillah," explaining that Josephine Strongin had "flitted in and out of my life, and still hovers occasionally in my consciousness."[20]

In *Mardi*, when Melville introduces Yillah, she is a distressed damsel whom the narrator rescues by killing the Polynesian priest who was planning to sacrifice her to the gods. The narrator, an American who lets himself be known locally as the "half-deity" Taji, feels persistent pangs of remorse about becoming a murderer, but he soothes himself by focusing on Yillah's ethereal beauty and purity. Her white skin and blue eyes make him think that perhaps he arrived just in time to redeem a long-lost European captive. But Yillah knows almost nothing of her origins: "she verily believed herself a being of the lands of dreams." She tells a strange story of getting spirited away from her birthplace and finding herself on "Oroolia, the Island of Delights," where somehow she was "snared in the tendrils of a vine," eventually becoming one of its blossoms, which then gave off a perfume that suddenly condensed into a mist, from which she reemerged as a human but all the more flower-like.

At times, Taji is "tranced into a belief of her mystical legends." Then again, he also suspects that the priest drugged her and spun fantastic yarns to get her to accept her destiny as belonging only to the gods.

Gradually, Taji helps her adjust to the wider world, and they fall in love—and for a short time Taji "thought that Paradise had overtaken me on earth, and that Yillah was verily an angel." In freeing her, he has achieved his own freedom.[21]

And then Yillah simply disappears. Taji spends the rest of the novel— which lasts another 450 pages—searching for her. She never turns up.

CHAPTER 14

The Happy Failure (1853–55)

Melvillean heroes never find what they're looking for: there are no happy endings. Sometimes, as in *Pierre*, the final tragedy is on a Shakespearean scale, with bodies strewn across the stage. Often, though, there is a survivor, like Ishmael; his lot is to continue on. Despite bitter destinies and the darkest of twists, Melville rarely offers any real closure. Ambiguity usually trumps calamity.

"Look not too long in the face of the fire, O Man!" says Ishmael. "There is a wisdom that is woe; but there is a woe that is madness." Of course, Melville could not respect any man "who dodges hospitals and jails, and walks fast crossing grave-yards, and would rather talk of operas than hell." The dread swamps and oceans of the world, of life, "the millions of miles of deserts and of griefs beneath the moon"—all must be acknowledged. Yet we also walk through landscapes of hope, inhabited by friends and co-laborers. "Believe not the artificial fire, when its redness makes all things look ghastly. To-morrow, in the natural sun, the skies will be bright; those who glared like devils in the forking flames, the morn will show in far other, at least gentler, relief."

Melville had a powerful resilience he could call on in his times of despair—a "Catskill eagle" in his soul that could "alike dive down into the blackest gorges, and soar out of them again and become invisible in the sunny spaces. And even if he for ever flies within the gorge, that gorge is in the mountains; so that even in his lowest swoop the mountain eagle is still higher than other birds upon the plain."[1]

After *Pierre*, Melville almost immediately wrote another novel, about an impossibly faithful wife who continues to love her sailor husband even though he leaves for years at a time and marries two other women in far-off ports. It was called *The Isle of the Cross*. But this book, too, turned into a failure: no one would publish it, and the manuscript is lost.[2]

Just as he was completing it, in the spring of 1853, with Lizzie expecting their third child at any moment, his mother decided that things had to change. "The constant in-door confinement with little intermission to which Herman's occupation as author compels him, does not agree with him," she wrote to her brother. "This constant working of the brain, & excitement of the imagination, is wearing Herman out, & you will my dear Peter be doing him a lasting benefit if by your added exertions you can procure for him a foreign Consulship."[3] Perennial family concerns; perennial efforts to find Herman some other way of earning a living. Sometimes Herman joined those efforts, but more often he observed from a distance, ambivalent, embarrassed that he so clearly needed a favor.

The odds actually seemed reasonable this time: Franklin Pierce had just been elected president and had immediately appointed his old college friend, Nathaniel Hawthorne, to be the consul at Liverpool. Hawthorne had Pierce's ear and was willing to give the president any letters of reference that could be collected. But how did Melville's character witnesses expect the president to react when they acknowledged that their acquaintance was "toiling early & late at his literary labors & hazarding his health to an extent greatly to be regretted"?[4] The assertions of Melville's insanity, in the immediate aftermath of *Pierre*, were a matter of public record. One headline had read, simply, "Herman Melville Crazy."[5] Not even the finest New England nepotism could overcome his reputation for defiant self-determination. A diplomat he would never be.

Melville continued on, tacking in the wind, deciding to write short stories for magazines in the hope of getting regular paychecks. Year after year, he seemed ready to succumb to tragedy and depression; year after year, he kept creating. His eagle soared and glided, its feathers rough and out of place, but its wings still strong. In story after story from these magazine years, the abyss beckons, but Melville's characters keep flying, keep searching for those thermal updrafts that might lift them back into the sunlight.

"Cock-A-Doodle-Doo! Or The Crowing of the Noble Cock Beneventano," December 1853

Our narrator is "blue," we learn, at the very start of the story, and "too full of hypos to sleep."[6] In other words, this tale begins the same way *Moby-Dick* does, for Ishmael is also seeking a way of "driving off the spleen": "whenever my hypos get such an upper hand of me, that it requires a strong moral principle to prevent me from deliberately stepping into the street, and methodically knocking people's hats off—then, I account it high time to get to sea."[7] But the narrator of "Cock-A-Doodle-Doo" is landlocked, in the Berkshires. He doesn't have to deal with the crowds and top-hat pretensions of the modern city, but, as he explains, he is suffering from a parallel combination of personal grief and social grievances: "In all parts of the world many high-spirited revolts from rascally despotisms had of late been knocked on the head; many dreadful casualties, by locomotive and steamer, had likewise knocked hundreds of high-spirited travelers on the head (I lost a dear friend in one of them); my own private affairs were also full of despotisms, casualties, and knockings on the head."[8]

In retrospect, the famous European revolutions of 1848 seem to signal a long-term trend toward liberal democracy—but Melville reminds us of just how brutally those revolutions were put down in the years immediately following their outbreak. And though it's tempting to assume that Americans have always embraced every technical "advance" with capitalistic excitement and opportunism, Melville also reminds us of just how skeptical and even angry some people were about the rapidity of modernization. In late July 1852, many Yankees found themselves questioning their "go-aheadism" when the steamboat *Henry Clay* caught fire and sank in the Hudson River, killing eighty-one passengers, including Nathaniel Hawthorne's beloved sister, Maria Louisa.[9]

In "Cock-A-Doodle-Doo," our grieving, dyspeptic country gentleman decides to go for a long, head-clearing walk—only to find the air "cool and misty, damp, disagreeable." Within a few minutes he is bent over, ascending a steep slope: "this toiling posture brought my head pretty well earthward, as if I were in the act of butting it against the world." The summit affords him a perfect view of the local valley, but his village is covered by "a great flat canopy of haze, like a pall. It was the condensed smoke of the chimneys, with the condensed, exhaled breath of the villagers, prevented from dispersion by the imprisoning hills." The landscape reflects back his "doleful dumps." He is reminded that his creditor will call for him as soon as he gets home.

Then—suddenly—"what a triumphant thanksgiving of a cock-crow! . . . Clear, shrill, full of pluck, full of fire, full of fun, full of glee. . . . It makes my blood bound—I feel wild. . . . Marvelous cock! But soft—this fellow now crows most lustily."[10]

I can understand why some readers have dismissed this story as "an extended dirty joke" about Melville's sexual frustration.[11] Mumford spent just a few words on it in his biography—enough to reinforce his suggestion that Melville was hopelessly repressed.[12] But I see the tale as a parable about coping with the everyday trauma of modernity.

The nameless narrator, like many of Melville's characters, seems almost impossibly isolated, with no discernible job or family. He lacks an essential reason to keep living. Occasionally he has charitable impulses, but he has nothing to spare; occasionally he feels some ambition to work—but "who would take the trouble to make a fortune . . . , when he knows not how long he can keep it, for the thousand villains and asses who have the management of the railroads and steamboats, and innumerable other vital things in the world. . . . Great improvements of the age! What! To call the facilitation of death and murder an improvement! Who wants to travel so fast?"[13] Though Mumford never commented on the politics of this story, he did make a mark next to this passage; I imagine he noticed that the narrator sounds almost eerily like Thoreau here.[14] But Melville's narrator (standing in for Melville himself) has not built his own shanty from discarded planks. Indeed, all he can think about is the second mortgage he's taken out on his estate, and his ruthless creditor, "who frightens the life out of me more than any locomotive—a lantern-jawed rascal, who seems to run on a railroad track, too" (in Melville's case it was a secret loan he had received from a man named T. D. Stewart to help him pay his mortgage—but now he was having trouble making his semiannual interest payments).[15] Instead of working his land and producing a simple sufficiency, he has bought into the new abstraction of the market—but finds he can neither fathom nor escape the system.

What saves him is not only the rooster's defiant crowing but the example of the stalwart workingman who owns the bird and refuses to sell it at any price. He is a sawyer, who resolutely supplies the narrator with sawn and split logs for his hearth, even amid blizzards—a man "tall and spare, with a long saddish face, yet somehow a latently joyous eye, which offered the strangest contrast. . . . I concluded within myself that this man had experienced hard times; that he had had many sore rubs in the world; that he was of a solemn disposition; that he was of the mind of Solomon; that he lived calmly, decorously, temperately; and though a very poor man, was, nevertheless, a highly respectable one."

While perhaps shaking our heads at the intellectual's romanticization of poverty and labor, and acknowledging the truth that the sawyer and his family have no recourse when a fatal illness attacks them in their shanty, we might also note that this secure, self-reliant workingman and his rooster inspire the narrator to a final, redemptive act of generosity and hard work: he buries the sawyer's whole family with his own hands and lays the gravestone, which he pays for himself—and proclaims that "never since then have I felt the doleful dumps, but under all circumstances crow late and early with a continual crow."[16]

"The Happy Failure: A Story of the River Hudson," July 1854

The action of this story is over within a couple of hours.

Our narrator's elderly uncle, an inventor, has spent ten dreary years constructing a "Great Hydraulic Hydrostatic Apparatus for draining swamps and marshes, and converting them, at the rate of one acre the hour, into fields more fertile than those of the Genessee." Now the plan is to test the machine on a deserted island in the Hudson River. The inventor is certain of his success: "this is the hour which for ten long years has, in the prospect, sustained me through all my painstaking obscurity. Fame will be the sweeter because it comes at the last. . . . Sustainer! I glorify Thee."

But the narrator, his uncle, and his uncle's African American servant, Yorpy, can't even get the machine out of its box.

For a few minutes, the inventor is devastated. Then, suddenly, he perks up and moves on. The wooden box could be quite useful, and "faithful old Yorpy can sell the old iron for tobacco-money." The nephew is confused; Yorpy is delighted. He thanks his dear, old master and tells him that after ten years of seeming insanity the inventor has finally become himself again. The inventor smiles, and agrees that "failure has made a good old man of me. It was horrible at first, but I'm glad I've failed. Praise be to God for the failure!"

His final advice to his nephew is simple: "Never try to invent anything but—happiness."[17]

"The Fiddler," September 1854

Another depressed, self-centered narrator. A poet. The story opens as he is reading the latest review of his work: "So my poem is damned, and immortal fame is not for me! I am nobody forever and ever. Intolerable fate!" Intolerable poet. His life is a cycle of ambition, frustration, desperation, spleen, and scorn: the artist's way in a capitalist society.

On the very first page of the story, though, the narrator meets his redeemer, a friend of a friend who happens by on a busy street, a middle-aged man named Hautboy, plump and ruddy and boyish and as sincerely jovial as the sawyer in "Cock-A-Doodle-Doo," if not quite so muscular. At first, the narrator, Helmstone, is uncertain: Hautboy has a warmly infectious zeal, but surely that must indicate the oversimplicity of his soul. Perhaps he is merely "acquiescent and calm," and "quite too contented," given the ills of modern society and the seriousness of the human condition. But a bit of conversation reassures Helmstone that

Hautboy can both recognize and transcend grim realities: "It was plain that while Hautboy saw the world pretty much as it was, yet he did not theoretically espouse its bright side nor its dark side. Rejecting all solutions, he but acknowledged facts. What was sad in the world he did not superficially gainsay; what was glad in it he did not cynically slur; and all which was to him personally enjoyable, he gratefully took to his heart." Hautboy seems to have found the secret to modern life: understand that there will always be both light and darkness, in a relation to each other that is both variable and unmeasurable.

And at the end of the story Helmstone discovers the secret to Hautboy's secret. As a young boy, he had been a violin prodigy, "an extraordinary genius" who toured the world's cities and "received the open homage of thousands on thousands." But a life of glorious, triumphant success turned out to feel overwhelming. So now, as an adult, he goes around town "teaching fiddling for a living" and spreading good cheer. "Crammed once with fame, he is now hilarious without it. *With* genius and *without* fame, he is happier than a king."[18]

Mumford marked that last passage with two dark pencil lines.[19] But I don't imagine he was as taken with the very last sentence of this brief tale: "Next day," Helmstone explains, "I tore all my manuscripts, bought me a fiddle, and went to take regular lessons of Hautboy."[20] Renouncing the desire for admiration is one thing. Must you also give up the desire to create?

"Jimmy Rose," November 1855

Our narrator, William Ford, an elderly gentleman, is indulging in some bittersweet retrospection. Ford has given up his "white-blossoming orchard" in the country and taken his "white hairs and white ivory-headed cane" to the city, where he has "become unexpected heir to a great old house" once inhabited by his departed friend, Jimmy Rose. The decrepit but stately building is in a neighborhood much like Pierre's, formerly residential "but now, for the most part, transformed into counting-rooms and warehouses. There bales and boxes usurp the place of sofas; day-books and ledgers are spread where once the delicious breakfast toast was buttered." Especially given the sad decline of Rose's fortunes, Ford is painfully aware of how commerce has remade the city, how people now rush about from wharf to stockroom focused exclusively on assessing the extent of their success or failure.

"Nevertheless," Ford noted, "in this old house of mine, so strangely spared, some monument of departed days survived. Nor was this the only one. . . . The street's transmutation was not yet complete." In various places, owners or managers of buildings had tried to substitute new-fangled features for outdated ones, but it was "as if the graft of modernness had not taken in its ancient stock." Ford seems to find pleasure in the interweaving of old and new, in his awareness of how continuity and change interact; he is especially charmed by some of his house's interior spaces, which have persisted despite occasional leaks and some "internal decay." There are impressive "timbers, huge, square, and massive, all red oak . . . , of a rich and Indian color," as well as "heavy-molded, wooden cornices, paneled wainscots, and carved and inaccessible mantels of queer horticultural and zoological devices." His wife and daughters plead with him to modernize the largest parlor: they want it to be "nice, genteel, cream-colored." But Ford cannot bear to cover the antique wall-paper, with its "massive festoons of roses" (even though they are so "be-draggled" as to look more like onions), and its "dimmed" and "blurry" but still "princely" peacocks: "so patiently and so pleasantly, nay, here and there so ruddily did they seem to bide their bitter doom" that Ford would "permit no violation of the old parlor." Besides, the ancient birds and flowers reminded him of Jimmy.

Jimmy retreated to this house, previously abandoned, when his import business went bankrupt from a combination of bad luck (two ship-loads lost in a gale) and "mad prodigality." Previously, his prodigal ways had been much appreciated among his acquaintances, for he had thrown the best "dinners, suppers, and balls" in the city, and he had become known for his "uncommon cheeriness" and his "sparkling wit" and his "glowing welcomes to his guests" and his "bounteous heart and board" and his "noble graces" and his "glorious wine" and his "cheeks that seemed painted with carmine, but it was health's genuine bloom, deep-ened by the joy of life." When everything collapsed, he had to flee and hide from his creditors, and when Ford tried to comfort him, Jimmy explained that he could no longer trust anyone, and pulled a gun.

But the important thing about Jimmy's story is that somehow he regained his dignity and joyfulness, despite never again having any money. When Ford finally rediscovered him, twenty-five years after his bankruptcy, it was immediately clear that Jimmy was "poor as any rat; poor in the last dregs of poverty; a pauper beyond alms-house pauperism; a promenading pauper in a thin, thread-bare, careful coat." And so his spirit ought to have been "dry, shrunken, meagre, cadaverously fierce with misery and misanthropy." Yet—"amazement! The old Persian roses bloomed in his cheeks." Jimmy would offer generous compliments to anyone who spoke with him, and he still knew how "to carry on a sprightly conversation." He was "rich in smiles." Determined to stay engaged with the world, he "kept himself informed of European affairs and the last literature, foreign and domestic"; his attitude remained so cheerful and open and eager that old acquaintances allowed him to linger in their parlors at teatime, where he swallowed piece after piece of buttered bread to stave off starvation. He kept his own past alive.[21]

Jimmy was the embodiment of the new age, in which the word "failure" could be applied not just to businesses but also, for the first time, to human beings.[22] But despite utter destitution, Jimmy managed to follow Ishmael's example and call on an inner source of peace that he had cultivated in better times: "even so," said Ishmael, "amid the tornadoed Atlantic of my being, do I myself still for ever centrally disport in mute calm; and while ponderous planets of unwaning woe revolve round me, deep down and deep inland there I still bathe me in eternal mildness of joy."[23]

And now, William Ford, gazing at the faded peacocks and roses on the walls of his parlor, seeks his own contented quietude, amid the rapidly changing city, by recalling his old friend's capacity to endure.

CHAPTER 15

Reconnaissance (1899-1925)

Mumford started taking walks through New York City in 1899, the year he turned four. He was guided by his German grandfather, a former head waiter at Delmonico's, who introduced Lewis not only to the city's great parks and museums and libraries but also to friends who ran book binderies and sold cigars and made boots, workers in the industrial economy who retained a high regard for craft and durability. After Mumford had become a grandfather himself, he recalled that almost all of these men prided themselves not on accumulation "but on their being fortunate enough to retire in middle life on a 'competency,' as they called it—enough to enable them to enjoy their leisure and their good health before their bodies became enfeebled. 'Enough is plenty' was a saying I can remember from my youth, before this became a heresy against the American way of life."[1] In time, sufficiency became one of Mumford's guiding principles, and the urban survey—or reconnaissance, as he often called it—became both his fundamental research method and a way of coping with his sense of trauma.

Cities, he thought, for all their drawbacks, should have everything a person needed, from the fresh air of a wooded path to the buzz of a community hall. Always on foot, he reconnoitered urban spaces to find out what he was up against, and to establish connections, to work his body and mind in ways that wove them into the fabric of his environment and that allowed that environment to become imprinted on his soul. Only once in his long life did Mumford drive a car: that was sufficient. (He almost crashed into a maple tree next to the driveway in

Amenia.) Cars were the ultimate paleotechnic machines, and their demands posed a direct threat to the culture of walking. People like Robert Moses, New York's "Master Builder" and one of Mumford's most hated foes starting in the 1940s, wanted to redesign entire cities in the name of automobility.[2]

Sometimes, though, the places Mumford encountered on his determined perambulations seemed to be at the root of his trauma, either because they sickened him directly or because he felt such a powerful empathy for the people who lived there. Committed to witnessing the worst injustices of Megalopolis and Coketown, he frequently found himself overcome by stagnant air, piercing sounds and odors, cramped quarters, close horizons, ugly smokestacks—by the "wretchedness and futility and waste" of neighborhoods that had been "developed by ruthless methods."[3] It was devastating both physically and spiritually.

Between the years 1912 and 1925, in his late teens through his late twenties, Mumford spent countless weeks in sickrooms and hospitals, suffering from constant colds, tuberculosis, and a hard-to-pin-down form of exhaustion.[4] When he recorded his feelings, he emphasized his overwhelming sense of "dissatisfaction" or "emptiness" or "futility."[5] At times, he thought of himself as an "invalid."[6] He took courses at several different New York colleges but didn't stay enrolled long enough at any of them to earn a degree (as it turned out, his lack of a B.A. did not prevent him from eventually teaching at places like Dartmouth, Stanford, Berkeley, the University of Pennsylvania, Harvard, and MIT). He also struggled consistently with the question of how he was going to make a living: his plays, poems, novels, and criticism were frequently rejected by publishers and periodicals, and he hated the various low-paying industrial and bureaucratic jobs he felt forced to take just to stay engaged in the money economy.

Perhaps the one constant during the first three decades of his life was his compulsion to walk through cities, no matter how he was feeling. He did surveys not only of every borough of New York but also of London, Edinburgh, Boston, Portland (Maine), Washington, D.C., Syracuse, Philadelphia, and Pittsburgh. And though his walks immersed him in the worst ills of modernity, they also distracted him from his anxiety and bolstered his stamina. His commitment to urban surveying reflected the responsibility he felt to accept reality, to uphold what Melville thought of as the Christlike virtues of "submission and endurance."[7]

The particular kind of reconnaissance Mumford did was pioneered by his intellectual mentor, Patrick Geddes; Mumford approached the task much more systematically once he started reading Geddes's work in 1914. He took pages of notes as he walked, and he often made pencil sketches of cityscapes, some of which he later turned into watercolors. Whenever possible, he studied not only the architecture and sociological phenomena but also the geography and geology of the cities he explored. Indeed, much of his spatial sophistication, as well as his engagement with biology and ecology, came directly from Geddes—first from Geddes's published writings and then through correspondence and direct contact.[8]

From Geddes's early work on evolution, Mumford learned "that no aspect of the living organism could be interpreted except in terms of the dynamic interacting, interpenetrating, all-enveloping whole in which it functioned. . . . Geddes's special endeavor was to apply ecological principles to the simplest and most complex social phenomena alike." All of society was biological, in other words, and all of biology was social. And everything had a history that would inevitably contribute to the shaping of its future.

Though Geddes eventually worked on city planning projects around the world (most notably in India and Palestine), his thinking was grounded in deep experience with community development in Scotland, his home country. During the early twentieth century, he had created a base in a remarkable Edinburgh building he called Outlook Tower. Mumford thought of it as "a new kind of laboratory-museum"; he sent his first letters to Geddes there, and in 1915 the Tower staff sent back "a little packet of pamphlets and books," which Mumford received, he later claimed, "with an elation" matched only by what he felt "upon the publication of my own first book."[9]

Geddes's Edinburgh writings emphasized the need for community members, not experts, to conduct extensive diagnostic surveys of their surroundings; Outlook Tower invited people in to start the process. The first goal was simply to give residents a bird's-eye view of their city and region. From the top of the Tower, on Castle Hill, they might gain some initial insights into topography and history: here they were, living in both a seaport and a hill fort, with unequally developed neighborhoods, with grand heights and dark alleys descending to a tangle of mews, courts, causeways, closes, and wynds. Then, coming in from the open air of the balcony, visitors passed through a curtain, one at a time, to a cramped, cell-like space, where they were encouraged to look inward for a couple of minutes. On the four floors below them, they would gradually descend through exhibits that opened wider and wider mental vistas, and all the while they were supposed to exercise their imagination, like a geologist analyzing layers of rock and trying to envision ancient processes of upheaval, metamorphosis, and sedimentation. How did we get here?

Visitors encountered maps, botanical specimens, graphs of climate fluctuations, diagrams of settlement patterns, photographs of vacant lots, old development plans, models of biological systems, and economic statistics, relating first to Edinburgh, then Scotland, then the United Kingdom, then Europe, then the World. The immediate hope was that they would come to embrace Geddes's local goal of "renovating old tenements, turning waste spaces into small public gardens, and . . . [building] much-needed student hostels in the Old Town of Edinburgh."[10] More broadly, Geddes wanted to present residents with dramatic "evidence of the necessity, practicability, and fruitfulness" of engaging with their city's "geographical situation" and "each important phase of its history from earliest to most recent times. Natural environment is thus never to be neglected without long-enduring penalties. Neither can historic phases be considered to be as past and done with; their heritage of good, their burden of evil, are each traceable in our complex present city: and each has a momentum, towards betterment, or towards deterioration respectively."[11] At the base of the Tower, thrust back into their community, visitors might walk away with burning questions but also with new ways of seeking answers in their everyday haunts and labors. Daily life was full of spurs toward reconstruction.

Mumford did not make it to Edinburgh until 1925, for what would prove to be a final visit with Geddes (they had spent time together previously in New York), but thanks to those books and pamphlets he received in 1915, he felt that he had visited the Tower in mind and spirit several times over. "Years before I met Geddes in person, he taught me how to take in the life of cities, both from inside and from outside, both in time and in space . . . , as a citizen and a worker, participating in the total life of a community, past, present, and prospective."[12]

Because Geddes was so focused on helping those whose lives seemed to have been impoverished by modernization, Mumford directed his surveys toward "the rankest and smokiest of factory sections, and the meanest and filthiest of slums," where "paint factories, soap works, sugar refineries . . . uglify the landscape while their vent-stacks poison the air" and the workers tried to survive in hovels and shacks and tenements. The sight of an infant, outside a "hut, by the gate, bawling piteously . . . left to crawl alone about in the filth," could send Mumford into spasms of guilt and confusion. In Pittsburgh, in 1917, he felt personally "[rebuked]" by the "flare of coke ovens" and the "spectacle of mill and mill-shack" and their "blank, overbearing tragedy . . . ; for of family life there is little, of social life less, and of communal life naught, and the daily round is simply a prolonged tussle in Sisyphean tasks whose profits reach only the pockets of mammonolaters in NY and Palm Beach."[13]

Instead of dismissing the urban environment as wrecked, though, Mumford walked through it with a sense of its internal contradictions, following Geddes's lead in seeing signs of promise everywhere—even along the chaotic waterfront, among the rough, overworked longshoremen, whose labor seemed "admirable" or even "essentially right in the fact that it was conducted in the open air and demanded muscular activity and physical alertness." The goal was always to turn one's vision toward offsetting forces and potential renovation. So, if workers found themselves confined to a "chamber of horrors" during business hours, maybe they would later be able to renew their acquaintance with "poplars and oaks" in an area like North Beach, in Queens: "its paths are well-marked out, its transit connections are convenient; and it has not yet been disreputably exploited. It is given over mostly to picnicking groves, some of which are spacious and beautiful." In the notes Mumford took of this particular reconnaissance, he acknowledged the

FIGURE 6. Mumford, "Mills from Bluff St., Pittsburgh," 1917.

likelihood that he had previously visited North Beach "with my grand-father—a good deal of the New York I've since rediscovered I first be-came acquainted with through him." But he was delighted to find that it felt both new and unspoiled.[14]

Mumford had a similar experience when he stumbled upon the play-ground at Seward Park, which had opened in 1903, the year he turned 8. Now, in 1916, as he wandered through "a clotted (but intensely human and sociable) neighborhood," he found the whole atmosphere to be "noisy, jolly, and happy." And his observations went far beyond nostalgia:

> I stand looking at the children scrambling around in little spasms of playfulness, at the baked apple and sweet potato man, at the groups of mellow looking elderly men, discussing affairs, or talking soberly about the weather; and I think: What limits are there to the power of these people, to whom organization and civil intercourse are (in con-trast to those who live in strictly private bourgeois neighborhoods) ordinary facts of their daily existence. . . . Why may they not thru the pressure of numbers and intelligence, tear down these nasty,

jerrybuilt cubby holes into which they crowd; make cleaner, sweeter homes for themselves, and create additional public works.[15]

Though sometimes beset by cynicism, given the intractability of class dynamics, Mumford generally had a Geddesian faith in the reconstructive power of ordinary people, as long as they had access to public space: cities could be oppressive, but they were not iron cages. It mattered how residents conscientiously chose to live in them. With the "Resorption of Government into the body of the community" as Geddes put it, "cities, towns, villages, groups, associations" would be able to "work out their own regional salvation."[16]

Mumford named his son after Geddes in 1925 because he felt that he owed his own salvation to the older man's tirelessly constructive holism. Geddes's writings and community work helped Mumford rediscover a youthful faith in the possibility of balancing theory and practice, city and country, science and art. The whole ethos of Outlook Tower confirmed his suspicion that, as Geddes put it, professional specialization would probably entail "knowing more and more about less and less."[17] Following his inclination to be a generalist might actually be the most useful and even radical thing Mumford could do. Moreover, to be connected to Geddes was to inherit a rich tradition of broad-minded and engaged scholarship, traceable all the way back to Alexander von Humboldt and including "aesthetic socialists" like William Morris and John Ruskin, "anarchist geographers" like Elisée Reclus and Peter Kropotkin, and the founder of the Garden City movement, Ebenezer Howard.[18] Invoking a poem by Walt Whitman, Mumford claimed that "what Geddes's voice did was to lead me away from the well-paved avenue to professional success: his was the Song of the Open Road."[19] Maybe wandering open-mindedly through cities could be not just a hobby but both a career path and a means of resisting the forces of linear, hierarchical Progress.

The only problem was that, in person, Geddes turned out to be more of a master than a mentor. Mumford would always be grateful to Geddes for his generous long-distance encouragement: "by its nature, correspondence happily is a two-sided affair." To be truly heard and appreciated by a respected elder—that experience can make a career, and the time and attention Mumford received from Geddes stayed with him into his old age. Indeed, Geddes's letters "have always remained before me as models, in their promptness and amplitude, for my own intercourse with the young." But alas, "when Geddes found a listener, he left little room for the latter to express himself on equal terms even though verbally he would call for 'criticism' and allowed (theoretically!) for dissent." Mumford ultimately categorized him as one of those intellectual giants who fail to recognize "the point at which their passionate absorption in their own work might lead to their committing spiritual violence on those around them."[20]

After a few years of writing letters, Mumford went to London in early 1920 to work as an editor with Geddes's close colleague, Victor Branford. Geddes himself was in Palestine, and still had commitments in India, and he offered Mumford a warm invitation to join him in either place, to help with his urban and regional planning projects and maybe organize his papers: the older man was a visionary, but not a particularly coherent or effective writer. So at first Mumford figured that London might be a jumping-off point for more distant destinations. After getting to know Geddes's inner circle, though, he started to sense that a direct apprenticeship to Geddes might actually hamper his development, and he also worried that a longer separation from Sophia (who had stayed in New York) might disrupt their intensifying relationship. In October, he decided to sail home. Lewis and Sophia were married the following year, and he did not meet Geddes until the aging polymath made a trip to New York in 1923—which triggered Mumford's gradual disenchantment with him.

Geddes's arrogance became apparent immediately, though Mumford recognized his own role in their clashes: "there were two demanding, self-absorbed egos to reckon with." It drove him crazy that Geddes would break engagements, double-book meetings, and assault him with "an unceasing volume of anecdotes, suggestions, and diagrammatic soliloquy." Perhaps just as difficult, though, was what Mumford came to think of as "the gap between our generations: his, heady even now with the hopes of endless progress through science, technics, and education;

mine, war-shocked, disillusioned, discouraged, unconsciously anticipating the even more formidable barbarisms that were to follow." Ultimately, Geddes was not Melvillean enough. And as if to underline the difference between them, Mumford started characterizing their relationship in Melvillean terms: it seemed that Geddes expected him to serve as nothing more than an amanuensis, but Mumford's response to Geddes's repeated queries along those lines was the same as that of Melville's infamously stubborn character, Bartleby the Scrivener: "I would prefer not to." Indeed, Mumford explained, Geddes "found that he had a scientific Bartleby on his hands, as loquacious as Bartleby was silent, but just as difficult to dislodge."[21]

Mumford never lost his veneration for Geddes's intellectual example, but he also resented that Geddes wanted him to devote his career to making sense of the older man's scattered, disorganized, rambling notes. When they parted in 1923, they were both emotionally exhausted, and when Mumford went to Edinburgh two years later, the New York pattern immediately reasserted itself. "Geddes drives me to tears, almost he does," Mumford wrote in his private notes. "He is perfectly lovable in his human moments; in fact he is enchanting. . . . But what can I do with a . . . pathetic tyrant who asks for a collaborator and wants a secretary."[22]

In later years, there were moments when Mumford was tempted to renounce his mentor: "What Geddes urgently demanded of me was an impossible lifetime of devotion as Collaborator (read docile filing clerk!), as Editor (read literary secretary!), or as Secretary (read handy drudge!). In short, the perfect disciple: his alter ego."[23] But they continued to write warm, expansive letters to each other until Geddes's death in 1932. Even in the face of deep demoralization, Mumford would always strive to follow Geddes's example of constructive engagement.

CHAPTER 16

Disenchantment (1853-55)

"To go up into a high stone tower," Melville wrote, in 1853 or 1854, "is not only a very fine thing in itself, but the very best mode of gaining a comprehensive view of the region round about." Mumford read this quotation in the fall of 1927, taking special note of it as he prepared to write his Melville biography. The sentiment no doubt reminded him of Outlook Tower, but his reading of Melville had helped sour him on Geddes's hubris with regard to comprehensiveness. The very idea of a comprehensive view, Mumford now realized, was a setup: it blinds you to the inevitability that you will always have blind spots.[1]

I wish I could offer a fuller view of Melville's life in the mid-1850s, but as usual I can only guess at his state of mind. In 1853, *The Isle of the Cross* was rejected; his third child was born—Elizabeth, known as Bessie; his family's attempts to procure a consulship for him went nowhere; and a fire at his publisher's warehouse destroyed hundreds of copies of his unsold books. Meanwhile, President Pierce, a pro-slavery New Englander, was starting to get attacked in the Northeast for his moral failings: *Uncle Tom's Cabin* had appeared in 1852, skewering the slave system, and political compromise seemed less and less viable. Perhaps Melville was relieved not to have a place in Pierce's administration, since some of his early magazine pieces were getting picked up by an ardently abolitionist periodical, *Putnam's Monthly Magazine*.[2]

He may not have been exactly happy in his failure as a novelist, but at least the magazine work was steady. His observation about stone towers appeared in a long series of sketches published by *Putnam's* in spring

1854 and entitled "The Encantadas, or Enchanted Isles"—popular names for the Galapagos (known at the time as the Gallipagos). Most of Melville's shorter works forsook his old seafaring themes, but occasionally he traveled back to the Pacific in his mind, perhaps searching for ways of improving his morale. The view from the tower overlooking the Galapagos, though, was not exactly enchanting.

The opening lines of "The Encantadas" assert that the islands look something like "the world at large might after a penal conflagration": they are piles of sharp, blackened, volcanic rock. "Take five-and-twenty heaps of cinders dumped here and there in an outside city lot," Melville suggested; "imagine some of them magnified into mountains, and the vacant lot the sea, and you will have a fit idea of the general aspect of the Encantadas." With one sentence, Melville managed both to condemn the modern city as a desert and to posit its burnt-over bleakness as stretching even to the supposedly paradisal islands of the Pacific. The enchantment of this place was more like a delusion. Indeed, Melville admitted to feeling as though a malignant charm had been cast on him during his time in the Enchanted Isles: now, back in so-called Civilization, whether he was immersed in "scenes of social merriment" or whether he had escaped "the crowded city to wander out July and August among the Adirondack Mountains, far from the influences of towns," he sometimes helplessly flashed back to those "Plutonian" mounds, those "dark, vitrified masses," those "Apples of Sodom." If he happened to be with any companions, they would inevitably express concern, spooked "by my fixed gaze and sudden change of air." He looked as though he had been visited by a spirit.[3]

Most often, when Melville was transported back into that place of "spell-bound desertness," what he saw was a ghastly, surreal image of the animal most closely associated with the Galapagos, as it dragged itself slowly, heavily, along the rocks: "the ghost of a gigantic tortoise, with 'Memento *****' burning in live letters upon its back." It's a vision out of Dante or Poe, but Melville said it came from a sailors' legend that the ancient tortoises housed the souls of "commodores and captains," who, as punishment for the exploitative cruelty of their command, were now condemned to tramp over "these hot aridities, sole solitary lords of

Asphaltum," always "in quest of pools of scanty water." Of course, the "wicked sea officers" could just as easily be slave drivers or factory overseers or office managers, now suffering the drudgery that they had inflicted upon others. Or, given Melville's reference to Sodom, they could be versions of Jonah, trapped in the body of an animal, but in this case without even the possibility of repentance and deliverance.

Melville briefly tried to redeem the symbolism of the Galapagos tortoise, which, "dark and melancholy as it is upon the back, still possesses a bright side; its calipee or breastplate being sometimes of a faint yellowish or golden tinge."[4] It's as if he recalled Father Mapple's sermon about Jonah in *Moby-Dick*: "But oh! shipmates! on the starboard hand of every woe, there is a sure delight."[5] Yet when you turn the tortoise over to appreciate its coloring, you are condemning it to death—a slow, agonizing death, since it will never be able to right itself, but it can survive for months without food or water. In the end, the tortoise can only be understood as representing the torment of "hopeless toil": "I have known them in their journeyings," Melville explained, "to ram themselves heroically against the rocks, and long abide there, nudging, wriggling, wedging, in order to displace them, and so hold on their inflexible path. Their crowning curse is their drudging impulse to straightforwardness in a belittered world." Progress, Melville knew, could never be straightforward.

In many of Melville's stories, the will to endure is the ultimate heroism, a rare force that can help offset trauma. But here, that kind of willpower becomes a permanent Purgatory. It's a "dateless, indefinite endurance." It's a charm you might never be able to shake. "The special curse, as one may call it, of the Encantadas . . . is that to them change never comes; neither the change of seasons nor of sorrows."[6]

That same sad, static atmosphere hovers over "Bartleby, The Scrivener: A Story of Wall-Street," which Melville wrote immediately before "The Encantadas": it was the first piece he published in *Putnam's*, in the late fall of 1853. Even though modernity is often associated with rapid change, Melville also took note of the ways in which new modes of living could be utterly stultifying. Whether your spirit is trapped in a tortoise shell on the Galapagos or stuck at the desk of a law office in downtown

Manhattan, you'll need to perform some serious mental labor to escape the evil spell and stop bumping into the dull, repeated obstacles with which the modern world is littered.

The nameless narrator of "Bartleby" is a pleasant, self-centered, perpetually befuddled lawyer who needs to employ a few clerks in order to continue entangling his clients in enough official documents ("bonds and mortgages and title deeds") to make them understand his indispensability. That is: he embodies modern bureaucracy in a capitalist society. At first, his fond tolerance for his employees' foibles comes across as charming: Turkey is a dedicated and energetic copyist in the morning but apt to spatter ink all over the office after his lunchtime tipple, which his boss willfully ignores; Nippers seems to arrive drunk and spends the early hours literally wrestling with his work table to get it into a more suitable position, but our narrator appreciates the good copying he does once he sobers up; and Ginger Nut, the office boy, is a "quick-witted youth" whom the attorney seems to respect for being so good at jovially avoiding any work besides serving as "cake and apple purveyor for Turkey and Nippers." Eventually, though, we are made to understand that the narrator can afford to be so forgiving only because he pays his workers so little and has gotten so good at scraping off a percentage of the profits earned by some of the wealthiest men in the nation. "I was not unemployed in my profession by the late John Jacob Astor," he says, with the winking double-negative diction of the supremely self-satisfied. Moreover, he is by nature a timid soul and will do almost anything to avoid confrontation.[7]

Enter Bartleby—also seemingly timid but simultaneously, it turns out, rather recalcitrant. Needing an extra hand, what with the reliable unreliability of Turkey and Nippers, the lawyer hires young Bartleby, "pallidly neat, pitiably respectable," partly in the hope that the new clerk's stolidity might help bring down the social temperature of the office. For a while, Bartleby works "silently, palely, mechanically," copying a huge number of documents, and our narrator is duly satisfied with his new investment. And then, suddenly, one day, when the attorney calls for Bartleby to come out from behind his partition and help him with some proofreading, there comes the scandalous objection:

"without moving from his privacy, Bartleby, in a singularly mild, firm voice, replied, 'I would prefer not to.'"

> What do you mean?
> I would prefer not to.
> *Why* do you refuse?
> I would prefer not to.
> You *will* not?
> I *prefer* not.

Most lawyers would have fired him on the spot. There were hundreds of men willing to earn a copyist's steady pay. But our narrator is cautious, disarmed, sympathetic, reluctant to make a scene, impressed by the lack of "uneasiness, anger, impatience, or impertinence" in Bartleby's refusal. Maybe he was asking too much of his employee? Gradually, though, Bartleby makes it clear that he is done working altogether. He does nothing but stare out the window at the brick wall of the building next door, which is just three feet away. When the lawyer decides to stop by his office on a Sunday, he finds that Bartleby has moved in—that in fact he never leaves the premises. And this act of claiming space, this occupation of Wall Street, in combination with the clerk's unwillingness to do his job, finally pushes the lawyer toward a questioning of all his assumptions about how modern society functions.

Bartleby's stance is infuriating in its inscrutability and seeming irrationality. It's impossible to blame the lawyer for wanting an explanation (Bartleby, he sighs, is "one of those beings of whom nothing is ascertainable").[8] And I can also understand the argument made by some critics that Bartleby must be another of Melville's representations of the dark, perverse side of Emersonian individualism: do you really want to "live wholly from within" if your inner voice has been reduced to passive-aggressive negation?[9] Bartleby's defiance, like Ahab's, will end in an ugly death. But it is to the narrator's great credit that he pauses long enough to formulate what I take as a slightly different critique of Emerson: even a person's innermost thoughts and drives, he seems to realize, are subject to cultural forces. The psychological and the societal are always in a dialectical relationship. To some extent, then, especially in the interconnected modern world, we are all complicit in any individual's seeming perversity. Indeed, as the narrator puts it, maybe that perversity is just a signal that we've been in the wrong all along, and "all the justice and all the reason [are] on the other side."

When the lawyer understands the extent of Bartleby's sense of isolation, it's as though he's waking from a trance: "For the first time in my life a feeling of overpowering stinging melancholy seized me. . . . The bond of a common humanity now drew me irresistibly to gloom. A fraternal melancholy!" Bartleby has nowhere to go, no one to turn to. The logic of the market tells the lawyer that if he is paying an employee, that employee should do his work or suffer the consequences—and the lawyer is a man of modern logic and methodical action. He should evict his uncooperating subordinate. But an older form of reasoning, based on sentiment and spirit, tells the lawyer that Bartleby is precisely the person he should be helping the most. Bartleby is not taking advantage of him but rather asking to be treated compassionately, as a fellow human being, with legitimate preferences. Why shouldn't the lawyer think of him as a member of his household, like an old-fashioned farmhand who took all his meals with the family, instead of as someone with whom he has a merely transactional and hierarchical relationship? Was the drudgery of bureaucratic capitalism any less impersonal or inhumane than slavery?

The ultimate tragedy of the story is that the narrator is unable to sustain his charitable impulse. Eventually he starts to worry about the rumors running "all through the circle of my professional acquaintance": to continue accommodating Bartleby would be to sacrifice his own reputation. And so "necessities connected with my business tyrannized over all other considerations." Unwilling to use physical force on his employee, the attorney, in his own act of "passive resistance," moves his office to another location. Then, when authorities track him down and seek his help in finding a new home for Bartleby, our narrator hardens his heart and denies any responsibility in the matter: "Bartleby was nothing to me—no more than to anyone else." Every modern American must look after himself. Left to his own devices, Bartleby decides that his final preference will be to decline all food, and so he starves to death in prison.[10]

Bartleby is a haunting character, inspiring interpretive obsessions for the last century, ever since the Melville Revival. Mumford read him as a dark mirror of Melville's mind, reflecting the writer's unwillingness to embrace the market: "People would admit him to their circle and give him bread and employment only if he would abandon his inner purpose: to this his answer was—I would prefer not to."[11] But it's the character of the lawyer who seems to haunt Melville himself, and who turns up again and again, in slightly varying forms, in the magazine pieces— perhaps never to greater effect than in the long story, "Benito Cereno," which appeared in *Putnam's* in the fall of 1855.

Captain Amasa Delano of Massachusetts—a real person, author of the now-obscure narrative on which Melville's story was based—comes across as faithful, good-natured, and somewhat oblivious. He collects seal skins, turns a tidy profit, expects his mates to keep the crew in line, and sleeps soundly. So when he sees a strange vessel approaching, rather haphazardly, in a "baffling" wind, with "vapors partly mantling the hull," under "creeping clouds," Melville's readers know that there are "deeper shadows to come," but Captain Delano remains unruffled. Perhaps the ship is in distress; perhaps he can help. He goes aboard, bearing several baskets of fish as gifts, and finds "a clamorous throng of whites and blacks, but the latter outnumbering the former more than could have been expected." They all seem to speak at once, delivering "a common tale of suffering": the ship is a Spanish slaver, but many of the Spaniards have died of fever or scurvy; they "narrowly escaped shipwreck" while rounding Cape Horn; and then they were caught in a dead calm and have now run dangerously short of food and water. Captain Delano takes it all in, but, Melville notes, it's always a little disconcerting to be dropped into the middle of a ship's society: "the living spectacle it contains, upon its sudden and complete disclosure, has, in contrast with the blank ocean which zones it, something of the effect of enchantment. The ship seems unreal; these strange costumes, gestures, and faces but a shadowy tableau just emerged from the deep."

The experience gets more and more shadowy and surreal as the action continues. Delano is eager to speak with his counterpart, Don Benito Cereno, and the Spanish captain does his best to converse, but he seems pale and twitchy, with "symptoms of an absent or moody mind." And though Delano would like to get the ship's full story in Don Benito's quiet, private quarters, he finds that the Spanish commander always has his personal black servant, Babo, by his side. On the one hand, Delano finds some "humane satisfaction" in witnessing "the steady good conduct of Babo," given Don Benito's clear debility; on the other hand, it seems strange that the Spanish captain is unwilling to dismiss the servant even for a few minutes, for a frank, commander-to-commander consultation. Delano, unlike President Pierce, is a liberal, antislavery New Englander, so he can accept that, under the circumstances, Captain Cereno has allowed his "cargo" to move freely about the ship. But even he starts to grow concerned as Don Benito becomes increasingly distant, or unhinged, or even disdainful, despite Delano's generosity and continued willingness to help. Hours go by; Captain Delano wavers between reassurance and suspicion while some of his men go to procure more provisions, but he steadfastly endures the uncertainty. Finally, still confused, he decides he can do no more and shoves off in his small boat—at which point Don Benito summons all his remaining energy and hurls himself over the side of his ship, landing at Delano's feet. Then Babo follows, dagger drawn, ready to murder his master. And suddenly the spell is broken, and all becomes clear, to Delano, and to the reader: "That moment, across the long-benighted mind of Captain Delano, a flash of revelation swept, illuminating, in unanticipated clearness, his host's whole mysterious demeanor, with every enigmatic event of the day." There had been a slave revolt on the ship; Don Benito was Babo's hostage; if Delano had uncovered their masquerade while onboard, he would have been killed immediately. But it never occurred to him that the black people might be in charge.[12]

Like Bartleby's employer, Captain Delano was so accustomed to the workings of the world, so enchanted with the status quo, that he could not recognize and understand true distress when he witnessed it. Bartleby was just stubborn; Don Benito was just tired and thirsty and a bit odd. Delano felt sympathy, even eagerness to offer assistance—but only a superficial assistance, which just made it easier for him to avoid the deeper, structural problems of injustice and inhumanity represented by the slave ship's very existence. Slavery was wrong—that he knew. But that its horrors might drive slaves to successful rebellion and brilliant deception was beyond his ken.

Captain Delano's complacency, his acceptance, his inability to acknowledge his own complicity, made him precisely the kind of American Melville wanted to address. It's true that Melville, headed for another of his Cape Horns, was struggling with family dynamics and writing failures, but a significant part of his turmoil, during this period, was political. He was clearly frustrated with his peers—well-intentioned, well-educated, white men of the Northeast—for doing so little to fight against the exploitation and abuse on which their social position rested. "Man should offset the malice and evil circumstance one finds in the constitution of the universe," Mumford wrote, in his commentary on "Benito Cereno": "instead, he aggravates it."[13]

The first installment of "Benito Cereno" came out in October 1855, and in the same issue of *Putnam's* there was an article arguing that Congress, by suddenly canceling the Missouri Compromise in 1854 and opening Kansas to slaveholders, had struck the nation's death blow. And the ensuing violence in "Bleeding Kansas" did in fact play a huge part in spurring the Civil War. Back in 1849, the black abolitionist Frederick Douglass had warned in a speech that "the slaveholders are sleeping on slumbering volcanoes." In "Benito Cereno," Melville used the phrase "slumbering volcano" to describe the Spanish slave ship, wondering whether it would eventually "let loose energies now hid." Captain Delano, in his narrative, had identified that ship as the *Tryal*, but Melville changed its name to the *San Dominick*, an explicit reference to the island of Santo Domingo, site of the Haitian Revolution, in which the black slaves had risen up to kill their masters.[14]

The fate of the republic was clearly on Melville's mind as he wrote his magazine pieces in the mid-1850s. He was not optimistic. Theorists of modernity have often emphasized the disenchantment of rationalism and industrialism, and while Melville clearly acknowledged that trend, he was even more concerned about how enchanted the leading citizens of modernity had become with the systems that secured their status and power. Americans needed to shake themselves out of their assumptions about success, Progress, citizenship, and nationhood. They needed to acknowledge the world's Bartlebys. Even kind, generous captains like Amasa Delano lacked any deep feeling for those below them in the social order. Indeed, "like most men of a good, blithe heart, Captain Delano took to Negroes, not philanthropically, but genially, just as other men to Newfoundland dogs."[15] But philanthropy, in the literal sense, is precisely what democracy requires: love of one's fellow human beings, no matter how different they might be.

CHAPTER 17

Counterpoint (1938)

"Life in the city," Mumford wrote, "takes on the character of a symphony." But he wasn't thinking of Mozart and Haydn. The music he heard in his mind was much more modern, more dissonant, ringing with different voices competing to be heard. At the heart of Mumford's vision of Renewal, especially in the 1920s and 1930s, was a commitment to the modernist avant-garde. He went to parties in Greenwich Village with the photographer Alfred Stieglitz and the painter Georgia O'Keeffe, where e. e. cummings read his erotic poetry and Aaron Copland played his latest compositions on the piano. It was Copland who wrote the syncretic score for the documentary film *The City*, which Mumford was working on in the spring of 1938 when he first slept with Jo Strongin. Mumford's idea of symphonic urbanism emphasized stimulation, possibility, variety, the constant intermingling of old and new. Jazz riffs might compete with folk melodies; clanging bells might interrupt the delicate plucking of strings. You had to struggle, sometimes, to hear the music of cities: "their conflicts are no less significant than their harmonies."[1]

In *The Culture of Cities* (1938), the second volume of *The Renewal of Life*, Mumford brought together all his interests, all his fields of study—all the voices in his head. Patrick Geddes sent him scrambling up towers for a view of the surrounding region; Catherine Bauer insisted that the city must be the creation of a democratic collective, rather than an all-seeing artist; Herman Melville reminded him that all vision is limited and that weak collectives fall prey to tyrants. More forward-looking than any other of his works, this book, Mumford explained on its very first page, was designed "to establish, for the purpose of communal action, the basic principles upon which our human environment—buildings, neighborhoods, cities, regions—may be renovated."[2] If *Technics and Civilization* was primarily a critique and a meditation, *The Culture of Cities* was primarily a blueprint—albeit a sophisticatedly provisional one, whose "principles" were often intentionally contradictory.

In a section near the end of the book called "Contrapuntal Organization," Mumford harked back to some of his earlier work to underline his Melvillean understanding of contingency: he would never "seek a harmony too absolute, an order whose translation into actual life would stultify the very purpose it seeks to achieve. The student of utopias knows the weakness that lies in perfectionism." Indeed, he would always cultivate communities "in which more significant kinds of conflict, more complex and intellectually stimulating kinds of disharmony, may take place." It's not that he was opposed to "good-fellowship"; it's that too much good-fellowship could lead to a dangerous complacency.[3] A robust culture of debate made it clear that the work of shaping the community would never be finished. "I promise nothing complete," Ishmael had said, when discussing cetology, and Mumford felt the same way about cities.[4] Under no circumstances should a city be allowed "to degenerate into a 'model community.'" As the Great Depression continued, despite FDR's efforts to put people back to work under countless New Deal programs, the cultural desire for simple, repeatable solutions became more and more desperate. But Mumford held his ever-shifting ground: "some of the highest products of the spirit have been achieved not out of small contentments, but out of great frustration, antagonism, disappointment, bitterness."[5] Though he remained fiercely committed to fighting for justice and equality, he didn't expect that life would ever get less tragic. It would be counterproductive to pretend that everyone could get along. Difference would always produce a certain amount of tension; the key was to embrace the tension and stay engaged.

When it came to urban planning, to uphold "the stimulus of variety, the shock and jostle and challenge of different groups" meant to uphold the public square. Much of Mumford's urban advocacy attempted to counter the abandonment of cities by wealthier white people seeking access to the private spaces of the suburbs. Mumford could understand how the "giantism of the metropolis" might leave people feeling isolated, alienated, demoralized: "small wonder that apathy sets in; or, to put it in its best light, that domesticity takes precedence over an effective political life." But democracy required mixing of all kinds. The typical suburb not only lacked gathering places, Mumford noted, but also tended to be "a one-class community"—in other words, hardly a community at all. It represented a "collective effort" by privileged people "to live a private life," removed from difference.[6]

A possible solution, Mumford argued, might be to bring some of the refreshing benefits of the suburbs to new urban neighborhoods—as in Sunnyside Gardens, where the Mumfords lived from 1925 to 1936. Designed by Lewis's friends Clarence Stein and Henry Wright in 1924, Sunnyside was meant to be simultaneously peaceful and provocative, with row houses and narrow apartment buildings oriented inward and opening on common green spaces, where children ran around and explored and adults took strolls and worked in gardens. The whole plan, in defiance of the suburban model based on isolated, freestanding, middle-class homes, fostered constant contact and an investment in a sense of commonality. It was a more deliberate version of Greenwich Village, whose spontaneous gatherings in the early 1920s had helped Mumford climb out of his depression. When dwelling places were understood "as social units," Mumford wrote, "with visible coherence in the architecture, with a sufficient number of local meeting rooms for group activities, as in Sunnyside Gardens, L.I., a robust political life, with effective collective action and a sense of renewed public responsibility," would have a good chance of developing.[7]

Moreover, the common areas at Sunnyside Gardens were understood as jointly owned property: like many other intellectuals in the 1930s, Mumford found himself not necessarily calling for a communist revolution per se but proposing a kind of renewed communalism as a force that could offset some of the worst tendencies of capitalism.[8] If your everyday experience of modernity was traumatic, it could help to recognize everyone's shared dependence on a viable habitat, and it was crucial to understand the Geddesian truth that life was sustained as much by "Mutual Aid" as by competition: it was time to give up solitary, bourgeois striving in favor of "symbiotic association." Indeed, Mumford had been deeply influenced by the rise of ecological science in this period, and well before such environmentalist heroes as Aldo Leopold and Rachel Carson he was insisting that social structures should be based on the simple truth that "every living creature is part of the general web of life. . . . If each particular natural environment has its own balance, is there not perhaps an equivalent of this in culture?"[9]

Perhaps the most fundamental balance in Mumford's vision was between city and country. Invoking one of his arguments from *Technics and Civilization,* Mumford embraced the Eotechnic model of decentralization, of life on a smaller scale and at a slower pace. The emphasis should be on the interpenetration of a town and its hinterland. Wherever people lived, they needed regular opportunities to interact with each other and with nature, like their ancestors had enjoyed, not just in a single, isolated common area but in "a *continuous* environment of public greens and open spaces."[10] Neotechnic sanitation was impressive in its ability to boost biological health, but the public pumps, fountains, and baths of the Eotechnic could claim both biological and social health benefits; the best sewage treatment system in the world was not worth so much as a solid network of community gardens or playgrounds. "Our capacity for effective physical organization has enormously increased," Mumford acknowledged; "but our ability to create . . . co-operative and civic associations . . . has not kept pace with these mechanical triumphs." Communities had to become invested in the environmental health of their entire region. A biotechnic society could not be achieved until "the landscape as a whole comes to mean to the community and the individual citizen what the single garden does to the individual lover of flowers."[11]

Drawing on Thoreau and George Perkins Marsh and Liberty Hyde Bailey, Mumford upheld the practice of reserving "primeval wilderness as a background for a civilized life," and he hoped that the sublime mountains and whispering forests and glassy lakes would inspire people to care about other parts of nature as well. While John Muir, founder of the Sierra Club, had helped Americans develop a deeper appreciation for the kind of land preserved in national parks, his exclusive celebration of wilderness "gems" had in effect relegated most environments to the waste bin: modern cities, for Muir, were already beyond help. But Mumford treated the entire landscape, from the alpine valley to the farm to the office buildings on Main Street, as a precious "cultural resource." His brand of environmentalism focused not on the negative goal of preventing damage but rather on the positive mission of "extending the range of the garden," nurturing respectful, varying blends of nature and culture in "every nook and corner of the earth," even the "less romantic areas." It's not that he wanted all wild lands to be domesticated; he merely asked that his fellow citizens recognize their responsibility to act as stewards in all their environmental decisions. Even if the common ownership of land was just a pipe dream or a thought experiment, people should behave as if they held a joint deed to the whole planet.[12]

Ultimately, Mumford's proposal to planners was to replace the megalopolis/suburbs/countryside model of development with a network of interconnected, midsized garden cities, each of which would have a system of parks woven into it and would also incorporate housing clusters, industrial operations, agriculture, and even a few wilderness areas. "The new type of regional center," Mumford explained, "would combine the hygienic advantages of the open suburbs with the social advantages of the big city, would give an equal place in its scheme to the urban and rural possibilities of modern life: in short, it would be a balanced environment."[13] Both the city and the country had their enchantments— their music—and the most potent effect was achieved when you could listen simultaneously for their different melodies.

Mumford desperately wanted to train his fellow citizens to become the right kinds of listeners and planners, people capable of perpetual renewal. The key, he suspected, was to provide them with regular opportunities to rediscover their surroundings, starting in elementary school (and each public school, he thought, ought to serve as a "community nucleus"). He had opened *The Culture of Cities* by explaining that his book was based "primarily on first-hand surveys, conducted in many different regions: beginning with a close study of my own city and region—New York and its immediate hinterland." By the end, Mumford was enjoining readers to make their own reconnaissances, and to encourage their children and students to do so as well, and to make the reconnaissance into a basic mode of living, which would eventually serve to transform both the design and the experience of all communities.[14]

The habit of exploration, "systematic contact with the environment," scientific observation: these practices would put people in touch with the full range of landscapes and modern phenomena, simultaneously shocking them and making them feel connected. Most importantly, they would become the kinds of citizens who could "contribute to our land-planning, our industry planning, and our community planning the authority of their own understanding, and the pressure of their own desires." Mumford certainly believed in expertise; only government action in the realm of urban design could counter the power of the capitalists, he figured, and professional planners would make better decisions than politicians. Meanwhile, though, he wanted to encourage a broad shift in consciousness, a groundswell of enthusiasm for the democratization of cities, for the "possibility of humanizing the natural environment and of naturalizing the human heritage." Like Geddes before him, he envisioned entire communities walking through the streets, reconnoitering local geographies and lifeways: "such surveys, if made by specialist investigators alone, would be politically inert; made through the active participation of school children, at an appropriate point in adolescent development, they become a central core in a functional education for political life. It is in the local community and the immediate region, small enough to be grasped from a tower, a hilltop, or an airplane, to be explored in every part before youth has arrived at the period of political responsibility, that a beginning can be made toward the detailed resorption of government."[15]

One might well accuse Mumford of idealistic naiveté and an unjustified confidence that what had worked for him would work for everyone. He failed to consider racial divisions, in *The Culture of Cities*, and never offered a clear enough political strategy to offset the overwhelming power of the ruling classes.[16] But there is promise in his embrace of the pedestrian survey, for a group of people tramping through a city and its region cannot be contained by the spaces of industrial capitalism. If there is room enough for them to be themselves, in all their difference, they might even be able to resist the power of demagogues and dicta-tors.[17] And in their "daily communion," their endless, joint tracings of the overlapping layers of history, lie opportunities to create a "collective work of art."[18]

Because Mumford moved to the countryside in 1936, and because he leveled such a trenchant attack on the general "devitalization" caused by crowding in great cities, many scholars have associated him more with a kind of bioregionalism than with urbanism.[19] But Mumford haunted cities all his life, and he never lost his faith in the cultural benefits of concentrated populations. "Here is where human experience is trans-formed into viable signs, symbols, patterns of conduct, systems of order."[20] Even in Amenia, the emphasis was on gathering with neigh-bors: "we were truly a community, close to one another, and the lake was our social magnet." Long conversations in the 1930s with his most intimate friend in the valley, the scholar-activist Joel Spingarn, had a huge impact on Mumford: as late as 1972, he felt called to publish a celebratory essay about Spingarn, who wrote "singularly Melvillian poems" and also, having helped to found the National Association for the Advancement of Colored People (NAACP), "was tireless in press-ing the case for racial equality upon his Dutchess County neighbor, Franklin Roosevelt," a descendant of Captain Amasa Delano.[21]

At the same time, Mumford acknowledged that part of Amenia's ap-peal lay in a kind of offsetting enchantment that was much harder to find in Megalopolis. If Melville had helped him understand the need for modern urbanites to be snapped out of their trances, he had also caused him to worry about the possible trauma of disenchantment. Mumford himself often craved "the full experience of the seasons and the ever-altering landscape," sought repose by wandering through more primi-tive environments, climbing to "the top of Oblong Mountain, where rattlesnakes nested on rocky ledges," or wading through the local "swamp, at whose edges the beautiful leaves of the elecampane flour-ished." And both of his children "found the country environment re-sponsive in a way that no city street can possibly be." They pressed flow-ers, woke up early and "went pollywogging," and gradually developed a sense of wonder, which Mumford thought might be the world's most precious gift.[22] The culture of the countryside offered Mumford and his family the kind of ancient awe that Ishmael found at sea, when he witnessed marvels like the "peaking of the whale's flukes"—which he proposed as "perhaps the grandest sight to be seen in all animated nature," even if the depth of its fascination would always "remain wholly inexplicable."[23] The more modern the City became, Mumford felt, the keener the human need for its "saving opposite."[24]

CHAPTER 18

Redburn (1839-55)

Though Melville was committed to following Emerson and Fuller and Hawthorne in creating a fresh, native literature, not beholden to British forms, he was keenly aware that the United States lacked the kind of deep history that could potentially offset some of the most wrenching trends of modernity. Especially as factories and offices became more widespread in the 1850s, as Kansas continued to bleed, as vulnerable families fell prey to inscrutable market fluctuations, many thoughtful Americans of Melville's generation wondered if their democratic experiment would ultimately justify the Revolution. Melville had been drawn to England's history and landscape since his very first voyage in 1839, which he revisited in *Redburn* a decade later: he had wanted to witness the "fine old lands" he had read about, "full of mossy cathedrals and churches, and long, narrow, crooked streets without side-walks, and lined with strange houses."[1] Perhaps, in the face of modernity's massive transformations, there was something to be said for such staunch, steady places.

Three of Melville's magazine pieces in the mid-1850s were self-conscious diptychs, juxtaposing a scene in the Old World with one in the New. The relationship between the two scenes generally implied that alleged American improvements might not have improved much of anything. In "Poor Man's Pudding and Rich Man's Crumbs" (1854), the class system seems equally vicious in both England and the United States, and the wealthy in both nations come across as equally haughty and oblivious to the affliction of those struggling to survive. But the psychological situation is clearly worse in America: "The native American poor . . . suffer more in mind than the poor of any other people in the world. Those peculiar social sensibilities nourished by our own peculiar political principles, while they enhance the true dignity of a prosperous American, do but minister to the added wretchedness of the unfortunate . . . , by furnishing them with the keenest appreciation of the smarting distinction between their ideal of universal equality and their grindstone experience of the practical misery and infamy of poverty."[2] Only in America, supposed Land of Opportunity, did people propose that the impoverished ought to blame their own failings for their condition.

In "The Paradise of Bachelors and the Tartarus of Maids" (1855), Melville depicted a luxurious gentlemen's club in London and a Berkshire paper factory in which women did all the coarsest jobs. Here, Melville was not only indicting the sacrifice of American womanhood to all-out industrialism but also echoing one of the themes he had developed in *Redburn*, about the unconscious dependence of the leisure classes on the skilled, competent labor of the scraping-by classes. Consider the attitude of travelers on a pleasure cruise toward the lowly, anonymous steersman: "they little think . . . what an important personage, and how much to be had in reverence, is the rough fellow in the pea-jacket, whom they see standing at the wheel, now cocking his eye aloft, and then peeping at the compass, or looking out to windward."[3] The London gentlemen in "The Paradise of Bachelors," just like first-class passengers lounging on a private deck, have the power and status to create a "refuge" for themselves, "quite sequestered from the old city's surrounding din." Of course, the women of the paper mill also inhabit a gated community, but their "Dantean gateway" is the kind at which one abandons all hope. Melville's naive narrator, impressed by the perfectly white sheets of paper being produced at the factory, invokes the hopeful "blank slate" theory of John Locke, who thought that both "the human mind at birth" and the entire New World offered clean, fresh opportunities for any free, enterprising individual. But what the narrator witnesses, as he stands "spell-bound and wandering in my soul," is a line of "blank girls" with "pallid faces," themselves transfixed, following the "rollers, wheels, and cylinders, in slowly-measured and unceasing motion," responding "in unvarying docility to the autocratic cunning of the machine."[4] A blank piece of paper might allow a privileged man to make his mark in the world, but the workers who produced that paper were not presented with parallel opportunities.

Melville's third diptych, "The Two Temples," is his only surviving short piece from this period that never saw publication—because its satire of an American institution was too obviously biting. In the English scene, our narrator, a lonely American wandering the London streets "without a copper," at first feels "forlorn, outcast," appalled by "the fiendish gaslights, shooting their Tartarean rays across the muddy, sticky streets." But then, suddenly, a friendly stranger offers him a ticket to a play, and once inside the old theater, he receives a free glass of ale from the usher, and he finds himself thoroughly enjoying the "most acceptable, right welcome, cheery company, to otherwise uncompanioned me." Though conditioned to have a prideful disdain for all charity, he winds up cherishing his new sense of solidarity and realizing that in fact "all your life, naught but charity sustains you, and all others in the world." Of course, this incident contrasts sharply with the same narrator's experience in the story's American scene, in which he walks three miles early on a Sunday morning to attend the service at New York's famous Grace Church (unidentified in the story but too easily recognized, according to the magazine editors who rejected the piece)—only to be barred from entry by the "fat-paunched, beadle-faced" sexton whose job it is to protect the sacred space from beggars and vagabonds. The narrator manages to sneak in through a door to the bell tower, though, and after a long climb he reaches a circular opening through which he can just barely peer down to the nave. High in a gothic tower, he knows he should feel exalted, closer to God, with a broader perspective, and he does his best to listen to the rector and "make my responses in the proper place." But he is not part of the community: "though an insider in one respect, yet I am but an outsider in another." Utterly alone, he comes to see the rector not as a spiritual guide but as some sort of hypnotist. "Book in hand, responses on my tongue, standing in the very posture of devotion, I could not rid my soul of the intrusive thought that, through some necromancer's glass, I looked down upon some sly enchanter's show."[5] In the United States, religion seemed merely a spiritual justification for commercialism, whereas in England even commercial events offered the possibility of true communion.

All these themes were anticipated in *Redburn*, Melville's meditation on what it had meant to travel to England at age nineteen, and walk through the streets of Liverpool for six weeks, and then return to New York. Just as Mumford would several decades later, Melville reconnoitered whatever modern cities he had access to, curious about how they shaped people's lives and how they compared to each other. In many ways, they seemed a lot like ships: sites of everyday trauma, often the result of brutally hierarchical relationships—but also sites of cosmopolitan fellowship, where eventually the sustained engagement with difference might help people rediscover a sense of commonality.

In a chapter called "Redburn Roves About Hither and Thither," our narrator explains that "wherever I have been in the world, I have always taken a vast deal of lonely satisfaction in wandering about, up and down, among out-of-the-way streets and alleys, and speculating upon the strangers I have met." Lonely satisfaction: suddenly, after *Typee*, *Omoo*, and *Mardi*, Melville has transformed himself from an island-hopper to a flaneur. He has become a poet of the city. And what his narrator finds most salient, all around him, is "poverty, poverty, poverty, in almost endless vistas"—despite the old city's narrow boundedness. In some of the better-off neighborhoods, Liverpool is "very much such a place as New York . . . , [with] the same elbowing, heartless-looking crowd as ever." But in other sections of the city are seemingly unprecedented "masses of squalid men, women, and children": "want and woe staggered arm in arm along these miserable streets." Redburn came to England in search of history, but what he discovers is a rapidly modernizing society with an entrenched industrial infrastructure and a newly concentrated population of exploited factory workers. In many ways, he is one of them, even if his job in the merchant marine is less modern. The problem is that most poor people are so beaten down by their circumstances that they are rarely capable of even the slightest connection. Sometimes, Redburn observes, "the very hardships to which such beings are subjected, instead of uniting them, only tend, by imbittering their tempers, to set them against each other."[6]

Redburn often acknowledges his own bitterness. Arriving in Liverpool with a precious guidebook, used and annotated by his now-dead father more than thirty years before, he at first feels "a soft, pleasing sadness" in contemplating his experience of cross-generational continuity. But then it turns out that many of his father's favorite sights are either gone or inaccessible. "Dear delusion!" Redburn cries. His inherited guidebook is "no more fit to guide me about the town, than the map of Pompeii." And he cannot abide this razing of history. "Is there nothing in all the British empire but these smoky ranges of . . . warehouses? Is Liverpool but a brick-kiln . . . ? This boasted England is no older than the State of New York." When he does finally stand upon some of the same flagstones his father stood upon, in "the fine quadrangle of the Merchants' Exchange," he comes close to weeping, as he contemplates his own "sorry apparel," and notices that people are "crossing the walk a little to shun me," and considers all the tribulations his father endured—"how he had been shaken by many storms of adversity, and at last died a bankrupt." The past is gone; the only continuity is that of failure and suffering.[7]

Hoping to redeem some part of the experience, Redburn attempts to visit a nearby "news-room" (a kind of library where one could read all the local newspapers) and the Lyceum, both of which were recommended in his father's annotations of the guidebook, and both of which appeal to a young man who prides himself on keeping up with current events. At the news-room, though, "a glance at my soiled shooting-jacket prompted a dignified looking personage to step up and shut the door in my face." At the Lyceum, a "crabbed old gentleman . . . , looking at me as if I were a strange dog with a muddy hide, that had stolen out of the gutter into this fine apartment . . . , shook his silver cane at me fiercely, till the spectacles fell off his nose," and then another "terribly cross man . . . took me by my innocent shoulders, and . . . , putting his foot against the broad part of my pantaloons, wheeled me right out into the street, and dropped me on the walk." So much for public engagement.

Scorned by "respectable" society, Redburn tries again to find solidarity among the poor, but his rambles yield more horror than recognition.

"Every variety of want and suffering here met the eye," he reports, "and every vice showed here its victim." He paces slowly past a line of beggars, sick and starving, "hollow-eyed and decrepit," the discarded refuse of a violently churning economy: "I remember one cripple, a young man rather decently clad, who sat huddled up against the wall, holding a painted board on his knees. It was a picture intending to represent the man himself caught in the machinery of some factory, and whirled about among spindles and cogs, with his limbs mangled and bloody."[8]

Wandering among the exploited poor, Redburn thinks also of enslaved people back in the States (slavery had been abolished throughout the British Empire in 1833). In fact, there are "painful" reminders of slavery all around him in Liverpool: "the Mobile and Savannah cotton ships and traders" at the dock; the "dingy, prison-like cotton warehouses"; and a monument depicting four men in chains that commands his attention for quite some time at the Merchants' Exchange. "These woebegone figures of captives" are meant to represent the major naval victories of Lord Horatio Nelson (who towers above the four defeated men), but Redburn "never could look at their swarthy limbs and manacles, without being involuntarily reminded of four African slaves in the market-place."

Even as his mind "[reverts] to Virginia and Carolina," though, Redburn takes solace in remembering that abolition is a practical possibility. If England's all-out commitment to manufacturing seems a dark shadow hanging over America's future, at least there had been real Progress in other areas of British society. The example of Liverpool is especially powerful, since, as Redburn remarks, "the African slave-trade once constituted the principal commerce" of the city, and when enough progressive Liverpudlians finally called the question, "the struggle between sordid interests and humanity had made sad havoc at the fire-sides of the merchants; estranged sons from sires; and even separated husband from wife." But the abolitionists had won—among them, a friend of Redburn's father, William Roscoe (a real historical figure), who wrote the famous poem "The Wrongs of Africa." Ultimately, the Nelson monument connects Redburn powerfully to the past, as he recalls with pride that his father visited Roscoe in Liverpool, and it also gives him concrete hope for America's future: if the sordid interests could be defeated here, then perhaps they could be defeated in Virginia and Carolina and Alabama and Georgia.

Redburn also takes pleasure in simply observing the freedom that black people enjoy on Liverpool's streets. There aren't many black Englishmen, but it's clear to Redburn that "the black cooks and stewards of American ships" love coming to England: they even hold themselves differently once they arrive. "In Liverpool indeed the negro steps with a prouder pace, and lifts his head like a man; for here, no such exaggerated feeling exists in respect to him as in America. Three or four times, I encountered our black steward, dressed very handsomely, and walking arm-in-arm with a good-looking English woman. In New York, such a couple would have been mobbed in three minutes; and the steward would have been lucky to escape with whole limbs." As in "The Two Temples," Melville's home country comes across as backward, ugly, roguish, in comparison to enlightened England. But in this case Melville's narrator is able to suggest a clear path forward: we could simply follow the lead of the British Empire and recognize black people's "claims to humanity and normal equality." Why is it, Redburn wonders, that "in some things, we Americans leave to other countries the carrying out of the principle that stands at the head of our Declaration of Independence"? The very spirit of our revolutionary break with England should now inspire us to follow England's example.[9]

Redburn's extended surveys of Liverpool certainly serve to broaden his sympathies, but he was already dissecting social hierarchies on the voyage across the Atlantic, during which he himself often felt "as if I were an African in Alabama." Since it was his first time at sea, he was often singled out both for ridicule and for the basest chores, and he had little chance of breaking into existing cliques. "I found myself a sort of Ishmael in the ship," he explains. Of course, the romance of the "glorious ocean life" occasionally captivated him—the "briny, foamy life, when the sea neighs and snorts, and you breathe the very breath that the great whales respire!" It was sometimes like being in a city that had unheard-of access to fresh air and open spaces. But more often it was a "miserable dog's life," for he was constantly "commanded like a slave, and set to work like an ass," forced to serve the "vulgar and brutal men lording it over me."[10]

One of the worst taskmasters was a sailor called Jackson, who "seemed to be full of hatred and gall against every thing and every body in the world," and who held an "extraordinary dominion . . . over twelve or fourteen strong, healthy tars." Redburn feels perpetually frustrated that his co-laborers don't band together to bring Jackson's cruel reign to an end. His resentment festers for a long time. After a while, though, he seems to push himself to recognize that Jackson has surely experienced his own share of abuse, that the world "had done him some dreadful harm"—that he was now quite sick, "consumed by an incurable malady"—and that in fact he could be quite friendly with strangers.[11] It's like the moment in *Moby-Dick* when Starbuck suddenly sees and appeals to Ahab's humanity: "Oh, my Captain! My Captain! Noble soul! Grand old heart, after all. . . . Let us fly these deadly waters! Let us home! Wife and child, too, are Starbuck's—wife and child of his brotherly, sisterly play-fellow youth; even as thine, sir, are the wife and child of thy loving, longing, paternal old age!"[12] Redburn eventually realizes that the people who seem most revoltingly different are precisely the ones whom we must try the hardest to understand and sympathize with. "There seemed even more woe than wickedness" to Jackson, Redburn quietly observes; ". . . and his wickedness seemed to spring from his woe; and for all his hideousness, there was that in his eye at times, that was ineffably pitiable and touching."[13]

There is some Jackson in all of us, Melville knew—himself included. Far too often, our traumas do indeed set us against each other. Melville was sometimes a tyrant in his own home, especially during his most intense writing years; his family feared his outbursts. It was helpful to all of them when he took time off to travel, to brush up against other people, to witness unfamiliar scenes. Wandering in his mind was sometimes insufficient. In the fall of 1849, after completing both *Redburn* and *White-Jacket* in a great flurry of machine-like productivity, he decided that it was time to go to sea again, and he sailed for England and the Continent, with dreams of continuing on to "Jerusalem & the Pyramids—Constantinople, the Egean, & old Athens!" The trip was a combination of pleasure and business, a chance to take a break from writing but also to gather new ideas and absorb new textures. He spent a couple of months mostly in London and Paris, negotiating a contract for the British edition of *White-Jacket*, lounging at gentlemen's clubs, and seeking out the best museums, where he took notes on various sculptures and paintings, including a few famous diptychs. There was money for further travels, and there were intriguing invitations, but it started to dawn on Melville that he was homesick. He missed Lizzie and tiny Malcolm—so much that he started to let go of his obsession with "procuring 'material.'" On Sunday, December 16, 1849, at 3 p.m., he sat smoking a cigar before a cozy London fire, and writing in his journal: "Would that One I know were here. Would that the Little One too were here. . . . I am all eagerness to get home." Ten days later, he was sailing back to America, feeling a little more human than he had in October.[14]

When he arrived in New York harbor, perhaps the scene was something like the one he had described at the end of *Redburn*: "The ship lay gently rolling in the soft, subdued ocean swell; while all around were . . . broad, milky patches, betokening the vicinity of scores of ships, all bound to one common port, and tranced in one common calm. Here the long, devious wakes from Europe, Africa, India, and Peru converged to a line, which braided them all in one." Worlds come together in the shared water of a busy port: it's the turbulent peace of interconnection. Redburn had noticed the same phenomenon in Liverpool, as perhaps Melville himself did back in 1839. In the novel's version of the story, Redburn immediately comments on how "all the nations of Christendom, and even those of Heathendom," unite at the Liverpool dock. "Here are brought together the remotest limits of the earth; and in the collective spars and timbers of these ships, all the forests of the globe are represented, as in a grand parliament of masts." Redburn then seeks to take in the sights and smells of one of the most exotic vessels, the *Irrawaddy*, from India: at first, an "oriental usher accosted me at the gangway, with his sword at my throat," but subsequently the swordsman behaved "very considerately" while Redburn enjoyed the "strangely woody" odor of the teak timbers and the "cocoa-nut fiber" rigging, and got acquainted with a large group of friendly "Malays, Mahrattas, Burmese, Siamese, and Cingalese."[15]

Crowded, cosmopolitan cities would always have their share of modern problems. Melville witnessed the worst kinds of degradation, viciousness, and apathy; people with different backgrounds and cultures, people of different classes and races, would almost always be suspicious of each other. But he also saw, in every major city, the concrete possibilities of the great American experiment. At the Liverpool dock, he imagined what each ship might contribute to the United States. Such a vision, he thought, should be enough, "in a noble breast," to "forever extinguish the prejudices of national dislikes. . . . You can not spill a drop of American blood without spilling the blood of the whole world. . . . Our blood is as the flood of the Amazon, made up of a thousand noble currents all pouring into one."[16]

Again and again, Melville would return to New York, the consummate American city, with its port, its warehouses, its offices, its tenements, its restaurants, its thronged and abandoned streets; again and again, he would find it simultaneously disillusioning and reenchanting.

CHAPTER 19

Radburn (1923-39)

Cities have always been mixed blessings, but they have been increasingly easy to criticize in the era of environmentalism. In conjunction with runaway industrial capitalism, they tend to stimulate overconsumption of most natural resources and overproduction of most forms of waste. They also concentrate toxins. For about half a century, urbanists have tried to avoid environmental issues, and environmentalists have denigrated urbanism.

In recent years, though, as climate change has announced itself more clearly, some scholars and activists have rediscovered the environmental advantages of urban concentration. Most significantly, cities offer crucial opportunities for energy efficiency. Lots of urbanites can live full, expansive lives without ever traveling by car. And thanks to the resurgent Garden City tradition, founded in early twentieth-century Britain by Ebenezer Howard and Patrick Geddes, some urban spaces are even starting to reattract the attention of nature-loving environmentalists.

What is so remarkable about Mumford is that, from the beginning, he was both an environmentalist and an urbanist.[1] Green City advocates have started to tout his ecological awareness, but it will be just as important, throughout the twenty-first century, to remind people of the political, cultural, and spiritual reasons to remake and reclaim urban spaces. Mumford was one of the most incisive, open-eyed critics of modern cities we've ever had. Yet he always remembered that youthful, idealistic embrace of urban possibility that he felt on his walks with his grandfather and that he rediscovered in books like *Redburn*.

Mumford even suspected that the fundamental stimulation for Melville's writing career may have come from those six weeks the young sailor spent in Liverpool: "all these scenes and people and apparitions were an essential part of his education," Mumford wrote. "Indeed, there is no better experience for a well-prepared lad than to be thrown in a strange city, not too remote in habit and culture from his original home, with long days for exploration, experience, meditation."[2] In 1839, about to turn twenty, Melville used his surveys of Liverpool to escape the immediate oppression of the merchant marine and to test himself against a broader reality. He found both misery and exhilaration, in ever-shifting degrees, and recognized that it would be ludicrous to describe an entire city as simply miserable or simply exhilarating.

Mumford, too, learned the lesson of honoring a city's offsetting forces.[3] Ultimately, *The Culture of Cities* would confront all the darkest challenges of urban life, but Mumford opened the book with a long paean to The City that seems to invoke Melville's enthralled descriptions of cosmopolitan Liverpool. "A sailing ship," Mumford wrote, "[or] a caravan, stopping at the city, may bring a new dye for wool, a new glaze for the potter's dish, a new system of signs for long distance communication, or a new thought about human destiny."[4]

Mumford had been making concrete, practical efforts to foster stimulating urban interchange since at least the spring of 1923, when he joined with some friends to launch the broad-minded Regional Planning Association of America (RPAA). The group's main goal was to build a Garden City in America, based on the two obvious English models, Letchworth (founded in 1905) and Welwyn (1920): the mother country, as Melville had noted, still had a few important lessons for its rebellious child. And Patrick Geddes, visiting Mumford in New York at the time, was able to reinforce that point when he attended one of the RPAA's earliest official meetings, at a worker's retreat called the Hudson Guild Farm in New Jersey.[5] Given Mumford's engagement with "the new ideas in conservation, ecology, and geotechnics," and given the involvement of his colleague Benton MacKaye, who was promoting what would eventually become the Appalachian Trail, the RPAA could even be considered a radical environmental organization. But Mumford's two closest friends in the group were the architect Clarence Stein and the planner Henry Wright, both of whom had helped design housing developments for soldiers and workers during the war; their emphasis was on transforming real estate from a profit-driven industry into a public-minded effort to create affordable, attractive, neighborly communities.[6]

Many members of the RPAA would get to work on large government projects in the 1930s under Roosevelt's various New Deal programs, but in the 1920s they had to rely on private funding, and so they started small—with Sunnyside Gardens. "The townplanner needs the aid of the poet," Mumford commented to Stein and Wright in 1924 as they worked on Sunnyside's aesthetic. But a financier can also be helpful: Stein succeeded in converting a real estate mogul named Alexander Bing ("developer of massive apartments and skyscrapers"), making the case, in Mumford's words, against "the general misdirection of effort in housing and planning during the nineteen-twenties, with its sprawling cities, its extravagant subdivisions, its areas of standardized blight, hastily sold off (under the aegis of the Own Your Own Home movement) to people already sufficiently insecure without this extra burden."[7] Just as ordinary 1920s Americans were encouraged to invest in the stock market (with ultimately disastrous results), so too were they bombarded by opportunities to secure mortgages on private, stand-alone properties that they couldn't afford (a pattern familiar to anyone who lived through the recession of 2008). Though some economics textbooks still teach that demand drives supply, modern history shows clearly that capital investments often come first, and then businesses use advertising to create more demand for their products. The supposedly archetypal American desire for homeownership did not arise from any "natural" inclination or grassroots movement; it is largely a construct of the real estate industry, which really started flexing its muscles during the boom of the 1920s.[8]

Alexander Bing, meanwhile, organized the City Housing Corporation, which immediately bought about seventy-five acres of land from the Long Island Railroad, aiming, in Bing's words, "to produce good homes at as low a price as possible." Always mindful of costs as they designed the units for Sunnyside, Stein and Wright—as Mumford noted—"doubtless sometimes allowed the inner quarters of the house to become a little cramped," even though the green spaces enclosed by the buildings felt quite expansive. This may have seemed like "excessive economy" to some, but the RPAA was keen to avoid "the fate of Forest Hills, the garden suburb built on Long Island before the First World War by the Russell Sage Foundation: meant to serve as a working-class community, but destined by the very generosity of its housing to become an entirely middle class, indeed upper middle class, community." Between 1924 and 1928, the City Housing Corporation built 1,202 family units, a mix of apartments and a few houses, and they were all occupied as soon as Sunnyside was completed. Bing had even turned a profit. A number of intellectuals, including Mumford and Wright, moved in, enjoying what Mumford cited as "an environment where space, sunlight, order, color—these essential ingredients for either life or art—were constantly present, silently molding all of us." But most of the residents, as a 1928 survey revealed, were mechanics, office workers, "small tradesmen," and salespeople.[9] Though the RPAA never addressed the structural racism of the housing market in Jim Crow America, the group did effectively call out class inequalities at a time when organized labor was struggling against the rising tides of upper-class hegemony and consumer culture.[10]

Sunnyside's success—its demonstration that not every working-class American aspired to the ideal of private, individualistic self-realization through suburban-style commodities—spurred the RPAA's most significant achievement, which came to be known as the "Radburn Idea." In 1928, Bing invested the money he had made at Sunnyside in two square miles of farmland in northern New Jersey, not far from New York, where the RPAA hoped to create a true Garden City, with a population of twenty-five thousand. That dream never became reality, largely because of timing: the town of Radburn was officially opened to inhabitants in May 1929, but within a few months the national economy had collapsed, and Bing's City Housing Corporation went bankrupt. Mumford, MacKaye, Stein, and Wright were all devastated that there would never be a buffer of wild land around Radburn—that no industries could afford to put down roots in the vicinity—that their proposed Garden City had been reduced to a bedroom community.[11] Yet they took solace in the very nature of the community's design, whose best features would be replicated in such far-flung places as Vallingby, Sweden; Chandigarh, India; and Kitimat, Canada.[12] Radburn itself, like Mumford's Melville biography, fell victim to Black Tuesday, but the Radburn Idea, like the broader Melville Revival, had legs.

As Clarence Stein explained, Radburn was intended as a place "in which people could live peacefully with the automobile—or rather in spite of it." Sometimes billed as a "Town for the Motor Age," Radburn adapted to the new reality of ubiquitous cars by strictly separating vehicular and pedestrian traffic. Instead of using the traditional gridiron street pattern, Stein and Wright built two self-contained neighborhoods they called Superblocks—large pieces of land surrounded by main roads but with no through-streets, only small access lanes leading to a series of cul-de-sacs where the houses were clustered, each in direct contact with the parks and gardens, which were arranged to form a kind of continuous "backbone."

One of Wright's contributions was to insist on having all the bedrooms and living rooms face the green areas, while the kitchens and bathrooms faced the access lanes. Meanwhile, pedestrian walkways connected all the private and public spaces, using a system of underpasses and overpasses where necessary, making it possible for children to get to any of Radburn's schools, playgrounds, and swimming pools (all integrated into the town's design from the beginning) without encountering a single car.[13]

Mumford took special pleasure in acknowledging that the idea for the underpasses and overpasses came directly from the plan used by Frederick Law Olmsted and Calvert Vaux for Central Park in the 1850s: "the educated man is he who can best make use of the wisdom of the past." And Stein was especially enthusiastic about how Radburn fought back against the dominance of the automobile. "In 1928," he noted, "there were 21,308,159 automobiles registered (as compared with 5 in 1895)." Both people and cars had been pouring into cities, and life on the urban gridiron pattern was astoundingly precarious: "pedestrians risked a dangerous motor street crossing 20 times a mile." Annually, in the twentieth century, there had been "more Americans killed or injured

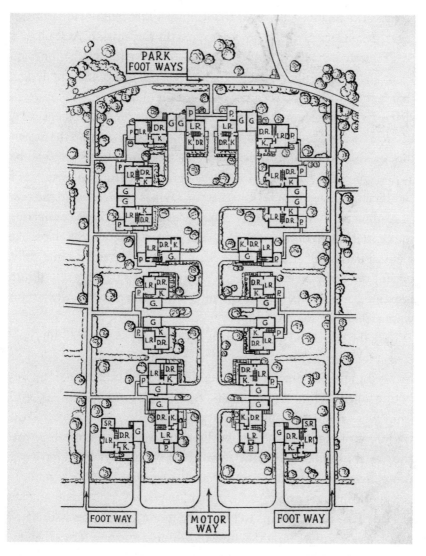

FIGURE 7. Clarence Stein, "Plan of a Typical Lane at Radburn," 1929.

in automobile accidents than the total of American war casualties in any year." Radburn would not contribute to those horrifying statistics. Moreover, it offered a restoration of "quiet and peaceful repose," removing all living spaces from the "bedlam" of "blocked traffic, honking horns, noxious gases."[14]

Even the financial vision of the Radburn Idea had obvious advantages, despite its inevitable foundering in the Depression. At Radburn, Stein asserted, the City Housing Corporation saved so much money on roads and public utilities, thanks to the town's compact, efficient design, that it could afford to keep "12 to 14 per cent of the total area" as green space. (Most developers leave as little open space as possible, because they can't sell parks, only houses.) Without through traffic in the Superblocks, the streets and lanes and water and sewer lines could all be 25 percent smaller than usual and of a "lighter construction"—and thus significantly cheaper. Stein said that the savings even "covered the cost of grading and landscaping the play spaces and green links connecting the central block commons."[15] Whereas property values near places like Central Park have almost always increased quickly and dramatically, driving out everyone but the very wealthy, the housing units at Radburn remained affordable because the town's fully integrated park systems were essentially free.[16]

Still, the social and political goals of the RPAA were not as fully realized at Radburn as Mumford would have liked. The residents were more firmly middle class than those at Sunnyside: Stein called them "mainly 'whitecollar'; salesmen, engineers, teachers, 'junior executives,' etc." They were almost all white, Christian, and college educated. So "the traditions of friendliness, neighborliness, and civic responsibility" that they established did not take as much work as they would have in a more diverse community. As Mumford emphasized, with a Melvillean sense of contingency, the designs that Stein and Wright implemented at Radburn "are not forms to be copied, but a spirit to be assimilated and carried further . . . , and in time transmuted into new forms that will reflect the needs and desires and hopes of another age." Stein could only agree: "Every job should be a laboratory. Customary plans, forms, or construction methods should be constantly questioned and analyzed. Fresh exploration and investigation [are] required to keep both architecture and community organization alive and contemporary."[17]

Today, Radburn is an unincorporated community within Fair Lawn, New Jersey—still a quiet, modest, leafy, solidly middle-class suburb, where you can sometimes smell the cookies baking at a nearby Nabisco factory. I spent a gray November day there in 2018, strolling along the pathways, exploring the underpasses, reading the historical markers, chatting with residents, digging in an archive. What I really wanted to know was how Radburn got its name. You can probably guess my suspicion: after all, the town was conceived in 1928, right when Mumford was working on his Melville biography. But I was wrong. "Radburn" was not a nod to one of Mumford's favorite city-surveying characters but rather a rushed mash-up of Old English terms, a coinage by Charles S. Ascher, the secretary of the City Housing Corporation, who was told on a Saturday that Mr. Bing would be giving a press conference on Tuesday and needed to know how he should refer to his new project. Ascher went to the New York Public Library, hoping to find inspiration in "the maps prepared by George Washington's campaign in New Jersey," but alas, there seemed to be "no human culture in our area, it was woods and marshes. The Saddle River ran through our town site, but there was already a Saddle River Township. I found a book on English place names which said that 'Rad' meant 'saddle'—so I added 'burn' and there we were."[18] "Burn" means brook or stream. As for "Rad," it can also mean reedy—or red.

Whether or not the town made Mumford think of Melville's adventures in Liverpool, he remained fond of it and often referred to it in his writings. He also visited sometimes. In June 1931, he and Catherine Bauer spent a few days together in New York, getting on each other's nerves more than usual, in part because some lousy weather made it impossible for them "to get out into the country." But, as Mumford wrote in his private notes, "it all ended happily enough: the last day we tramped around Radburn . . . , and had one of our old happy times in bed."[19] Not too long afterward, Bauer became the executive director of the RPAA and even did some research on Radburn. Ascher claimed that it was Bauer who helped them figure out "how many sites to set aside for church buildings" (some construction continued at Radburn during the first years of the Depression). "Her interviews with the national councils of many denominations showed that all the Protestant denominations could share a Community Church, which the Reform Jews would also share"—a determination which, as a Reform Jew, I find amusingly believable.[20]

Bauer was one of the RPAA members, along with Stein and Wright and a few others, who applied the Radburn Idea to some important New Deal projects in the 1930s. While Bauer landed at the United States Housing Authority (USHA), continuing her advocacy for communitarian architecture and public housing for low-income workers, Stein and Wright went to the Resettlement Administration (RA) to work on its Greenbelt Towns initiative. Directed by Rexford Tugwell, the RA was one of the more obviously socialistic New Deal agencies, and Tugwell agreed with almost all of the RPAA's principles. In Stein's considered opinion, the RA's most famous accomplishment, the new town of Greenbelt, Maryland, "carried out and developed the Radburn Idea more fully and completely" than had Radburn itself, thanks to the resources and clout of the federal government—though even in this case there were clear drawbacks and failings. With plenty of space to incorporate wild lands, Greenbelt became more of a true Garden City than Radburn, but, like its predecessor, it had trouble attracting industry and overturning structural inequalities. It quickly came to resemble many other white, middle-class suburbs around Washington, D.C., housing mostly federal workers who had to commute more than a dozen miles each way.[21]

Still, Greenbelt's symbolism mattered, especially in Mumford's ongoing crusade to promote communalism, ecological awareness, and equal opportunities—to "make the good things of our civilization available to all its members" and thus prepare the way for "a bolder and more humane generation, less victimized by the false gods of finance."[22] In the face of an ongoing Depression, not to mention entrenched racism and the resistance of powerful lawmakers and business interests, not only the RA but also the USHA and the Public Works Administration (PWA) managed to plan new towns across the country that were designed to accommodate former mine workers, black farmers, black factory workers, and virtually any other underemployed or otherwise struggling Americans who might be interested in cooperative housing and businesses, affordable rents, and easy access to workplaces, shopping, schools, community centers, and open space.[23] Greenbelt, in particular, demonstrated the democratic advantage of creating a city that, in Mumford's words, incorporated "the primeval and the rural."[24] When

Stein wrote about Greenbelt, he emphasized that its "essential shape . . . was indicated by nature," and he quoted MacKaye, the wilderness advocate, to seal his point: "The basic achievement of planning is to make potentialities visible. . . . Planning is revelation."[25] Mumford, Stein, MacKaye, and Bauer all contributed to the documentary film, The City, shown at the New York World's Fair in 1939, and they chose Greenbelt to serve as the modern exemplar of what a city could be. As Aaron Copland's music soars and twitters in the background, the camera shows children cycling through underpasses, families digging up carrots, young men walking to work. And then the narrator takes over, reading Mumford's script: "We fathers have a little time to watch our kids and play with them. They see us in the daytime. The people who laid out this place didn't forget that air and sun are what we need for growing, whether it's flowers or babies. . . . In this new scheme of things, the school becomes the center and the focus of activities. Here boys and girls live and re-live the life around them, getting the measure of our bigger world and shaping it anew . . . , facing the good and bad."[26]

Though Mumford, committed to life as a writer, chose not to work directly for the New Deal, his ideas fit better with the political culture of the 1930s than with that of any other period in his career, and upon the publication of The Culture of Cities in 1938 he reached the first peak of his popular fame (there would be another in the 1960s). Some of his 1920s proposals that had come across as radical now seemed almost mainstream. And it would be a source of bitter frustration for the rest of his life that World War II interrupted the New Deal and knocked most of the country back onto the mass-manufacturing military-industrial track (perhaps the United States would have become locked into that kind of economy anyway, but the war effectively killed many alternatives). Meanwhile, though, Mumford appeared on the cover of Time magazine in 1938 and even responded positively to a couple of requests that he come out of his seclusion in Amenia to do some new reconnaissances and propose development plans, for the city of Honolulu and the whole region of the Pacific Northwest.[27]

In Oregon and Washington, as he toured the landscape, he relished "the great simplicity of the towering Douglas firs," but he surprised his hosts by focusing on the need to rethink the region's boom towns, Seattle and Portland, which, after supplying the Klondike Gold Rush in the late 1890s, had almost immediately become congested and "blighted." Yes, local planners ought to put a stop to such "anti-social actions" as "the mining of the forests" throughout the region. But an even higher priority was "the 'reforestation' of urban culture."[28]

In Honolulu, where he stayed for five weeks with Sophia, Geddes, and Alison, Mumford thought often of Greenbelt, and in his report he wound up recommending low-cost housing, ample common areas, pedestrianism, the broad diffusion of parks and greenery throughout the city, and an advisory planning council, composed of ordinary citizens, to "provide a useful public check" on the more official directors of development. He also invoked Melville, as someone who understood how places like Hawaii might offer the chance to slough off some of "the restrictions and burdens imposed by . . . 'Snivelization'" and to embrace "the privilege of confronting the primeval forces of the ocean and the sun."[29]

For Mumford, the whole trip to Paradise was a strange and intense experience, full of both confrontations and evasions. Looking back on it many decades later, he especially remembered the terror of his vigil at Sophia's hospital bed as she battled a virulent strain of pneumonia (successfully). But the Hawaiian sojourn was also memorable for the unusual closeness Lewis felt with his often-distant thirteen-year-old son, when they woke up early and strolled "to the sea for our dip, a dip in that calm ocean, smoothed by the coral reef, whose temperature at every hour of the day or night was just right for swimming in." And Mumford also recalled the pleasing thrill of writing flirtatious letters to Jo Strongin, his Yillah, the "*pure spirit*" who would remain forever beyond his reach: "the sharp heathen voluptuousness of the island has me in its grip," he told her.[30]

Earlier in the year, when Lewis had suggested that the whole family go to Hawaii, Sophia had responded with joy and affection: "In all this curious world, my very dearest, I'm so thankful for the reality of you. . . . I don't know whether to weep that when we were young we didn't consciously know what beauty was in store for us, or whether to rejoice that approaching middle age seems glorious with the thought that you and

I are to spend it together. I love you."[31] She didn't know that Jo was continuing to pursue her husband, and that Lewis was continuing to lead her on. When Sophia fell ill, Lewis felt that his "long dreamt-of idyll turned into a nightmare."[32] But when she recovered, he went back to thinking about Jo. "Melville spends a whole chapter in 'Moby-Dick' dwelling on the nature of Delight," he wrote to her; "and now I can add a paragraph or two to all he could say about it. I have packed the tiny phial of ginger perfume I picked up in Hawaii to send away to you. . . . I doubt if it can even faintly give you a sense of the dark woods beneath the jagged mountains on the windward side of Oahu where, stumbling over stumps through an ancient forest, near an old Hawaiian temple and sacrificial ground, I came upon the ginger plant, growing with . . . heavy stems, broad leaves, sweet rank odor, heavy and pungent, like some anesthetic invented to allay the pains of thwarted lovers. If you had popped out from behind the great dark mango trees, when I first saw the ginger wild, I should not have been surprised."[33]

In truth, there is no "whole chapter" about Delight in *Moby-Dick*. Just before the final, fatal encounter with the white whale, the *Pequod* does meet a ship called the *Delight*, but it turns out she is "miserably misnamed": Moby Dick has just shattered one of her boats and killed five of her men. Mumford was more likely thinking of the long passage about Delight in Father Mapple's sermon about Jonah. Of course, the chaplain is less concerned with tropical indulgences than with spiritual fortitude. "Delight is to him whose strong arms yet support him, when the ship of this base treacherous world has gone down beneath him. . . . Delight is to him, whom all the waves of the billows of the seas of the boisterous mob can never shake from this sure Keel of the Ages."[34] Delight, in other words, is virtually impossible to cling to—as Mumford well knew.[35]

CHAPTER 20

Revolutions (1848-55)

On a "miserable rainy day" in December 1849, Melville found himself prowling around London, torn between his homesickness and his hunger for new material. He tried to go to the British Museum, but it was closed. At a silversmith's near the Strand, he "bought a solid spoon for the boy Malcolm—a *fork*, I mean. When he arrives to years of mastication I shall invest him with this fork—as of yore they did a young knight, with his good sword." A silver *spoon*, I suppose, would have been too ironic even for Melville. After dallying in several "old book stores about Great Queen Street & Lincoln's Inn," he also bought a gift for himself: a map of London from 1766. "I want to use it," he wrote in his journal, "in case I serve up the Revolutionary narrative of the beggar."[1]

He was thinking of an obscure memoir he had read called *The Life and Remarkable Adventures of Israel R. Potter*, about a common American soldier in the Revolution who had been captured by the British near Boston Harbor and wound up spending the next forty-eight years in England before finally making it back to the United States. Potter's story seems to have appealed to Melville on many levels. Perhaps most obviously, it was a potential debunking of the gloriousness of the American Revolution. It also arrived in his lap as a premade diptych, offering an extended opportunity to compare conditions in the Old World and the New. And Potter's life as an impoverished exile was generally rich in historical, political, and metaphysical themes: in an increasingly interconnected and abstracted world, what did it mean for an ordinary person to struggle for Independence? Having had enough of his heroic Revolutionary grandfathers—General Peter Gansevoort, famous for his defiant defense of Fort Stanwix against a superior British force, and Major Thomas Melvill, who participated in the Boston Tea Party—Herman decided to adopt a Revolutionary outcast as his ancestor.

The question of Revolution haunted Melville all his life, but it was especially urgent in the aftermath of the European revolutions of 1848. In mid-March of that year, he was with his friend Evert Duyckinck when tidings of the uprising in France reached New York: it looked like the monarchy might be overthrown again, and New Yorkers showed their support for the French workers and students by pouring into the streets. Evert's brother George had written vividly from Paris to say that thousands of young citizens had erected makeshift barricades using "doors, boards, carriages, whatever came to hand."[2] In turn, Evert told George that "A Walk in Broadway to-day is a thing of excitement, the news of the Revolution in Paris having imparted to every one that vivacity of eye, quickness of intelligence and general exhilaration which great public events extend to private ones."[3] Over the next several weeks, Louis-Philippe gave up his throne, Queen Victoria took refuge on the Isle of Wight rather than confront angry mobs of unemployed Englishmen, and revolutionaries marched in Germany, Denmark, and Hungary. Melville noted everything and decided to bring these great public events into his private study, weaving them into the ever-expanding manuscript of *Mardi: And a Voyage Thither*. In fact, Taji's quest for Yillah winds up taking him to an allegorical archipelago whose islands stand in for different countries experiencing various forms of political unrest. Some of the book's funniest passages deal with a rumbling volcanic isle whose rival valleys are divided into such kingdoms as Franko, Ibeereea, Latianna, Vatikanna, Tutoni, Zandinavia, and Muzkovi.

Alas, after only a few months, most of the European revolutions were being repressed, in some cases brutally, and the disillusionment stuck with Melville for a long time—as he noted, for instance, in the despotic "head-knockings" passage of 1853's "Cock-A-Doodle-Doo." Then, in *Clarel* (1876), his book-length poem about a pilgrimage in the Holy Land, he referred back to 1848 as evidence that all goodness and wisdom would eventually be countered by the fatal combination of "malice" and "ignorance":

> And what is stable? Find one boon
> That is not lackey to the moon
> Of fate. The flood ebbs out—the ebb
> Floods back; the incessant shuttle shifts
> And flies, and weaves and tears the web.
> Turn, turn thee to the proof that sifts:
> What if the kings in Forty-eight
> Fled like the gods? Even as the gods
> Shall do, return they made; and sate
> And fortified their strong abodes;
> And, to confirm them there in state,
> Contrived new slogans, apt to please—
> Pan and the tribal unities.[4]

Too often, "revolution" ultimately means restoration: the wheel comes all the way around again. And, as in the French Revolution of 1789, rebellions against the existing order may result in total chaos, or even a Reign of Terror. "He who hated oppressors," Melville wrote, in *Mardi*, "is become an oppressor himself."[5] We think of revolutions as marking radical change; they also, Melville noted, mark radical continuity.

But the legacy of the American Revolution was still a wide-open question in the years following 1848. In the world of *Mardi*, Melville laid out the uncertainty by introducing readers to the republic of Vivenza (one part of the continent-sized island of Kolumbo), which had recently declared Independence from the smaller island of Dominora, ruled by the grasping, warlike King Bello. While Dominora invoked "Old Times," resting on its past accomplishments and sense of history, the young nation of Vivenza seemed to be Mardi's greatest hope for democracy: "the foremost and goodliest stripling of the Present," Vivenza also "brims with the future." There had been no restoration of the monarchy here; instead, ordinary citizens governed, and worked the land with "stout hearts and arms," planting themselves in the "boundless fields, that may be had for the seeing." "We are all kings here," say the citizens of

Vivenza—all equal, all our own sovereigns. Taji and his search party visit Vivenza's impressive Temple of Freedom, take in "the rejoicing hum of a thriving population," and think to themselves that surely, in this lively nation, "Yillah will yet be found."[6]

Some of Taji's companions, though, react more skeptically to what they identify as Vivenza's "braggadocio." They understand why Vivenza might still be keen to defy Dominora, but they counsel moderation. Now that the young country is becoming more mature, it should "not fail in a reverential respect for its parent." Indeed, its citizens ought to recognize the debt they owe to Dominora: "As an army of spurred and crested roosters, her people chanticleered at the resplendent rising of their sun. For shame, Vivenza! Whence thy undoubted valor? Did ye not bring it with ye from the bold old shores of Dominora, where there is a fullness of it left?" King Bello was showing more restraint these days and had recently overseen some important reforms, such that Taji and his party begin to wonder whether Dominora, with its well-preserved buildings and woodlands and its garden-like landscape, might even be the more progressive nation.

"There's not so much freedom here as these freemen think," comments one of Taji's guides, as they tour Vivenza. "Ah, ye republicans!" says another, after reading a plaque claiming that "In this republican land all men are born free and equal." Just outside the vaunted Temple of Freedom, they find a "man with a collar round his neck, and the red marks of stripes upon his back." And they note how the "fiery and intractable" southerners of Vivenza swear "that if the northern tribes persisted in intermeddlings, they would dissolve the common alliance, and establish a distinct confederacy among themselves."[7]

Their questions come to a head when news arrives in Vivenza that there has been an enormous eruption in Franko, and the lava fires have been followed by numerous political conflagrations. Most citizens of Vivenza support the revolutionaries abroad: "Who may withstand the people? The times tell terrible tales to tyrants!" But Taji and his party stumble on intriguing evidence of dissent. A "clamorous crowd" has gathered around a tree, onto which an anonymous writer has tacked a rather substantive scroll, which eventually gets read aloud: "In these boisterous days, the lessons of history are almost discarded. . . . Yet, per-adventure, the Past is an apostle." How likely is it that this republic will last? Vivenza has not received a divine "exemption . . . from all the or-ganic causes, which inevitably divide mankind into brigades and bat-talions, with captains at their head. Civilization has not ever been the brother of equality." Moreover, given the persistence of social hierar-chies and human weakness, and the ubiquity of evil, mightn't it be use-ful sometimes to have a strong leader? Monarchies are not inherently wrong. "Better be the subject of a king, upright and just; than a freeman in Franko, with the executioner's ax at every corner. . . . Better be secure under one king, than exposed to violence from twenty millions of mon-archs, though oneself be of the number." And speaking of freedom: "Though King Bello's palace was not put together by yoked men; your federal temple of freedom, sovereign-kings! was the handiwork of slaves." Even in this promising republic, "poverty is abased before riches . . . ; any where, it is hard to be a debtor . . . ; every where, suffering is found." So no citizens should ever be too sure of their society's Pro-gress. "Students of history," the scroll's author concludes, "are horror-struck at the massacres of old; but in the shambles, men are being murdered to-day. Could time be reversed, and the future change places with the past, the past would cry out against us, and our future, full as loudly, as we against the ages foregone."[8]

At the start of the nineteenth century, hardly any Americans had questioned the value of their Revolution. The colonists suffered under the yoke of Britain; now they were free. Progress had been made. His-tory was on their side. By the 1830s, though, all the Revolutionary he-roes were gone, and there was virtually nothing uniting the republic anymore.

When Melville wrote his revolutionary doubts into *Mardi* in the summer and fall of 1848—in chapters 145 through 163 of a sprawling, fantastical manuscript—he at least wrapped them in layers of comedic roguery. Witness a semi-divine king and a pompous philosopher accus-ing each other of having written the anonymous screed on the scroll: "My lord," says the philosopher, "I am amazed at the indiscretion of a demi-god. . . . I recognized your sultanic style the very first sentence."

Hah! "I am astounded at your effrontery," replies the king. "I detected your philosophy the very first maxim. Who posted that parchment for you?" A reader could be forgiven for not considering the criticism of Vivenza too conscientiously.[9]

But when Melville took up his doubts again in 1854 and began spinning his own version of Israel Potter's life story, he took a very different approach: the lack of national unity now constituted a true cultural crisis, he thought, and he wondered if the republic's foundations had been shaky from the start. Though the resulting piece of fiction does have picaresque elements and a bit of vivacious tricksterism, it is mostly a direct confrontation with the grim side of the American Revolution. By this time, Melville had befriended Hawthorne, and gone back to Shakespeare, and decided that "man, 'poor player,' succeeds better in life's tragedy than comedy": tragic tales are simply more compelling; they seem truer to life.[10]

There is no chance that the reader will miss Melville's dark satire in the twistings of the tale, in part because *Israel Potter: His Fifty Years of Exile* (1855) is not just Melville's only historical novel but also his only serialized novel, and it is so fast-paced as to make one question his authorship. Instead of chapter-long, meditative tangents, we get tight, biting observations packed into single sentences. Melville was an established magazine writer by this time, and he correctly recognized that serialization could be a decent financial strategy, so long as he kept his readers engaged: "There will be very little reflective writing in it," he promised his editors; "nothing weighty. It is adventure."[11] Yet it is adventure that explicitly reverses the direction of Progress. "How little he thought," Melville writes of his lowly hero, "when, as a boy, hunting after his father's stray cattle among these New England hills, he himself like a beast should be hunted through half of Old England, as a runaway rebel. . . . This little boy of the hills, born in sight of the sparkling Housatonic, was to linger out the best part of his life a prisoner or a pauper upon the grimy banks of the Thames."[12]

Here was a Revolutionary story most Americans of the mid-nineteenth century had never heard. A solid, stalwart young man of the Berkshires, a wood-chopper, a stone-wall builder, fights at the Battle of

Bunker Hill, where the patriots are famously instructed not to fire until they can see the whites of their enemies' eyes. Israel obeys the order and is rewarded with "a musket-ball buried in his hip, and another mangling him near the ankle of the same leg." Then the British seize him and ship him to England in shackles—where he almost immediately escapes— and is almost immediately caught again—and then escapes again, and this time falls in with some high-up American sympathizers, who enlist him as a courier, supplying him with coded letters for Benjamin Franklin in Paris. The great philosopher-diplomat drinks cognac, womanizes, and speaks in charming aphorisms: "At the prospect of pleasure," he tells Israel, "never be elated; but, without depression, respect the omens of ill." The ill omens, for Israel, are many, and once back in England he gets "kidnapped into the naval service" and forced to serve as foretopman on one of his majesty's ships—not the *Undaunted* or the *Unconquerable* but the *Unprincipled*.[13] From there, Israel gets transferred to a small English cutter, which is in turn captured by an American vessel commanded by John Paul Jones, who brings Israel along to help with his brutal assault on the British coast. In the confusion of a sea battle, Israel winds up aboard another English frigate, where he successfully passes himself off as a lowly member of the crew, until the ship finally lands and he once again becomes a refugee. Then, for the next forty-five years, he wanders the streets and sewers of London, working when he can as a brick-maker and mender of chairs, fearing constantly that he would either be imprisoned as an American or impressed back into the royal navy if he claimed to be an Englishman. It is only through a seeming miracle that he is finally able to meet with an American consul (after Britain and the United States establish cordial relations), who arranges passage for him back to New England. An old man, ready to die, he arrives in Boston on the Fourth of July 1826—the very day, infamously, on which both John Adams and Thomas Jefferson left the world, marking the final demise of America's heroic, Revolutionary generation.

Has Israel achieved Independence? Well, at almost no point in the story does he seem to exert any control over his fate; he is mostly a cog in the war machine, a tool in the industrial economy, a long-suffering drudge obeying others' commands. Melville says of some sailors in a

Revolutionary naval battle that they "stood and toiled in mechanical magic of discipline. They tended those rows of guns as Lowell girls the rows of looms in a cotton factory." The comparison was anachronistic, but Melville's readers would have understood immediately: those sailors were being exploited, to such an extent that they became automatons, lacking any sense of their own responsibility. Who benefited from the American Revolution? Thousands of patriots sacrificed their lives for Freedom and Independence, but the new American republic was founded on slavery, and on webs of transatlantic commerce, and there was a clear social hierarchy, at the top of which sat southern plantation owners and northern businessmen. Certainly, opportunities arose for some ordinary Americans. But the U.S. government, strapped for cash ever since the republic's founding, would not even give old Israel a pension for his military service.[14]

By the time Israel made it home, slave labor was producing enough cotton to supply manufacturers in both Old and New England. Though Thomas Jefferson had dreamed of a nation of humble, democratic, agrarian freeholders (and part of that dream did come true), much of America was looking more and more like Liverpool and Manchester, as Melville noted several times. His story about the female workers at a Berkshire paper factory, "The Paradise of Bachelors and the Tartarus of Maids," came out in April 1855, the month after the last installment of *Israel Potter*. And while that diptych seemed to be drawing a contrast between the gentlemen's clubs of London and the women's workshops of America, one could alternatively see it as mapping working-class England onto the northern United States, and aristocratic England onto the southern United States (the "terraces, gardens, broad walks" of the gentlemen's clubs remind the narrator explicitly of "old Virginny").[15] In effect, Melville suggested, the American Revolution gave birth to a second modern England—but slavery lasted much longer here, and, by the way, all of the highest-quality manufactured goods (and the best book critics) still came from the mother country.

So when Melville described Israel's descent into the industrial Underworld of London—in two chapters called "Israel in Egypt" and "In the City of Dis"—he was using England's past to comment on America's present. If you took the long view, though, despite this immediate sense of restoration or replication, the Industrial Revolution actually did seem to be something new. Bricks, to take an example from Israel's direct experience, had been made for thousands of years, but the modern scale and speed of production meant that brick-makers were now slaves to furnaces and simple machines, and they moved to an automatic rhythm. "All night long, men sat before the mouth of the kilns, feeding them with fuel. A dull smoke—the smoke of their torments—went up from their tops." And meanwhile they had to shovel clay into a hopper, where it was ground and churned and spewed out into a trough, from which it then had to be slapped into molded trays and finally scraped smooth. Israel took no pride in his labor, had no sense that he was participating in anything constructive; nothing grew beneath his fingers. "Who ain't a nobody?" he asked, echoing Ishmael. "All is vanity and clay."[16] And the brick-making scene echoes the scene in *Moby-Dick* where the sailors of the *Pequod* fire up the "try-works" to boil their whale fat into oil, bringing an infernal industrial power to the ancient arts of sailing and hunting: "With huge pronged poles they pitched hissing masses of blubber into the scalding pots, or stirred up the fires beneath, till the snaky flames darted, curling, out of the doors to catch them by the feet. The smoke rolled away in sullen heaps. . . . The ship groaned and dived, and yet steadfastly shot her red hell further and further into the blackness of the sea and the night."[17]

Israel's brick-mills and brick-kilns are just outside London, but the actual cityscape reflects their dominance in the new order of things. The great River Thames is "one murky sheet of sewerage," crossed occasionally by a "black, besmoked bridge." Israel finds his only solace in "glimpses of garden produce, the blood-beets, with the damp earth still tufting the roots," which allow him to imagine "the green hedges through which the wagon that brought them had passed." But generally, in London, "whichever way the eye turned, no tree, no speck of any green thing was seen; no more than in smithies. All laborers, of whatsoever sort, were hued like the men in foundries. The black vistas of streets were as the galleries in coal mines; the flagging, as flat tomb-stones minus the consecration of moss; and worn heavily down, by sorrowful tramping, as the vitreous rocks in the cursed Gallipagos, over which the convict tortoises crawl."[18]

Stranded in this Tartarus, Israel feels like a "trespassing Pequod Indian, impounded on the shores of Narragansett Bay." Israel becomes an Ishmael. "All hands seem to be against me," he says. And his struggle, like Melville's, becomes the fundamental one of finding a will to continue on: he seeks "with stubborn patience to habituate himself to misery, but still hold aloof from despondency." As Israel slaps mud and clay into molds for bricks, he is "thereby taught, in his meditations, to slap, with similar heedlessness, his own sadder fortunes, as of still less vital consideration," and he tries to embrace "the reckless sort of half jolly despair" of the typical factory worker. "In his dismallest December," he clings to the occasional feeling of "a momentary warmth in his topmost boughs." He bends over, and feeds the fire, and catches at the hints of heat.[19]

There is one memorable moment in Melville's narrative when Israel suddenly snaps himself out of his mechanical routine and takes decisive action. He is sailing with John Paul Jones; an enemy ship passes too close, sending its jib-boom sweeping across the deck, where Israel grabs and holds it, helping Jones to knit the two vessels together with a coil of rigging. It's an act of wild bravery. But what follows is an infamous sequence of mutual barbarities. It's as if the two ships have entered "a co-partnership and joint-stock combustion-company," as if two "Siamese twins, oblivious of their fraternal bond, should rage in unnatural fight"—as if the Revolution were really a civil war. The antagonists hurl grenades at each other, fire cannons methodically at point-blank range. Jones even succeeds in igniting a long row of the enemy's ammunition, and "the fire ran horizontally, like an express on a railway" (another anachronistic description, but similarly potent for Melville's readers). "I have not yet begun to fight," says Jones, when the English captain asks him to yield, and by the end of the battle about half of all the sailors on both ships will be dead or wounded. Melville finishes his account of the carnage and asks: "What separates the enlightened man from the savage?"—a question that recalls an earlier passage in the book, about "those tragic scenes of the French Revolution which levelled the exquisite refinement of Paris with the blood-thirsty ferocity of Borneo; showing that broaches and finger-rings, not less than nose-rings and tattooing, are tokens of the primeval savageness which ever slumbers in human kind, civilised or uncivilised." The wheel comes around again, with cogs this time, as Melville's America, the glorious young republic, grinds its way toward its own fraternal battles.[20]

CHAPTER 21

Misgivings and Preparatives (1938–39)

Melville grew more cynical between *Mardi* and *Israel Potter*, but his pessimism about the United States had taken hold even before 1848, in the wake of the 1846 war with Mexico launched by President Polk, who clearly wanted to extend the territory where his fellow southerners could hold slaves—even if he didn't acknowledge that goal as the source of his bellicosity. In *Mardi*, the author of the scolding scroll refers to Polk fairly explicitly: "your great chieftan, sovereign-kings! may not declare war of himself; nevertheless, he has done a still more imperial thing:—gone to war without declaring intentions. You yourselves were precipitated upon a neighboring nation, ere you knew your spears were in your hands." This was the conflict over which Thoreau famously went to jail, not wanting his taxes to support slavery and imperialism. To Melville, the war confirmed that those who once revolted against oppression had now become the oppressors. "Evil," says the author of the scroll, "is the chronic malady of the universe, and checked in one place, breaks forth in another."[1]

Mumford didn't really enjoy reading *Mardi* (it does drag), but he thought that it marked the sharpening of Melville's political voice. He referred to the book as "a savage parody of the whole economy of Western Civilization, and its lofty Christian professions."[2]

In the fall of 1938, just back from Paradise, Mumford began to lose his basic faith in Western Civilization. He had always complemented his exacting criticisms with a commitment to reconstruction. But now evil was breaking forth again, and no one seemed to be responding. Why was the rise of European fascism going unchecked? How to understand this "paralysis of world-barbarism"? Despite the success of *The Culture of Cities*, Mumford felt that he had to make a drastic shift in his approach. The basic western ideals, "the decencies and sanities," were no longer sufficient.[3] What seemed necessary, now, was an Ahab-like defiance.

His plan had been to start work on the third volume of *The Renewal of Life*, but instead he transformed himself into one of the world's foremost antifascists, and within a few months he had produced an angry scroll of his own, different from anything he had written before. *Men Must Act* was hammered onto doors and trees around the United States and England early in 1939, provoking a fair amount of vitriolic condemnation.[4] His stance was a lonely one. After *Kristallnacht*, the "Night of Broken Glass" in Germany, in November 1938, which Mumford referred to as "the bestial outbreak against the defenseless Jews," more people acknowledged that the Nazis might pose a broad threat to European democracy and humane society.[5] But, especially in the United States, most liberals, still traumatized by the Great War, clung to a reflexive isolationism that increasingly drove Mumford toward desperation. A few of his prominent friends—Frank Lloyd Wright, Malcolm Cowley, Charles Beard—not only insisted on a policy of appeasement toward Hitler, Mussolini, and Franco but also denounced antifascists like Mumford and the poet Archibald MacLeish as dangerous warmongers.

The stakes seemed impossibly high, and Mumford's assertive moralism tended to make political rifts feel all the more personal. Mumford argued that the fascists had to be confronted immediately, with harsh sanctions and military might, because they had already proven themselves to be terrorists with world-conquering ambitions; "peace is not worth while having," he said, in *Men Must Act*, "if its preservation enslaves or exterminates peaceful men."[6] On the other side, "pragmatic" liberals claimed that the fascists would eventually be satisfied with a certain amount of regional power, and that countering their influence would require too many sacrifices. "Is meeting force with force the only way you see now?" asked Frank Lloyd Wright, in a searingly condescending letter to Mumford, disclaiming his previous admiration for Mumford's architectural writing. "Then I am sorry for you—you amateur essayist on culture."[7]

Mumford's voice did change in *Men Must Act*: it often harangues, accuses, excoriates. It reveals his bewilderment at how good people could stand by and allow evil to spread—how they could even rationalize their acceptance of murderous violence against tens of thousands of civilians (the Nazis had already invaded Austria and Czechoslovakia). In the past, he had reserved his most incisive criticisms for profiteers and exploiters, but now, all around him, he saw "self-indulgence" and "meek acquiescence" and "hypocritical pretense" and "wishful waiting" and "childish credulity" and "sheer inertia."[8] And if there were no people he could count on, it no longer made sense to emphasize renewal; this moment required an awakening and a counterattack. Mumford almost never stopped envisioning a better future, but in this case he wanted his readers focused exclusively on the present and the past: "The one kind of *ism* that no intelligent man should hold today is optimism. There has probably not been a time when the outlook for humanity was so black since the fourteenth century, the century of the Black Death. To fancy that fascism will sweep over the world and leave America untouched, merely because we wish to be let alone, is to imagine that we will be protected by a miracle."[9]

At the same time, though, Mumford made it clear that his willingness to fight stemmed from his commitment to the same humanistic and democratic values he had always celebrated as the West's fundamental heritage. He wanted to protect society's belief in "the participation and consent of the governed"—in "free inquiry and free choice"—in "unity by inclusion." He wanted every single individual to have the opportunity to lead a life that was "meaningful and purposive . . . , formative and creative." Indeed, he understood much of fascism simply as an extension and exacerbation of the same threats to Western Civilization that he had been tracking and attacking for two decades—the threats of industrial capitalism. Ordinary people in Europe and America were already suffering from a kind of everyday trauma that made it difficult for them to act as responsible citizens. "Each day brings with it a burdensome routine: the anxious efforts at punctuality, the necessity for speed and machinelike efficiency in production, the need to suppress personal reactions." Fascism was the tool employed by cynical demagogues to take advantage of people who had grown accustomed to "automatism and compulsion." So Mumford's antifascism was ultimately compatible with his long-standing efforts to combat the underlying shell shock of modernity.[10]

The Culture of Cities had required the bulk of Mumford's attention in the mid-1930s, but as early as 1935 he had also made a point of lashing out against Hitler and making the connection between political absolutism and "the forces of physical destruction and mental disintegration released by the massive technological equipment of modern states." And by the spring of 1938, months before the Allies' notorious appeasement of Hitler at Munich, Mumford was already issuing a "Call to Arms" in the *New Republic*, arguing that "an atmosphere of foggy unreality hangs over current discussions of peace." He feared that the "principle of 'live and let live,'" so popular in consumerist democracies, had turned most Europeans and Americans into affable denialists: "Surely, these people say to themselves, turning away from the latest fascist barbarity in the morning paper, the world cannot be so bad as that; or if it is for the moment, it cannot long remain so."[11]

Even if *Men Must Act* had a new, shrill urgency to it, then, it was really just an elaboration of Mumford's Melvillean realism. In a way, Mumford had been preparing for this sort of extreme case ever since the Red Scare in the aftermath of the Great War—certainly since his immersion in Melville in the late 1920s. In 1929, Mumford had emphasized how important it was that "Melville was a realist, in the sense that the great religious teachers are realists."[12] Melville had asked the basic moral question: how must good people respond to the existence of evil? Of course, there were evil elements in every society: for years, Mumford had called out "intransigent industrialists" and "native fascist organizations like the original Ku Klux Klan."[13] But it did feel a bit different when fascists were running national governments. In all of his previous works, Mumford had gotten away with being an Ishmael—a somewhat removed observer and interpreter. Now he had to reckon more directly with the white whale.

Could the example of Captain Ahab help Mumford explain his new conviction that the violence of fascism had to be met with the violence of righteousness? Maybe; but I don't think he ever reconciled his conflicting interpretations of Ahab. Mumford asserted quite forcefully that "in one sense, Ahab achieves victory: he vanquishes in himself that which would retreat from Moby-Dick and acquiesce in his insensate energies and his brutal sway."[14] We can all admire Ahab for not giving in to what Ishmael calls "that intangible malignity which has been from the beginning"[15]—for not becoming a mere tool of evil, for avoiding the path of so many fascist enablers and cooperators. And yet Ahab could not control his own malignity, so he also becomes the archetypal totalitarian dictator who manipulates ordinary toilers, exploiting the "state of acute frustration" that defines everyday life for so many moderns. Imagine all those German citizens, grasping for a way of explaining their bitter sense of entrapment in the overwhelming world: "out of their impotence they project an omnipotent Leader. And in order to achieve expression of their now maimed impulses, they collectively follow the example of Captain Ahab in 'Moby Dick': blindly, desperately, they seek revenge."[16] Scapegoats are offered up, and suddenly people who used to seem reasonable and well-intentioned are willing to man the boats and hurl harpoons wherever they're directed to.

Mumford's confusion about Ahab, and about who was responsible for the spread of fascism, invests all of *Men Must Act* with an ambivalence that belies its sometimes-belligerent tone. It is the book of a truly divided mind, written in a period that Mumford thought might be parallel to the final decline of the Roman Empire.[17] "The situation is a real test of my philosophy," he noted, in October 1938: "if I can write a book that rings true in the present world, my beliefs ought to hold water for any conceivable society or any moment of the individual's life: not fair weather philosophy for these days."[18] But how do you argue that you're trying to preserve a particular form of Civilization when that Civilization also produced the evil you're fighting against?

Well, at the very least, you have to be honest about the past, and about the drawbacks of what you're proposing. And then you can start to make careful distinctions between the admittedly flawed ideal you want to uphold and the all-too-similar but nevertheless pernicious ideology that you need to dismantle.

Mumford's knowledge of history made him fully aware that a military mobilization in the United States would probably lead to the mass murder of civilians; to the suspension of basic civil liberties; to the exacerbation of prejudices; and to the sacrifice of resources that ought to go toward "the building of workers' houses," toward "the re-building of cities," toward "furthering the processes of education and culture." Mumford hated war, and he knew that to live under what Patrick Geddes called "wardom" was to risk losing a society's investment in the future. He knew that his liberal opponents, arguing for isolationism, were absolutely right about the realities of fighting back. But he had decided that "the universal reign of fascism" would be "far more brutal and disastrous than war itself."[19]

Mumford understood that the United States was not an ideal refuge for those fleeing Europe: "I do not forget that the treatment of minorities in America, above all the treatment of the Indian and the Negro, has pages that have been as black as any that the fascists have written." But the United States still upheld the rule of law, and laws could be changed to help accommodate refugees. Like Melville defending the rights of starving Irish immigrants in *Redburn*, Mumford insisted that his nation open its gates for any "victims of fascist persecution," no matter what. "The basis of our present immigration policy is one of the least defensible things in our public law: equaled perhaps only by the denial of the vote in the South to the Negro. Our existing immigration law deliberately discriminates between the immigrants on the fascist basis of 'race.'" The infamous Immigration Act of 1924 had been a response to "pseudo-science" and nativism and a reactionary inwardness in the aftermath of World War I. But the Great Depression and the New Deal should have reminded Americans that "equity and justice" were also part of the national heritage, and that "to preserve our civilization we must be ready to give the world more than we get." As long as representative government survived, a new wave of empathy could result in a more humane policy.[20]

Mumford also knew that the United States had become an Empire after the Spanish-American War, had followed the criminal example of the European powers, with their "spurious doctrines of racial supremacy" and their pathological greed. But at least, under democratic empires, it was possible to defy racism and imperialism, and throughout modern history dedicated rebels had "actively fought against the tendency to seize and exploit distant lands" and had "freely opposed the dirty brutalities that accompanied this process. Such critical voices were heard all over the world." Indeed, all of "the evil forces that exist in a democracy are exposed to criticism and open to correction," whereas "those in a fascist state are sealed against even the majority's opinion."[21]

Yet Mumford also worried that Americans had gone too far in thinking of the classic Bill-of-Rights freedoms in absolute terms. Probably his most controversial proposal in *Men Must Act* was that it was time to limit the rights of any self-proclaimed fascists within the United States: those who declared an open, political allegiance to Hitler or Mussolini should have their citizenship withdrawn or be deported. "With a free society as our goal," he asserted, "we must restrict freedom to those who would destroy it. These are bitter paradoxes."[22] Bitter indeed, and vulnerable to abuse—for instance, when FDR incarcerated more than one hundred thousand Japanese Americans based solely on their ancestry (a move Mumford condemned). Still, liberalism had to be offset by realism.

In fall 1939, Mumford and his family moved back to New York City: he and Sophia both wanted to be more involved in antifascist activism, and they felt that Geddes, now fourteen, would benefit from going to high school in a more cosmopolitan setting than Amenia (though they never sold their farmhouse there). It was an equivocal time. "We have lived to see strange things," Mumford wrote to a friend. The city, at least, both familiar and new, was always stimulating: "I feel that I have much still to learn; and that at any rate, every sight, every person, every building, has something fresh to say." But the world was undeniably in crisis. "Not to be in trouble or pain at the present moment, not to feel baffled and empty, is to be outside the experience of our generation and therefore inhuman. I almost feel a little guilty when I find myself enjoying a free day, as it occasionally comes to one." Clearly, though, even the simple act of writing a letter to a friend could help Mumford gain some purchase on both his private and public grief: "On the other hand, I smile too, when I catch myself, as I did the other night, pleading earnestly, zealously, for—guess what!—law and order! Twenty years ago those were the tags of a reactionary; and one did not suspect then that they were, like most conservative sayings, the leftovers of an earlier revolution: that of the seventeenth century, which, faced with the caprices and uncertainties and terrors of despotism, opposed to these political vices the concepts of law and order: the first stop beyond despotism!!"[23] The wheel was coming around again.

Earlier in the year, Mumford had finished his work on the documentary film *The City,* and he had given up on trying to have a sexual relationship with Jo Strongin. Now he wondered if he might be ready to take up *The Renewal of Life* again, to enter into "that long communion with other books which is part of the incubation period" for any great piece of writing.[24] But, despite the excitement of urban living, he worried that his own creative process had come to depend on the alternative freshness of rurality: "It is the apple tree that gives me my sense of the bounty of the countryside," he wrote, just before departing Amenia; "yes, and the wild strawberry jam, served the morning after it is picked in the middle of June. All this we are leaving, for no one knows how long." The transition perplexed him, and put him in a retrospective mood. The previous few years had been "chequered with domestic tribulations, work done under great strain, the intensive effort of conceiving and finishing a big book, and a long journey to the lands west last summer." He tried to tell himself that "they have been good years in all the underlying things that make life good: Sophy and I have experienced rare moments of beauty together, moments of high understanding and deep respect, moments of passion and gay intensity." But, ever the realist, he also acknowledged that "there have been gritty stretches in between . . . stretches when I feel as if I were living in the wrong family, a stranger and an outcast among people who would never be companions or intimates."[25]

"Misgivings and Preparatives" is the title of the chapter in *Pierre* in which the main character comes to grips with the new reality of his half sister and gets ready to renounce his family. It's the moment in the novel when he becomes an Ishmael; within a couple of days he will abandon the Berkshires for New York City. The rest of the story is fairly bleak, but there are occasional glimmers of hope and engagement with the world. During the long stagecoach journey to the city, Pierre picks up an obscure philosophical pamphlet called "Chronometricals and Horologicals," and Melville inserts some of it into the novel. The pamphlet is largely about acknowledging that "the history of Christendom for the last 1800 years . . . , in spite of all the maxims of Christ," has been "just as full of blood, violence, wrong, and iniquity of every kind, as any previous portion of the world's story."[26] This was Mumford's favorite part of the book: "the chapter on Horologicals and Chronometricals in *Pierre*," he wrote to a friend, in 1944, "I look upon as one of the best essays on morals any American had ever written."[27] He referred back to that chapter regularly for the rest of his life. In writing *Men Must Act*, in confronting the reality of fascism, Mumford had started to think of himself primarily as a moralist. Over the next decade, he would collect dozens of books on the history of religion. He later noted that, as of 1939, he had realized that he was "living in the same kind of world that Origen, Augustine, and Jerome lived in": the American Empire, like the Roman in the third and fourth centuries, was corrupt and crumbling.[28] And he, too, was becoming something of a martyr, addressing his disenchanted epistles and impassioned homilies to a passive, indifferent society.

CHAPTER 22

The Piazza (1856–57)

Melville would have preferred not to follow Pierre's example in abandoning his Berkshire estate, but he had been defaulting on his loan payments regularly throughout the 1850s. His domestic tribulations were coming to a head. By the spring of 1856, it became clear that he would have to sell at least half the land at Arrowhead, including some of his most treasured trees.

The property's purchase price, back in 1850, had been $6,500. Thanks to Justice Shaw, Melville had immediately been able to pay $3,000 to the estate's owner, Dr. John Brewster. And there was an agreement on a ten-year mortgage of $1,500. As for the additional $2,000, Brewster had generously allowed Melville to delay payment until he found a buyer for his house in New York City—which happened in the spring of 1851. But, profits from that transaction not being sufficient, Melville found himself needing to acquire an urgent, hefty loan from his friend T. D. Stewart (he kept it secret because he knew Lizzie would disapprove): $2,050, to be repaid within five years, at 9 percent interest. Melville used all the New York cash and some of Stewart's to complete the purchase of Arrowhead, but now he had to make annual mortgage payments to Dr. Brewster (every September 14) and biannual loan payments to Stewart (on the first day of May and November): his debt totaled $3,550. Earnings from books and magazine pieces allowed him to stay current with Brewster (until 1855, at least), but the installment of November 1, 1851, was the only one he ever paid to Stewart. The entire balance would come due on May 1, 1856. On April 14 of that year, in a panic, he submitted a notice to the Pittsfield *Sun,* advertising "80 acres, more than half well wooded, within a mile and a half of Pittsfield village by the County road."[1]

In truth, the 1851 loan from Stewart had been necessary not because Dr. Brewster was pressing Melville for money but because, late in winter, the enthusiastic new farm owner had launched some extensive renovations at Arrowhead, without waiting for the ground to thaw. In particular, Melville yearned for a porch, that perfect communicating point between culture and nature, "combining the coziness of in-doors with the freedom of out-doors"—from which he would be able to see Mount Greylock, the highest peak of the Berkshires, said by some to resemble a whale. The porch would be added to the house just below Melville's study. In local terminology, it would be known, rather grandiloquently, as a piazza.[2]

Five years later, flummoxed by his debts, Melville spent a lot of time pacing his piazza, and much of his writing from this season is set at Arrowhead. Having given his readers naval battles with Israel Potter and slave revolts with Amasa Delano, he now turned inward. And his 1856 depictions of his domestic life seem consistent with what we know about his intensifying financial strain and his deteriorating health. He was tired of fighting just to keep up his morale.

In "I and My Chimney," published in March in *Putnam's,* Melville offers us a narrator plagued by sciatica and by a busybody spouse who desperately wants to modernize their cozy, crumbling farmhouse. (Lizzie pointedly noted in her copy of the story that "all this about the wife applied to his mother"—which is not entirely implausible, given what we know of Maria Melville.)[3] The narrator tries to explain that he is purposely lagging "behind the age," that he has brought their family to the country specifically to escape the city's "terrible alacrity for improvement, which is a softer name for destruction." Like Mumford railing against skyscrapers (they blocked the light and discouraged social interaction), Melville's narrator laments that virtually every well-to-do urban gentleman has become "a meddlesome architectural reformer," who wishes only to build a higher building than that of the landlord next door. "Such folks, it seems to me, need mountains for neighbors, to take this emulous conceit of soaring out of them." Of course, the era's predominant direction of displacement was from the countryside to the rapidly expanding cities, but it was typical of Melville to struggle against the prevailing winds, especially when they were filling the sails of entrepreneurs and captains of industry.[4]

The narrator spends time digging in his cellar, dreaming of "striking upon some old, earthen-worn memorial of that by-gone day when, into all this gloom, the light of heaven entered, as the masons laid the foundation-stones." He wants to enjoy his deep connection to the past, wants to sit "in the comfortable shadow of my chimney, smoking my comfortable pipe," perhaps reading the essays of "old Montaigne," while eating "old cheese" and drinking "old wine." But his "enterprising" wife is "spicily impatient of present and past," seeming to live "in a continual future" of "schemes" and "expectations." She would like nothing more than to be done with her husband's cherished chimney forever: what the house really needs, she thinks, is a more open, spacious floorplan, which she would keep sleek and clean, with no more smoke and ash. For her: the crisp lines of an "elegant modern residence," entirely under "female jurisdiction," fully approved by the fire-insurance company and "the man who has a mortgage on the house." For him: a picturesque decay, "secret recesses," layers of history, lots of space for a "mossy old misanthrope," a "dozy old dreamer like me," to wander through, with the rooms laid out in so "labyrinthine" a way that "you seem to be forever going somewhere, and getting nowhere. It is like losing one's self in the woods; round and round the chimney you go, and if you arrive at all, it is just where you started, and so you begin again, and again get nowhere."[5]

Two months later, in the May issue of *Harper's*, the defender of the chimney becomes the discoverer of a seemingly haunted piece of furniture in "The Apple-Tree Table." In the first story, the narrator admits that he is "sometimes as crippled up as any old apple tree"; in the second, he surreptitiously squeezes his brittle body into his house's attic (off limits by order of the insurance company) to find that within some gnarly, twisted apple tree there had been a solid enough core to make "a very satanic-looking little old table, indeed." The rediscovered antique takes its place in the household, much to the discomfort of the narrator's family, especially when the table starts to emit a clear and precise ticking sound, as if bitterly clocking the unknown years it had been abandoned and forgotten. "Spirits! Spirits!" cries the narrator's daughter, invoking the famous Fox sisters of upstate New York, Spiritualists who held se-ances in the early 1850s and claimed to communicate with the dead through a system of knockings and rappings (they were cracking the knuckles in their toes). But it turns out that in this case the sounds are coming from two insects gradually gnawing their way out of the table.[6]

This was in fact a familiar story in antebellum New England; Melville may even have read the version that Thoreau wove into the end of *Walden* (published in 1854). Apparently, the eggs of certain insects can lie dormant for several decades after being laid inside the bark of a thriv-ing tree; can remain dormant for several more decades after said tree has been shaped into a table, which in turn gets locked in a garret; and can then produce living beings after the table is brought down into more temperate regions and placed near a snug fireplace. And though Mel-ville's skeptical and bemused tone in "The Apple-Tree Table" may seem to mock Thoreau's transcendental celebration of renewal, the narrator also clearly appreciates the experience of wonder sparked by the pecu-liar sounds: "In a strange and not unpleasing way," he "gently oscillated" between spiritual and scientific impulses, as he tried to understand what was happening. And then, once the mystery is seemingly solved, the narrator's daughter clings to her faith that the newly hatched insect has a deeper meaning: "say what you will, if this beauteous creature be not a spirit, yet it teaches a spiritual lesson. For if, after one hundred and fifty years' entombment, a mere insect comes forth at last into light, itself an effulgence, shall there be no glorified resurrection for the spirit of man?"[7]

Melville, of course, isn't sure. It's hard to read his tone at the end of the story. His narrator enjoys the way the past has come to life, but he also distances himself from both the dry, crusty explanation of the local learned naturalist and from the spiritual exuberance of his daughter. While his family gets ready to move on, he seems stuck in a kind of limbo. What *is* the difference between life and death? Ishmael remarked that, in our understanding of such questions, "we do not advance through

fixed gradations, and at the last one pause:—through infancy's unconscious spell, boyhood's thoughtless faith, adolescence' doubt (the common doom), then scepticism, then disbelief, resting at last in manhood's
pondering repose of If. But once gone through, we trace the round
again; and are infants, boys, and men, and Ifs eternally."[8]

Mumford owned a volume called *The Apple-Tree Table and Other
Sketches*, dating from 1922, the very beginning of the Melville Revival
(the editor explained that he had compiled it to meet the "growing
demand for accessible reprints of Melville's work," sparked especially
by Raymond Weaver's 1921 biography). Inside the front cover, Mumford
listed some page numbers and made one substantive comment: "The
Apple-Tree Table—I and My Chimney. In each case a man with one particular inanimate object that he venerates and cleaves to against the
protests of his family. A table, a chimney, a feeling of isolation: nothing
more. What does this symbolize?"[9] Just like Melville, Mumford wallowed in uncertainty. But he also decided, once he was ready to write
his Melville biography, that the prose in these stories probably reflected
a "frayed and knotty feeling within . . . , the anxiety and weariness of the
last five years, the incessant round of writing, and, further plaguing him,
instead of giving relief, the equally endless round of the farm."[10] As of
the previous year, when Frances (known as Fanny) was born, there were
four small children to feed and care for (Malcolm turned 7 in 1856, Stanwix 5, Bessie 3, and Fanny 1); and the debts loomed; and Melville's back
pain and eyesight were worsening; and Lizzie was starting to sound like
the wife in "The Apple-Tree Table," who at first thinks that the ticking
sounds her husband hears are the hallucinations of a shameless drunk:
"Poor old man—quite out of his mind. . . . Do, do come to bed. I forgive
you. I won't remind you of it to-morrow. But you must give up the
punch-drinking, my dear. It quite gets the better of you." Melville was
desperate for his own, quiet space, where he could commune with the
past and feed his imagination, where he could try to renew himself—
where he could feel pleasantly lost and enjoy not getting anywhere.

The piazza, in other words, had not been fully effective. But he still
went to it in search of inspiration; it still provided fresh air and views of
Mount Greylock; it was still a place where fact and fancy might meet.

He went to it even in winter, the season of its construction: "once more, with frosted beard, I pace the sleety deck, weathering Cape Horn."

Melville wrote that sentence in the winter of 1856, in a story that came to be called "The Piazza"—the introduction to a new collection of some of his magazine pieces, published in the spring as *The Piazza Tales*. He was, indeed, approaching Cape Horn again. Perhaps this new book, full of stories that had already succeeded in the popular press, might provide him with enough cash to satisfy T. D. Stewart on May 1. May Day. "The Piazza" was a cry for help. But Melville was a realist: he knew that no book, however briskly it might sell, was going to save him from himself. His narrator paces the piazza and stares out at the hills, daydreaming, seeking a measure of solace in a gentle spring shower, which then brings a rainbow: "if one can but get to the rainbow's end, his fortune is made in a bag of gold." Talk about an eternal If.[11]

A true country gentleman—a Glendinning, for instance—would have built a panoramic wrap-around porch, so as to enjoy the "upland pasture," with its alley of maples, to the east; and the ancient apple orchard to the south; and the "Hearth Stone Hills" to the west; and of course Greylock, to the north, "like Charlemagne among his peers." (*Pierre* was dedicated to "Greylock's Most Excellent Majesty.") But, as Melville explains in "The Piazza," he was constrained by finances: "the house was wide, my fortune narrow. . . . Upon but one of the four sides would prudence grant me what I wanted." If he had to choose only one view, it would be Greylock, also known as "Saddleback," for its double hump, which turned a pure white when the snows came. Melville's wealthy neighbors, though, less interested in sublime scenery, thought it rather ridiculous that this crackpot author would build his porch facing the coldest blasts of air in the valley: "Piazza to the north! Winter piazza!"[12]

Melville's narrator tries to make the most of it. He stares out at "the purple of the mountains," finding the scene's "vastness" and "lonesomeness" to be "so oceanic, and the silence and the sameness, too," that he was "often reminded of the sea." It's a rather cold comfort, but the sea does make him think of long journeys, and ultimately the view from his piazza inspires him to escape his rut and take an "inland voyage to fairyland." One afternoon in late autumn, he catches a glimpse of something glinting in the woods, "high up in a hopperlike hollow or sunken angle among the northwestern mountains." He wonders: a signal of some sort? A window? Eventually, almost a year later (he had to stew about it first), the beacon draws him out into the forested glens, though the immediate spur to this quixotic trip is his sudden feeling that he can no longer stand being trapped in his house, this domestic space of his own creation where he has recently been confined to his sickbed: "I could not bear to look upon a Chinese creeper of my adoption, and which, to my delight, climbing a post of the piazza, had burst out in starry bloom, but now, if you removed the leaves a little, showed millions of strange, cankerous worms, which, feeding upon those blossoms, so shared their blessed hue as to make it unblessed evermore—worms whose germs had doubtless lurked in the very bulb which, so hopefully, I had planted."[13]

In some ways, Melville (or his narrator, if you prefer) finds just what he was looking for in the hills: warm air, berry bushes, enfolding greenery, a landscape both revivifying and calming. As he climbs, his prose becomes more and more poetic, building on rhythmic, Shakespearean iambs: "and here, among fantastic rocks, reposing in a herd, the foot track wound." He doesn't know exactly where to go, but he proceeds "with faith." Finally—wonder of wonders—he comes to a "fairy-mountain house" that is perfectly integrated into an insular clearing, an enchanted grotto, with a glorious view back onto the valley, and the tiny cottage turns out to be inhabited by a shy maiden, "like some Tahiti girl." Paradise regained.

Yet the young woman's eyes make her seem significantly older, as if weighed down by some tragedy, as if the prospect before her seems closed. What ails her? "I don't know," she says, ". . . but it is not the view, it is Marianna." (She is named for a Shakespeare character, who in turn inspired a famous 1830 poem by Tennyson, about the pain of isolation and separation from a loved one.) For Melville, Marianna embodies the vague and rarefied suffering of daily life, of a solitary routine: she sits alone and sews. All she can dream of is the sure happiness of the person who lives in the one distant farmhouse she can see at the foot of the mountains. "I looked, and, after a time, to my surprise, recognized, more by its position than its aspect or Marianna's description, my own abode, glimmering much like this mountain one from the piazza." His festering, corrupted, bankrupt estate was her promised land?

The mirroring gets more and more intense, until it overwhelms the story, which cuts off abruptly. Both Melville and Marianna, though ensconced in rural retreats, are living under an industrial-style energy regime—"her brother, only seventeen, had come hither . . . to cut wood and burn coal"—which allows certain members of each household to avoid hard labor and engage in other activities but also leaves them suffering from "weariness and wakefulness together," as Marianna puts it. "Brother, who stands and works in open air, would I could rest like him; but mine is mostly but dull woman's work—sitting, sitting, restless sitting." Woman's work for Marianna, writing work for Melville, each in a remote house, gazing through a "mirage haze." Their reality is a kind of Purgatory. The view from the piazza, like the view from the grotto, and like the view from a box at the theater, can still arouse, can still spark a person's fancy: "yes, the scenery is magical—the illusion so complete." But what's the value of living with pent-up energy, of persisting restlessly through a life you know to be utterly artificial? We've reached an impasse. "Every night when the curtain falls, truth comes in with darkness. No light shows from the mountain. To and fro I walk the piazza deck, haunted by Marianna's face, and many as real a story."[14]

In fact, *The Piazza Tales*, despite the enigmatic gloom of its introductory parable, did quite well. One of the earliest reviews called the book "decidedly the most readable" that Melville had produced "since *Omoo* and *Typee*." Several reviewers claimed that even the disaster of *Pierre* had now been redeemed, and Melville seemed almost reborn: "in his rich descriptions, his wonderfully striking narrative, his exquisite, short hand hitting off of absurdity," Melville surely "wears the palm of superiority among our native sketchers." Thoreau's friend William Ellery Channing opined in the New Bedford *Mercury* that *The Piazza Tales* should be purchased by all those "who love strong and picturesque sentences, and the thoughtful truths of a writer, who leaves some space for the *reader* to try his own ingenuity upon,—some rests and intervals in the literary voyage." The Philadelphia *Evening Bulletin* even asserted that Melville's new collection "will doubtless have an extensive sale as a summer book."[15]

But Melville couldn't wait for the summer. Pressed hard by T. D. Stewart, he wrote a confessional letter to Justice Shaw, explaining all his financial bungles and begging for yet another bailout.[16] Within a few weeks, Lizzie also wrote to the Judge, to let him know how concerned she was about her husband's physical and mental health.[17] (Melville's longer-term writing project in 1856 was *The Confidence-Man*, a text which Mumford considered to be hard evidence that Melville's "torments and suspicions had, for a brief while, taken on a pathological character.")[18]

Over the next few months, Shaw provided enough cash for Melville to pay off Stewart and also buy a ticket on a steamship bound for Britain. Melville would then proceed, after his visit with Hawthorne, to make a head-clearing pilgrimage to the Holy Land. He had also wanted to visit Shakespeare's grave, but that would have to wait for the return trip. Lizzie, meanwhile, sent her sons to board with various aunts and uncles for a few months; she and the girls went to Boston to live with her father.

"The Piazza" was published with a poignant Shakespearean epigraph, from *Cymbeline*: "With fairest flowers, / Whilst summer lasts, and I live here, Fidele—. . . ." The next line in the original reveals that the speaker is in mourning: "I'll sweeten thy sad grave."[19]

In December, having stopped in Constantinople for a couple of days to see the sights, Melville may have thought back to that epigraph when he came across a widow screaming out her grief, sprawled on "a new grave—no grass on it yet. Such abandonment of misery! Called to the dead, put her head down as close to it as possible; as if calling down a hatchway or cellar; besought—'Why don't you speak to me? My God!—It is I!—Ah, speak—but one word!—All deaf.—So much for consolation.'" The image lingered in Melville's memory: "This woman and her cries haunt me horribly." He was losing faith in both language and communion.

When he finally made it to the graveyard at Stratford-upon-Avon the following May, he found it "cheerless, melancholly." And by the time his steamer arrived in New York, at the end of the month, he had probably decided to abandon his career as a writer.[20]

CHAPTER 23

Faith (1940–43)

On June 14, 1940, the Nazis occupied Paris. The United States maintained neutrality. Mumford decided that he needed to write another book. Ten days later, he had finished the first draft of *Faith for Living*.

This time, though he still wrote with urgency and passion, Mumford took a calmer tone. He was done with Ahab; *Faith for Living* brought him back to Ishmael, in the moment just after the sinking of the *Pequod*, when he was "buoyed up" by Queequeg's coffin and floating in the "soft and dirge-like" waves.[1] "At best," Mumford explained, in a prefatory note, "this book is a testament for survivors, if ever they reach shore. . . . I but remind the reader of those durable ideals of life which in the past have kept humanity going during its most anguished and shattered moments."[2] *Faith for Living* was a flower on Melville's grave, an affirmation that "in 'Moby-Dick' Melville was optimist enough to provide a 'happy ending,' namely someone left to tell the tale."[3] One resilient survivor is enough to revive a civilization, to keep the story going.

Mumford's new book was divided into seven sections, each with an epigraph; the first and last epigraphs are quotations from Melville. Striking an overtly religious note, the first comes from *Clarel*, Melville's five-hundred-page Holy Land poem. The verses suggest that Satan is on the prowl, in the guise of an entrepreneur who is training the ideal disciple: "Vindictive in his heart of hearts, / He schools him in your mines and marts." And in fact the first half of *Faith for Living* elaborates the argument that fascism is an outgrowth of the exploitation inherent in industrial capitalism—which means that antifascism must consist "in part in offsetting the debilitating effects of our too mechanized environment and our too impassive routine." Democracy is the best weapon against Satan, but faith in democracy requires citizens who are "self-governing, self-acting, and self-respecting."[4]

The second half of the book lays out a vision for how individuals might conduct their lives in a countercapitalist society. In a sense, it boils down the recommendations of *Technics and Civilization* and *The Culture of Cities* to their spiritual essences. The final epigraph, for a section entitled "Sacrifice and Salvage," is just one line of a short poem called "Old Counsel": "All hands save ship! has startled dreamers." It seems to underline the need for societal disenchantment: every sailor must snap out of his profit-oriented trance, "his familiar routine," and always be ready to jettison everything onboard.[5] More broadly, Mumford was proposing a pivot from modernity's fetishization of the material to an older emphasis on beliefs: mere physical survival is worth much less than the persistence of humane principles. "For life is not worth fighting for," Mumford wrote: "bare life is worthless. Justice is worth fighting for, order is worth fighting for, culture—the co-operation and communion of the peoples of the world—is worth fighting for." If you die struggling for a noble cause, your life and death will have meaning for future generations, and the cause has a better chance of being sustained: "the best consolation for the dying is the thought that others, equally good, will carry on their work: that is the comfort the father and mother derive from their children, that the teacher derives from his student, that comrades and colleagues pass on to each other."[6]

Perhaps the book should have been called *Faith for Living and Dying*, for at its core is the problem of confronting death. And though Mumford always retained a fierce skepticism about religious institutions (one dark chapter of *Faith for Living* is called "Temptations of the Churches"), he nevertheless turned to historical Christianity as the tradition most capable of reversing the new trend toward the denial of mortality. "Modern society," Mumford thought, "rests on a gentleman's agreement to forget death—death and all its stark anticipations." In our embrace of security and comfort, we take pains to hide "the slaughter-house, the prison, the hospital, the slum, the asylum, the battlefield, the sewer, and

the garbage pile." But Christianity ascended from the ashes of the
Roman Empire by explicitly emphasizing what "the Romans refused to
face: the inevitability of their disintegration as a society and of their
death as individuals." Indeed, "the fact that the Christian Church arose
in the classic Time of Troubles" gave it a "great capacity for administer-
ing to the defeated, the brow-beaten, and the hopeless. This faith was at
home in the presence of Death." It was Christianity's historical context
as much as the specific teachings of Christ that spurred the widespread
acceptance of a faith based on love, peace, charity, "and, above all, the
capacity for sacrifice." The true Christian "must give up life daily in
order that he may live," must always demonstrate "an athletic readiness
to face abstentions, poverties, curtailments of pleasure and power, for
the sake of love."[7]

Of course, many Christians embraced sacrifice for the sake of a
promised reward in the afterlife, but Mumford conscientiously neglected that aspect of Christianity. For him, what mattered was the way
in which Christianity was similar to Judaism: both religions, he thought,
drew their "tough capacity for survival" from the experience of shared
suffering, which tended to encourage empathy. In modern times, economic values had largely replaced religious values, but the stubborn
persistence of Christian empathy was "shown by the miner who risks
his life to save his fellows trapped in the mineshaft, by the lineman who
risks electrocution to pull a comrade away from a live wire, by the physi-
cian who enters the plague-stricken house." Such faithful sacrifices
could, in turn, spark acts of creation and continuance: "it is only by the
capacity to surrender one's own private life for that other life one brings
into the world that the race can survive."[8]

Birth offsets death. To Mumford, the rediscovery of a humanist
Christianity entailed recognizing that our values must constantly be
reborn. Ultimately, he was after "a measure of concord which is the fruit
of love. This has no guarantee of permanence in political life, any more
than in marriage; but it may be perpetually recovered and reinstated."
Indeed, Mumford encouraged his readers to think of "birth" in the
broadest possible terms, not merely as "the physical departure from the
mother's womb: it embraces the other crises of life: the constant

re-births of purpose and vision that are necessary if the soul is not to be paralyzed by calcareous deposits of habit." Though Mumford never abandoned his analysis of social structures and systems, in *Faith for Living* he went further than ever before in insisting that saving society required the saving of individual souls. Entranced moderns like Captain Delano or Bartleby's boss could be manipulated by fascist dictators; responsible, engaged human beings were perpetually primed for self-government and social renewal. "Man truly lives by scrapping and rebuilding his dead selves," Mumford insisted—"which is to say, by being born again. This holds as much for communities as for personalities." We are all dormant insects in an apple-tree table—but we need to burrow our way out no matter what the climatic conditions.[9]

If we also cultivate a sense of history, then we will always be prepared for the next struggle: "no matter how strange may seem this stark wasteland we now confront, Man has walked here often before." Only in the modern era had people started to forget or deny that "hardship, difficulty, and poverty are normal aspects of life." Regular trips back into the past remind us that we have repeatedly been dominated by "radical evil," by sin, by Satan, by "illness, error, defeat, frustration, disintegration"— but also that some of our most important and enduring cultural adaptations have arisen during dark times.[10]

The Great Depression, Mumford noted, had impoverished the entire nation, but FDR's massive New Deal agencies had offered not just jobs amid scarcity but also chances to pause and reflect and create, through their "projects in music, drama, literature, and the graphic and plastic arts": "more vital culture has come out of the sobering poverty of the depression than ever came out of the riotous period of so-called prosperity in the twenties." Think of the photographs of Dust Bowl migrants and black sharecroppers; the recordings of plaintive and joyous folk songs; the interviews with former slaves; the new hiking trails carved into canyons and forests; the colorful murals depicting every type of labor. Mumford never suggested that a phenomenon like poverty was "natural" or salutary; rather, he argued that it had to be accepted as a grim reality (for it would never disappear completely) and then addressed aggressively in the name of the common good. That was a social goal, but it would spring from the clear moral conviction of individuals who had taken time to grapple with the perpetuation of injustice—who had looked at the photographs and read the oral histories and come away with a commitment to act.[11]

Mumford's plan to cultivate such individuals focused on three "areas that have always been life-sustaining, life-preserving, life-forwarding. One is the family. The other is the land. And the third is the self." His faith for living, in other words, followed his favorite Eotechnic patterns, with all their benefits and blind spots. Even if the overall vision seems somewhat provincial in the twenty-first century, the downshifting to a more human scale and a gentler pace remains timely. Mumford imagined his fellow citizens balancing "the spiritual and the practical" sides of their lives, observing a sabbath, taking time for contemplation and the cultivation of "humility" and "selflessness," writing family histories, gathering around the hearth—but also growing much of their own food, working with their hands, splitting rails and cutting trails. It was no "accident, in our own American Golden Day, that Henry Thoreau was a pencil maker and surveyor, that Herman Melville was a sailor." Yet, as Mumford noted in the chapter called "Life Is Better than Utopia," physical labor is also fraught with challenges and even threats. To be a good sailor, you must learn to enjoy the breezes while also girding yourself to weather the gales and the captain's tyrannical rages. The goal isn't to create a perfect society: "perfection itself would mean death." Our eternal "antagonists," like the figure we call Satan, transform life from a superficial "pageant passing before the eyes of bored spectators" into "a high drama that awakens exaltation by pity and terror."[12]

Faith for Living was conceived in the city, amid the stimulation of both antagonists and collaborators. Even after France fell, most Americans clung to their isolationism. Mumford's closest friend, the Harvard psychoanalyst and fellow Melville scholar Henry Murray, accused Lewis of taking a fascistic tone in his antifascist writings, using "machine-gun phrases" to try to "forcefully impel people" to agree with him: "if everyone stood up and spoke as you do, there would be no community, no comradeship."[13] But Mumford spent as much time as he could with the more like-minded Waldo Frank, a boon companion since the early

1920s and the author of *The Rediscovery of America* (1929) and *Chart for Rough Water: Our Role in a New World* (1940).[14] Mumford also made a new friend who proved just as influential as Frank: the Christian realist Reinhold Niebuhr, author of *Moral Man and Immoral Society: A Study in Ethics and Politics* (1932) and one of the foremost advocates for U.S. intervention in Europe. The coffee shops of New York offered Mumford, Frank, and Niebuhr frequent opportunities to discuss strategies and plans; at one point Mumford and Frank decided to jointly resign from the editorial staff of the *New Republic*, and later, with Niebuhr, they tried to start a new magazine that would be committed to "staying the forces of barbarism" and upholding a form of western culture that blended, in Niebuhr's formulation, the "religious emphasis upon love" with the "rational ethic" that "aims at justice."[15]

At the same time, though, *Faith for Living* bears many marks of the countryside.[16] As Mumford acknowledged, retrospectively, he owed much of his philosophy to "the ever-altering landscape" of Amenia, to "the full experience of the seasons" afforded by his "shabby" country cottage— "in no sense . . . the house of our dreams" but rather "the house of our realities. . . . Without such an underlayer of rural experience I could hardly indeed have written 'Faith for Living.'"[17] Many of the most powerful sections near the end of *Faith for Living* argue for the importance of struggling against the weather, of sinking roots in the soil, of imagining Conservation not merely as the efficient use of resources but as a determination to spend time "laboring *on* the land, laboring *with* the land, laboring *for* the land." For Mumford, "deliberate first-hand contact with nature and man" was "the very basis of communal health." The nation's young people, instead of living "like sleepwalkers . . . , dead to everything but . . . the flickering shadows on the screen," ought to be "toughened off in lumber camps, on fishing boats, behind the hay-wagon and the threshing machine, on the road gang and in the quarry"—not to increase economic output but rather to foster "a loving awareness of one's environment" and an "intimate knowledge of our human background that will guide effectively our efforts to make the community itself a high work of art." Mumford's environmentalism, like his promotion of urban surveys, encouraged constant engagement with the landscape, wherever one might be.[18]

FIGURE 8. Mumford in 1940.

And, in a climate of fear and alienation, his readers responded—perhaps, in part, because enough of *Faith for Living* was reassuringly reminiscent of the most constructive sections of *Technics and Civilization* and *The Culture of Cities*. The book sold twenty thousand copies in its first year, making it Mumford's biggest hit, and it did even better in England than in America, as Winston Churchill exhorted the troops and as British civilians desperately tried to keep calm and carry on. (Britain was fighting for its life: one whole edition of Mumford's book went up in smoke when the printing facility was hit during a Nazi air raid—eighty-seven years after a number of Melville's unsold books succumbed to fire.)[19]

Despite its harsh realism and its demand for sacrifice, *Faith for Living* managed to boost people's morale: stripped of "material abundance," they embraced "comradeship, art, and love"; they planted gardens; they found that old ideals could help "offset the deprivations."[20] Of course, not all readers were enthusiastic: one review called the book "Lewis Mumford's 'Mein Kampf,'" arguing that it added up to little more than pro-war propaganda.[21] But many others embraced Mumford's humanistic program. His loving celebration of "religion, ethics, and esthetics" so impressed the leaders of Stanford University that they invited him to be a keynote speaker at their fiftieth anniversary celebration in 1941—which then led to his appointment the following year as head of their new School of Humanities.[22]

As soon as Mumford had moved to New York, in the fall of 1939, he had dived into the reading he needed to do for the third volume of *The Renewal of Life*, and he turned back to that project right after he finished *Faith for Living*. His son, meanwhile, struggled through three years of high school (at three different schools), before heading west in the summer of 1942 for some experience on a Washington ranch. That September, the family was reunited at Stanford, in Palo Alto, California, where Geddes would attend the local public school and complete his secondary education. Lewis had tried to finish his book, to be called *The Condition of Man*, over the summer, but without success; now it was time to focus on writing the lectures for his humanities course.

Within just a few years, Stanford would become notorious as an incubator for electronics companies and a handmaiden to the (not-yet-named) Military Industrial Complex.[23] And even by the early 1940s, American culture had established that there were no fields "as important as science and technology and economic organization." But Mumford insisted that only the humanities could hold society together. It was only in "poetry, disinterested thought, the free use of the imagination, the pursuit of non-utilitarian activities, the production of non-profitmaking goods, the enjoyment of non-consumable wealth," that people could find "the sustaining values of a living culture. To be alive is to hear, to see, to feel, to touch, to shape, to manipulate, to think, and create: then to intensify all these experiences through an organized system of recording and preserving and reproducing them."[24]

Moreover, fields like history, literature, art, and philosophy could give students a reason to persevere in a time of war. At the end of Mumford's first year at Stanford, a pregnant student whose husband was in the navy thanked him for debunking the materialist "fairy tales" she had been raised on, which "taught us that we lived in a world where everyone had a right to be happy and where he would certainly achieve happiness if he managed to get a sufficient income. That kind of philosophy isn't very useful to us now, when we have to say good-bye to our lovers or our husbands whom we've just married and may never see again." In place of those fairy tales, Mumford's course had given her an entire heritage to fight for: "I am *glad* to have my baby, whether my husband comes back from the war or not. I have something to give the child now, and if my man dies he won't die in vain." Ultimately, Mumford's lectures, like *Faith for Living*, had been about birth and death—and the making of meaning. "Who can study the nature of man in all its manifestations," he asked, at the first annual conference of the School of the Humanities, in May 1943, "its animal inheritance, its historic social roots, its personal and communal choices, its many unplumbed potentialities, without having a better grasp on his own life, a better insight into his own duties, purposes, and opportunities?"[25]

That summer, Mumford moved back to Amenia to finish his book; his son turned eighteen on July 5 and entered the army two weeks later.[26] Geddes had actually applied to attend Stanford in the fall, but he didn't have the grades. The apologetic rejection letter, dated February 19, 1943, was addressed to Professor Mumford.[27] Though Geddes was a much more engaged student once he started going to school in California (his parents thought he was hoping to impress his girlfriend back East), he had actually been considering the army since the Pearl Harbor attack of December 7, 1941—after which the United States had finally entered the war. Lewis told him at the time that he and Sophia would have to talk it over, but meanwhile he was "proud of your desire to take part in this fight and to serve your country promptly. I don't like the idea of your getting into uniform before I do; but I must admit that you can probably be of more use as a soldier than I could be; and this is a time when each of us must find what he can do best and do it with all his might."[28]

Lewis and Geddes had a complicated relationship, but in California they became closer than they had ever been before, because Geddes stopped getting into trouble (he got kicked out of a boarding school in Vermont, after having performed poorly at Bronx Science in New York) and started peppering his father with questions about Western Civilization. "Where the guy picks it all up is beyond me," Geddes wrote to his girlfriend, "but it's there for the asking, which is just what I have been doing."[29] Western Civilization was still on Geddes's mind when he wrote some essays about American values as part of his army training— though he signed them "Jack Mumford," a name by which no family member ever called him.[30]

In the fall of 1943, Geddes was in boot camp, first in California and then in Oregon, preparing to be deployed overseas. Lewis was still in Amenia, having negotiated a term off from teaching. The plan was to return to Stanford in January, and in November Lewis wrote a long letter to his son saying that he and Sophia and Alison wanted to make sure they would get some time together on the West Coast before Geddes had to leave.

The letter is full of history, ethics, nature, love, and guilt. "Today is a dark day that began with rain, which changed to snow, the first snow of the season," Lewis wrote. He and Sophy had gone out walking and found the earth soft, saturated with moisture; they had seen a fox, the biggest one they'd ever encountered. It was Armistice Day, November 11, and Lewis remembered celebrating with his naval company in the streets of Boston exactly twenty-five years before. But now he realized just how premature that celebration had been: "The mistake that my generation made—and I was as much at fault as anyone—was to . . . stop thinking about the wicked world across the Atlantic and avoid shouldering any of the responsibility for preserving and enforcing the peace." It wasn't fair that the sons were now being sent to fix the mistakes of the fathers, but it was right and noble for the sons to go—despite the obvious danger to their bodies and the peculiarly modern danger to their souls. "Because the individual soldier wields more power than ever before and has been forced to become more brutal in his tactics, it is wise to build up in yourself every possible resistance to brutality, by

means of increased self-control and increased kindliness and forbear-
ance in your dealings with other people. Don't wait till the war comes
to an end to recondition yourself to being human. . . . Err on the soft
rather than the hard side."

Lewis closed by showing his own tenderness: "Grandma Mumford
is here, making cookies, and she has just told me to send you a big arm-
ful of her love. And here's a fatherly embrace in addition." The letter was
typed, but at the bottom it says, in inked cursive: "Your loving dad,
Lewis."[31]

CHAPTER 24

The Metaphysics of
Indian-Hating (1856-57)

Early November, 1856. Melville has arrived in Liverpool. In a couple of days he'll track down Hawthorne, and they'll huddle on the sand hills along the Irish Sea, and it will be clear to the older man that his friend has lost his faith.

But first Melville wants to revisit old haunts: he hasn't been to this city since the summer he turned 20; he is now 37, with poor vision, a faltering career, back pain, four young children, and a disapproving, impatient father-in-law. It's a rainy afternoon when he checks in at the White Bear Hotel and sits down for a meal. Then: "After dinner went to Exchange. Looked at Nelson's statue, with peculiar emotion, mindful of 20 years ago" (it had been 17).[1] He stares at the "four naked figures in chains . . . , seated in various attitudes of humiliation and despair"—as he put it in *Redburn*.[2] He is thinking about his own humiliation and despair. But he is also thinking about injustice. Though we still imagine Melville as perpetually tortured by inner demons, his grief was almost always linked not just to private disappointments but also to his indignation about public affairs—especially to his sense that his country was abrogating its ideals.

In characterizing this era of Melville's life, Mumford and other scholars had good reason to emphasize stories like "I and My Chimney" and "The Apple-Tree Table": Melville was clearly struggling to make space for himself, on an estate he couldn't afford and in a market economy he couldn't understand. A typical modern writer, he both suffered from a sense of isolation and yearned for larger blocks of uninterrupted solitude. But along with the domestic dramas he produced during these months of self-disgust, he also published a piece called "The 'Gees" (March 1856, *Harper's*), which deepened his assessment of race and racism in western society.

One of the reasons Melville was such a "philanthropist"—so eager to embrace the humanity of all races and nationalities—was that, as Ishmael says, "a whale-ship was my Yale College and my Harvard," and the whaling industry brought together every different kind of person, including, of course, "actual cannibals" like Queequeg, as well as "Feegeeans, Tongatabooans, Erromanggoans, Pannangians, and Brighggians."[3] Melville worked alongside all of them, and understood, with Shakespeare, that they all bled, and were all fed by the same food, and were all warmed and cooled by the same summer and winter. Even on a whale-ship, though, there were hints of slavery and capitalist exploitation, for some captains liked to stop at Fogo, one of the Cape Verdean islands, to pick up the so-called 'Gees, a notorious biracial people (from the mixing of a colony of "Portuguese convicts" with "an aboriginal race of negroes"), who were thought to have "a natural adaptability . . . to hard times generally"—and thus got stuck with the foulest, most grueling jobs. Melville's satirical sketch paints the captains who recruit 'Gees as slave raiders, since their recruitment strategy involved sneaking onto Fogo at night and putting their chosen sailors "under guard with pistols at their heads." The 'Gees themselves, meanwhile, come across as stalwart, hard-laboring shipmates who, after gaining some experience, usually demanded more humane treatment. Alas, like free blacks in the North coping with the resentment of the white working class, the natives of Fogo often earned the "disdain of regularly bred seamen," because "the 'Gees undersell them, working for biscuit where the sailors demand dollars."[4] Racism and capitalism reinforce each other perfectly, because they were born and bred together. And their partnership, Melville suspected, may have been permanently buoyed up by the American Revolution.

These are also the jolly themes of *The Confidence-Man*, which turned out to be the last novel Melville wrote, and whose manuscript he delivered to his publisher in October, just before sailing to Britain. As Mumford noted, the book is virtually "unreadable," full of bitter, cynical humor, impossible contradictions, and devilish manipulations.[5] Yet it is also scathingly political. Melville had been working on it for at least the previous year, and during that time slaveholders and abolitionists had been pouring from Missouri into Kansas and viciously attacking each other; the U.S. Supreme Court had started considering the Dred Scott case, which originated in St. Louis and called into question the notion that slaves who arrived in Free states could actually claim freedom; and the federal government had been seizing as much Indian land on the plains as it could, implementing its new Reservation policy and clearing the way for more white settlers and railroads.[6] So Melville's decision to have his con-man do business aboard a Mississippi steamer called the *Fidèle*, out of St. Louis, suggests a basic lack of faith in his nation's future.

Melville's main character, a shape-shifter who dons different disguises in different chapters, spends a great deal of time either trying to sell actual products to the passengers or trying to sell them on the idea that they needn't worry about their society's sins: they should have confidence in the system and in humanity. The con-man, in other words, is Satan—or maybe a senator from the South—and he wants you to feel both genuine fondness for all the nation's faithful slaves and genuine equanimity about the existence of slavery. It serves his purpose if you imagine yourself as a philanthropist and act like a misanthrope: that's only human. But our diabolical river guide truly comes into his own in the very middle of the story (though there is no real story, just a series of dialogues)—during his long discourse on what Melville calls "the metaphysics of Indian-hating." Here he offers some basic advice on how to get ahead in a rapidly expanding nation, without really thinking about it.

In fact, avoiding thought is crucial: the metaphysics of Indian-hating turns out to be similar to the psychology of fascism. From the con-man's perspective, the nation's backwoodsmen, its Daniel Boones, are the truest Americans, patriotic pioneers who push the frontier ever westward, relying only on themselves and their own judgment. That judgment is formed largely by "histories of Indian lying, Indian theft, Indian double-dealing, Indian fraud and perfidy, Indian want of conscience, Indian blood-thirstiness, Indian diabolism": on the frontier, in other words, judgment is just "the instinct of antipathy against an Indian." If your horse has been stolen, your crops eaten, your woodlot burned—it was Indians. Your survival may depend on an instantaneous decision, so the decision must be automatic. Don't think—just pull the trigger. The con-man explains that the true American drinks in with his mother's milk the sense that all those around him have suffered some direct outrage at the hands of Indians. And then every additional hint of Indian violence just confirms his conviction: "the thought develops such attraction, that much as straggling vapors troop from all sides to a storm-cloud, so straggling thoughts of other outrages troop to the nucleus thought, assimilate with it, and swell it." By the time he reaches adulthood, the American is a willing avenger, killing Indians mechanically, whenever they get in his way—defending all the pure, innocent settlers from frontier terrorism.[7]

Melville had identified the bait and switch, the con game, at the very core of American nationalism. The Revolution confirmed that the colonists were honorable citizens, the victims of terrible oppression, fighting for their basic, God-given rights. And they would never surrender that identity—no matter how many Africans they enslaved, or how many Indians they killed, or how much land they stole.

The whole proposition of the United States, then, was based on bad faith. But the average American would always consider himself reasonable and blameless, simply taking advantage of his opportunities, claiming his fair share. He went about his business. He was, in Melville's words, the classic "moderate man"—who also happened to be "the invaluable understrapper of the wicked man."[8]

There was a real Confidence-Man in antebellum America, manipulating as many moderate men as he could find—a notorious, gentlemanly criminal, on whom Melville's character was based. He started in New York, but he had also turned up in New Orleans, at the mouth of the Mississippi, and he made all the newspapers: "The Original Confidence Man in Town," read a headline in the Albany *Evening Journal* on April 28, 1855.[9] Since 1849, Samuel Willis (or Samuel Williams, or Samuel

Thomas, or Edward Stevens, or William Thompson) had been in and out of jail for running the same scam. He would approach a stranger, pretend to recognize him, ask him politely for his trust—or confidence—and then ask him even more politely for the loan of a pocket watch or a few dollars. It frequently worked.[10] The trick seems thoroughly urban, but it also played well in frontier regions, where everything was fluid, where everyone was a fleeting acquaintance, and where there were several different currencies in use, which spurred the publication of booklets known as Counterfeit Detectors (and there were also counterfeit Counterfeit Detectors).[11]

Melville had actually traveled to the Mississippi Valley back in 1840, seeking his fortune, and ever since then he had wanted to believe in the "western spirit" as the key to American Progress. In a strange chapter of *Israel Potter*, the main character, in keeping with his propensity to encounter famous personages like Benjamin Franklin and John Paul Jones, winds up meeting Ethan Allen, leader of Vermont's Green Mountain Boys—and Allen comes across as the embodiment of frontier capability. His is the true form of confidence. He has been captured by the British and is being held prisoner in England, but he seems to Israel completely unbowed, showing a "ferocious" defiance to his guards and a "wild, heroic sort of levity," a "barbaric disdain of adversity." His outfit is "a half-Indian, half-Canadian sort of a dress, consisting of a fawn-skin jacket," and a "bark-like belt of wampum," and "old moccasins riddled with holes." In other words, he lives and behaves like a defeated but noble Indian, and when the British commander asks for his loyalty in exchange for "a major-generalship and five thousand acres of choice land in old Vermont," his response is: "You, *you* offer *our* land? You are like the devil in Scripture."[12] It's a haunting moment, and it anticipates some of the dialogue in *The Confidence-Man* about Indian-hating, for one of the con-man's interlocutors suggests that the *true* backwoodsman is not an Indian-hater at all but rather someone who adopts Indian ways and learns to live in harmony with Indians, sharing the wild land and steering clear of society's degeneracy. Indeed, this interlocutor sees fit to mention Pocahontas and Massasoit and Red-Jacket and the Five Nations as representatives of the various "federations and communities" of "heroic" Indians who had often cooperated with American settlers. The whole story of the archetypal Indian-hater, a frontiersman named Colonel John Moredock, is ultimately about the transformation of a hearty westerner, described as brave, skilled, hospitable, convivial, generous, and benevolent, into a thoughtless killing machine, through a kind of brainwashing.[13] From Melville's perspective, the frontier, like a whaleship, was a place for bracing physical activity and enriching cross-cultural exchange, but it had been corrupted by smooth-talking men peddling the righteousness of individualistic opportunism.

During his own time on the maritime frontier, Melville had witnessed firsthand the brutal hypocrisy of Christian Civilization in its dealings with native peoples, and from the beginning of his career he consistently wove his vindication of so-called "savages" into his writings. One of the reasons he remained so resentful at being known primarily as the author of *Typee* and *Omoo* is that readers tended to embrace the tropical adventures of those novels and dismiss or even scorn their politics. It's not that Melville romanticized native peoples as flawless or even particularly honorable; he just insisted, again and again, that they be understood as fellow human beings.

Near the beginning of *Typee*, the narrator, Tommo, abandons his ship in the Marquesas, fleeing his "servitude" under the "unmitigated tyranny of the captain." But what kind of welcome can he expect from the natives, who are known as "inveterate gourmandizers of human flesh"? Well, they turn out to be relatively friendly—when not under attack. Melville filled in some history: back in 1814, a U.S. frigate had arrived on the Typees' island, sending a military force inland with a seemingly arbitrary "design of conquest." The Typees beat them back, killing several of the "Christian soldiers"; the surviving Americans "consoled themselves for their repulse by setting fire to every house and temple in their route," so that in the end "a long line of smoking ruins defaced the once-smiling bosom of the valley." From then on, the Typees were said to meet any ships approaching their island with a "deadly hatred" in their eyes. "Thus it is that they whom we denominate 'savages' are made to deserve the title." Indeed, back in "Civilization," the average, moderate man is shocked to hear of the "massacre" perpetrated by the natives against "all Christendom," and he cries out for "justice": "how we sympathise for the unhappy victims, and with what horror do we regard the diabolical heathens, who, after all, have but avenged the unprovoked injuries which they have received." Happily, since Tommo arrives on the island with only one companion, and they come in flight, the Typees "embrace the strangers" with the old "instinctive feeling of love" they used to show for overseas visitors, before their disillusionment. One of the main reasons Melville wrote his first novel was simply to let Americans know that he had rediscovered some native peoples in their (as it were) pre-savage state, and they were the most civilized cannibals you could imagine: "They deal more kindly with each other, and are more humane, than many who study essays on virtue and benevolence."[14]

Since several reviewers of *Typee* insisted that the author's political observations were "prejudiced and unfounded," and complained explicitly about the book's "slurs" against Civilization and "praises of the life of nature, *alias* savageism," Melville decided to make his arguments even more pointed in *Omoo*.[15] This time, in the book's early pages, he depicted a scene of Christian barbarity that he had witnessed himself, in which his captain, from the safety of his rowboat, fired on some natives who had gathered on the beach. "Wanton acts of cruelty like this are not unusual on the part of sea captains," Melville commented drily, ". . . and this too as a mere amusement on the part of the ruffians. Indeed, it is almost incredible, the light in which many sailors regard these naked heathens. They hardly consider them human. But it is a curious fact, that the more ignorant and degraded men are, the more contemptuously they look upon those whom they deem their inferiors."[16] Americans had an opportunity to become less ignorant by reading *Omoo*, but of course it's a rare reader who allows a book to upend his prejudices. Horace Greeley, the famous publisher of the New York *Tribune*, found *Omoo* to be "unmistakably defective if not positively diseased in moral tone," predicting that it would "very fairly be condemned as dangerous reading for those of immature intellects and unsettled principles."[17]

Alas, it was one of Melville's core convictions that unsettled principles were precisely the mark of a *mature* intellect; everything he ever wrote was addressed to the kind of ideal reader who would want to

consider long discourses on unanswerable questions. He freely acknowledged the human desire for certainty, the yearning to take leaps
of faith. But he couldn't even tell whether it was water or vapor that
came out of a whale's spout: "My dear sir, in this world it is not so easy
to settle these plain things. I have ever found your plain things the knot-
tiest of all."[18] So how could he be expected to make a pronouncement
on the morality of bringing Christianity to Tahiti? On the one hand, the
narrator of *Omoo* is profoundly moved by the choristry of several con-
verts at a Sunday service, as they "sang right joyously, despite the solem-
nity of the tune." On the other hand, as soon as the singing was over,
they turned "fidgety and inattentive" or depressed and listless. It soon
became clear to the narrator that though almost all the natives were now
outward Christians, their faith was superficial; many of them frequently
got together in secret and "solemnly revived all their heathen customs."
And his own happiest times in the islands came when he sought out
remote communities where the natives could still hold traditional
dances more frequently, despite the fact that such ceremonies had been
"prohibited by law, as indecorous." In the end, Melville had no desire to
hide his ambivalence: "Doubtless, in thus denationalizing the Tahitians,
as it were, the missionaries were prompted by a sincere desire for good;
but the effect has been lamentable."[19] Melville had always intended to
write the kinds of books that could make his readers, in Thoreau's words,
"dangerous to existing institutions."[20]

The Confidence-Man was Melville's most dangerous book, and the
reviewers, across the board, were even less sympathetic to it than Greeley had been to *Omoo*. Since it had been published on April Fool's Day,
1857, the notices were starting to pile up as Melville finished his Grand
Tour and returned to New York at the end of May. They probably rein-
forced his decision to give up writing. "It is like his other recent works,"
said the Albany *Evening Journal*, "a story in which the incidents and characters are chosen with a view to convey a theoretic moral, not a vivid,
graphic delineation based upon real life, like 'Type' and 'Omoo.'" Another reviewer confessed that he closed the volume "finding nothing
concluded, and wondering what on earth the author has been driving
at." Another believed that the book's "artistic or mechanical execution

is wretched." And several were offended: "The world is not made up of cheats and their victims," and only an embittered miscreant would cry injustice while living in a free, democratic republic, rich with economic opportunities (that is, until the Panic of 1857 took hold in August). But maybe such acid nonsense was all that could be expected of "one of the vilest of those runaway sailors who escape from work, and from the disagreeable things of civilization, and give themselves to the indulgences of a brutish life among the savage inhabitants of the islands in the Pacific." Such were the metaphysics of Melville-hating.[21]

Melville may have decided to stop being an author as early as the previous November. From Liverpool, he let his mother know that he was "aware of the necessity of cessation from writing."[22] And there is a steady flow of defeatism in the journal he kept as he proceeded to Constantinople, Cairo, and Jerusalem, and then back to England by way of Greece and Italy. The steady flow, though, is as notable as the defeatism: this is the journal of a still-working writer, and not a few of the entries suggest an intention to develop the material further—which he did, in the lectures he gave between 1857 and 1860 and in *Clarel*. Melville took notes on almost every single day of his trip, describing landscapes and holy sites and ruins and museums and eccentric characters—recording the weather and snatches of dialogue—asking "What in God's name were such places made for, & why?"[23] The heat and aridity were ever on his tongue, and at times he was utterly spent. But he continued on, seeking some kind of repose. "When one has found the worst that can be said against the world," Mumford wrote, about this period in Melville's career, "one must still live in it, and eventually Melville resigned himself, and lived. The crack which began to open like the gaping earth in Moby-Dick, that widened with a shiver in *Pierre*, became a foaming abyss in *The Confidence Man*. As he was on the point of falling into that abyss, Herman Melville withdrew, and the wide fissure closed—or seemed to close."[24]

It truly was a crisis of faith, another Cape Horn—but the world still engaged him. Reading through a hotel register in Jaffa (known as Joppa at the time) and finding the entries "apparently flattering to the host, but really derogatory to the place," he noted: "Something comical could be made out of all this." Despite his eye trouble and "general incapacity" and "singular pain across chest & in back," he opened himself to all the strange sights and the "millions of fellow beings" who doubted "much of our morality & all of our religion." Indeed, he treated his trip like an intensive course in the humanities, covering architecture, archaeology, world religions, and art history. It was just the sort of trip Mumford enjoyed taking, and he recognized Melville as a fellow "Pilgrim," seeking solace in the creations of the world's cultures, renewing his commitment to putting his own suffering in perspective by appreciating and reinterpreting "the life around him" and all of "what he had inherited from the past."[25]

On the Bosporus Strait, Melville found that the "Mosque of Achmet" produced a "beautiful effect," with its "20 small cupolas or domes," its "verandah without, and a colonnade within," its "fountain in the middle," its "columns of variously colored marbles and mosaic." Egypt's pyramids catapulted him back into ancient times and left him stunned: "Never shall forget this day. . . . Arab guides in flowing white mantles. Conducted as by angels up to heaven. Guides so tender. . . . I shudder at [the] idea of ancient Egyptians. It was in these pyramids that was conceived the idea of Jehovah. . . . After seeing the pyramid, all other architecture seems but pastry." In Rome, the Coliseum reminded him of Mount Greylock, and he loved the cafés, and loved strolling along the "avenues of olives" and the "bowered walks of stone." The notes he took on statues and paintings would serve as inspiration for poems and transportive daydreams for the rest of his life. And, again and again, he wrote about the graceful blending of natural and cultural landscapes, and of past and present: "Walked across the sand to the Adriatic shore. Calm waters. Long wide beach.—Through the glassy lagoon to Armenian Convent. Admirable retirement from the world . . . , the Lido a breakwater against the tumultuous ocean of life.—Garden, convent, quadrangles, cloisters,—View from the library window—isles—The city in the distance. Portraits of noble bearded old Armenian priests. Old printing presses."[26]

When Melville arrived back in Britain, though, his thoughts shifted homeward and toward the future: within a few weeks, he would be facing his family for the first time in more than half a year, and he would need to find a new way of making a living. It's hardly a shock that when he stopped by Stratford-upon-Avon, just before embarking for New York, he found Shakespeare's grave depressing.

Yet Oxford, which he visited just before Stratford, turned out to be the "most interesting spot I have seen in England." He was deeply impressed by the university's stability and endurance, but the effect was not over-awing like that of the pyramids. "It was here I first confessed with gratitude my mother land, & hailed her with pride. . . . Pulpit in corner of quadrangle. Deer. Garden girdled by river.—Meadows beyond. Oxen & sheep. Pastoral and collegiate life blended. . . . Amity of art & nature. Accord. . . . Garden to every college. . . . Sacred to beauty & tranquility. . . . Has beheld unstirred all the violence of revolutions."

Melville was committed to the idea of America, and to American ideals—to freedom, justice, democracy, and Christian charity. But he found nothing more galling than the hypocrisy of Americans who refused to acknowledge that their nation had never lived up to those ideals. For a few hours, on a Sunday afternoon in early May 1857, he seems to have wished he could forgo his American attachments and simply become an Oxford don. Forget about reading what the reviewers had to say about his books: he would just lecture on art and history and wander these gardens and meadows. Here was a cultural landscape in which he could invest some confidence, a community that could help him face his critics: "I know nothing more fitted by mild and beautiful rebuke to chastise the ranting of Yankees."[27]

CHAPTER 25

The Darkness of the Present Day (1944)

In early January 1944, back at Stanford—nicknamed The Farm, since the university's land had previously served as Leland Stanford's rural retreat—Mumford did his best to embrace Northern California's tranquil climate, in the midst of war. Winter in Palo Alto was a season of gentle rain and new blossoms: "the tall geraniums were in bloom, and there were even fresher spring flowers." Lewis, Sophia, and Alison "settled down again in the familiar house on Alvarado Row," just before the start of the term.[1] Having completed *The Condition of Man* at the end of the fall, Lewis hoped that university life would feel like a respite.

His own condition, though, seemed to worsen as soon as he resumed his teaching: he came down with bronchitis, and that, combined with his frustration at not yet getting to see his son, left him "tired and feeble . . . , sluggish and insufficient." But then, suddenly, Geddes was granted a furlough from his posting at Camp Adair, in Oregon, and he surprised his family by turning up in the middle of the night and sneaking into his bedroom, leaving a note on the door wishing his parents and sister a Happy New Year.[2]

To Lewis, desperate to have faith in his son's willingness to sacrifice, Geddes seemed to have become more "poised, self contained. . . . All signs of the old discontent or uncertainty or confusion had vanished completely. Spiritually he had tightened up: he was a man with a purpose." One morning, Geddes came along to his father's class "The

FIGURE 9. Lewis, Sophia, and Geddes at Stanford, January 1944.

Nature of Personality," and when one student commented on "the wholly negative character of war," Lewis took the opportunity to argue that "men who actually fought knew comradeship and experienced love, sometimes to a degree far beyond their civilian experience. . . . War, which plainly brutalized men, also raised some of them to a saintly level." Lewis noted that, afterward, Geddes admitted to being "tempted to join me in the discussion, on my side, against the doubters, with illustrations out of his own experience"—though of course he had not yet seen combat. Geddes also said that he wanted to keep attending class for the rest of the week, but he never again woke up in time, and Lewis decided to let him sleep.[3]

A few years later, Lewis still remembered bits of a conversation they had while "skirting the bare hills that lie behind Stanford," golden brown even in the wet season; they strolled through "rolling fields, with the fennel growing wildly in the footpath, with the radio mast in the distance, and a blimp, dipping and sawing in the clear sky." Geddes wanted "to share the intimate details of his training," wanted his father to understand what it felt like to handle grenades and to stand in swampy water for hours at a time. He wanted Lewis to be able to picture the scene when a young, "undersized" major found "a man's portrait of his wife among his soldierly gear": the major "had not merely confiscated it, but had torn it up in front of the man's eyes." Though Geddes never wavered in his desire to fight fascism or his willingness to risk his life, he did bristle both at the ruthlessness of military culture and at civilian disengagement. "A soldier is denied the right to live a normal life free of greater hardships," he observed, "and yet he must stand by and see the people who are supposed to be supporting him fight among one another to maintain the useless devices of pure pleasure that belonged to a fatuous pre-war era."[4]

Mumford was enough of a realist to acknowledge his son's alienation along with his fierce commitment to freedom and justice. But that acknowledgment took a toll. Lewis and Sophia were perpetually torn "between our convictions as citizens and our more private hopes and wishes." Once Geddes went back to Oregon, after a stay of eight days, both parents began to break down. "I find myself waking up in the middle of the night," Sophia wrote to her son, "and thinking about you and about the other boys at war and hating civilians, and hating being a civilian. We ought all be in it equally." She was suffering from severe back pain, and Lewis admitted to feeling "old and ill, as I had never felt my years or my body's heaviness before." The proofs had arrived for *The Condition of Man*; within a few weeks, he had to read through them, make corrections, and use them to prepare an index, while continuing to teach. Before the end of February, he had decided to apply for another leave of absence so that he could return to Amenia as soon as the winter quarter was over.[5]

The Condition of Man came out in May, just as Geddes was arriving in North Africa, on his way to the front in Italy. But by this time he was falling out of touch: "The recent absence of letters," he explained in June, "has not been from lack of filial affection or sense of duty but rather because of censorship restrictions hampering my form. It's pretty hard to write when you are permitted to say nothing." One thing he did manage to say, in a way that made a huge difference to Lewis, was that he understood both why his father had withdrawn from Stanford and why he had gone there in the first place. "I hope you haven't entirely given up on that theory of education," Geddes wrote. The problem, he thought, was that "you were, as usual, a bit in advance of your time (not to mention the dodos that inhabit most universities). It seems to me that after the war would be a better time to start a new one."[6] In fact, it wasn't just poor health that had spurred Lewis's quick departure from Stanford: as early as the summer of 1943, after the federal government had taken over part of campus for the training of new soldiers, Mumford had commented in his private notes that universities were starting to seem like "the last place in which to expect renewal."[7] His 1944 leave of absence wound up being a permanent resignation, though he continued teaching college courses on the East Coast, off and on, until 1975.

In *The Condition of Man*, Mumford turned back to renewal as his central purpose, though he also admitted that this was a wartime book, making "the colors" of this volume "somewhat more somber" than those of *Technics and Civilization* or *The Culture of Cities*. The New Deal had reaffirmed America's dreams of equal opportunity and common cause, but ultimately the Depression had bled directly into the war, meaning that most Americans had been coping with radical instability for fifteen years. Still, Mumford insisted on the hope inherent in the process of rediscovering the past. If you push your vision further and further back, he explained on the book's first page, you'll find that "not once, but repeatedly in man's history, has an all-enveloping crisis provided the condition essential to a renewal of the personality and the community. In the darkness of the present day, that memory is also a promise."[8]

Volume 3 of *The Renewal of Life* is a grandiose history of Western Civilization, going back to ancient Greece and Rome (not just the monasteries and urban settlements of the Middle Ages); it feels as all-encompassing as *Moby-Dick*. Initially, it sold better than the first two volumes, but the reviewers were ambivalent, underlining the book's solemn tone and its overwhelming emphasis on dissolution (first Greece and Rome fall, then the Christian era devolves into the Dark Ages, and then we're confronted with all the self-destructive power of modernity). In truth, as Mumford always reminded people, each analysis of decline in the book is accompanied by a discussion of reconstruction (its original working title was "Crisis and Renewal").[9] But it's also undeniable that, lacking a focus on technology or cities or any other concrete social structure, this volume seems more abstract and less political. Instead of proposals touting the potential of biotechnic innovation or citizen science or the democratic shaping and use of public space, we get broad suggestions relating to culture and values and personhood, more in the vein of *Men Must Act* and *Faith for Living*.

The pivot was entirely deliberate: Mumford was striving for something fundamental, a discussion of the very "purposes and ends of human development," which he ultimately identified as "the whole personality and the balanced community." He believed that "a remolding of the self and the super-ego is an inescapable preliminary to the great changes that must be made" throughout the western world. Indeed, it's not that he neglected the need for shifts "in public policy, which must be argued before an electorate and decided by the democratic process, so as to enlist the full and open participation of those most concerned." The point was simply that people had to wake up before they could be expected to embrace full citizenship. And it seemed better to emphasize a subtle reshaping of consciousness than dramatic political action, for Mumford shared Melville's distrust of revolutions: "Revolution in the light of the constant miscarriage of every revolution from 1789 onward is nothing more than the form through which a decadent civilization commits suicide." Basically, the first order of business was to cultivate human beings who would never allow demagogues to sway them, who were self-critical enough to resist movements like Nazism; the world could have no more of Melville's "moderate men." "The danger to human society today," Mumford asserted, "does not come solely from the active barbarians: it comes even more perhaps from those who have in their hearts assented to the barbarian's purposes." Look to your heart, Mumford was saying. And fortify it with an understanding of our ancestors' sacrifices and our vast inheritance.[10]

The new "organic person," Mumford argued, "must be in dynamic interaction with . . . every part of his heritage."[11] That interaction, that engagement, had actually defined humanness for hundreds of years. It was only in modern times that people lost the everyday opportunity to hear their elders tell stories about the past. And now children were being born into a traumatized culture that no longer knew what it meant to be human.[12] Mumford, in his writing and his teaching, tried to offer people an open-minded embrace of both change and continuity, a deep awareness of the layers of time.

We are temporal beings: "Man alone lives in a time-world that transcends the limitations of his local environment: the world of the past, the present, and the possible; or, if you will, the real, the realizing, and the realizable." Human consciousness of time—that flash of memory, that daydream about the future—is a constant source of wonder. But during the so-called Age of Reason, which turned its back on the past and declared Progress to be inevitable, societal leaders insisted that "history is only the record of superstitions, frauds, miseries, and lies." That scorn is still with us—especially, as Mumford noted, in the United States, where in the 1920s "it became popular to say that only contemporary history was important; whereas the truth is that all history is important *because* it is contemporary and nothing is perhaps more so than those hidden parts of the past that still survive without our being aware of their daily impact."[13]

In particular, "long-forgotten traumas in history" continue to have an influence specifically because they have been forgotten—because society has never reckoned with them fully. "Both the ancestry and posterity of Grief go further than the ancestry and posterity of Joy," Melville commented, in *Moby-Dick*. Indeed: as Mumford pointed out again and again, America's mistreatment of Native Americans and African Americans, dating back to the seventeenth century and still largely unacknowledged, left deep scars on everyone. Only "the perpetual rediscovery and reinterpretation of history" make true progress possible; when we are actively "re-thinking it, re-evaluating it, re-living it in the mind," the past stops controlling us and in fact becomes our best tool for "the creation and selection of new potentialities." In a crisis, Mumford thought, all the members of any community "must confront their collective past as fully as a neurotic patient must unbury his personal life," and the result might be a sudden, liberating flood of understanding: as you start to see how you got to this point, you might also see how to get beyond it.[14]

The Condition of Man is a series of reckonings. Mumford, contrapuntal thinker that he was, always plumbed the countercurrents within any historical epoch. But it is also helpful to consider his occasional over-simplifications about different eras, his broad characterizations of trends and cycles in the West over the last two thousand years. "Roman culture," he asserted, "was choked by its material advantages" and its "parasitism." The spirit of Christianity rose up in part to check Rome's excesses. But then the ethereal, ideal, pure love of God had to be brought back to earth in the Middle Ages, and there was a reorientation toward the fellowship of life in a guild, toward the idea of a "co-operative commonwealth," toward "the love of a man and a woman, the love of parents for children, the love of friends and neighbors: the natural prelude to every sublimation, to every wider sharing, of love." There was even "cultural intermixture" sometimes, as when Christians, Jews, and Muslims managed to coexist in southern Spain; "such regeneration as actually occurred" in the Middle Ages, Mumford thought, "can be attributed to the fresh mingling of cultures." But some communities always defined themselves in opposition to others. The Enlightenment of the eighteenth century, with its rational universalism, was a necessary corrective, given the traumas of the Crusades and the Spanish Inquisition. And Romanticism, with its "sanative belief in the vital and the organic," was a corrective to the Age of Reason's arid faith in mastery.[15]

Meanwhile, the most ambitious nations had embraced capitalist expansion, and the opening of the "New World" ushered in the era of modernity, leaving us with the dilemmas captured so suggestively in *Moby-Dick*. Like Melville, Mumford felt that he had inherited a culture dominated by individualism—a "world of isolates, presided over by isolatoes." And, as Melville had shown, the modern West of the previous three hundred years was a society of imperial conquest, though "contempt and guilt mingled with this whole process of exploitation." The exploiters did their best to justify the appropriation of native land, the abuse of native peoples, the co-opting of native practices, even while realizing that they should have treated the New World as an opportunity to rethink the "possibilities for human existence and charitably share their own blessings with those of the original inhabitants." Aboard the

Pequod, each sailor ultimately became a "private man, indifferent to politics," a mechanical laborer, doomed to "servile conformity." Yet each sailor also harbored the potential to reunite with his fellows, retaining a dim sense of what a "better commonwealth" might feel like. Whenever you're ready to conclude that human beings are selfish, ungrateful, and passive, you must remember that "there is equal historic evidence" showing that they are "also loyal, honest, ready to face danger, indifferent to personal gain when principles are at stake."[16]

Ultimately, Mumford's study of western history led him to seek a kind of conscientious balancing of all the different historical trends he identified. His engagement with the burgeoning science of ecology bubbles up constantly in *The Condition of Man,* but his main concern was to apply the idea of ecological equilibrium to culture. Thinking back to the rise of Christianity, he wanted to recapture "a healthy tension between animal needs and ideal ends." Thinking back to the Middle Ages, he celebrated Dante's realistic confrontation with evil and earthly suffering as well as his enduring faith in spiritual redemption—or, more broadly, his balancing of "common daily life" with a "sense of the eternal and the infinite." And thinking back to the dawn of modernity, Mumford insisted on remembering how certain "counter-movements" like "Protestantism, romanticism, and democracy" had always helped to offset "capitalism, militarism, scientism, and mechanization." In fact, he argued that "all of these institutions made positive contributions to human culture: even militarism." His own son had come to embody the ideal of military sacrifice, had learned in basic training to confront the darkest truths about himself and the world: "the outer discipline he had gone through he had accepted as inner discipline." What mattered was the balancing, the offsetting of forces, the combination of self-development and self-restraint, the constant, compensatory readjustment. And, of course, the ideal of balance was offset by the ever-present reality that "all equilibrium is necessarily unstable and is constantly upset by the continued act of growth."[17]

Mumford's own equilibrium was particularly unstable in the summer of 1944. He tried to ignore the reviews of *The Condition of Man,* tried to enjoy the sales figures, tried to find solace in gardening and swimming and sleeping in, tried to tell himself that he was enjoying a "vacation" at home in Amenia.[18] But for his entire adult life, he had defined himself primarily through his work. Now he was avoiding even the smallest professional tasks; his writing was limited to letters, mostly to Geddes. After D-Day (June 6), the Allies seemed assured of victory, but the Axis seemed bent on drawing out the violence as long as possible. Throughout that endless summer, Mumford "gathered together candy, pipes, cigars, [and] . . . yards and yards of rawhide laces" for care packages, and he wrote to his son at least five times a week. He lived "from moment to moment in benign outward days," telling Geddes about the games he played with Alison, who had turned nine in the spring, and about the mild weather they were having, and the abundance of vegetables he was harvesting, and the "fine batch of currant jelly Sophy was putting aside for his return." His letters "kept up a cheerful, gossipy tone"—though "once Geddes had gone into combat it was impossible, I am afraid, altogether to hide our deep concern, which must have been visible between the lines."[19]

Geddes's letters were always mixed—both glib and grim, sometimes in the same sentence. "I celebrated my birthday," he wrote from Italy in mid-July, "by coming as close to getting killed as I ever want to. I felt the machine gun bullets passing my shoulder. Two of my buddies were hit by the same burst. It's a great life if you like excitement." He was a committed soldier, with a matter-of-fact bravery that led him to volunteer as an advance scout: the Nazis were anchored in the northern mountains, holding the so-called Gothic Line, and it was Geddes's job to move forward until he drew fire, thus revealing the Nazis' exact positions. It was clear to everyone he served with that he preferred to be in the thickest action, though he also insisted that he had "a lot more to do with my life than die during this war." He was proud of his alertness and precision—"I guess my years of hunting were of some use after all"— but also honest about the horrific conditions, the vulnerability, the fear: "I've seen men almost unable to walk from nervous exhaustion. I was awake and moving around for all but six hours of my first six days. . . . My conception of time in terms of days and nights was completely gone. . . . It's the whine and crunch of shells and the mutilated bodies of your buddies and friends that tears a man to pieces." In combat, you're trapped in a perpetual present; it's hard to feel human. But writing letters to his parents sometimes brought him back to himself, and to empathy: "Well, don't strain yourself wondering or worrying about the grimness of it all. If I weren't rough enough to take it I wouldn't have gotten this far and I can still laugh five or ten minutes after a barrage. You needn't lose any sleep either, thinking that you should be up here. This is a young man's war. It's your job to take care of the States, you have the needed experience in that line. We don't. We can take care of this end and I'd call it a fair division."[20]

Lewis followed his son's progress as well as he could. He knew that the tactical objective was Monticelli, on "a rocky broken ridge with a cone-shaped peak, three thousand feet high, wooded three-quarters of the way up, but lacking in concealment of any sort for the last six hundred feet of the slope. . . . I have never seen this territory, but in a photograph the country looks like the barren desiccated ridges one finds in New Mexico or Arizona." The Nazi positions, Lewis learned from various reports, "were protected by pillboxes and dugouts, tunneled deep into the mountain and carefully camouflaged." This would be the Germans' last line of defense in Italy.[21]

Geddes managed to write every four or five days, sending love, musing on faith, continuing to delve into the painful divide between modern soldiers and modern civilians: "it's hard for men, who live only because they co-operate, to explain things to people who live only as semi-isolated individuals. A front line soldier will almost always *give* you half of his last dollar or one of his last two cigarettes. An American civilian finds it hard to lend you half of his surplus. A man who has gone but a few hundred yards with death in his footsteps and the fear of God in his heart appreciates his fellow man just a bit more than before. The returning front line soldier will find himself, first shocked and then embittered by this difference in outlook. This will be one of the problems of a post-war world."[22]

One night in August, Alison had a nightmare that Geddes was killed, and Lewis and Sophia had trouble consoling her: "she had awakened with tears in her eyes and she kept on sobbing softly, even while she snuggled close to her mother." From then on, Lewis felt, the family's "false peace was quietly shattered." In mid-September, Geddes's letters stopped coming. Lewis and Sophia collected photographs to send to him, and collected stories from other parents about how sometimes they had gone three months without news from their sons: "That was war." But on October 10, there was a telegram: Missing In Action. They wrote him one more letter. Then, on the seventeenth, two days before Lewis's forty-ninth birthday, the final word came: Geddes had been hit by enemy gunfire, "between the 12th and 15th of September, just before we broke the Gothic Line. He was killed instantly." There must have been an eyewitness—but one who had lost track of the days. Lewis and Sophia waited until the next morning to tell Alison. She "lay silent for a moment, and then, in a thin, remote voice she said: 'Life will never be the same again.'"[23]

CHAPTER 26

More Gloom, and the Light of That Gloom (1856-76)

Chapter 9 of *Pierre* has dueling titles: "More Light, and the Gloom of That Light"; and "More Gloom, and the Light of That Gloom." It's about Pierre's doubt, self-distrust, and indecision. He has received the truth about Isabel and his father—probably. And with that illumination, he "droops into nameless melancholy." How can he redeem Isabel and also spare his mother? At least he has always been told that "Gloom and Grief" are "the selectest chamberlains to knowledge"—the keys to reality. He picks up "the Inferno of Dante, and the Hamlet of Shakespeare." He reads: "All hope abandon, ye who enter here." Then: "The time is out of joint;—Oh, cursed spite, / That ever I was born to set it right!" Both books wind up trampled at his feet, their pages "torn into a hundred shreds." By morning, Pierre does come to a resolution, affirming that it can help to read about other people's struggles, and that "the deepest gloom precedes the day." But Melville wouldn't want us to mistake resolution for clarity. In fact, the angst of the previous evening will haunt Pierre for the rest of his short life: "Impossible would it be now to tell all the confusion and confoundings in the soul of Pierre."[1]

Impossible, too, to tell much about Melville's life and career after 1856. But we know a few things. After he arrived back in the States in May 1857, he informed his in-laws that he was "not going to write any more at present & [wished] to get a place in the N.Y. Custom House."[2] That didn't work out until 1866. Meanwhile, he went on the lecture circuit and wrote poetry. According to some notes Lizzie made after Herman's death, he had "a severe attack of what he called crick in the back" in March 1858, and "he never regained his former vigor & strength."[3] Still, he was relatively active, even braving Cape Horn in 1860 on a voyage from Boston to San Francisco, with his brother Tom as captain. During that trip, he sent some warmhearted letters to his children and enclosed "a little baby flying-fish's wing for Fanny," who had recently turned five (the same age as my youngest child when, 154 years later, I found myself in an archive staring at that wing, glued to a brittle piece of paper). "Now, my dear Malcolm," he wrote, from the Pacific ("Off the coast of South America, On the Tropic of Capricorn"), "I must finish my letter to you. I think of you, and Stanwix and Bessie and Fanny very often; and often long to be with you. But it can not be, at present. The picture which I have of you and the rest I look at some-times, till the faces almost seem real.—Now, my Dear Boy, good bye, and God bless you. Your affectionate father, H Melville."[4]

The next spring, in late March 1861, when Melville went to Washing-ton, D.C., to shake the new president's hand and try to get a government job, he sent back a note to his wife, and today it is the only letter from Herman to Lizzie known to have survived. It is full of his characteristic realism—"as yet I have been able to accomplish nothing in the matter of the consulship"—but it also bespeaks a comfortable, abiding love. It describes the cool air of the early spring, and the sunshine on budding bushes, and the "magnificent flowers" at a White House gala, and the pleasure of getting "lost among the labyrinths of halls, passages & splen-did corridors" of the new Capitol building. He signed it "Thine, My Dearest Lizzie—Herman."[5]

Then there was the wagon accident in November 1862, and the final abandonment of the Berkshires for New York City in 1863. Melville vis-ited the war zone in Virginia in the spring of 1864 and published *Battle-Pieces* in 1866. In December of that year, he signed on at the New York Custom House. The job either settled him down or made him crazier, or both, and by May Lizzie thought she would have to leave him. Then Malcolm shot himself in September. And then: virtual silence, until *Clarel* came out, in June 1876.

FIGURE 10. The Melville children, c. 1860 (L to R: Stanwix, Fanny, Malcolm, and Bessie).

No one knows exactly when Melville started writing his "Poem and Pilgrimage in the Holy Land" or how steadily he labored over it, but the bulk of the work was probably done in the 1870s.[6] Despite its dependence on Melville's travel journal from 1856–57, *Clarel* is a distinctly postbellum book, full of haunted images of sad processions—barefoot hermits holding candles, monks with torches, downcast maidens linking arms and singing strange melodies—that recall the grave-decorating ceremonies immediately following the Civil War. But it is also a Centennial book, published just days before the grand celebrations of July 4: after one hundred years of "Independence" and "Progress," Melville was asking his fellow Americans to pause in their self-congratulation and look backward as well as forward. They were busy drinking toasts to the ongoing conquest of the New World; he offered them the deep perspective of Antiquity.

Desperate to forget all the recent unpleasantness, 1870s Americans had turned their eyes away from cemeteries and toward glorious

FIGURE 11. Herman, c. 1861.

railroads, vast mineral resources, sublime scenery, and a series of wars pitting the white men of the North and South against the so-called "savage red men" of the West.[7] To Melville, though, who was grieving for his son, and then, as of 1872, for his mother, it was precisely the traditional rituals of mourning, repeated year after year, in honor of both continuity and the passage of time, that could endow a place with history and render it a pilgrimage site, "tingling with kinship through and through."

FIGURE 12. Herman in 1868.

Clarel was a long reminder that Gloom and Grief are the only constant stars by which we can navigate. But, unlike *Pierre*, this book suggested that a navigator who adopted the spirit of a pilgrim might feel as though he were perpetually on the threshold of a chapel, even when confronted by a desert, or a boundless ocean, or a blank, barren city. To stop the modern press of days and dwell with human suffering is to become "stable in time's incessant change" and also feel "the intersympathy of creeds."[8]

Clarel (rhymes with Carol) is a lost seminary student from the United States, struggling with his Protestant faith, constantly "irked," full of modern spleen. He has come to the Holy Land to slow down, to turn back, to expose himself, to relive the scenes of scripture, to absorb other perspectives: "Yes I am young, but Asia old. / The books, the books not all have told. . . . / Our New World's worldly wit so shrewd / Lacks the Semitic reverent mood." The first person he meets is a "Black Jew" from Cochin, India, and eventually he will spend time not only with Jews but with many Muslims and Catholics, not to mention Greek Orthodox monks, a Lutheran minister from England, and various apostates, including several fellow exiles from America.[9] Almost immediately, Clarel realizes how starved he has been for companionship, and finds himself drawn to stranger after stranger—both those who seem to share his doubt, and those who seem utterly assured in their faith.

He will never know exactly what he's looking for. Most of his love interests are beautiful, brooding men (one of them strongly reminiscent of Hawthorne), but he falls hardest for a woman named Ruth, the embodiment of mercy. And she finds Clarel to be bright and refreshing, despite his confusion. Ruth is American, born on the prairies. Now she's in Jerusalem because her father, Nathan, a fervent convert to Judaism, wished to have a fuller spiritual life than he could in his original homeland. But Nathan is suddenly killed by Arabs, who consider him an invader of their lands (he had also been considered an invader by the Natives of the American West). As soon as Clarel gets word, he goes to comfort Ruth, but the local rabbi turns him away: only Jews may be present for the rites of mourning. Desperate for distraction, Clarel immediately joins a group of pilgrims setting out across the desert for Bethlehem. By the time he gets back to Jerusalem, Ruth has also died, from fever or grief.

Clarel starts out an Ishmael, and ends an Ishmael—alone and adrift, but committed to persisting. In a passage at the end of the book that Mumford found particularly remarkable, Clarel, after briefly considering suicide, suddenly realizes that his pilgrimage has actually left him with a will to live: "Spurn—I'll endure; all spirit's fled / When one fears nothing.—Bear with me, / Yet bear!—Conviction is not gone."[10] Faith is not what he needed, to live in the modern world—only conviction. Not God—only human fellowship, and landscapes imbued with history and beauty, and the realistic understanding that "the world is rent /

With partings," and that mortality is precisely what creates meaning: "Emerge thou mayst from the last whelming sea, / And prove that death but routs life into victory."[11]

Melville devoted most of this book to the philosophical dialogue of the pilgrims with whom Clarel travels—a group almost as diverse and disputatious as Ahab's crew. And there are constant invocations of *Moby-Dick*, from references to a famous ship-destroying whale to a pilgrim's story of a failing compass needle (it spun "like an imp," because of some metal cargo)—recalling the scene aboard the *Pequod* on the morning after a magnetic storm, when Ahab wondered why, against his orders, his ship was sailing away from the sunrise: "lo! The two compasses pointed East, and the Pequod was infallibly going West."[12] *Clarel* is in fact just as ambitious as *Moby-Dick* in its roaming search for ways to navigate the modern world, and it is a worthy sequel. Melville was asking, again, how to cope with our unhealing wounds and our unanswerable questions—and with the hopeless conflict between naive religion and hubristic science. Your needle might point true for a time, but it will eventually falter, and meanwhile the night sky, previously sparkling with beacons, now seems a dead black. The Three Kings found Jesus, but Clarel won't: "Nor failed they, though by deserts vast / And voids and menaces they passed: / They failed not, for a light was given—/ The light and pilotage of heaven: / A light, a lead, no longer won / By any, now, who seekers are: / Or fable is it? But if none, / Let man lament the foundered Star."[13]

The New World, with its supposed Democracy and its embrace of reason, had functioned as a new lodestar, a new source of hope and progress. For the Revolutionary generation in America—for Melville's grandfathers—Deism had offered a comfortable reconciliation of God (the Divine Watchmaker) and Nature (the Benign Garden), and by the 1830s the United States seemed to have set a steady course of liberal reform. The light of Science was shining brightly. But in Melville's day, America's unity of purpose not only collapsed but came to seem impossible: "Prone, prone are era, man and nation / To slide into a degradation?" asks a character in *Clarel*, already suspecting the answer. Much of the conversation among the pilgrims revolves around the dangers and failures of modernity. With the rise of Geology and Evolution, they know that they can no longer turn to the Bible for timeless morals, but they are also disgusted by the greedy, cynical Go-Aheadism of scientific and technical development. If not religion, then "what shall stay / The fever of advance?" Melville felt sure that people "get tired at last of being free—/ Whether in states—in states or creeds. / For what's the sequel? Verily, / Laws scribbled by law-breakers, creeds / Scrawled by the free-thinkers, and deeds / Shameful and shameless. . . . / Who's gained by all the sacrifice / Of Europe's revolutions? Who?" There had to be some sort of counterweight to the fetishization of Progress. There had to be a way to remind the idealistic revolutionaries that even if their dreams of equality were genuine, the wheel would always come around again: "Come, thou who makest such hot haste / To forge the future—weigh the past."[14]

One of the most memorable of the pilgrims is an American called Ungar, part Indian and part Catholic, who insists repeatedly that only a deep reckoning with history can redeem modernity. He should know: he has not only inherited the "Indian's hopeless feud / Under the white's aggressive reign" but also served in the Civil War. As soon as he starts talking, the other Americans in the group can tell that he has been scarred, like the whole nation, by the "immense charred solitudes / Once farms," and the "chimney-stacks that reign / War-burnt upon the houseless plain," and the "hearthstones without neighborhoods," and the North's "misrule after strife," and the "dust from victor heels"—that he must live with "disgust / For times when honor's out of date / And serveth but to alienate." His is the voice of conscience—or perhaps of Melville's self-hatred, for his complicity not just in the corruption of Reconstruction but in the general devastation visited on the Earth by his own kind: "The Anglo-Saxons—lacking grace / To win the love of any race; / Hated by myriads dispossessed / Of rights—the Indians East and West. / These pirates of the sphere! Grave looters—/ Grave, canting, Mammonite freebooters, / Who in the name of Christ and Trade / . . . Deflower the world's last sylvan glade!"

But what Ungar ultimately cannot abide is the way that white Anglo-Saxons use their pride in the innovation of Democracy to help obscure their criminal history. For him, Democracy is promising only when it explicitly sets out to check and balance past abuses. That is the very meaning of Democracy: it arose as a means for the People to take power from the elite and spread it among themselves as evenly as possible. Its deepest significance lies not in its newness but in its organic connectedness to history: "The future, what is that to her, / " asks Ungar, "Who vaunts she's no inheritor? / 'Tis in her mouth, not in her heart. / The Past she spurns, though 'tis the past / From which she gets her saving part."[15]

No wonder Mumford loved this book; no wonder he devoted some twenty pages to it in his Melville biography. Frustrated by the escapism of the Roaring Twenties, he immediately understood Melville's condemnation of the escapist Gilded Age and the Wild West: American culture was based on a flight from history. The Indian Wars on the plains started immediately after the Civil War, and the transcontinental railroad was completed in 1869—the same year that Buffalo Bill first appeared in a dime novel, ready to save innocent white settlers from marauding savages. But Melville's evocation of the "storied ground" of the Holy Land, with its burial mounds and stations of the cross and layers of civilizations and ancient pilgrimage routes and thousand-year-old palms and monasteries built into cliffs, was meant to remind readers that the past is inescapable—and also, thanks to its "saving parts," potentially generative.[16]

Mumford certainly acknowledged the reasons that Clarel, with its "aloofness" and its "stale poetic airs," was Melville's "most neglected" work.[17] Indeed, the book's 18,000 lines, its monotonous meter, its tangled diction, its tragic narrative, its oppositional politics, its abstract philosophy—all made the poem, as Melville himself admitted, "eminently adapted for unpopularity."[18] Lizzie went even further: she called it a "dreadful incubus of a book," because in the end it seemed to possess Herman. Instead of spending time with her and the children, instead of allowing the years to mellow their grief, he would lock himself in his study after a full day of work at the custom house and wrestle with his doubt. Writing still meant a great deal to him—was still at the core of his identity—but this regimen seemed far from healthy for a man over fifty. Lizzie felt that the book had put Herman in "a frightfully nervous state," and the stress of the final pre-publication corrections had "undermined all our happiness."[19] It was *Moby-Dick* all over again.

Like *Moby-Dick*, though, as Mumford well recognized, *Clarel* harbors a certain amount of determined hope. It reveals a writer "who had approached, and was slowly finding peace."[20] The rediscovery of historical continuity can have a powerful emotional impact, as when one of the pilgrims suggests that Cicero, who lived in the troubled century before Christ, composed works that "would serve to read / For modern essays. And indeed / His age was much like ours: doubt ran, / Faith flagged." Other people in other times have suffered and struggled, and have persevered, and gained perspective.

The landscape, meanwhile, though changeable, is renewed every morning in familiar ways: "The gray of dawn. A tremor slight: / The trouble of imperfect light / Anew begins. In floating cloud / Midway suspended down the gorge, / A long mist trails white shreds of shroud." Clarel remains mostly isolated and alienated among the pilgrims, as he trudges through the wilderness, always "vacillating" and "irresolute." But every now and then there is a flask set up "in evening arbor"; several cups touch "brink to brink / In fair bouquet of fellowship"; there are songs, and comic masquerades, and sabbath days of rest, which help offset the pilgrims' traumas. "The heat," says one of them, "the burden of the day, / Life has its trials, sorrows—yes, / I know—I feel; but blessedness / Makes up."[21]

Little by little, Clarel realizes that all the seemingly steadfast pilgrims carry as much doubt with them as he does—that "Pisa's Tower confirmed in place" is a better metaphor for religion than the right-angled edifice of the Church. "Faith leaned from the beginning," says a particularly sensible pilgrim; "yes, / If slant, she holds her steadfastness." The whole pilgrimage becomes a meditation on patient acceptance of doubt, and Clarel takes another steady step while listening to a sailor-pilgrim (the same one who told of the spinning compass needle) describe the resolute pilgrimages of Galapagos tortoises, "which better may abide life's fate / Than comprehend. What may man know? / (Here pondered Clarel;) let him rule—/ Pull down, build up, creed, system, school, /

And reason's endless battle wage, / Make and remake his verbiage—/ But solve the world! Scarce that he'll do: / Too wild it is, too wonderful."[22] Pierre's inability to solve the world drove him toward death, but Clarel, even after the bitterest of confoundings, could still appreciate wildness and wonder.

Mumford owned a rare, two-volume first edition of *Clarel*. Only about 350 copies were printed, of which just over 100 were sold, and 220 were sent to the paper mill to be pulped in 1879, at Melville's request.[23] Mumford's copy had been discarded from the New York Public Library in the fall of 1927; a friend who worked there passed it on to him, with an inscription referring to an evening they had spent together with Josephine Strongin, who had already captured Mumford's attention, though their affair wouldn't begin for another decade. Mumford noticed that the pages of the two volumes had never been cut: he was the first to read them.[24] Later, in September 1944, he wrote a letter to his friend Van Wyck Brooks, a scholar of nineteenth-century American literature, that said not a word about Geddes being on the front lines in Italy but went on at length about Melville: "Maybe our final title to greatness will be the fact that we are the sole living Americans who have read *Clarel* from end to end!"[25]

If you do read *Clarel* from end to end, you will wind up where you started, in Jerusalem (which Melville sometimes shortened to Salem). It's different from *Moby-Dick* in that way: it reinscribes circular, cyclical time. The pilgrim goes out and then comes all the way back again, in what Mumford thought of as "the mood of humility"—a mood sometimes adopted by communities as a kind of spiritual reinforcement after they have been "racked by war, pestilence, slavery, and sheer fatigue of living." Mumford was adamant that "although Clarel returned from his pilgrimage to find himself bereft, the experience of love had given him something: the love that would have redeemed the universe for Captain Ahab and kept him from his deadly contest with the whale, now was a pledge of his own redemption for Melville." Read *Clarel*, Mumford urged, and you will feel Melville slowing down and coming home to solid earth; you will find "the germs of a new feeling about life." Mumford imagined Melville's career as "a June evening. . . . In half an hour the scene changes from the most brilliant activity and ecstasy to utmost passiveness. Bats swoop silently in the air; a chill comes up from the river; darkness is cool as well as silent. Is all over? Not yet. Presently the fireflies make a warm firmament of the fields, and in the pale rising of the moon, the earth itself takes on another glory. There are fireflies and moonlight and the domestic chirp of crickets in the night of Melville's life, its last quarter century—not silence and unrelieved blackness."[26] As Lizzie lamented, the final push to publish *Clarel* had taken a toll on both of them—but at least there had been some kind of happiness to be undermined—some light in the gloom—some sense of a new equilibrium and repose, even after they had lost their son.

CHAPTER 27

Survival (1944–47)

Throughout his life, Mumford experimented with the visual arts, making pencil drawings and watercolors of landscapes, his friends, and himself. In the late spring of 1944, having fled from Stanford, and feeling anxious about Geddes, he started sketching with soft colored pencils, as a kind of therapy.[1] He would work in the garden, and take long walks, and then sit somewhere and gaze. Some of the scenes he captured show Amenia's valley in all its expansive lushness, with orchards and meadows and wild hills. Other landscapes feel more constrained. If the date on the back can be trusted, Mumford made a particularly dark sketch on his forty-ninth birthday, two days after hearing that Geddes was dead.[2]

There is a broken barbed-wire fence, a blackened tree, an interrupted path, and a tangled thicket. The curving dirt track in the foreground welcomes the eye into the scene, but from there every route is blocked, except for one possible opening in the upper right between a patch of brown hillside and another charred and stunted tree: the only way forward is over fire-scarred ground. I'm not entirely sure of the geography, but that bit of bare earth might be the "semi-circular sandpit a few hundred yards behind our house, where the meadow drops abruptly to the river," and where Lewis and Geddes used to test the guns they carried with them on hunting expeditions—a piece of land that, Lewis attested, "haunted my consciousness in an overwhelming fashion the week before Geddes went into the line for the last time: it had become a symbol of his life, his talents, our special intimacy as father and son."[3]

FIGURE 13. "Pasture at Foot of Old Mitchell Place," 1944.

Both Lewis and Sophia sank into their grief. They both had special intimacies with Geddes, but they also fought with him, and like all thoughtful parents they questioned many of their parental decisions. So guilt mingled with the pain of loss that fall and winter, as they looked through family albums and reread letters, wondering if they had been too free with Geddes, or too strict, or if he had suffered from neglect when they turned their attention to antifascist activism. "On one of our brief afternoon walks the other day," Lewis wrote, in December, "... Sophy and I were discussing the quality of our lives during the last half dozen years.... We both agree that, far more than the fact that we were 'aging' and too often ill, the pressure of the outside world, the anxieties and dangers connected with the widening triumphs of tyranny and the necessities of war, have robbed our domestic life of the fulfillment it might have had, and of the gaiety and animation it might have afforded to both our children, who instead lived under our lengthening shadows."[4]

This was an evasion of sorts, but it was better to blame the war than each other—something they were unable to avoid completely as they considered Geddes's teenage struggles in light of their own temperamental differences. Sophia and Geddes had stormed at each other passionately, but they were always close; Lewis had maintained a somewhat mystified distance, showing his deep love with perhaps too much subtlety (he was also absorbed in his own affairs, both literary and amorous). Almost immediately after they got word of Geddes's death, Lewis had the idea of writing a book about him, and asked for Sophia's help, since she was the keeper of family records. But she wasn't yet ready for so direct a confrontation with their loss; they had another child to raise, after all. Grief sometimes brought the family closer together, but it could also exacerbate resentments. By the following summer, Lewis had to admit that "Geddes' death has torn our lives asunder in more than one way. One of the ways in which I least suspected it would is in increasing the disturbance between Sophy and me."[5] It was as if they had each come separately to Father Mapple's New Bedford chapel, where every whaleman or whaleman's widow was "purposely sitting apart from the other," each with a "silent grief" that seemed "insular and incommunicable."[6]

While Sophia focused on day-to-day practical realities, Lewis wavered between efforts to work through his anguish and to distract himself. Most immediately, he wrote poems. They were all about war and death; a few were published, as Lewis noted, "despite their imperfections."[7] One bore the title "For Those Bereaved in War," and its refrain— "Death comes to every household"—suggests Mumford's compulsion to reckon with his trauma in a way that might be helpful to other members of a war-torn society.[8] He was trying to be true to his own urgings in *The Condition of Man*, that modern citizens ought to shake themselves out of their denialism and their fetishization of security, that they ought to relearn the art of facing history and mortality with openness and grace.

But Mumford acknowledged, in December 1944, that "the emotional strain of reflecting on Geddes's life and on what might have been often becomes almost unbearable."[9] The season had turned frigid—this would be the worst winter the Mumfords had ever endured in their drafty farmhouse—and Lewis noted that "the outer cold of the weather" only served to reinforce "the inner cold of grief."[10] He had a few infected teeth that had to be extracted, and then came heart palpitations and circulatory problems. "The very blood disappears from the surface of the body," he wrote; "and the limbs are stiff."[11] To his friend Henry Murray he confessed that he was mired in "a period of Melvillian grief and gloom"—the worst he had ever experienced. "The reality cuts much deeper than any preliminary anxiety."[12] Sophia was right: it was too soon to write a book about Geddes. For the moment, the act of pondering Geddes's past just underlined the fact that his future had been stolen. And meanwhile, the war still raged.

In August 1945, Lewis was devastated by the news that his nation had dropped two atomic bombs on civilians: this was not what Geddes had fought for. He managed to listen to the first couple of minutes of President Truman's radio address about the end of the war, but soon he found himself stumbling outside. Immediately, he "started for the sand-pit by the river, so deeply associated in my mind with Geddes's life and death, weeping and sobbing unrestrainedly. Next to the actual announcement of his death, it was the bitterest moment of my life: bitter and lonely as no other had been before."[13]

He still couldn't write the book about Geddes, but he decided to dedicate one to him. *Values for Survival*, published in 1946, was meant to "clarify the issues of the war and to point to the tasks and the duties of peace. Geddes felt that the war would not be over nor peace won till the soldiers who participated in it knew what they had been fighting for. So in a special sense this is his book: and the writing of it is my filial obligation to him; a labor of love for the Geddeses who come out of the war."[14] Many of the essays in the book, mostly on politics and education, had been written in the late 1930s and early 1940s: they are companion pieces to *Men Must Act*, *Faith for Living*, and *The Condition of Man*, explaining and justifying Mumford's antifascism stance and his efforts at Stanford to demonstrate the enhanced relevance of the humanities in dark times. Modern society was producing comfortable consumers, but no amount of consumption would bring comfort under a fascist regime. The conditions of modernity required people who would scrape and claw to survive despite "the chill of disaster and the ugliness of error," who would find fulfillment in human solidarity and sacrifice in the face of senseless violence. "From the Odyssey to Moby Dick, from Isaiah to Dante, the great masters of reality have cultivated the tragic sense of life and have enabled men to survive, with courage and faith, even in a crumbling world."[15]

Some of the most compelling prose in *Values for Survival*, though, was freshly inspired by the horror of the atom bomb. Many other thinkers were already worrying that after a certain number of nuclear explosions "the planet itself may be made permanently uninhabitable," and Mumford joined them in embracing ecology as a check against atomic warfare: the spread of radiation across the globe quickly confirmed "the interdependence of the entire world of life" and the truth that "all creatures live by complicated partnerships." But Mumford was one of the first writers to look for the historical and psychological trends that had made the bomb possible—that had allowed human beings to decide that it was acceptable to kill tens of thousands of their fellow human beings in a matter of seconds (and here he was also thinking of the incendiary bombs dropped on Tokyo and Dresden). Drawing on his reading of Melville, he pointed to a general distancing of individuals from the consequences of their actions: modern citizens seized the main chance, consumed whatever was made available to them, assumed their own innocence as mere cogs in a grand machine, and thus trained themselves not to worry about where their food, or land, or bricks, or paper, or oil, or comfort, might have come from. It seemed to Mumford that as our machines had gotten more powerful, we had simply started deferring to them: "Modern technics . . . has produced a race of moral robots." The problem of the bomb was the problem of "the ideological insulation of the technician." Perhaps Melville's "moderate man" was the same man who was willing to press the button that opened the bomb bay door—and the same man who went along with the Nazis. So Mumford boiled down his "Program for Survival" to the immediacy of relationships—to love, understanding, and sacrifice—to "increasing tenderness, increasing sensitivity, increasing practical regard for . . . all man's millions of co-partners and helpers in the animal and vegetable world."[16]

For Mumford, whose life and career were profoundly influenced by the tender nurturing of his German grandfather, the most vexing issue was probably the complicity of ordinary German citizens in the crimes of Nazism. And his need to explore their seemingly robotic acquiescence spurred him to some of the most creative writing he ever did, in the final section of *Values for Survival*—a collection of five long, stylized letters to five different composite German personalities, based on several of his actual friends and acquaintances. Was the problem just an old, inbred "respect for army discipline, respect for law, respect for authority"? he asked Frau Maria Z. in Lübeck. "Did you close your eyes when the police came for your communist neighbor, who lived in that little allotment Siedlung near-by?" Did Dr. Hermann K., architect and city planner in Hamburg, simply appreciate "what progress had been made under National Socialism in unified planning"? Did "the worship of power, the cult of the supermen," destroy the "capacity for self-criticism"?

Mumford's prose in these strange epistles conscientiously balances an accusatory rage at his correspondents' willingness to accept state terrorism with a respect for their deep cultivation. And at the very end of the book he finds hope in addressing the Unknown Citizens who might be "born in the defeat of the German armies, in the wreck and dissolution of the German state, growing up in the midst of ruined cities"—who might embrace a "re-dedication to life"—who might devote themselves "to the non-German, to that which is universal and essentially human." If you want to rejoin the world community, he says, "instead of priding yourself on your race and caste, you will blot out these fantasies of Aryan and Germanic purity, and pride yourself on your actual fusing together of many races and strains, on the democratic breaking down of the lines of caste."[17]

Mumford was finally able to cling to hope again, and his rediscovered interest in the future helped him turn back to the past. After *Values for Survival* had been published, he thought he might be ready to write the book about Geddes, and Sophia reluctantly agreed to help him, by marshaling the family records and sharing her own recollections.

Green Memories (1947) is Lewis's most lyrical book, full of love and wistfulness and poignant observation. Since "death comes to every household," he assumed that his story would contribute to the gradual healing of his community. But most of all, this book was for himself: it was an intimate effort to make his son come alive again, to defy the horrible truth that "the dead do not die once, but endlessly."[18]

Geddes was a defiant child; Lewis went so far as to suggest that his son had "a touch of Ahab's pride and fierceness." But this was just the kind of perspective that made Sophia continue to question the whole project: what would readers gain from learning about Geddes's flaws and struggles and his parents' self-critical guilt? Lewis tried to reassure her that, as in all of his writings, he would strive for balance above all, and in fact he consistently offset darker comments with lighter ones. Despite Geddes's "generalized grievance against Moby-Dick," Lewis attested, "another part of him remained quite unscathed, as jaunty and imperturbable as Ahab's second mate, Stubb."[19] Indeed, from the beginning, Lewis was aware of "great problems in form to be solved in doing such a memoir as 'Green Memories,' for the burden of my tale is a sad one, not only at the end but even at the beginning; and yet one must at every page do justice to the vitality, to the high spirits, to the undauntedness that was Geddes, too."[20] And so he wound up signaling this dilemma at the very start of the book, explaining that "if this were a piece of music one might compose it in one of two modes." The first would be a "happy version," the version predominantly "brought forth by his mother's memories," figuring Geddes as a wild, sunny river. The other, stemming more from Lewis's recollections, might be written "in the mode in which Melville wrote *Redburn* and *White Jacket*. Then one would show a landscape overhung from the beginning with dark clouds, and only fitfully would the sun pour through them."[21] Neither *Redburn* nor *White-Jacket* is a dismal book, but both of their main characters, versions of the young Melville himself, struggle with the world's rigid hierarchies and bitter injustices.

In the end, Mumford welcomed quite a bit of Sophia's sunshine into *Green Memories*, especially when he took the story to the Melvillean paradise of Hawaii, where "Geddes had one tantalizing glimpse of Heaven, a visible, palpable Heaven." He had just turned thirteen, after a year "when his temper was intolerable and his manners worse," but now he got to spend his days swimming and surfing and fishing, "sometimes not even coming back for lunch, but getting hot dogs and coca-cola on the beach." For a boy who was "at one with Nature and all of Nature's ways," who liked nothing better than to be outside, Hawaii felt like home. Lewis sometimes led him on hikes through bamboo forests, where they found guavas and hidden waterfalls, and once they "stumbled by accident on a Hawaiian feast," where some elders, the island's rightful inhabitants, were baking a pig in the earth and "insisted on treating us to a generous helping," whose succulence and flavor they never forgot. On such expeditions, Lewis and Geddes felt that they were "never far away from the aboriginal world of magic, the world of Kahunas and Shark Gods, of stone altars deep in the jungle, the world that Melville had revealed in *Typee*"—a world where, as Melville put it, "there were none of those thousand sources of irritation that the ingenuity of civilized man has created to mar his own felicity."[22]

When Sophia fell ill in Honolulu and had to be hospitalized, Lewis and Geddes would visit her together in the morning, and then when Lewis went back in the evening, Geddes would stay home and put Alison to bed, "with a patience and a good will, with a sympathy and an understanding," that he had rarely shown before. The whole experience, Lewis thought, "brought Geddes and me together as perhaps we had never been before: no longer just father and son, but two Men of the Family, standing shoulder to shoulder, and bearing our common responsibilities. Just as our earlier sense of comradeship is attached for me to the sense of us walking home along the Leedsville road, after a hunt, with my arm around his shoulder, singing." And the next year, when Geddes turned fourteen, he started to read Melville, "and he went through, not merely *Typee* and *Omoo*, but *Moby-Dick*, too."[23] His interest even led him to Lewis's Melville biography—the only one of his father's books that he ever read.[24]

Mumford did not suppress his disappointment at Geddes's recalcitrance in the classroom, and at the drinking habit he developed during his troubled high school years. Lewis could not understand why his son was unable to work in any disciplined way, why he resented all routines, even at the two progressive boarding schools he attended in Vermont, especially given the rugged scenery and the freedom he had from parental authority. "Like Bartleby in Melville's story, he looked around him and said: 'I know where I am.'" Of course, Bartleby is simultaneously perverse and heroic, and Lewis simultaneously decried and admired his son's instinct for resistance: "a few Geddeses would be a guarantee against fascist dictatorship in any country."[25]

In his rebelliousness and his wildness, Lewis thought, "Geddes was renewing the spirit Thoreau had brought to the American landscape."[26] And, most important, as he grew older, he gradually learned to channel that spirit. He seemed fully engaged with his studies when he took some courses at San Jose State in the spring of 1943, having completed his high school degree in December. He even expressed interest in becoming a field biologist. Then, as Lewis attested early in 1944, over the course of his military training, Geddes "achieved a degree of self-control, personal direction, and integration that I would regard as admirable at any age level."[27] Just after hearing of Geddes's death, Lewis told Henry Murray that his final impression of his son had been surprisingly solid: "the Ishmael and the Ahab in him, that had once seemed to promise only ultimate defeat, if not doom, had been mastered by an angel of light: approaching life from the dark end, from the moment of his birth when he refused food, he at last had come to the end of the tunnel and had found sunlight, too."[28] Indeed, by the time Lewis was writing *Green Memories*, he no longer thought of Geddes as comparable to a Melville character but rather to Melville himself, who also took a fair amount of time to reach maturity: "From the combination of inward brooding and outward action, which was so deep in the grain of his life, an imaginative writer might have been born: that was not the least of his resemblances to Herman Melville, the Melville, who after a season of rough adventuring awoke at twenty-five to discover that he had a mind."[29]

Murray had actually advised Mumford not to write *Green Memories*, or at least not to publish it. He worried that Lewis might err too far on the side of Melvillean realism, might come across as overly harsh in the way he treated Geddes's failings. "I believe in the Rousseau model—expose yourself," he wrote to Lewis; "and even, if necessary, in the *Pierre* model—expose your parents—but not in the Expose your Child idea."[30]

That rebuke stung Mumford, but the two men had been friends for almost two decades, since discovering a shared interest in Melville (Murray reviewed Mumford's biography very favorably), and they would weather this gale just as they had their disagreement over the stridency of Lewis's antifascism.[31] In fact, Murray's concern meshed with Sophia's, and Lewis wound up taking it quite seriously. He tried to tell the truth, but he also tried to withhold judgment: "what a father writes about his son must needs be fragmentary, hesitant, and partial." His brand of Melvilleanism, in this book, would simply emphasize "the complexities and contradictions that inhere in such a record."[32]

Mumford did expose some of his own mistakes, including a potentially fatal one. Toward the end of August 1944, Lewis sent a letter to Italy with news of the death of Geddes's childhood friend, John Duffy—"news that we conveyed to him, not without misgivings and debate, for we did not want to add to his burdens by giving him our own grief to share, yet we felt that for the grown man he had become, one who was going through the ordeal of facing death almost daily, it would be a betrayal to withhold something that so deeply concerned him." Realism won out. But "many times since then we have gone over that decision and wondered whether, roundaboutly, it had lowered his vitality and so made him less cautious and alert than he might have been at the last fatal moment." Geddes responded to John's death with a lonely and inexpressible grief, in the very last letter his parents received from him, just days before he himself was killed. "I feel as if I had lost a brother," he wrote. "What more there is in my mind can only be felt, not said or written. There are no words. . . . There's nothing more that I can say."[33]

Lewis thought back to that last letter months later, when the army sent a packet of all the "relics found on Geddes's body," including a photograph that Lewis had taken during Geddes's last furlough, at Stanford. Why, Lewis wondered, had Geddes chosen to carry this particular image with him? It was different from virtually every other picture they had of Geddes: it showed not "the tough, kindly, humorous soldier," nor the "gay, laughing Geddes." Rather, he appeared with "his brows knotted and his face tense: if it expresses any emotion, it expresses anxiety, perhaps even fear. In that choice, Geddes did not flatter himself; but unless I misread him, he revealed the ultimate dread we all tried to suppress, he most manfully of all."[34]

In the end, Mumford took some solace in the complex memorial he had created to honor Geddes's life. "Certainly," he wrote to Murray, "the book is a far better one than I could have produced without the dialectic struggle that ensued with you and with Sophy." But he knew that Sophy had found the whole process less than cathartic, and he was so exhausted that he wondered if he might be approaching another Cape Horn in his life: "*Green Memories* may have taken more out of me than I had supposed."[35]

Back in June 1944, in Amenia, the two of them had drawn closer in their shared concern for Geddes's safety. One day, in a glade surrounded by birch trees, they experienced what Lewis described as one of their "most perfect unions . . . , not less so because the hard unyielding ground gives a sharpness to one's movements. . . . The rays of our delight penetrated every corner of our selves, cleansing, sweetening, purifying, perfuming our whole being; the relaxation appeared on our faces in a smile that did not vanish in the hours that followed. We have had such hours together before; but during the last few years they have been too infrequent. But now they had come back again, as real as the best moments of our youth, as youthful as the highest moments of love's reality."[36] After Geddes's death, though, and especially after *Green Memories* came out, they found middle age to be mostly bitter and bewildering. "In the act of writing the book," Lewis told Murray, "matters that had been 'settled' and buried for years rose again to the surface of our lives, and the deep temperamental differences between us, too, became actively separatist."[37]

Over the next few years, Lewis would try repeatedly to start work on volume 4 of *The Renewal of Life*. But he felt heartbroken, and alone. He wrote throughout the summer of 1947, just after he sent the corrected proofs of *Green Memories* to the publisher, but not a single page seemed "usable."[38] Memories of Geddes haunted him, virtually every hour of every day.[39] Though the war was long over, he saw few prospects for renewal at either the personal or the civilizational level.

That November, Lewis had to give a lecture on Melville at Dartmouth College, in Hanover, New Hampshire, where he and Sophia and Alison had started spending the school years after Geddes's death, so as to feel more connected to a community without having to give up country living. The lecture was going to focus on *Pierre*, but when Mumford tried to reread the novel, as he explained to Henry Murray, he "found it unbearable and finally desisted." One can sometimes overdose on reality and the tragic sense of life. Yet Mumford found other texts for his lecture; he was "full of caustic Melvillian contempt," that fall, "but not Melvillian despair." At the dawn of the atomic age, he felt that the world "now looks as black and ashen as Melville's own interior in his worst years," but Melville had more than enough good years to offset the bitterness of a book like *Pierre*. "There is much about Melville I still want to discuss with you," he told Murray, and there always would be.[40]

CHAPTER 28

The Warmth and Chill of Wedded Life and Death (1876–91)

Two weeks after America's Centennial, on July 18, 1876, a disappointed reviewer for the Springfield *Republican* advised readers to go back to Melville's novels instead of picking up *Clarel*: "Herman Melville's literary reputation will remain, what it has fairly become, a thing of the past."[1] The *Republican*, based in western Massachusetts, had previously treated Melville as a local celebrity, so this must have been a bruising blow. Other jabs and gibes, often more mean-spirited, would follow: "We have to note the unusual phenomenon of a poem in two volumes— *Clarel*, a versified account of a pilgrimage in Palestine, not remarkable either for elevation of sentiment or for poetic excellence."[2]

By February of the following year, Lizzie was worrying that Herman had gotten even more "*morbidly* sensitive," that he might be reliving the trauma of the reviews he'd received for *Mardi*—and *Moby-Dick*—and *Pierre*—and *The Confidence-Man*.[3] Yet at the end of March he wrote a remarkable letter to his brother-in-law in which he seemed almost dismissive of his own pain. His only priority now, he claimed, was "good-fellowship." He had found himself more and more attracted to "nepenthe"—the magical drug that Helen of Troy added to her wine in *The Odyssey* to quiet her sorrow and help her forget her grief. If Melville's reputation was a mere memory, so be it, for his ambition, his restless desire for recognition, his absolute commitment to reality, were also things of the past. "You are young," he wrote; "but I am verging upon three-score, and at times a certain lassitude steals over one—in fact, a disinclination for doing anything except the indispensable. At such moments the problem of the universe seems a humbug. . . . At my years, and with my disposition, or rather, constitution, one gets to care less and less for everything except downright good feeling. Life is so short, and so ridiculous and irrational (from a certain point of view) that one knows not what to make of it, unless—well, finish the sentence for yourself."[4]

What remained indispensable to Melville was the writing of poetry—for a limited audience of family and friends, and for himself. With regard to commercial publishing, he now adopted Ahab's defiant attitude toward the selling of whale oil: "Nantucket market! Hoot!"[5] Melville would chase his whales, and enjoy those boon companions who happened to share his love of the chase. So, for instance, with the letter he wrote to his brother-in-law, he enclosed a poem. "What the deuce the thing means," he said, "I don't know; but here it is."[6]

It was called "The Age of the Antonines," referring to the period of peace and prosperity (the years 98 to 180 C.E.) that Edward Gibbon identified as immediately preceding the decline and fall of the Roman Empire: "While hope awaits Millenial years, / Though dim of late the signs, / Back to the past a glance be cast—/ The Age of the Antonines!" Seemingly relieved of doubt, and eager to express his scorn for the demagoguery and denialism of the present, Melville became unabashedly nostalgic: "We sham, we shuffle, while faith declines: / They were *frank* in the age of the Antonines!" The Roman Empire had reached its pinnacle in a time "ere the sting was dreamed to be taken from death," when people were willing to face the world's tragedies and their own flaws, when they cared about more than being "blatantly free."[7] Alas, Melville's golden years were playing out in the Gilded Age, the ultimate era of avoidance and superficiality, when Americans trained themselves to look away from corruption in government and corporations and to enjoy whatever gaudy distractions they were offered. Gibbon had argued that the Antonine rulers, who included such luminaries as Marcus Aurelius, wielded "absolute power," but for a few generations, at least, they governed "under the guidance of virtue and wisdom" and "were pleased with considering themselves as the accountable ministers of the laws."[8]

Earlier in life, Melville might have been skeptical of such a characterization, but now he embraced the opportunity to find solace and hope in history. "Ah," he wrote, "might we read in the Future's signs, / The Past revived in the Antonines!"[9] Though the signs weren't promising—Rutherford B. Hayes had just been inaugurated as president, and he was no Marcus Aurelius[10]—Melville remembered Lincoln and allowed himself to imagine that America could in fact produce thoughtful, fair-minded leaders.

Eventually, he did publish "The Age of the Antonines," in a collection he called *Timoleon, Etc.*, which came out in May 1891, a few months before his death, in an edition of just twenty-five copies. He had used the same approach in 1888 for a volume called *John Marr and Other Sailors: With Some Sea-Pieces*, and though Melville thought of these as more or less private printings, one of the twenty-five copies of *John Marr* fell into the hands of someone who arranged to review it for the New York *Mail and Express*.[11] And even after he published *Timoleon*, he kept writing: before he died, he had selected a number of additional poems for a collection with the title *Weeds and Wildings Chiefly: With a Rose or Two*—though it didn't appear until 1924, once the Melville Revival was under way. What Raymond Weaver called "The Long Quietus" was actually, as Mumford insisted, a period of steady work. But it's also true that the work was quieter.

It was a quiet time of life. "The days pass," Mumford wrote of these years, "and one day is like another: there is comfort in monotony." Melville traveled to his office at the custom house on foot, by horse car, and, later, by the new elevated train above Third Avenue. In the evening he usually escaped to his study, and there, Mumford imagined, "with his pictures, his books, his glass of brandy to seduce sleep, the day ends in a solitude and a hush—tolerably." There may even have been moments of easy affection with Lizzie, and Mumford had solid evidence with which to picture Herman as a quirkily doting grandfather to Fanny's two daughters: "he bounces them on his knee, makes noises like wind whistling through the rigging, sings a stave of an old chanty, walks with them in Central Park."[12] Fanny's older child, Eleanor, noted that

FIGURE 14. Herman in 1885 or 1886.

Melville enjoyed growing roses in his backyard garden, and she recalled his intimate jokes and nicknames, and the sweet, sticky figs he saved for her as treats, and his "thick . . . , tight curled . . . , firm and wiry" beard, which he allowed her to pull and squeeze.[13]

Both Eleanor and her sister, Frances, acknowledged that their mother had been slightly afraid of her father, for in her own childhood she had witnessed "his moods and occasional uncertain tempers," his "impatience, and even anger."[14] When Mumford interviewed Fanny (she was in her early seventies by then), they had a "pleasant, genteel" conversation, but he had to swear in advance not to mention Melville's name while they were talking.[15] It was Eleanor, though, who now possessed Melville's private papers, including his journals, and she invited Mumford to her home on Martha's Vineyard to spend several days reading through the manuscripts and chatting. Eleanor confirmed in person what she had written out for Raymond Weaver in 1921, and her sister would later say much the same thing in her own memoir: Grandpa, as they called him, seemed playful, dreamy, calm, and kind. "He made a brave and striking figure," Eleanor wrote, "as he walked erect, head thrown back, cane in hand, inconspicuously dressed in a dark blue suit and a soft felt hat."[16] The younger Frances found her grandfather somewhat "mysterious," but she had vivid memories of the "great delight" on his face when he took her to ride the swan boats or to see the lifelike wax figures at a small museum on Fourteenth Street.[17] Though it was true that he was distracted enough to lose her once during an excursion to Central Park, she didn't hold that against him. "He is benign even when his thoughts are elsewhere," Mumford concluded, "and occasionally downright jolly."[18]

Lizzie, of course, knew that Herman would never quite escape his demons. Throughout the 1870s, despite his diligent work inspecting unloaded cargo and making sure all the appropriate fees and duties were paid, the family was still impoverished; he still sometimes felt like a failure and an exile. And he had no job security: "Of course there have been removals," Lizzie wrote to a relative, "and he may be removed any day, for which I should be very sorry as apart from everything else the *occupation* is a great thing for him—and he could not take any other post that required head work, and sitting at a desk."[19] Though everyone in his circle commented on his remarkably upright posture, his eyes continued to fail, and he had pain in his hands, and his heart was weak. He still paced heavily, in seeming frustration, behind the locked door of his study. By the 1880s, as Lizzie noted, he often found his job "too onerous for a man of his years, and at times of exhaustion, both mental and physical, he has been on the point of giving it up, but recovering a little, has held on, very naturally anxious to do so, for many reasons."[20] Gradually, though, he had been inheriting bits of money, and when Lizzie's half brother Lemuel Shaw Jr. died in 1884, she received enough to make them both feel truly comfortable for the first time. In December 1885, at the age of sixty-six, Herman resigned from the custom house.

Now he was free to wander into bookstores and curio shops, and he seems to have found great joy in purchasing the latest volumes and collecting prints of whaling ships. His granddaughter Frances remembered his study being lined with "books, books, books," but there were also shelves and mantels where he had stashed "pictures, statuary, vases, or ornaments which pleased him."[21] One bookseller's apprentice later recalled being a frequent "bearer of bundles of books to the Melville house," and he testified that "when the author was at home I was certain to receive a modest but welcome tip." To this young man, Melville came across as consistently amiable: "I particularly recall his gentleness of manner and his pleasant smile. I never found him to be the misanthrope that many authorities accuse him of having been; it is difficult for me to believe that he was a disappointed man—if he was he did not permit his disappointment to come out into the open."[22]

The disappointment and grief did sometimes come into his poems, though: they were not all works of rosy retrospection. He was not addicted to nepenthe. His late works feature images of tempests and drifting shipwrecks and abandoned graves. In *Clarel*, a knowing reader might have perceived Melville's effort to work through the trauma of Malcolm's death; in *John Marr*, Melville is newly but familiarly haunted by the loss of his second son, Stanwix, who died at age thirty-five, under uncertain circumstances, in the German Hospital of San Francisco. The news came just two months after Melville retired. Two years later, *John Marr* appeared, and on its first page the title character builds a coffin, and buries his wife and child, and then ponders the small earthen mound he has made on the seemingly endless prairie.

"John Marr," like several of Melville's other late poems, is preceded by a headnote in prose (the headnote for the poem "Billy in the Darbies" eventually became the novella *Billy Budd*). In this case, Melville immediately sets up an inner tension that seems to reflect his own experience of old age: "While the acuter sense of his bereavement becomes mollified by time, the void at heart abides." A former sailor, John is now stranded inland, bereft, "kinless," but he has developed an "honest stillness"; he wants to stay near the fresh grave and tend to it.

In his loneliness, he turns to memories of his former shipmates: "one cannot always be talking about the present, much less speculating about the future; one must needs recur to the past, which, with the mass of men, where the past is in any personal way a common inheritance, supplies to most practical natures the basis of sympathetic communion." Especially in a nation of confirmed isolatoes and speculators, there will be no Union without a communal dedication to interrogating history. The actual poem at least suggests that John is still able to feel a sailor's sense of solidarity: "Nor less, as now, in eve's decline / Your shadowy fellowship is mine." But he can't share it with the chastened prairie pioneers who actually surround him. He finds them lacking not only "sympathy" but also "geniality, the flower of life springing from some sense of joy in it"—and he starts to resent them. He wishes he lived closer to "the remnant of Indians thereabout—all but exterminated in their recent and final war with regular white troops, a war waged by the Red Men for their native soil and natural rights." Hoping merely for a little comfort in his retrospection, he finds himself analyzing the metaphysics of nineteenth-century American history, regretting the "unintermitting advance of the frontier," condemning each "successive overleaped limit of civilized life," aghast at all these "places overpopulous with towns overopulent . . . , now everywhere intersected with wire and rail." Ultimately, he falls back on his ghosts, though his relationship with them is ever in flux: "He invokes these visionary ones,—striving, as it were, to get into verbal communion with them, or, under yet stronger illusion, reproaching them for their silence."[23]

Toward the end of *John Marr*, perhaps thinking back to his Battle-Pieces, Melville included two shipwreck poems that he labeled as "Sea-Pieces." Even while attempting to rediscover the good fellowship of his maritime companions, he recalled that their commonality was often forged in the face of the ocean's terrors. "The Haglets" tells of the aftermath of a sea battle, when the victorious crew of a man-of-war dip their beards in casks of wine and dream of carrying treasure home to their wives and sweethearts—only to lose their way and founder in a storm. Nature, for a time, had seemed so keen to support their cause, and they had felt so relieved at the outcome of the fight, that they chose to ignore the strange quivering of the compass needle and the portentous birds of the poem's title, which flew unrelentingly behind their ship after having wheeled and screamed overhead while the enemy frigate sank. "But who a flattering tide may trust, / Or favouring breeze, or aught in end?" The wind turned, the tempest rose, and the sailors did not see the warning of the lighthouse until the moment before they struck land. Now there is only a "decayed and coral-mossed" stone marker on the shore, which Melville envisions on a night when meteor showers light up the breaking waves: "And up from ocean stream, / And down from heaven far, / The rays that blend in dream / The abysm and the star."[24]

The second Sea-Piece, "The Aeolian Harp," just reinforces the bittersweet riskiness of revisiting memories. There is a harp on the windowsill of a coastal inn, "stirred by fitful gales from the sea," and it, in turn, stirs Melville: "Listen: less a strain ideal / Than Ariel's rendering of the Real. / What the Real is, let hint / A picture stamped in memory's mint." The lookout on a yardarm calls out, "Wreck ho, a wreck!" But the old brig hasn't sunk. Melville remembers staring out in awe at the "waterlogged" and "forsaken" ship, overgrown with weeds, "overwashed with every wave," silent and dark, rotten, yet still solid enough to do harm. We all have these wrecks, and we can't predict when they'll surprise us: "From collision never shrinking, / Drive what may through darksome smother; / Saturate, but never sinking, / Fatal only to the *other!* / Deadlier than the sunken reef / Since still the snare it shifteth, / Torpid in dumb ambuscade / Waylayingly it drifteth."[25] The wind blows across some strings; you walk past a sand pit; you read a familiar verse; you approach the shore and suddenly smell the sea. Sometimes you keep walking; sometimes your limbs seize up, and the waves of memory crash over you, and you are saturated.

John Marr ends with a sequence of seven short poems called "Pebbles." In relation to the all-encompassing sea, the poems suggest, we will always feel small and fragmentary and tossed about—but perhaps, eventually, we may wind up smooth and rounded. "Healed of my hurt," says the surprising first line of the final poem, "I laud the inhuman Sea." The firm reality, the undeniable otherness of the non-human world, is perhaps what gives meaning to humanness. The sea is "pitiless," but also "wholesome."[26] When your memories are overwhelming you, it might be bracing to immerse yourself in actual surf.

Many of Melville's late poems are remarkable for their thematic balance of constraint and compensatory pleasure, and their meter is less broken, more musical. They acknowledge an old man's inability to go back to the ocean and see new shores—but in *Timoleon* Melville included several poems under the heading "Fruit of Travel Long Ago," many of which suggest that he carried both the ocean and the desert within him, for the poems hark back to the healing he experienced on his Mediterranean voyage of 1856–57, when he relished the elegance and power of Egyptian, Greek, and Italian architecture, when he gazed for hours at "The Attic Landscape": "'Tis Art and Nature lodged together, / Sister by sister, cheek to cheek; / Such Art, Such Nature, and such weather, / The All-in-All seems here a Greek." And these memories helped deepen his ongoing exploration of what it means to be an artist—to give form to fleeting, ethereal thoughts and feelings, to dwell with the contradiction of wanting both to be immersed in life and to ponder it:[27]

> In placid hours well pleased we dream
> Of many a brave unbodied scheme.
> But form to lend, pulsed life create,
> What unlike things must meet and mate:
> A flame to melt—a wind to freeze;
> Sad patience; joyous energies;
> Humility—yet pride and scorn;
> Instinct and study; love and hate;
> Audacity—reverence. These must mate
> And fuse with Jacob's mystic heart,
> To wrestle with the angel—Art.

Melville no longer wrote passionate letters to fellow artists, nor sought out friends for long evenings of drink and ontological heroics. He declined the invitations of various clubs and literary societies, even those that met just a couple of blocks away from his house, at Delmonico's, where Mumford's German grandfather was working as a waiter.

But he graciously welcomed anyone who came to visit, and he used Delmonico's as the setting for a series of poems called "At the Hostelry," in which he gathered several long-dead Italian artists for a debate about the Picturesque—whose fundamental characteristic is the juxtaposition of seeming opposites, resulting in scenes that are both "furious and serene."[28]

Though he often stayed absorbed in his own memories, he also read more and more widely, turning especially to the so-called Systematic Pessimists, people like James Thomson and Arthur Schopenhauer, who somehow found a charm in "the philosophy of disenchantment," who had learned from Buddhism to find peace in loss, who turned away from striving and simply accepted life in "the city of dreadful night."[29] Melville's younger granddaughter, Frances, also seemed to enjoy these writers, sometimes piling their books into architectural structures on the study floor: "A set of Schopenhauer pleased me most—they were not too heavy to handle and of a nice palish blue color."[30] Of course, Melville enjoyed them more for their realism. To a correspondent who was sending him Thomson's best-known works in the mid-1880s, Melville asserted that he himself was "neither pessimist nor optimist," but he particularly liked reading Pessimism "as a counterpoise to the exorbitant hopefulness, juvenile and shallow, that makes such a bluster in these days—at least, in some quarters."[31]

It would be fairly easy to make the case that Melville was predominantly a Pessimist throughout most of his career. Toward the end of it, though, perhaps more than ever before, he also revealed some powerful Romantic tendencies. While his daily life was circumscribed in the dark city, his imagination often wandered back to the bright meadows of the Berkshires, and *Weeds and Wildings* consistently celebrates his earnest affection for Nature. It is full of simple testaments to the beauty of underappreciated plants, from clover and dandelions and buttercups and goldenrod to the rarely flowering American Aloe. And its dedication is a long tribute to Lizzie and to their forty-four years of marriage, recalling a "specimen" of four-leafed clover that Herman discovered "by the wayside on the early forenoon of the fourth day of a certain bridal month, now four years more than four times ten years ago." He felt he had been lucky, through all their shared tragedy, through their poverty, through his failures and rages. And he had been lucky to continue writing into his old age, even without recognition or appreciation. If he did not have any blossoms to show for the second half of his career, then, as with the American Aloe, perhaps it was "owing to something retarding in the environment or soil." He begged her to receive these poems in the same spirit she had shown when accepting a bunch of red clover he had picked one October in the Berkshires, after an early snow: "the genial warmth of your chamber melted the fleecy flakes into dewdrops rolling off from the ruddiness. 'Tears of the happy,' you said."[32]

Mumford was touched by the dedication of *Weeds and Wildings*; it suggested a kind of redemption in the Melvilles' marriage. Life, Melville knew, was waning: he acknowledged that these sweet, fanciful poems bore "indications, too apparent it may be, of that terminating season on which the offerer verges."[33] And in contemplating death, Mumford thought, Melville had rediscovered love—"love, which has its philosophic equivalent in the desire to merge oneself with the universe and surrender to it."[34]

Melville's acceptance of mortality comes across especially powerfully in one of the last poems he worked on, called "Pontoosuce," or "The Lake," which Mumford thought was "perhaps the finest Melville wrote." The verses show him gradually confronting "death and emptiness of being, and he draws his faith from that spectacle in which the great religions have found their sustenance, in the march of the seasons, the rhythmic cycle of life, the ecstasy, the agony, the tragedy of the dying god, and his annual resurrection and renewal."[35] It is a perfect Berkshire scene, just northwest of Arrowhead. Melville stands on a forested bluff over the clear, blue lake, with its Indian name, with fields and orchards and mountains and barns in the background. Bathed in "Autumnal noontide, I look out / From dusk arcades on sunshine all about." But then the chastening thought comes to him: "All dies! and not alone / The aspiring trees and men and grass; / The poet's forms of beauty pass, / And noblest deeds they are undone, / Even truth itself decays, and lo, / From truth's sad ashes pain and falsehood grow." He is coming undone with grief, when suddenly the spirit of the lake appears: a woman, wearing a strange wreath of pine sprigs and moss and fresh, crumbly soil. She sings; and he is released:[36]

> "Dies, all dies!
> The grass it dies, but in vernal rain
> Up it springs, and it lives again;
> Over and over, again and again,
> It lives, it dies, and it lives again,
> Who sighs that all dies?
> Summer and winter, and pleasure and pain,
> And everything everywhere in God's reign.
> They end, and anon they begin again:
> Wane and wax, wax and wane:
> Over and over and over again,
> End, ever end, and begin again—
> End, ever end, and forever and ever begin again!"
> She ceased, and nearer slid, and hung
> In dewy guise; then softlier sung:
> "Since light and shade are equal set,
> And all revolves, nor more ye know;
> Ah, why should tears the pale cheek fret
> For aught that waneth here below.
> Let go, let go!"
> With that, her warm lips thrilled me through,
> She kissed me, while her chaplet cold
> Its rootlets brushed against my brow,
> With all their humid clinging mould.
> She vanished, leaving fragrant breath
> And warmth and chill of wedded life and death.

CHAPTER 29

Chronometricals and Horologicals (1944–51)

The chill of wedded life is such that sometimes spouses need years to rediscover each other. It wasn't just their disagreements over *Green Memories* that drove Lewis and Sophia apart; within a couple of months of Geddes's death, Lewis already suspected that the shadow of grief would dim the light of love for a long time to come. It was somewhat strange—especially considering what he and Sophia had navigated in the past: "even during the bitterest period of turmoil or estrangement, from 1930 to 1938, we were buoyed up by a lively faith in each other, and an intense enjoyment of the good moments and days we shared." Or maybe it wasn't so strange, since, even if Sophia might have agreed that there had been plenty of passion in the 1930s, she never stopped feeling the scars of Lewis's emotional betrayals. In any case, as of December 1944, their relationship seemed "bleak and meager." Yes, they had come together blissfully during the summer, in a mutual expression of anxiety about Geddes. But their shared loss didn't create the same sense of commonality.[1]

Occasionally, Lewis found some comfort in Nature, especially the following summer, during his rambles through the fields and forests around Amenia: "There has never been such a year for wild bergamot," he wrote; "indeed, all the weeds and wildings have been doing magnificently."[2]

But the next few years were dominated by mourning, haunting, isolation, and a general sense of ineffectual struggle. It would be a long trip around the Horn. Not until he had been through "the actual experience of grief" did he "understand how it drives sexual energies back into the unconscious, as the coming of winter drives the sap down to the roots of a tree."[3] Looking back much later, he referred to the period between 1945 and 1949 as one of "low vitality and poor productivity." And then he found himself with a prostate condition that gave him a constant feeling of "mental heaviness" for several more years. He and Sophia did not manage to renew the vibrancy of their marriage until the mid-1950s.[4]

Meanwhile, Lewis dreamed of his son. The phone rings, and Sophia calls from the other room: "It's Geddes. He wants to speak with you." Then Geddes is in a river, during the war, swimming easily and gracefully, pulling a boat next to him as he does the backstroke; he ties it fast to a landing place, so his fellow scouts will be able to make a quick getaway. Somehow, Lewis is watching from the bank, and as Geddes climbs out of the water they find each other and embrace, and Lewis whispers: "Darling: you don't know how much I *admire* you." But then Geddes dives back into the river, and as soon as he comes up for air, he is hit by a sniper.[5]

Early in 1948, Mumford wrote that "there is scarcely an hour of the day when the image of Geddes does not pass through the mind, or become the object of thoughts, affectionate or regretful, proud or bitterly self-reproachful." The dreams had become less frequent by then, but at the end of January he received a visit from Geddes that lasted the entire night. "He had come back," Mumford wrote, "maturer than ever, but gay and outgoing in every fashion: the report of his death had been false." For someone like Mumford, this was especially befuddling, because he had already published *Green Memories*; would he now have to write a new afterword? Thankfully, his authorial angst dissipated quickly, allowing him to express his "tender and overwhelming love." And Geddes "reciprocated it with the same degree of feeling. We planned a climb together; we spent a day or more in each other's company; and it was such an overwhelming relief to have him back with us once more!" Mumford wallowed in "the reality of it, the intensity of it"—especially "the indications of further growth, maturity, acceptance of life" that he saw in this spectral version of his son. He was deeply grateful for the renewed connection, for the gift of presence. But then this "blessing" was suddenly "snatched away, and I still feel bereft, almost as bereft as if he had really come back home and then gone off again into the zone of danger."[6]

A couple of months later, Lewis and Sophia had an actual visit from a young man named Colin Raubeson and his wife: "They are the couple to whom we have pledged Geddes's insurance till he gets through college."[7] Almost immediately after Geddes was killed, Lewis and Sophia had agreed that they would donate any federal life-insurance payments to "other young people, who had some of Geddes's promise, so that they might have the opportunities for development and for service that in his own case were prematurely cut short."[8] It seemed the best way to honor their son, who had written such compelling letters home about the selfless generosity of his fellow soldiers, and who had worried so earnestly about whether veterans would be able to adapt to civilian life. Now Lewis and Sophia took solace in supporting Colin's education with $45 a month, and in getting to see firsthand how much wisdom returning soldiers had to offer when they were lucky enough to come home to sustaining relationships.

A sense of comradeship with the men of Geddes's generation was in fact the best thing to arise from the publication of Green Memories, Lewis felt. The book received only a few "half-hearted notices," and its sales were terrible; Mumford thought it had been as badly neglected as Clarel, in part because it came out at precisely the same time as Death Be Not Proud, by the journalist John Gunther—another remarkable memoir about the death of a son, which became a best seller, perhaps because it dealt with the much less political subject of cancer.[9] In any case, Mumford wrote, the "sting" of his book's poor reception was at least partially offset by "the letters it has elicited, particularly from the young, who feel that it is their book and has said something for their generation, in particular has recorded the withheld grief of men in combat, who lost their buddies and who, when they came back, found no one to understand their feelings."[10] And, bizarrely, Mumford received four offers from Hollywood to turn Geddes's life story into a film. "Though we gave a flat 'No' to all of them," he explained to a friend,

"Hollywood being what it is, I was happy to realize that there was enough of the generic and the common in the story, which seemed to me so very special and private as I told it, to tempt the movies to make a bid for the book solely on its merits, and not because it had attracted public attention or sold well."[11]

Green Memories had been a challenge to write, but Mumford had relished the experience, for the book was "of a more imaginative and 'literary' nature" than anything else he had ever published, and he had always fancied himself as much an artist as a scholar. In the mid-1950s, he would enjoy taking up this mode again in the autobiographical essays that would eventually become *Sketches from Life*. Meanwhile, though, he found himself wondering whether a serious intellectual could expect to wield any influence at all in a fast-paced, entertainment-crazed, mass society, regardless of which genre he might choose for his work: "I might as well write lyric poetry, if I knew how, for all the effect my writings actually have."[12] Perhaps he would become as obscure as Melville.

Despite fleeting moments of renewal, the years after Geddes's death felt more and more like a time of fading success for Lewis, in both his professional and his personal life. He could not get any purchase on the follow-up to *The Condition of Man*, and he felt as isolated in the work he did in opposition to nuclear testing as he had in his early antifascist activism. "Another failure," he wrote, in reference to his futile efforts to "arouse reaction against exploitation of [the] atom bomb," which made the cool reception of *Green Memories* feel like even more of a defeat. Indeed, though Mumford railed against the atomic age with his usual earnestness, he now harbored "the corrosive belief that a civilization so far in decay as ours" might not even be capable of confronting its moral backsliding.[13]

Mumford's faith in the resilience of his family had also been eroded, in part because he had reached that overwhelming age at which one sometimes has to take responsibility for both the younger and the older generation. His mother's moderate health concerns had gradually devolved into the "private nightmare" of severe dementia.[14] Elvina Mumford had been spending summers with the family at Amenia in the mid-1940s, but by the fall of 1946 she had become so incoherent and unpredictable that Lewis decided she needed professional care in a nursing home. It was a wrenching move for everyone. As I know from having tried to care for two parents with Alzheimer's disease, there is great potential for trauma when basic identities and expectations are compromised. Sometimes your presence and assistance are welcome; sometimes not. You always wonder if there's some other approach you could take, if there's some surer way of conveying your love and caring; you always know that you're not doing enough. Lewis found a small, family-run facility in Hanover, New Hampshire, where his mother seemed relatively comfortable. But he was still committed to living in Amenia during the summers, and in the fall of 1948 the family moved to New York City, so that Alison, like Geddes, could taste the opportunities afforded by a larger high school. Though Lewis visited his mother fairly regularly, or at least occasionally, he wasn't certain that she wanted to go on living or that his efforts made any difference. "Geddes's premature death," he wrote, on New Year's Day, 1949, and "my mother's belated death," which would not arrive for almost two more years, "each weigh upon me in different fashion, bringing to the surface my own weaknesses and inadequacies as father, son, husband. And in a sense that load will never be lifted."[15]

Mumford's private writings through these years dwell, in particular, on his perceived failings as a father. He excoriated himself for not visiting Geddes more often when he was struggling at boarding school in Vermont. And he worried that, in his grief, he was neglecting Alison, hoping lamely that Sophia would compensate for his self-absorption. In truth, he still paid close attention to his daughter, taking her on long walks and commenting on her reading, her engagement with politics, her memories, her friendships. When she turned sixteen he wrote a poem for her, just as he had done for Geddes. But Lewis would always remember her fifteenth birthday, when he had promised to take her to Boston but never made the time. Until a couple of weeks before they found out Geddes had been killed, Lewis was still telling Alison a long series of stories about a family of cats—stories full of "harmless mischief" and "carefree fantasy." Each time he finished a tale, he noted, Alison would ease herself back "with a glow of gratitude in her eyes—'Oh! You are such a wonderful Daddy.' No storyteller ever had a fuller reward." But it proved almost impossible for Lewis to recapture that mood of innocence with his daughter.[16]

Instead, even though Alison was only nine and a half when Geddes died, Lewis seemed to shift immediately toward a concern for her adulthood. Deprived of all his hopes for Geddes's future, he stopped noticing Alison's need for fun and affection and started envisioning the day when his daughter would be old enough to become his heir and literary executrix. A year after Geddes's death, he started writing strained letters to her—not to be read until someday far in the future—offering various explanations and instructions relating to financial matters, family history, and his private papers. What possessed him to suggest to her that she ought to be guided by Geddes's harsh criticism of consumer culture and perhaps give away his half of her inheritance? What possessed him to insist that, once he himself was gone, she ought to consider publishing his most personal writings and exposing his deepest secrets? There is a determined self-flagellation in these letters, and a heedlessness of the burden he was placing on his daughter. But there is also a noble desire to be utterly true to his ideal of applied realism. He wanted Alison to brace herself, and then to pay special attention to his "Personalia," the notes that he wrote "in the darkest crises or the ugliest confusions of my life. These items tell much about my marriage, much about my own difficulties and weaknesses, much about my relations with other women than Sophia. . . . My own sense of reality, in the world crisis through which we are moving, was sharpened by my own experience of sin and suffering, by the realization that I, thinking myself virtuous and well-balanced, had committed sins as dark as those of one of Dostoyevsky's heroes. Knowing myself, I better understood the weaknesses of the world I was living in; had I sinned less, had I suffered less, had I lacked the courage to face these painful facts, I would have been less capable of repentance and radical renewal."[17]

We are not necessarily the best judges of our own capabilities, and many of us rationalize our failings, but what strikes me about Mumford during the 1940s is that he consistently chose Life, all of it, the sweet and the bitter, again and again, despite grief, despite guilt, despite a keen knowledge of his unfixable flaws.[18] Whether or not he actually repented or achieved radical renewal, he continued to move in those directions, insisting to himself that failing was better than not making the effort. At the end of 1947, thinking back to a psychiatric evaluation he had undergone earlier in the year, he captured the paradox of his emotional life during this period, his peculiar combination of despair and stubborn confidence: "The Rorschach disclosed deep pain and depression, almost to the suicidal point; but it also showed that I had exceptionally high creativity—though not fully 'used'—and remarkable balance between the emotional and the intellectual, the extrovert and the introvert, sides of my nature; so that I actually incarnated, as shown by the test scores, the ideal of balance I have held up in my work."[19] Maybe he would never again delight in fatherhood; maybe he would never again connect deeply with his daughter; maybe he wouldn't be able to stifle his egotism or prevent Sophia from sometimes resenting his inner balance; maybe he wouldn't be able to rediscover his basic faith in human decency. But he would try.[20]

Perhaps his most remarkable effort during these years was his lonely crusade to convince his countrymen that the atomic bomb marked a truly new epoch in human history—a stunning position for someone with such a powerful awareness of historical continuity—and that it therefore demanded a profound rethinking of both ethics and government. "Gentlemen," he wrote, in a 1946 magazine article meant to shock people out of their daze: "You Are Mad!" He was addressing every "general, admiral, senator, scientist, administrator"—but also all the rest of us moderate men and women who "keep our glassy calm" and "view the madness of our leaders as if it expressed mankind's traditional wisdom and common sense."[21] Earlier that year, in Hanover, Mumford had organized a group of less passive citizens to submit a petition to Congress and President Truman demanding an immediate halt to weapons development and a rigid inspection regime overseen by the recently created United Nations.[22] "The presence of this new source of energy," Mumford wrote, "makes every other form of military power, and every claim based on it, negligible. Nothing will be proof against a suicidal anxiety except an absolute submission to a universal standard of humane conduct: a morality built on new foundations to repair the world we have devastated during the last thirty years."[23] Yes, in a way, the dropping of the bomb just confirmed the moral collapse of the previous three decades and even the timeless human capacity for violence. But it also signaled the ease with which the entire world might now be destroyed, which in turn would require conscientious world governance, consistent civic engagement, and some sort of check against anguish and despondency.[24]

Mumford's own anguish, and his catastrophic imagination, drove him to pronouncements that were just as unpopular as his early calls for military intervention against fascism. As the Cold War got started, most scientists and politicians were pushing for the United States to redouble its efforts at nuclear weapons production so as to stay "ahead" of the Russians. Mumford wanted to know how they had simply accepted the murder of civilians and the unleashing of radiation in the world. Having acquired the power to annihilate all life, had they simply become nihilists? He worried that, as the arms race progressed, more and more of his fellow citizens would simply give up, "like Bartleby . . . , and have nothing further to do with life." And after the inevitable nuclear war, if there were any survivors, Mumford assumed that "the trauma left on the human psyche [would] be far worse than that from any previous fear or terror, even the melting of the icecaps."[25] Yes, polar melting is an old anxiety, dating to the late nineteenth century, when Euro-Americans became obsessed with the myth of Atlantis and the drowning of civilization. As prescient as he was, even Mumford could not have prophesied that this seemingly outdated paranoia would become our postmodern, late capitalist reality.[26]

In his writings against the bomb, Mumford seemed to be attacking his countrymen at a moment of victory—like Melville warning northerners not to gloat after winning the Civil War—and he wound up feeling utterly isolated. But his anti-nuclear position did not cost him as dearly as his antifascism. Even as he continued to rage, and to fear that he was becoming an irrelevant pariah, friends like Henry Murray were encouraging him to keep writing, and to find a more constructive way of framing his reactions to the atomic age. What forms might renewal take in an era of nihilism? He didn't really get rolling on the final installment of *The Renewal of Life* until 1949, but as early as the summer 1947 he had an epiphany about it: "volume four, I have come to believe, must be a positive, yea-saying, ideal-searching, directive book: it should discuss, not what is, but what may be and must be, in a fashion that none of the other volumes has yet done. Though the form will not be that of a utopia, the material itself must consist mainly of ideal forms and patterns: they must be centered on the ideal personality, the ideal community. There is no use telling people a thousand miles from land, clinging to a frail life raft, that the chances are against them: if they are ever to reach land, one must, after surveying the situation realistically, suppress every defeatist thought and rather concentrate their spiritual strength on their eventual triumph, picturing their rescue, the port they will reach, the things they will finally do and the food they will eat."[27]

The Conduct of Life (1951), whose title was taken from an 1860 collection of Emerson's essays, sought to encourage free thought and action at a moment of fear and constraint—at the start of a Red Scare that would turn out to be far more virulent and damaging than the one following the Great War. Already, in 1950, Mumford had written an "Open Letter to the American People," condemning the rise of McCarthyism, urging his fellow citizens "to cease regarding those who differ from them as if they were agents of a foreign power."[28] Like Emerson, Mumford celebrated intellectual independence and communal solidarity; in dark times, he upheld humility, sacrifice, self-appraisal, cross-fertilization, and mutual aid. "What people need now," he realized, "is not information, facts, or verified propositions: what they need is a new attitude, the product of hope, imagination, love, and desire."[29] And so *The Conduct of Life* is even less empirical, less grounded, than *The Condition of Man*. It poses ethical questions, offers spiritual counsel, and connects religion with ecology in a grand vision of interdependence and unity. It is a self-consciously middle-aged guide for the perplexed, dealing with issues Mumford felt he couldn't have handled back when his focus was on technology and urbanization. "By the time men reach middle age," he wrote, in a section of the book called "Eternity, Sex, and Death," "even the seemingly fortunate have some inkling" of things like "disintegra-tion" and "loss," "ills" and "evils."[30]

Now, at fifty-five, he was ready to argue that although the current threats to humanity were "more appalling than ever before, the reward for facing them and overcoming them promises also to be greater." Indeed, western society had been suffering from a long illness, but the experience of convalescence would be that much more exhilarating—even granting the truth that illness would inevitably take hold again later. Healing was not automatic, but it was always a possibility. "When the lethal contents of Pandora's box were released, the Gods, taking pity on man, left him with one gift that would enable him to survive every natural plague or human mischief: Hope."[31] As Emerson argued in the book Mumford used as a model, you can't deny Fate, or Nature, or the multifarious limitations on our lives—but you can face them, and offset them, through acts of vital, exuberant creation. "Let us build altars," Emerson wrote, "to the Beautiful Necessity."[32]

The atomic bomb created a rift in human history, but one could still draw on the wisdom of the past. Even the most drastic change could not negate continuity entirely.[33] To observers like Emerson and Melville, the conflicts of the 1850s seemed as world threatening as the conflicts of the 1940s would to Mumford, and they wrote books and essays and poems in order to anchor themselves, to gain some purchase on the passage of time, to establish connections to long traditions of resilience in the face of destruction. Now Mumford could look to these forebears for reminders that renewal begins with a belief in dynamic subjectivity, in the agency of "the individual human person; for it is he who precipitates change in the social order by first initiating a profound re-grouping of forces and ideal goals within himself."[34]

In 1947, Mumford was unable to reread *Pierre*, but by 1949 he had gone back to his favorite section of the novel, the pamphlet by the philosopher Plotinus Plinlimmon called "Chronometricals and Horologicals," which Pierre reads during his stagecoach ride from the Berkshires to New York City. And the lesson of that pamphlet found its way to the very heart of *The Conduct of Life*. It is both an ethical and a historical lesson, about the need to balance modern, absolute time with local, traditional, relative time. In Melville's day, as Mumford explained, scientific time was set by the Royal Observatory at Greenwich, "and every vessel setting out from London checks its ship's chronometer by Greenwich time" (a necessary practice if the crew wanted to be able to calculate its longitude during its voyage). "But by the time the ship reached, say, China, its captain would discover a startling discrepancy between his own accurate chronometer and the local clocks or sundials. If the captain tried to conduct the day's business by a schedule that kept to his own Greenwich time, he would be sleeping by daylight and making sociable calls when his Chinese neighbors were in bed." Such are the world's ambiguities, the messy realities of the dialectical relationship between continuity and change. "Our ideals," as Mumford observed, "however imperative and absolute, must nevertheless reckon with the fact that we live in the realm of the historically conditioned, subject to pressures and environmental limitations that cannot be entirely put aside. In other words, the moral ideal is a compass point, not a destination."[35] Yes, set your watch, and steer by the compass—but also trust the local timekeepers, and be prepared to adjust your course. There will always be moments when the impish needle starts to quiver and spin.

Mumford offered *The Conduct of Life* as a work of synthesis, a gathering-up and honing of what he considered to be his most important ideas about renewal. So his most devoted readers would have found many of the book's proposals to be familiar. In the three previous volumes of the series, and also in *Men Must Act* and *Faith for Living*, Mumford had gradually developed these clarion calls: for the honest acknowledgment of evil and the commitment to counter it; for the acceptance of mortality; for the communal resorption of government; for vigilant resistance to automatism; for spiritual awakening; for contrapuntal and polyphonic thinking; for the open embrace of otherness; for hybridity; for public service; for the welcoming of challenges; for ecology, and devotion to the land and all life; for pausing, in solitude, to meditate or daydream; for all the arts and sciences; for justice; for organic holism and unity; for softening, and empathy, and love.

In the specific American context, Mumford also demanded repentance, and perhaps even restitution, for "the historic errors made by our forebears in displacing the Indian and enslaving the Negro." Moving forward always entailed looking backward—always entailed a reckoning—and a recognition of the link between individual mindsets and the culture at large. Mumford wanted his society to be "entirely candid" with itself, "as unsparing as Melville's Pierre tried to be."[36]

If, as Mumford argued, *Typee* was Melville's *Walden*, then *The Conduct of Life* was Mumford's own Thoreauvian experiment, undertaken at a time when his grief had driven him into a kind of withdrawal, and he was moved to philosophize about what he lived for. "Most men, Thoreau observed at a far more favorable moment in Western culture than this, live lives of quiet desperation." More thoroughly than ever before, Mumford understood his compatriots' overwhelmedness, but he still clung to the faith that they could rouse themselves and work "toward conscious, directed, passionate commitment and participation."[37]

Some reviewers and, later, scholars found *The Conduct of Life* to be overly moralistic and rationalistic, and perhaps relevant only to white, male, apolitical intellectuals.[38] But you can generally count on Mumford to be more self-critical than his readers. If the book does have a few passages in which he sounds elitist or Puritanical—for instance, when he condemns Americans' addiction to "soporifics and aphrodisiacs, television and motor trips and sports"—there are many more in which he expresses the depth of his "fellow-feeling" for all humanity and idealizes "the cultivation of an exquisite sensitivity and an incomparable tenderness," and offers all the emotional encouragement he can muster, and admits his own flaws and confusion. Mumford may celebrate the ideal of balance, but he also consistently repeats his qualification that "man's constant re-shaping of himself, his community, his environment, does not lead to any final state of equilibrium." There is no goal, no solution, no paradise—only a constant dwelling, a muddling through, sustained by hope, determination, inclusion, flexibility, resilience.[39]

If you know where to look, you can see Mumford dwelling with his own grief as you read these chastened pages. He quotes an unidentified "American soldier in combat during the Second World War"—and it turns out to be Geddes, musing on the solidarity and generosity of his battalion.[40] And Mumford surely had his mother in mind when he began commenting on the universal human need for meaning and purpose: "When the brains of the aged begin to break down, they sometimes maintain a vegetative existence, without memory or hope; and with what lingering spark of mind remains they will often resent this state as life's final indignity: they eat, they breathe, they move, often in perfect health: but in a meaningless world. That is neither life nor happiness." Even Mumford's fairly abstract meditations on love probably reflect his resigned sense that his own marriage was in a long eddy. He had always believed in "the essential sacredness of sex," but only in middle age did he accept that it might be cyclical, and that its ebb and flow might in fact be the fundamental source of its significance—"for it is out of sex, in the dual roles assumed by the passionate lovers and the compassionate parents, that the gospel of love itself was born. Here ecstasy and union: there detachment and sacrifice."[41]

Along with Pierre, Captain Ahab makes a few appearances in *The Conduct of Life*, standing in for the modern man who denies the cycles of the tides and remains "fanatically concentrated upon a single end," setting his chronometer to absolute time and steering only by the magnetic pull of Moby Dick.[42] And just like Pierre, he refuses to adapt, refuses to deviate from his mission. "Oh, devilish tantalization of the gods!" Ahab exclaims, turning away from Queequeg and his coffin, after pondering the harpooner's efforts to copy his own tattoos onto the coffin's lid. The strange, "twisted tattooing," the "grotesque figures and drawings," seemed to Ahab like hints of "a complete theory of the heavens and the earth, and a mystical treatise on the art of attaining truth; so that Queequeg in his own proper person was a riddle to unfold; a wondrous work in one volume; but whose mysteries not even himself could read, though his own live heart beat against them; and these mysteries were therefore destined in the end to moulder away with the living parchment whereon they were inscribed, and so be unsolved to the last."[43] It is always tempting to try to read the hieroglyphs, for we were born to interpret—but Ahab would not be distracted, could not abide the uncertainty. That defiant single-mindedness has its place and time, and Mumford had appreciated it during his period of antifascist crusading. But now, a decade later, he wanted to yield to mystery, wanted to find at least a temporary balance between the chronometrical and the horological. A mature modern man, he felt, in search of ideals "worth living for and worth dying for," would learn "to ask questions for which, in the limits of a single lifetime or a single epoch of culture, he will never find the answer." Mumford did have a purpose, an agenda, a whole series of suggestions: his contingent interpretations of the past were meant to stake at least a provisional claim on the future. At the same time, though, he understood that "those who wish to qualify as guides, must do so under the constant discipline of humility."[44]

The great gift, the great joy, of that discipline is the recognition that old stories, told respectfully and openly, can be thoroughly renewed. After all, Mumford asserted, the humility of the mature modern man, "born of self-awareness, has another side to it: confidence in his own powers of creation. *Confidence in creation:* a sense of the rich potentialities of life and of endless alternatives."[45] The tattoos will always be there, not hiding one particular truth, but awaiting your willingness to make meaning of them.

CHAPTER 30

The Life-Buoy (1891; 1924-29)

Herman Melville and his coffin were lowered into the ground at the end of September 1891, at Woodlawn Cemetery, in the Bronx. On his writing desk Lizzie found a spray of weeds and wildings, including the ballad "Billy in the Darbies," about a young sailor facing death.

When I first encountered that title, I imagined the Darbies as an island group, perhaps near the Encantadas—or the Ambiguities. Then I learned that "darbies" is mariner slang for manacles. Billy was in a makeshift brig, waiting to be hung the next morning, for an ambiguous offense: "A jewel-block they'll make of me tomorrow, / Pendant pearl from the yard-arm end / Like the eardrop I gave to Bristol Molly—/ O, 'tis me, not the sentence they'll suspend." At first Billy thought he was dreaming, but he soon accepted his reality. He had spent his time in the navy as a foretopman, high above decks, gazing thoughtfully out to sea. Now he was ready to slide into the depths: "But Donald he has promised to stand by the plank; / So I'll shake a friendly hand ere I sink. / But—no! It is dead then I'll be, come to think. / I remember Taff the Welshman when he sank. / And his cheek it was like the budding pink. / But me they'll lash me in hammock, drop me deep. / Fathoms down, fathoms down, how I'll dream fast asleep."[1]

The time had come; the judgment had been pronounced. He was neither bitter nor remorseful. Just resigned. Maybe even slightly bemused. He seemed to be asking: is this really how it ends?

In *The Conduct of Life*, Mumford wished that everyone might be granted the time and space to stare at the ocean. "Herman Melville quite rightly called the whaling ship he sailed on his Harvard College," Mumford wrote; "indeed one may well trace to his long meditations on the maintop much of the originality of vision he brought into the world."[2]

Yet the meditative, visionary life has its dangers. Near the end of *Moby-Dick*, when Ahab is finally closing in on his prey, a sailor goes up to the masthead for the sunrise watch, only to tumble down in a dreamy haze, to the horror of his shipmates: "He had not been long at his perch, when a cry was heard—a cry and a rushing—and looking up, they saw a falling phantom in the air; and looking down, a little tossed heap of white bubbles in the blue of the sea." One of the crew ran to the stern and grabbed the ship's life-buoy from "where it always hung" and hurled it overboard. The sailors watched the "long slender cask" as it bobbed on the waves. "But no hand rose to seize it, and the sun having long beat upon this cask it had shrunken, so that it slowly filled, and the parched wood also filled at its every pore; and the studded iron-bound cask followed the sailor to the very bottom, as if to yield him his pillow, though in sooth but a hard one. And thus the first man of the Pequod that mounted the mast to look out for the White Whale, on the White Whale's own peculiar ground; that man was swallowed up in the deep."

It was an ill omen. The immediate task, though, was to replace the life-buoy. Starbuck searched for another cask; he found none "of sufficient lightness." So Queequeg came forward, making "certain strange signs and innuendoes."

"A life-buoy of a coffin!" cried Starbuck, starting. But after the initial shock, he recognized the cannibal's wisdom, and called on the ship's carpenter, who went for his hammer and calking-iron and pitch-pot and set to work.

And then Ahab, attracted by the racket, came up from the cabin-gangway and accosted the trusty carpenter, who had previously made him a new leg from the jawbone of a whale. "Here now's the very dreaded symbol of grim death," Ahab muttered, "by a mere hap, made the expressive sign of the help and hope of most endangered life. A life-buoy of a coffin! Does it go further? Can it be that in some spiritual sense the coffin is, after all, but an immortality preserver! . . . Will ye never have done, Carpenter, with that accursed sound? I go below; let me not see that thing here when I return again."[3]

The carpenter finished the job, and Queequeg's coffin was hung up in the life-buoy's accustomed place.

Melville had thought about publishing "Billy in the Darbies" in *John Marr and Other Sailors* in 1888, but his prose introduction to the poem just kept expanding.[4] Perhaps he never really wanted to finish it; after all, ever since his early cetological studies, he had been deeply suspicious of any pretention to completion or comprehensiveness. When he turned seventy in 1889, he explained to an acquaintance that he had "lately come into possession of unobstructed leisure, but only just as, in the course of nature, my vigour sensibly declines. What little of it is left I husband for certain matters as yet incomplete, and which indeed may never be completed."[5] But he did eventually indicate that "Billy in the Darbies" should be placed at the end of what became a novella of some 350 manuscript pages and that the work of prose should be entitled "Billy Budd, Sailor (An Inside Narrative)."[6]

Early in 1888, the manuscript was about 70 pages. Then, after an intense burst of writing in November, Melville found that the story had doubled in length. He logged another revision the following March, and another in April 1891, after struggling through heart problems and skin infections in 1890.[7] Though he worked periodically over the five and a half years of his retirement—and of course he did manage to put finishing touches on quite a number of poems—he was sometimes confined to his bed, and his mind occasionally seemed a thorny tangle. One acquaintance who wrote a long essay about him shortly after he died noted that Melville had suffered from "a lingering and painful illness," though his family averred that he had "manifested heroic fortitude, and patience, and also a considerate regard for those who attended him which commanded their admiration as well as their gratitude."[8]

The pages of "Billy Budd" that Lizzie found in her husband's study were a jumble of scrawled insertions, corrections, cancellations, reworkings, reminders, and provisional decisions, marked in ink, pencil, and an assortment of colored crayons. Most of the writing was his, but some was hers: in the last years of his life, instead of locking his study door, he had welcomed Lizzie back in as a copyist and collaborator, the way he had at times in the early years of their marriage. And Lizzie was solicitous of his posthumous reputation, encouraging friends and admirers to compose memorial tributes and even republish some of his novels. She seems not to have made any effort to get "Billy Budd" into print, though. Instead, she put the muddled manuscript in what one visitor called "a japanned tin cake-box," together with Melville's travel journals and remaining poems. The box passed from Lizzie to her older daughter Bessie, and then to Bessie's sister Fanny, and then to Fanny's older daughter Eleanor—who insisted that it was a bread box, not a cake box, and who opened it for Raymond Weaver in 1919, the year Melville would have turned one hundred. Weaver brought out the first edition of "Billy Budd" in 1924, though he used a title that Melville had discarded: "Billy Budd, Foretopman."[9]

Eleanor had always been enthralled by the box. Early in the twentieth century, Lizzie would occasionally invite Eleanor to join her for long evenings in the parlor, on the rare occasions when an admirer of Herman's writings came to call. Eleanor, in her early twenties, knew that she was being primed to become the steward of her grandfather's reputation. While Lizzie guided the conversation, Eleanor would gaze around at Melville's old books, and at the portrait of him that hung over "the white marble mantelpiece," and at "the precious box of manuscripts," placed prominently on "the same table where he used to write." Sometimes, they would even leaf through the pages of "Billy Budd" and several "fugitive, discarded, or rewritten poems." When Raymond Weaver turned up, after the Great War, Eleanor finally felt as though her grandfather might be resurrected.[10]

———

Captain Ahab sometimes dreamed of dying, and he told his dreams to his private harpooner, Fedallah, a mysterious Easterner with dark skin and "a glistening white plaited turban, the living hair braided and coiled round and round upon his head." Fedallah was also a prophet.

"Have I not said, old man," Fedallah whispered, "that neither hearse nor coffin can be thine?"

To Ahab, the prophecy meant that he would drown.

"But I said, old man, that ere thou couldst die on this voyage, two hearses must verily be seen by thee on the sea; the first not made by mortal hands; and the visible wood of the last one must be grown in America."

And Fedallah also claimed that Ahab could only die if he, Fedallah, died first; and that if he himself did die, then even in death he would continue to serve as Ahab's "pilot," would continue to lead him on toward his prey.

Well, then, Ahab concludes, "I have here two pledges that I shall yet slay Moby Dick and survive it."

Fedallah's eyes lit up "like fire-flies in the gloom," and he gave his captain yet another pledge: "Hemp only can kill thee."

This last assertion caused Ahab to cry out, laughing, for he assumed it meant that he would one day die on the gallows—sometime well after he had accomplished his great task. For the moment, he thought, he could not be killed: "I am immortal then, on land and on sea. . . . Immortal on land and on sea!"

The first hearse turns out to be Moby Dick himself: Fedallah gets tangled in his harpoon line, and his corpse winds up pinned to the whale's back, "his distended eyes turned full upon old Ahab."

The second hearse is the *Pequod*, with its cosmopolitan crew and American timbers, smitten by the brow of the enraged whale and doomed to sink in a whirlpool of its own making.

Ahab, just like Fedallah, dies by the hemp of his own whale line, but not before cursing Moby Dick, and the universe, and all humanity: "Sink all coffins and all hearses to one common pool!"

As it happened, Ishmael did not sink; he was not onboard the *Pequod* when it foundered. He had been flung out of his whaleboat and was now floating in the waves, watching from a safe distance. He was the immortal storyteller.

"When the half-spent suction of the sunk ship reached me, I was then, but slowly, drawn towards the closing vortex. When I reached it, it had subsided to a creamy pool." And then, suddenly, "owing to its great buoyancy, rising with great force, the coffin life-buoy shot lengthwise from the sea, fell over, and floated by my side. Buoyed up by that coffin, for almost one whole day and night, I floated on a soft and dirgelike main. The unharming sharks, they glided by as if with padlocks on their mouths; the savage sea-hawks sailed with sheathed beaks. On the second day, a sail drew near, and nearer, and picked me up at last." Queequeg's caring forethought had saved him.[11]

When the ship's chaplain came to see Billy Budd during his last night alive, the young foretopman seemed "serene," greeting his visitor politely, almost "cheerfully"; the man of God understood right away that he "had no consolation to proffer which could result in a peace transcending that which he beheld." Nonetheless, he gave his standard "clerical discourse," and Billy acknowledged it considerately, in the way that "the primer of Christianity" was accepted "long ago on tropic isles by any superior *savage*, so called. . . . Out of natural courtesy he received, but did not appropriate."

Perhaps Billy had no need of salvation, for he seemed "wholly without irrational fear" of his own death—a "fear more prevalent in highly civilized communities than those so-called barbarous ones which in all respects stand nearer to unadulterated Nature."[12] Indeed, Queequeg had thoroughly enjoyed carving his coffin, and when he lay down in it to make sure of the fit, while suffering from a life-threatening fever, he had shown a perfectly "composed countenance." "*Rarmai*," he murmured; "it will do; it is easy." Billy was as innocent and natural as the "soothing savage" who had become Ishmael's "bosom friend" and "inseparable twin brother"—and savior.[13]

If Billy was resigned to his death, though, the same could not be said for most readers of *Billy Budd*, who have generally found his execution to be both a travesty and a tragedy. Billy was genial, humane, noble, kind; he made just one mistake, in a moment of passion.

"It was the summer of 1797," Melville tells us. Britain was at war with France. That spring, the British Navy had endured the so-called Great Mutiny, and though the government made certain concessions to the sailors, and many of the mutineers immediately redeemed themselves with Lord Nelson at the Battle of Trafalgar, nevertheless, every naval warship now operated under clouds of suspicion and resentment. Billy had been serving on a homeward-bound merchant ship called the *Rights of Man*, whose owner "was a staunch admirer of Thomas Paine." But an outward-bound fighting ship called the *Bellipotent*—the Power of War—turned out to be short of men, so her lieutenant boarded the *Rights* and immediately selected Billy for impressment. The captain of the merchantman protested that Billy was his best sailor, a "peace-maker," loved by all the crew; the lieutenant tossed back his tumbler of grog and said, "Yes, I know. Sorry." Billy had the face of an angel, and, in this case, the external was a true reflection of the internal. The only flaw that anyone ever noted in Billy was a slight speech impediment, a stutter, which arose when he was under stress.

Billy's story takes very little time to unfold; there is hardly any action in Melville's final work of fiction. Like the early novels, it is mostly meditative, a bundle of historical, philosophical, and psychological tangents. But its tone is more resigned, its mood more reposeful. In *Redburn* and *White-Jacket* Melville offered a passionate plea for refugees and all the poorer classes, and his condemnation of flogging was just one element of a broad social critique that couched a sincere hope for reform. *Billy Budd* looks backward much more than forward. With a quieter realism, it tracks the transition from a society celebrating freedom and universal rights to a society defined by internecine warfare.

Billy is transferred from the *Rights of Man* to the *Bellipotent*, and he is immediately adored by his new crewmates—everyone except John Claggart, the master-at-arms, who acts as "a sort of chief of police charged among other matters with the duty of preserving order on the populous lower gun decks." On the surface, Claggart seems friendly and relaxed and even forgiving, but his inner spirit is roiled with envy and an elemental antipathy: like everyone else, he is drawn to Billy, but he also feels personally affronted by Billy's popularity and absence of malice, not to mention his "good looks, cheery health, and frank enjoyment of young life." Claggart is a form of the devil, forced to reckon with an angel. Gradually, he enlists some henchmen to help him frame Billy as the instigator of a mutinous conspiracy, and the climax of the story comes when Claggart brings his accusation to the honorable Captain Vere, whose very name signals his commitment to truth, and whom Melville describes as mindful, modest, firm, clear, and utterly reliable.

Vere is shocked by the charge of mutiny, for he has observed Billy at his post and was already thinking about promoting him. He ponders Claggart's motives and decides to clear the matter up in a private meeting, calling together the accused and the accuser in his cabin. And so the story's three main characters are assembled, staring at each other, in a scene saturated with suspicion and ambiguity. By the end of the story, all three will be dead.

Captain Vere calls upon Claggart to repeat his allegation to Billy's face, and the master-at-arms rises to the performance. Billy immediately goes into a kind of shock; he stands "like one impaled and gagged." The captain, still certain of Billy's innocence, can't fathom his silence. "Speak, man!" he says. "Speak! Defend yourself!"

Billy tries to speak—and fails. Vere then realizes that Billy is a stutterer and reaches out to soothe him, tells him that there's no hurry: they can wait for the words to form. So Billy tries again, more insistently now— "efforts soon ending for the time in confirming the paralysis, and bringing to his face an expression which was as a crucifixion to behold." Then, suddenly, in a violent spasm of frustration, Billy lashes out and strikes Claggart on the forehead, and the master-at-arms falls and instantly dies. And just as instantly, Captain Vere knows what the consequence will be: "Struck dead by an angel of God! Yet the angel must hang!"

They are at war. The Articles of War say that attacking an officer is a capital crime; the reason for the attack is irrelevant. Claggart's death cannot be covered up. The captain will have to convene a court-martial on the ship, right away. The court will convict. Billy will pay the price of his action.

Captain Vere waged a war within himself, a "clash of military duty with moral scruple—scruple vitalized by compassion." He could have spared Billy and tried to explain the situation to his crew; he could have kept Billy in shackles and sailed home, deferring responsibility for Billy's fate to a proper court. But Duty prevailed—and Order—and Necessity. Billy was a good man—fundamentally, chronometrically. But horologically, he had lost his temper and killed a superior officer. Some days later, as Vere was pursuing his nation's military mission, he was struck by a French musket ball, and as he lay dying, he murmured to his attendant: "Billy Budd, Billy Budd"—but without remorse.

On the night of the accusation, though, when Vere told Billy that he would be executed in the morning, the captain also managed to convey his fierce, fatherly belief that Billy had never intended to commit either mutiny or murder. And that was enough for Billy. His moral absolution made the legal punishment palatable, and he found himself letting go. Standing at the yardarm at sunrise, he uttered his final words: "God bless Captain Vere!" And a few minutes later, his body was wrapped in his hammock, which had been "ballasted with shot," and a plank was tilted, and the men of the *Bellipotent* watched Billy Budd slide into the sea, in his "canvas coffin."[14]

———

At the beginning of *Moby-Dick*, Ishmael leaves Manhattan in disgust and sets out to find a whaling ship in Massachusetts. He arrives in the town of New Bedford on a "very dubious-looking, nay, a very dark and dismal night, bitingly cold and cheerless." The daily packet boat has already sailed for Nantucket, where he is bound, so he'll need to find a bed right away, though he is low on cash. And he'll have to stay in New Bedford for two nights, because it's Saturday, and there is no packet boat on Sunday. He passes up the first two inns that he comes to, "The Crossed Harpoons" and "The Sword-Fish," for they seem "too expensive and jolly." Then he finds a place that looks adequately "dim" and "dilapidated," with a sign saying "The Spouter-Inn:—Peter Coffin." "Coffin?" he thinks. "Spouter?—Rather ominous in that particular connexion."

But the inn "looked as if it might have been carted here from the ruins of some burnt district, and as the swinging sign had a poverty-stricken sort of creak to it, I thought that here was the very spot for cheap lodgings." And it is here that Ishmael shares a bed with Queequeg, who at first comes across as a terrifying savage but eventually starts to seem "a clean, comely looking cannibal." Ishmael wakes up on Sunday with "Queequeg's arm thrown over me in the most loving and affection-ate manner. You had almost thought I had been his wife." After break-fast, they both wind up in the Whaleman's Chapel, listening to Father Mapple's sermon about Jonah: "And eternal delight and deliciousness will be his, who coming to lay him down, can say with his final breath—O Father!—chiefly known to me by Thy rod—mortal or im-mortal, here I die."

With some surprise, Ishmael notices that there is a large oil painting on the wall of the chapel, just behind the crow's-nest pulpit, which is reachable only by a side ladder and system of ropes. The painting de-picts "a gallant ship beating against a terrible storm off a lee coast of black rocks and snowy breakers. But high above the flying scud and dark-rolling clouds, there floated a little isle of sunlight, from which beamed forth an angel's face; and this bright face shed a distinct spot of radiance upon the ship's tossed deck, something like that silver plate now inserted into the Victory's plank where Nelson fell." There will be tempests, the painting seems to say, and treacherous reefs, but you must cling to hope and faith: "beat on, beat on, thou noble ship, and bear a hardy helm."

A very different kind of painting, Ishmael noted, hung in the entry-way of The Spouter-Inn, one that was "so thoroughly be-smoked, and every way defaced, that in the unequal cross-lights by which you viewed it, it was only by diligent study and a series of systematic visits to it, and careful inquiry of the neighbors, that you could any way arrive at an understanding of its purpose." Mostly, it consisted in "unaccountable masses of shades and shadows"; its overall effect was of "chaos be-witched." Ishmael found it a "boggy, soggy, squitchy picture," infuriating in its vagueness, in its virtual uninterpretability—though at the same time he had to admit that there was a "sort of indefinite, half-attained, unimaginable sublimity about it that fairly froze you to it. . . . It's the Black Sea in a midnight gale.—It's the unnatural combat of the four primal elements.—It's a blasted heath.—It's a Hyperborean winter scene.—It's the breaking up of the ice-bound stream of Time." It could be almost anything dark and mysterious. But before leaving for Nantucket, Ishmael spun out a final theory: "The picture represents a Cape-Horner in a great hurricane," he decided; "the half-foundered ship weltering there with its three dismantled masts alone visible; and an exasperated whale, purposing to spring clean over the craft, is in the enormous act of impaling himself upon the three mast-heads."[15]

———

Billy Budd has inspired more interpretations than any other of Melville's writings except *Moby-Dick*. It is more ambiguous than *Pierre*; it is built to be debated. It is also unfinished, and the instructions Melville left about its structure were not entirely intelligible. But a few formidable scholars have worked through the evidence and agreed on a relatively authoritative text, and what is perhaps most clear from it is that Melville's final additions and emendations were meant to throw everything even deeper into doubt.[16] Melville himself seems not to have decided whether he approved of Captain Vere.

A reviewer responding to Weaver's 1924 edition of *Billy Budd* thought that Melville was "telling the story of the inevitable and utter disaster of the good and trying to convey to us that this must be so and ought to be so—chronometrically and horologically."[17] Christ must be crucified. The perpetual offsetting of light by darkness was a spur to bring more light into the world. Billy's shipmates on the *Bellipotent* would always honor the courage of his sacrifice: they preserved "the spar from which the foretopman was suspended," and even for those who had never known him, "a chip of it was as a piece of the Cross."[18] But did they think of Vere as Pontius Pilate?

Billy Budd has been made into a film and an opera. It has been effusively admired by such writers as Hannah Arendt, W. H. Auden, Albert Camus, E. M. Forster, and Thornton Wilder. Scholars and critics and artists have offered interpretations that could be characterized as ethical, aesthetic, political, historical, sexual, autobiographical, psychoanalytical, and mythical. Virtually all of them can be supported by the text.

Billy Budd is about the stigma of homosexuality: "Claggart could even have loved Billy but for fate and ban."[19]

It is about the tensions of modernity: "Billy Budd was like a young horse fresh from the pasture suddenly inhaling a vile whiff from some chemical factory."[20]

It is about Melville's struggles as a father; it is about the acceptance of death; it is about Buddhism; it is about Melville's ever-tormented first cousin, Guert Gansevoort, who infamously accused three men of mutiny aboard the USS Somers in 1842, resulting in their immediate execution; it is about America's loss of innocence; it is about how the Civil War failed to resolve anything.

Weaver was initially unimpressed with Billy Budd (the characters seemed to him mere symbols), but by the time he put out a new edition of the story in 1928, he had decided that it perfectly embodied Melville's hopeful realism: "There is, of course, in this type of tragedy, with its essential quality of encouragement and triumph, no flinching of any horror of tragic life, no shirking of the truth by a feeble idealism, none of the compromises of the so-called 'happy ending.' The powers of evil and horror must be granted their fullest scope; it is only thus we can triumph over them."[21]

Mumford read the 1928 edition of Billy Budd as he was working on his Melville biography, and ultimately he endorsed Weaver's interpretation, though he also deepened its historical resonance: "These are the fundamental ambiguities of life: so long as evil exists, the agents that intercept it will also be evil, whilst we accept the world's conditions: the universal articles of war on which our civilizations rest." In the United States, in particular, racked by constant warfare and bitter divides over race and class, even the good citizens were now complicit, for modernity had knit everyone together in a web of relationships, for better and worse. Mumford thought that Melville, at last, had acknowledged this "situation as a tragic necessity; and to meet that tragedy bravely was to find peace, the ultimate peace of resignation, even in an incongruous world."[22]

Mumford also noted that Melville dedicated *Billy Budd* to his old shipmate Jack Chase, the beautiful, poetical hero of the main-top in *White-Jacket*, who had such "an abounding air of good sense and good feeling" that he made all the main-top-men feel like "brothers, and we loaned ourselves to each other with all the freedom in the world." He embodied Melville's ideal of intimate solidarity. In his last years, Melville may have resigned himself to death and devils, to grief and degradation and all the limitations of democracy. But he also clung to the bluff honor of those sailors who had shown him, in his youth, what a "fraternity of fine fellows" could accomplish.[23] There was good in Billy Budd; there was good in Captain Vere. They were both doomed, and they were both flawed, but in their short time together they could help buttress their community and offset the evil and weakness of the world's Claggarts. When Billy used his last moment alive to pronounce a blessing on his captain, his words "had a phenomenal effect. . . . Without volition, as it were, as if indeed the ship's populace were but the vehicles of some vocal current electric, with one voice from alow and aloft came a resonant sympathetic echo."

And then another phenomenon followed. The silent signal was given, and in silence all watched as Billy, dressed in white, but catching "the full rose of the dawn," was silently suspended. And the men, having witnessed executions before, were stunned to see Billy's body showing no signs of spasm, but just dangling in perfect stillness: "in the pinioned figure arrived at the yard-end, to the wonder of all no motion was apparent, none save that created by the slow roll of the hull in moderate weather, so majestic in a great ship ponderously cannoned."

The sailors talked about it endlessly. None of the men who had "beheld the prodigy of repose in the form suspended in air" would ever forget Billy Budd's death. For the rest of their days, the memory of that scene had the power to lift them up from the depths of hopelessness.[24]

CHAPTER 31

Man's Role in Changing the Face of the Earth (1951-62)

Though Mumford's soul never really found repose, and though his body would not fully merge with the world for another four decades, his mind lingered more and more frequently on the sustaining peace of ecology, on the potentially deep connections, both physical and emotional, between human beings and their surroundings. "So it follows that part of our love must be expressed by our relation to all living organisms and organic structures," he wrote, in *The Conduct of Life*: "some of our love must go to sea and river and soil, restraining careless exploitation and pollution: the trees and wild creatures of the forest, the fish in the rivers, are as subject to our affectionate care as the dogs or the cats who live in closer dependence on us."

Just like Melville, Mumford often yearned for fellow-feeling and a sense of commonality as he entered his late fifties. And like Rachel Carson, whose first best seller, *The Sea around Us*, came out a few months before *The Conduct of Life*, Mumford sometimes found what he needed in nature more readily than in society, though both Mumford and Carson also worried that the culture-nature bond had never been more threatened. "Consider the systematic wiping out of the natural landscape," Mumford lamented, "and the withdrawal from rural occupations and rural ways that took place during the last century: the spread of megalopolitan deserts undercuts love at its very base because it removes man's sense of active partnership and fellowship in the common processes of growth, which bind him to other organisms."[1] In the second half of his career, Mumford gradually lost faith in society, but he clung to the redemption latent in environmental relationships, where death at least sometimes led to renewal, as today's weeds and wildings faded and crumpled and were folded into tomorrow's fertile soil.

Even during the years when Alison was in high school and the family was based in New York, Lewis spent summers in Amenia, tending his garden. And after Alison started at Radcliffe in 1952, though Lewis often taught semester-long classes at the University of Pennsylvania or MIT, Amenia once again became the Mumfords' home base. They cherished their house in the valley. It grounded them, connected them to nature, stored their memories, gave them perspective. In December 1953, returning to Amenia from Philadelphia, Lewis sighed, and celebrated his "joy at the first glimpse of the house, still standing under the bare maples, in all its angular outlines; the sense of peace that enfolds us as soon as we enter the door; the feeling, after five minutes, that we have spent all our lifetime here and have never been away. Even the empty places in the house, the great inner vacancy left by Geddes's death, never to be filled again . . . , only makes the house that much more dearly a part of our lives; since the unused rooms, the fishing gear or the old toys we catch occasional glimpses of, remind us the more poignantly of a darkness and an emptiness that will never vanish, that indeed we must cherish as the negative equivalent for the joy of our present fulfillment."[2]

Mumford was finally rounding the Cape, but the last few years had been especially difficult. On the first day of 1953, he felt he was foundering, as low as he'd been "since the year following Geddes's death."[3] His courses on urban design at the University of Pennsylvania seemed pointless, and an operation to remove his prostate in August 1952 seemed to leave him "sleepy and foggy" all fall, a condition exacerbated by another "run of ailments" that only served to confirm his anxieties about aging.[4] He even got caught in the vortex of McCarthyism, when a conservative congressman from Michigan publicly accused him of having joined the Communist Party back in the 1930s.[5] "The confidence I had in 1940 about our ability to fight fascism without being infected with it," he admitted to a friend, "has proved unsound."[6] Moreover, the poor sales and reviews of *The Conduct of Life* had siphoned off any sense of accomplishment he might have attained after completing his twenty-year effort to spur Renewal. His capstone volume inspired "the worst press I had so far received in the whole series."[7] But he took a revitalizing trip to England in the spring of 1953, with Sophia and Alison joining him for a summer of touring in France and Italy. "Europe I still find deeply exciting," he said; "and full of vitality, too, whatever it may have been from 1938–1948."[8] The old cityscapes of Paris and Venice, the layers of history, the remnants and persistents, once again helped him rediscover an appreciation for human striving and creativity. He and Sophia were finally reconnecting, and he was finally beginning to incubate some new ideas for long-term book projects. By August 1954, he was writing to Henry Murray that "I scarcely dare to confess the utter happiness of the last six months, though it's inconceivable it should last a day longer. Such inner Peace!—as if the world were saved and I had been there, passing the buckets, when the damnable fire was put out."[9]

Of course, the world hadn't been saved, and Mumford had in fact been growing increasingly alarmed by the fascism of McCarthyism, by nuclear testing, and especially by the clear spread of environmental degradation. Among the many horrors unleashed by World War II was the nightmare of global contamination caused by new chemicals, plastics, and radioactive isotopes. Alas, many of the key insights of ecology arose when scientists and doctors started tracking the effects of radiation around the various test sites for nuclear bombs—first A-bombs, especially in the deserts of the American West, and then, as of 1952, H-bombs in the South Pacific. All around the world, radioactive isotopes lit up the environmental networks and systems on which all life depends, appearing, soon enough, even in the milk of nursing mothers.[10] In November 1953, Mumford gave a lecture at the American Philosophical Society in Philadelphia in which he admitted to being plagued by visions of the "millions of lives exterminated, of slow-dying cripples and embryological monsters in various species, of vegetation wiped out, ecological partnerships ruined, water supplies contaminated, soil and atmosphere permanently poisoned." Did the scientists and politicians not sense "the traumatic effects on the personality of our present preparations for these events, and the worse traumas to be anticipated from their becoming an actuality"?[11]

Mumford's own accumulated traumas, both personal and societal, would encumber him for the rest of his life; they darkened the tone of many of his late writings. His entire generation of intellectuals struggled to make sense of their role in two world wars and a globe-spanning Depression, struggled to face the violence and injustice seemingly inherent in what they had formerly thought of as Western Civilization. But by the mid-1950s Mumford was once again rediscovering his resilience, drawing on deep reserves of determination and—this was a word he tended to avoid in his earlier writings but now used frequently— love. The renewal of his relationship with Sophia, in particular, helped him cope with the world's iniquity and humanity's failings, helped him continue to offer constructive proposals despite his sense that his public profile was fading. In November 1955, Sophia wrote a journal entry suggesting how far she and Lewis had come: "I am deeply grateful to him for his strong sense of life and of love; for his belief in the power of love, and for his conscious leading of our life in the paths of love."[12] A particular dream visited her again and again, during these years, in which she continually discovered new spaces in their house in Amenia—a dream that brought delight to both of them, as they shared intimacies late into the night. "Yes, in the good old house there are new rooms," Lewis wrote in 1956, "at the end of passages one thought one had thoroughly explored long ago."[13]

In the summer of 1955, Mumford called on his newfound fortitude to confront some of the most sobering realities of the present, as co-chair of a landmark international symposium called "Man's Role in Changing the Face of the Earth." The event was dedicated to George Perkins Marsh: his *Man and Nature* of 1864, sprawling but pointed (its subtitle was "Physical Geography as Modified by Human Action"), not only served as inspiration for Mumford and many other conference participants but also offered both a baseline and a wide-ranging agenda. Remarkably, the proceedings of the conference were published the following year in a tome of some 1,200 pages, and it fell to Mumford to write the concluding remarks. How to bring together disquisitions on fossil fuels, energy limits, and climate; on per capita metals consumption, ocean harvests, and "technological denudation"; on forests and grasslands and invasive species and air quality in cities; on population, transportation, and "man's transformation"? It was, arguably, the most thorough environmental reckoning yet undertaken, though it was not nearly radical or ecological enough for Mumford. How to move the conversation forward, toward more unity and diversity, toward cooperation and communion, toward cautious restraint and caring?

"Too much of our discussion here," Mumford posited, ". . . has dealt with proposals for man's exercising control over nature without reference to the kind of control he must exercise over himself." The Bomb was ever on his mind: "Atomic energy by itself is a neutral thing, obviously. It promises nothing; it threatens nothing. It is we who do the promising; it is we who exert the threat. What makes nuclear power a danger is the fact that it has been released in a world savagely demoralized by two world wars, the last of which turned into a war of unlimited annihilation." Here was another chance to remind people that technology determined very little—that the Bomb might seem brand-new, but its challenge to culture and ethics and history was anything but. Indeed, he argued, "the danger we face today was prophetically interpreted a century ago by Herman Melville in his great classic of the sea, *Moby-Dick*. In that epic the mad Captain Ahab drives his ship and his crew to destruction in his satanic effort to conquer the white whale—the symbol of all the powers outside man that would limit or lame him. Toward the end, as his mad purpose approaches its climax, Ahab has a sudden moment of illumination and says to himself: 'All my means are sane; my motives and object mad.' In some such terms, one may characterize the irrational application of science and technology today. But we have yet to find our moment of self-confrontation and illumination."[14]

Mumford, treating Melville like an old friend or family member whose stories had become second nature, did not get the citation exactly right: this "glimpse" of self-knowledge actually comes early in the story, just after Ahab has convinced the entire crew to swear an oath of allegiance to him in his quest to kill Moby Dick. Ahab knows that his passion has stirred his men, that they are now as one: these are the sane means. Even Ishmael, the distant observer, admits to having "a wild, mystical, sympathetical feeling."[15] But that sense of solidarity had been generated in the insane pursuit of impossible vengeance. The problem is that though Ahab can perceive his own insanity, and did so at an early stage, he still can't change it: it is beyond his will. As Mumford ultimately understood, despite the casualness of his Melville reference, rational self-confrontation is virtually impossible, so the dark side of life must be countered by an equal and opposite brightness—by "the force of love."[16]

The final paragraphs of Mumford's essay at the end of *Man's Role in Changing the Face of the Earth* all serve the argument that only "a redeeming and all-embracing love" could help human beings "to rescue the earth itself and all the creatures that inhabit it from the insensate forces of hate, violence, and destruction." Many of the symposium's scholars, calling on technical data and rigorous research techniques, had pointed to alarming trends in various environmental cycles and relationships. But Mumford noted that there was also "a palpable undercurrent of love all through this conference"; indeed, he would never forget how individual speakers expressed their "love of the seashore," and "love of the soil," and "love of the ecological pattern," and "love of the peasant economy," and "love of a primitive Indian community." Approaching his sixtieth birthday, Mumford went full Romantic, invoking "love in all its meanings: love as erotic desire and procreativeness; love as passion and aesthetic delight, lingering over its images of beauty; love as fellow-feeling and neighborly helpfulness, bestowing its gifts on all who need it; love as parental solicitude and sacrifice; love as the miraculous capacity for overvaluing its own object and, thereby, glorifying and transfiguring it, releasing for life something that only the lover can see." He still worried that the power of science and technology could "turn out to be more self-destructive than ignorance and impotence," but he also maintained his faith in "the compensating processes of life," which might eventually "foster a new kind of personality, whose all-lovingness will in time offset these dangerous tendencies."[17] Only love could counter both the malice of Moby Dick and the hubris of Captain Ahab.

At this same time, in 1955, Mumford was also completing a short book to be called *The Transformations of Man* (published in 1956), which offered readers a condensed, accessible history of humanity, combined with a meditation on cultural evolution and an injunction to embrace a pluralist universalism, a sense of commonality, a "One World culture." In some ways, the book was just an abridgement of the last two volumes of *The Renewal of Life*, but it also developed a polemical argument that Mumford was quite excited about. Humanness, he insisted, was not defined by "the Promethean theft of fire"; it was not technology "that turned man into a creature so different from his primordial self." Rather, what truly mattered in human history was "the Orphic gift of music"—our "playfulness" and "artfulness," our "capacity to dream," our "intuition that there is more in nature than meets the eye," our interest in imagining the outlines of another's consciousness, our drive to create and interpret, our passionate engagement with "the unknown, indeed, the unknowable." If you were a student, then, and you wanted to prepare yourself to help remake the world, you would have to think of your education not instrumentally, as the acquisition of technical knowledge, but humanistically, as a historical exploration of meaning-making. Societal renewal would come from each person's making "time to play and experiment, time to learn, time to take in not merely the immediate environment but the remembered experience of his kind, time to grope in dream toward a distant future." Renewal would come from the desire to fill white pages with stories about white whales, as long as the stories retained a "sense of wonder and mystery." Renewal would come, ultimately, from imaginative "acts of love and sacrifice and devotion," from "a sense of being 'all in the same boat,'" from "the close chain of sympathetic responses in which man first securely established himself as irrevocably human: these friendly eyes are the indispensable mirror in which the self beholds its own image."[18]

Unfortunately, *The Transformations of Man* was barely noticed. "The failure is complete," Mumford wrote: "the rejection absolute."[19] He was too far out of step with the individualistic, consumerist 1950s. Perhaps the book's failure made Mumford think of Bartleby, who, according to Melville's narrator, had probably lost his faith in humanity while working "as a subordinate clerk in the Dead Letter Office at Washington. . . . Sometimes from out the folded paper the pale clerk takes a ring—the finger it was meant for, perhaps, moulders in the grave; a bank-note sent in swiftest charity—he whom it would relieve, nor eats nor hungers any more; pardon for those who died despairing; hope for those who died unhoping; good tidings for those who died stifled by unrelieved calamities."[20] Or perhaps Mumford was still pondering *Moby-Dick* and remembered the scene where the *Pequod* meets the *Jeroboam*, and Ahab pulls a letter from his mailbag addressed to the *Jeroboam*'s chief mate—who, it turns out, has recently been killed, by the white whale himself, with a casual flick of his tail: "the luckless mate, so full of furious life, was smitten bodily into the air, and making a long arc in his descent, fell into the sea at the distance of about fifty yards."[21] The American reading public, traumatized by two world wars, stunned by atomic blasts, fleeing to the suburbs, sinking into leather armchairs, was not primed to pick up books about the unknowable.[22]

Yet Mumford continued on, taking up the literary challenge of his autobiography, going on long country walks with Sophia, and launching a new urban history project meant to solidify his stature as the century's leading advocate for humane cities. One of the solaces of age, perhaps, is that you're better prepared for dead letters, and though the missed connections might not be less painful, they sometimes seem easier to offset. In the summer of 1957, Lewis and Sophia crossed the Atlantic again and were hosted by friends and colleagues in Holland, Belgium, France, Italy, and England, where they attended lavish dinners and garden parties, investigated ancient ruins and war monuments, and chatted with artists, architects, and scholars. It was just as therapeutic a trip as Melville's tour through Europe and the Holy Land a century earlier.

During their time in Tuscany, the Mumfords visited Geddes's grave, up in the burnt sienna hills. Lewis did a little lecturing and a little research, and in London there was a dinner put on for him at the House of Lords, in honor of his being awarded the gold medal of the Town Planning Institute. At sixty-one, finally feeling as though the trauma he shared with Sophia had brought them closer together, Lewis found himself putting *The Transformations of Man* behind him and preparing to write another book. Sophia remained more aware than he of the tension they would always have to navigate, but she also recognized how important it was to their relationship for Lewis to perpetually renew his passion for ideas: "When he comes on a passage he wants to share with me his whole face is aglow, his eyes soften, his mouth is mobile—you feel his whole being responding to the thought."[23]

Lewis was in good health, and thanks to his various professorships and his magazine writing—especially his regular architecture column, "The Sky Line," in the *New Yorker*—his finances were more stable than ever before. Over the next three years, he worked steadily on what many critics and scholars (though I don't count myself among them) consider to be his masterpiece, *The City in History* (1961), which won the National Book Award for nonfiction in 1962.[24]

Mumford himself acknowledged that his new book drew heavily on *The Culture of Cities*, and that certain beams and struts from "that earlier edifice" had been "preserved under a quite different building." Indeed, he hoped that his carefully selected remnants would "give the book an organic continuity and solidity that would have been lacking, perhaps, had I ignored the earlier structure and, like a speculative builder with a bulldozer, levelled the whole tract. In this it reflects with symbolic aptness the historic growth of the city itself." For me, that's too clever a justification, and the new book doesn't feel particularly fresh. I strongly prefer the more radical politics of the original, written in the vibrant 1930s, when Mumford still had faith in public space and contrapuntal communalism. Most of the passages Mumford retained from *The Culture of Cities* are straightforwardly historical; meanwhile, the older book's proposals for collective renovation have been replaced by somewhat chastened explanations of the multiplying challenges of Megalopolis, ranging from pollution to congestion to mechanization to desperation. *The City in History* dwells on trauma, trying to show how "the power to command, to seize property, to kill, to destroy," became concentrated in early cities under the rigidly male institution of kingship—how urban structures created "a focal center for organized aggression"—how the "mass extermination and mass destruction" perpetrated by the Mesopotamians and Sumerians and Aztecs foreshadowed the horrors of World War II's ghettoes and concentration camps.[25]

Still, as always, Mumford included some light with the gloom, and ultimately *The City in History* laid out a passionate defense of urbanity against the trend toward suburbanization and highway building. The book also shared many themes with other classic works of this transformative moment in American cultural history, like Jane Jacobs's *The Death and Life of Great American Cities* (1961), and Rachel Carson's second best seller, *Silent Spring* (1962), and Betty Friedan's *The Feminine Mystique* (1963). If Mumford's book was less cutting-edge, it was also more integrative, encompassing aspects of the other three books in its argument against sprawl, which poisoned the air and water, and destroyed old neighborhoods, and tended to isolate women in stultifying roles. Don't let the nation become one big Los Angeles, he begged, with its formerly glorious environment now "befouled by smog," and its design catering exclusively to the needs of the automobile, such that the next logical step in the city's development would be "to evict the remaining inhabitants and turn the entire area over to automatically propelled vehicles." Though scholars have made much of various feuds between Jacobs and Mumford—she disliked parks and preferred denser housing, for instance—they both ultimately celebrated healthful urban living spaces, and cooperation, and pedestrianism, and civic structures that, in Mumford's words, had been "designed to make man at home with his deeper self and his larger world, attached to images of human nurture and love."[26]

It was an era of awakening in America. "The final mission of the city," Mumford wrote, on the last page of *The City in History*, "is to further man's conscious participation in the cosmic and historic process. Through its own complex and enduring structure, the city vastly augments man's ability to interpret these processes and take an active, formative part in them."[27] Many Americans were at last emerging from their suburban bomb shelters, shaking off their Cold War paranoia, turning toward the civil rights movement, pouring into the streets. The culture of the 1960s, like that of the 1930s, was energetically public-spirited, and readers seemed to rediscover Mumford as a writer whose gravitas could bolster their radicalism. Friedan, Jacobs, and Carson have all enjoyed a more enduring popularity, in feminist, urbanist, and environmentalist circles. But in the 1960s Mumford's influence surged: he experienced a true renewal, as publishers reissued his books, and he was bombarded by offers of honorary degrees, awards, and speaking engagements (many of which he declined, so as not to be distracted from his work, though he found the appreciation deeply gratifying). His perspectives resonated in the culture of the moment, but he also played an important role in changing the face of that culture. Once again, for a few years, it seemed possible to envision a society remade not in the image of the machine but rather according to human scales and values, with broad civic participation, and invigorating green spaces, and a commitment to reckon with the past, and equal opportunities to shape history.

CHAPTER 32

Revival (1919–62)

Nobody could have predicted the renewal of Melville's reputation. Over a few decades, his works went from obscure to canonized, from derided for opacity and even insanity to celebrated for edgy modernism and sophisticated social criticism. And, a century after his rediscovery, we still don't have a thorough explanation for why the Melville Revival happened. Somewhere, Melville's spirit is chuckling.[1]

Raymond Weaver, who in college had "begun *Typee*—and stopped at the beginning," wrote his 1919 *Nation* article about Melville at the casual suggestion of his colleague in the Columbia University English department, Carl Van Doren.[2] In 1917, Van Doren had thought enough of Melville to include a few pages about him in the new *Cambridge History of American Literature*, in a section dedicated to a few minor writers contemporaneous with the era-defining James Fenimore Cooper. The general study of American literature was just getting off the ground at the time; even its defenders were careful not to claim that any New World authors had ever reached the heights of European literature. But *Moby-Dick*, Van Doren said, boasted an "extraordinary mixture" of "vivid adventure, minute detail, cloudy symbolism, thrilling pictures of the sea in every mood, sly mirth and cosmic ironies, real and incredible characters, wit, speculation, humour, colour."[3] The suggestion seemed to be that some readers might find the epic of the white whale almost as exciting and entertaining as one of Cooper's *Leatherstocking Tales*. Though Van Doren knew of hardly anyone who truly appreciated Melville's lively wit, he believed he saw some signs, perhaps especially in

England, that critics were starting to come around: "Of late his fame has shown a tendency to revive." Weaver definitely caught the bug and began reading Melville more and more deeply, "with gaping wonderment and incredulity."[4] Suddenly, *Moby-Dick* seemed to him less an adventure than an "allegory" of American history, or a "psychological synthesis" of the American character, or a "transcendental" work of "spiritual daring," or a lesson in "woeful wisdom" and "uncompromising despair" that was nevertheless delivered "genially and painlessly," as if Melville had "made pessimism a gay science."[5] Melville somehow arose from the depths of modernity to become a clear-eyed, affable guide to the postwar world, an expert in artful perseverance in the wake of trauma.

Meanwhile, Virginia Woolf also noticed Melville's centenary in 1919 and published a tribute in the *Times Literary Supplement*. To Woolf, it was *Typee* and *Omoo* that seemed most relevant, since she was keenly aware of how, during the war years, the peacefulness of the South Seas had been increasingly invoked as the perfect antidote to the fracturing of European modernity. Just a few months before Woolf wrote her article on Melville, W. Somerset Maugham had published *The Moon and Sixpence*, in which the main character, modeled on the painter Paul Gauguin, abandons the conventions of bourgeois society to find freedom and beauty in Tahiti. And in the previous year, Woolf had penned a review of the collected poems of Rupert Brooke, who was best known at the time for going to the South Seas to rediscover his emotional stability, just after having suffered a nervous breakdown, and just before getting drawn into the Great War, in which he was killed. (A line from Brooke's 1914 poem, "Tiare Tahiti," provided F. Scott Fitzgerald with the title of his 1920 debut novel, *This Side of Paradise*.) What was remarkable about Melville, from Woolf's perspective, was his recognition in the Marquesas not only "that this simple, idle, savage existence was after all remarkably pleasant" but also that his perception of the pleasantness stemmed in part from his own society's overcivilization. Woolf suggested that Melville came across as uncertain, torn between the indolent indulgence of the islands and the restlessness of his well-educated mind. But, she thought, he justly condemned his colonizing compatriots for always bringing "the diseases of civilization along with its benefits." In the South Seas, Melville had become thoroughly "engrossed in the lives and customs of the natives," and long before the ascendancy of anthropology, he clearly appreciated the value of cultural difference.[6]

Throughout the 1920s, the Anglo-American South Seas craze developed hand in hand with a new cultural relativism, which was based, like the Melville Revival, at Columbia, thanks in large part to the anthropologist Franz Boas and his many students—including Margaret Mead, whose best seller, *Coming of Age in Samoa*, came out in 1928, making Melville seem that much more germane and prescient.[7] At the turn of the century, the Spanish-American War had transformed the United States into a genuine empire in the Pacific, launching a renewed celebration of American power and Manifest Destiny but also a renewed cultural politics of anti-imperialism, as exemplified by the increasingly scathing writings of Mark Twain. When the American journalist Frederick O'Brien went to the Marquesas in 1914, it was with a distinctly Melvillean spirit, to escape from his home country's "sky touching buildings" and its "artificially lighted cages of a thousand slaves to money-getting." And his first book about his travels, *White Shadows in the South Seas*, the second-best-selling work of nonfiction in 1920, condemned the metaphysics of colonial racism and exploitation.[8] Despite the Civil War and the abolition of slavery, the pall of white supremacy had returned to darken America's empire, and the author of *Moby-Dick* was being invoked to help remind all white Americans of their long-standing complicity.[9] By the time *Coming of Age in Samoa* came out, the KKK had been revived all across the United States, and it felt as though Americans were at war with each other again, as the imperialists trumpeted their skyscrapers and stock markets, while the cultural relativists suggested that the supposedly primitive peoples of the world might actually be wiser, happier, healthier, and more just in their social relationships.[10] For decades, Boas had been arguing against any singular High Culture and urging Euro-Americans to recognize the inherent value of all the world's different cultural systems, each with its own internal logic. And Mead's work ultimately echoed Melville's in suggesting that 1920s Samoans, like the nineteenth-century native peoples whom Melville encountered, had developed cultures notable for their communal care

and their fostering of resilience—qualities largely absent from the neurotic, individualistic cultures of the modern West. "Realising that our
own ways are not humanly inevitable," Mead wrote, "nor God-ordained,
but are the fruit of a long and turbulent history, we may well examine in
turn all of our institutions, thrown into strong relief against the history
of other civilisations, and weighing them in the balance, be not afraid
to find them wanting."[11]

Mumford thought that obscurity had descended on Melville because
he was too radically critical of his home culture. Melville had seen
through modernity even in its earliest incarnations, when most Euro-
Americans were still enraptured by "felt slippers and warm bellywash,"
as Mumford put it in his 1926 book, *The Golden Day*[12]—and when they
still dreamed of a "neatly ordered material universe." "In thought and
experience," Melville had "broken outside this neat, cosy, Victorian" culture and had come to realize that "he doubted progress. He could not
believe that Liverpool had a higher civilization than the South Seas."[13]
His complacent compatriots could not countenance his disbelief. By the
1920s, though, modern comforts had come so far that many Americans
were starting to worry about growing soft and flabby, and most dreams
of order and security had been fractured. Melville's criticisms seemed
more and more timely. And his strange experiments with style and form,
his interest in flouting everything that readers expected from particular
genres, meshed perfectly with the inclinations of those cutting-edge
twentieth-century artists and intellectuals who thought of themselves as
modernists. Melville would have fit right in with the people Mumford
befriended in New York in the 1920s and 30s: Alfred Stieglitz, making
abstract photographs of clouds that were meant to evoke music; Aaron
Copland, composing music as a form of collage; Georgia O'Keeffe, painting the sexual organs of flowers; e. e. cummings, writing about sex in
surrealistic fragments.[14] As Mumford noted in 1924, "people have criticized *Moby-Dick* because it is formless and full of irrelevancies; but the
truth is that the irrelevancies are an essential part of its form, and had
Melville attempted to reduce the bounds of his universe to the scene
required for a slick story of the sea, that universe would not have been
the multitudinous and terrible thing he sought to create."[15]

D. H. Lawrence called *Moby-Dick* "one of the strangest and most wonderful books in the world." William Faulkner fingered it as the one novel he wished he had written. E. M. Forster suggested that it was "full of meanings; its meaning is a different problem. . . . Nothing can be stated about *Moby Dick* except that it is a contest. The rest is song."[16] It is somewhat difficult to find an important English or American modernist of the 1920s–1950s who did not embrace Melville. Ralph Ellison's experimental novel, *Invisible Man*, begins with an epigraph from "Benito Cereno," and the book's prologue riffs on an incident from the opening pages of *Moby-Dick*, when Ishmael briefly listens to an African American preacher sermonizing on "the blackness of darkness." (For Ellison, the key phrases become "the darkness of lightness" and "the blackness of blackness." And by chapter 3 of *Invisible Man*, Ellison has also invoked Mumford, somewhat teasingly, by having his narrator visit a derelict bar/brothel/gambling den/insane asylum/veterans' club called the Golden Day.)[17]

Melville gained so many admirers in the 1920s thanks mostly to Raymond Weaver, not just because his 1921 biography was so widely read and highly regarded but also because he saw to it that many of Melville's writings were reprinted, or published for the first time. His influence was clear on the decision by the Constable publishing house of London to bring out a sixteen-volume set of Melville's complete works between 1922 and 1924; volume 13 was Weaver's edition of the previously unknown *Billy Budd*, which especially enthralled E. M. Forster, who later wrote the libretto for Benjamin Britten's operatic adaptation. (*Billy Budd*, in its perfect ambiguity and relative brevity, also became a favorite assignment in college literature courses within just a few years.)

American publishers followed Constable's example and quickly offered new editions of every Melville novel except *The Confidence-Man*, which still seemed either too insane or too radical a condemnation of capitalism. But as soon as Mumford's biography of Melville came out, in the spring of 1929, it supplanted Weaver's, and it would remain the most influential piece of Melville scholarship through the 1930s and 1940s, until the explosion of work in 1951 to commemorate the centenary of *Moby-Dick*.[18] Even Weaver's old colleague Carl Van Doren endorsed Mumford's book; he was instrumental in getting it picked up by the Literary Guild of America and wound up penning the article explaining the editorial board's selection. Mumford's biography, he thought, had gone "further than any studies yet produced in defining Melville's genius, setting it in relation to the age and surroundings in which he lived. . . . Here is a striking account of the standards, prejudices, repressions, discouragements which prevailed in the American Victorian age, which handicapped Melville from the start, and which kept him from being understood by his contemporaries."[19]

Indeed, this deep contextualization of Melville's career was both one of Mumford's most significant accomplishments and one of the pillars of the Melville Revival. Most of the Revivalists understood Melville as a man of his time. He was relevant in the twentieth century not because his genius was somehow "timeless" but because he responded so trenchantly to the debates and conflicts of the era he was living through, and because some of those debates and conflicts had persisted to the present moment. Even those who actively shape their culture are themselves shaped by it. "One cannot separate a man from his social environment," Mumford wrote, in *Herman Melville*: "a society lives in a man: a man is a creature in society; the inner world is less private and the outer world less public than people habitually and carelessly think."[20] In Melville's case, the new, fast-paced world of railroads and con artistry and racial violence would cast a long shadow.

It's not that Weaver's approach was ahistorical. But his near-exclusive emphasis on the first few years of Melville's career meant that he had almost nothing to say about how Melville tracked the sweeping national tensions of the 1850s, or the aftermath of the Civil War, or the empty decadence of the Gilded Age. Mumford, conversely, in his revisionist zeal, consistently emphasized Melville's keen understanding of American modernity as a devil's bargain, in which the self-focused upper- and middle-class white folks had agreed not to think about the dark side of expansion and mechanization and commercialization.

In the works of the 1850s, Mumford thought, Melville's real aim was to "penetrate the leathery optimism and the cast-iron self-righteousness of antebellum America." So *Pierre* contained not just a searing psychological exploration of Melville's family history but also "realistic caricatures of the slums of New York." "Bartleby" dealt not just with inner perversity but also with the outer realities of capitalism, in offices and factories—with "the pervasive prison of dull routine and meaningless activity." And though Mumford found *The Confidence-Man* less than coherent, he saw in its fragments a clear denunciation of the cynical Go-Aheadism that seemed innocently to uphold the ideal of "a prosperous and efficient life" but that turned out to be based on slavery and the theft of land from Native Americans—and on the summary rejection of an older set of values "that would place friendliness and natural intimacy above cold circumspection, that would make every alien soul a friend, and would place the needs of man above the safety of property."[21]

Even in the poetry of the postbellum years, Mumford discovered a profound engagement with historical trends. Abolitionism had won out, but Melville saw that scientific racism had just grown stronger; the slave masters of the Old South were no more, but many Americans fell under the yoke of "new agents of exploitation." What was the good of a "free" labor system given "the sacrifice of the worker's welfare to profits"? In his thorough contextualization of *Battle-Pieces*, Mumford suggested that Melville had started writing again, after his long withdrawal, because he recognized that "the prime issues of the great conflict were silenced, rather than settled, by the decisive victory of the North." After all, the North was still full of vicious racists, opportunistic industrialists, and greedy speculators. "What was saved" by the North's victory was "not freedom and equality, the freedom of voluntary association and local initiative, the equality of access to an unlimited amount of utilizable land: what was left was just the opposite of these things, servility and inequality." From Mumford's perspective, Melville mattered because he had accurately diagnosed the ills of American modernity as soon as the earliest symptoms started to appear, and for readers in the disease-ridden 1920s, the uncanniness of Melville's prescience might provide a salutary jolt.[22]

After the jolt of World War II, though, a new gap seemed to open between past and present. Melville had not predicted the atom bomb. While Mumford's historical reading of Melville's work had resonated powerfully throughout the 1930s, by 1945 the western world was registering a kind of trauma that even Mumford suspected had never been seen before. Americans and Europeans did not stop reading Melville, but their sense of his relationship to time and history began to shift. Living through what they perceived as an utterly new and different era, they needed works that rose above the context in which they had been created. If Melville had once seemed a grounded social critic and a modernist experimenter, he now took on the role of universal metaphysician. In the 1920s, *Moby-Dick* had come across, in Mumford's words, as "one of the first great mythologies to be created in the modern world, created, that is, out of the stuff of that world, its science, its exploration, its terrestrial daring, its concentration upon power and dominion over nature." But by the late 1940s the book became a myth removed from time altogether, capturing the tragedy of the human condition, or the perversity of human nature, or the fragility of human communities.[23]

Thanks in part to the Melville Revival, but also to the rise of contemporary writers like Robert Frost (whom Mumford got to know at Dartmouth in the 1930s) and Zora Neale Hurston (who studied anthropology with Franz Boas), as well as Fitzgerald and Faulkner, American literature was now becoming a respectable academic field, and scholarly studies of U.S. authors began to proliferate. As the Cold War got under way, it was also useful to have a distinctly American literary tradition to extol. But at this same moment, literary studies took a turn toward what would come to be known as the school of New Criticism, which embraced self-referential formalism and tended to scorn historical context. In other words, just when Melville's reputation was becoming solidly established, many of the critics and scholars who were producing new writing about his career were emphasizing the timelessness of his aesthetics and his metaphysics. To them, Mumford's approach seemed outdated. Melville entered the canon, then, not so much as a sailor, or a New Yorker, or a lover of trees, or an observer of race relations, or a critic of modernity, but as a Genius Philosopher and Artist.[24]

Mumford was bothered by some of the trendy approaches to Melville, but he did not entirely disapprove of the new scholarship, especially since his old friend Henry Murray had produced some of it.

Anyway, who could deny the timelessness of Melville's appeal? By 1951, Mumford recognized that his Melville biography had been superseded by the recent work of such critics and scholars as F. O. Matthiessen, Jean Simon, Richard Chase, Newton Arvin, Leon Howard, and Jay Leyda, and he seems to have enjoyed seeing all the new editions of *Moby-Dick* pouring from the nation's presses. Mostly, his attention was elsewhere: 1951, after all, was the year he published the final volume of *The Renewal of Life*. But he did take the time to read Murray's powerful 1951 essay, "In Nomine Diaboli," which offered a fresh interpretation of *Moby-Dick*, in honor of the book's one-hundredth birthday.

Lewis and Henry, or Harry, as he was known to friends, had been talking Melville for almost twenty-five years; in 1947, Lewis had even said that "my friendship with you, dear Harry, is the best reward I got for writing my study of H.M." When Lewis first sought him out, in 1928, Harry, already a well-known Harvard psychologist, cut a dashing figure in the Melville Revival. In Mumford's first letter to the esteemed "Dr. Murray," he explained having heard a rumor from Raymond Weaver that "you had a great deal of firsthand data about Melville's life which you would not divulge to anyone, as you intended to do a psychological study of him." The rumor was entirely true—and for the rest of his life, Murray would be infamous for secreting documents and never actually publishing the Melville book that he was always working on. Yet he immediately shared some of his materials with Mumford, and the two men, similar in myriad ways, became very close.[25]

Their relationship quickly transcended their shared obsession, but Melville's presence always hovered in the background. "Dear Harry," Lewis wrote in February 1952, "It was good to see your whalespout again; and in a few weeks . . . I hope to jump into my whaleboat and go after you." On a few occasions they seemed to be hunting each other, and they had some difficult disagreements, about Melville as well as about Lewis's "machine-gun" prose style and his public honesty about his son's failings. But throughout their friendship they enjoyed a deep mutual trust; in their letters, they discussed religion and ethics and psychoanalysis, war and politics and history, fame and death and money and sex. Murray was as much of a renaissance man as Mumford, with degrees in history, biology, biochemistry, and medicine (most of his graduate training was at Columbia) and an allegiance to both Freud and Jung, in addition to Melville. Unlike Lewis, Harry had chosen the stability and prestige of an academic appointment; he helped direct Harvard's Psychological Clinic from 1927 until 1962, and he influenced as many people in psychology and psychiatry as Boas did in anthropology. But he remained restless and ravenous in his explorations. He and Mumford were essentially soul mates, even if they feuded at times like brothers. Harry was happily married, but also happily involved in a decades-long affair, and Lewis became friendly with both Harry's wife and his lover. The two men prodded each other, confided in each other, comforted each other. "Dearest Harry," Lewis wrote, shortly after Geddes's death, "dearest and most loving of friends: Your letter yesterday was the only one that brought us any sort of consolation, not because it erased our grief, but because it truly participated in it and even deepened it, if that were possible."[26]

Lewis and Harry also offered long, thoughtful responses to each other's writings, and the commentary could be simultaneously encouraging and critical. In the case of Harry's *Moby-Dick* essay, Lewis testified to having read it "with unbounding admiration and delight last night. It is not merely the very best thing you have written, in its clarity, its penetration, its subtlety, its charity, its depth; but it is the very best thing anyone has written on Melville: volumes have been written without saying half as much. . . . I had been a little worried over the fact that your long researches on Melville hadn't yet come to full fruit in a whole book; but after this essay . . . I feel no misgivings whatever. Rest easy! It is not by the quantitative results that good thinking and feeling shall be judged."[27] Mumford, of course, published about five times as much as Murray over the course of their careers.

"In Nomine Diaboli" invokes the scene from *Moby-Dick* in which Ahab and his blacksmith forge a new harpoon and "baptize" it in the name of the devil, with the blood of the three "pagan" harpooneers, Queequeg, Tashtego, and Daggoo.[28] For Murray, Ahab himself is "an embodiment of that fallen angel or demi-god who in Christendom was variously named Lucifer, Devil, Adversary, Satan." And Moby Dick, in addition to being "a veritable spouting, breaching, sounding whale," is also "the projection of Captain Ahab's Presbyterian conscience, and so may be said to embody the Old Testament Calvinistic conception of an affrighting Deity and his strict commandments." The novel, in other words, was meant to express Melville's hopeless frustration with New England Puritanism. But Murray, being Murray, added a psychological layer to his interpretation: Melville had also depicted "an insurgent Id in mortal conflict with an oppressive cultural Superego."[29]

Mumford was intrigued, certainly, and he granted the brilliance of his friend's heuristic flourishes. But he was not convinced. Perhaps Ahab did have certain devilish qualities; perhaps he was a fascistic dictator; perhaps his trauma had reduced him to pain and rage. Yet, as Lewis wrote to Harry, there were times when Ahab seemed the very "spirit of man, nay the superego itself, the frail and lonely spirit that nevertheless, while the ship remains afloat, keeps his command; but this superego has been tamed by the very nature of the force it contends against, and by allowing itself to become the image of the thing it hates . . . becomes in the end its victim." The white whale, meanwhile, might sometimes come across as oppressively haunting, in the manner of a Calvinist's conscience, but more often Mumford thought it represented "something more primitive, the chaotic and undirected primordial energies, random motion, accident, all those forces outside of man that so often countervail his efforts and, through his very efforts to understand their irrational nature, seem directed against him and his purposes."[30] To Mumford, Melville's characterization of Ahab went beyond sympathy for the devil: there was a nobility to the maimed captain's defiance, a basic sense of human purpose, an insistence on carving out meaning. He was hubristic and manipulative and violent—but didn't those qualities merely make him a figure for "Modern Man; and is not the Atomic Bomb his final progeny"?[31] It did not seem satanic to Mumford, but rather quintessentially human, to draw one's compatriots into a desperate effort to offset senseless chaos, by any means necessary, even if the means might ultimately make the world even more chaotic.

In 1962, in the thick of the Cold War, and on the heels of Mumford's success with The City in History, he was offered the chance to reprint his Melville biography. In the new preface, he saluted the scholarship of Henry Murray—but only his friend's work on Pierre, not Moby-Dick.

And he also made a point of complaining broadly about the "new breed of critics," especially the academics who no longer took his biography seriously. Mumford found it especially galling that some of them had turned *Moby-Dick* into "a subversive undercover attack upon Christianity, a theory that makes mock of both the literary qualities of *Moby-Dick* and the religious content of *Clarel.*" It was true that Melville had his doubts about religion, especially in light of modern science, but he also tried all his life to be faithful. The white whale did not represent the Church. Mumford did propose many different symbolic possibilities for Melville's works; he was willing to consider religious typologies, psychoanalytic tropes, political allegories. In the end, though, he judged his historical analysis to be just as important as his literary interpretations. Ultimately, he explained, the Melville biography had been "in effect an enlargement, in terms of a single life, of the study of 'American Experience and Culture' I had opened in *The Golden Day*."[32]

Ralph Ellison, though he generally admired Mumford—"I have owned . . . , and have learned from, most of his books"—objected to *The Golden Day* because the antebellum period had hardly been golden for African Americans.[33] But between *The Golden Day*, which came out in 1926, and *Herman Melville*, published in 1929, Mumford revised his understanding of the age of American Romanticism, developing a more nuanced and significantly darker perspective on the era—thanks in large part to Melville's keen awareness of injustice, hypocrisy, complacency, exploitation, and alienation.

Even with its emphasis on Melville's "tragic sense of life," though, Mumford's biography had come across as too sanguine to some reviewers—including Henry Murray.[34] There were times, over the years, when Mumford agreed with Murray's assessment and lamented that his sheltered innocence had prevented him from diving deeper into the abyss: "it was only after the book had been published and our son was close to death and all the weak bricks in my own internal structure had fallen about me, so to say, that I had an insight into Melville's dismay, his exacerbation, his despair, his insight into evil, and all that went with it."[35] In the end, though, Mumford stood by his original approach, whose relative balance was one of the main justifications for publishing a new edition of the biography.

After so many years of Revival, after so much "admirable scholarly work" had come out, it was a leap of faith to think that anyone would want to read so ancient a tome. But Mumford was willing to wager that his open-ended treatment of "Melville's desperation and despair" would strike a chord with the present generation. Indeed, his biography had carefully embodied Melville's own fascination with uncertainty, ambiguity, contingency, and possibility, and the early 1960s felt like a time when anything could happen. Scholars had found some key documents in the intervening years, but, Mumford thought, "by now it seems likely that the most gaping holes in the evidence will never be satisfactorily filled." His book honored the gaps: "Against the current ideal of literary scholarship, which leaves little to the author and less to the reader, my book remains a tacit protest."[36]

Henry Murray, like many other Revivalists, had done so close a "dissection" of Melville that he wound up feeling a deep "disenchantment" with him, which Mumford never shared, and which he sometimes resented in his friend. "Your autopsy of Melville," he wrote to Harry, "is so thoroughgoing that even the Last Trumpet would hardly suffice to bring the various organs and parts together again." Mumford had tried to capture the whole man, in all his complexity, and though he found Melville "frightful" at times, he also loved him, and would always be grateful for his fellowship, for the sense of connection and solidarity he found in his writings, parallel to the "shock of recognition" that Melville himself described when he first read Hawthorne.[37] Melville had sparked Mumford's curiosity and imagination—had kept him consistently engaged with the past—had brought him as much light as gloom.

"Beneath the mask you'll come upon the dark New England," Mumford wrote, in a 1943 poem: "Dark as a face that's sailed around the Horn and blistered under the equator. / That's it. . . . The smoke-charred soul of Melville standing alone, grim as a chimney when the house is gone. / Here is a proper home and what is more a destination; / This is what makes one hunger for the walnut-bitter hills / And poke around the tunneled root cellars of old farmhouses, / Where, at winter dawn, a pin of light between the rocks / Shines like a sun."[38]

CHAPTER 33

Call Me Jonah (1962-82)

The Mumford Revival of the 1960s did not equal the Melville Revival of the 1920s, but it gave Mumford a solid platform from which to launch his critiques and proposals. By the mid-1970s, when he became an octogenarian, he had turned mostly to autobiographical writings. But in the 1960s, he embraced the spirit of the age and railed against mainstream culture and politics. He was a relatively angry old man. As the Cold War lurched on, as hundreds of thousands died in Vietnam, as slums expanded, as machines took over more aspects of life, Mumford sought to shine a light on American recklessness and superficiality—to combat "the dire insufficiencies of current one-generation knowledge. If we do not take the time to review the past we shall not have sufficient insight to understand the present or command the future: for the past never leaves us, and the future is already here."[1]

Like many writers, Mumford often fretted about whether his words would make any difference, but in the 1960s, tens of thousands of readers picked up his books, and dozens sent him fan letters. Many Americans were in fact reckoning with broad historical traumas, embracing the civil rights movement, and environmentalism, and feminism, and the struggle for peace. Use of the word "Mumfordian" spiked upward, referring both to Mumford's characteristic concerns and to people who considered themselves his followers. Over the course of the decade, publishers put out new editions not just of *Herman Melville* but also of *The Story of Utopias, The Golden Day, Technics and Civilization, The Condition of Man,* and even *The Conduct of Life.* And Mumford completed one last magnum opus, a popular two-volume rethinking of the history of technics called *The Myth of the Machine*. *Technics and Human Development* appeared in 1967, followed by *The Pentagon of Power* in 1970. Mumford had become one of the most celebrated public intellectuals of the twentieth century. Yet he still sometimes felt obscure and misunderstood, as most writers do. "At the end of almost half a century's writing," he noted in his private journal in 1967, "I cannot see that my work has had any real influence in any of the fields I have touched. Even old friends, who should have known me better, have often regarded me as a 'hysterical' prophet of doom, denying the disintegration I had exposed and turning away from the personal reorientation I urged."[2]

Mumford was never a doomsayer, but he himself acknowledged taking on the mantle of a prophet, just as Melville had done. "Call me Ishmael," the narrator says at the beginning of *Moby-Dick*, inviting us to think of him as a wandering outcast whose voice will echo across the world's wild spaces. In 1972, Mumford received the National Medal for Literature, and the title of his acceptance speech was "Call Me Jonah." He felt he had been chosen to speak difficult truths, just as Jonah had been commanded by God to tell the people of Nineveh that they would have to change their evil ways. But he admitted that, like Jonah, he often failed: sometimes he overcompensated, allowing his tone to become too righteous; sometimes he fell mute and fled from the confrontation, as Jonah had fled from the Ninevites, only to wind up getting swallowed by a whale. At least, Mumford noted, one could always turn back to Melville's "telling version of this singular story in *Moby-Dick*: the classic interpretation of Jonah's moral dilemma that one finds in Father Mapple's sermon." For his part, he fully accepted Father Mapple's denunciation and castigation. He read the preacher's words "again and again, and each time the sermon gets better and better." Over the course of decades, he had been trying to internalize the lesson: "Whenever Truth commands us, we must obey it and utter it aloud whether our friends and neighbors and countrymen like it or not." Yet Mumford also spoke freely about how hard and confusing a mission that was, how much ambiguity he saw in the story of Jonah. "First I begin to identify my own life with Jonah's," he said, "and then Jonah himself turns into the whale, not the Biblical whale but the whale in . . . *Moby-Dick*." In the modern age, how could anyone be sure of Truth? In the modern age, wouldn't the prophet himself be just as complicit as every other member of society? Mumford would continue to try to speak out, forcefully but cautiously, as "neither a pessimist, nor an optimist, still less a utopian or a futurologist." He would offer a prophecy of uncertainty and humility, sometimes in the form of criticism, but perhaps more often in the form of "gratitude"—aimed especially at "those nameless voices" that he had heard, "coming from the distance and the deep, when I was entombed in the belly of the whale. Their response to my words has given me faith to struggle out of that darkness and rise up into the sunlit air again."[3]

Throughout the 1960s and into the mid-1970s, Mumford continued to climb into his pulpit, searching for the right words to help his crewmates steer the ship. His mood was often perturbed, his tone polemical: the weight of evidence in the twentieth century suggested that modernity was tending toward darkness. But he still always made a point of invoking hope and possibility.[4] Reflecting on the 1967 war between Israel and Egypt, he admitted fearing for the future, given the horrors that the present conflict brought to mind: "the First World War, the Turkish massacres, the Second World War, the Soviet concentration camps, the Nazi extermination camps, 'strategic' (extermination) bombing—Warsaw, Rotterdam, London, Coventry, Hamburg, Dresden, Tokyo, Hiroshima, then Korea, Vietnam, and more civilian extermination. And now the Near East. No wonder the younger generation loathe this world and find no good whatever in it; they have known nothing else, and it is easy for them to believe that there never has been anything but fraud, hypocrisy, malevolence, and violence." At the same time, though, Mumford immediately recognized that "the crisis brought out many of the old decencies, the old moralities, the old heroisms that have enabled the human race to survive both natural and man-made catastrophes." He was particularly impressed by the response in cold and stoic Switzerland: "something had taken place that had been unimaginable before this moment: the high school students, never given to demonstrations, had marched in public to show their solidarity with Israel."[5]

FIGURE 15. Lewis in 1973.

Perhaps the Swiss were trying to atone for their sins in World War II, as the Italians had done in constructing a particularly poignant memorial that Mumford celebrated in 1963 for its capacity "to remind us, in today's Purgatory, of the Inferno." The Ardeatine Cave memorial is essentially a mausoleum built into a hillside on the outskirts of Rome, where Nazi soldiers and their Italian collaborators executed 335 civilians in 1944. "In this cavelike structure," Mumford wrote, "one is not merely alone with the dead; one is close to their final moment of agony. So far from making that moment easier for the visitor, the architects have sought to intensify it." Indeed, a visit to the site was like a "descent into hell," but it was "a descent followed by a promise of redemption as one returns to the daylight world." To remember is not exactly to make amends, but a humane architecture could at least help societies work through the traumas of the past.[6]

Alas, Mumford found "more aesthetic life in this Roman monument, dedicated to the dead, than there is in most of the recent multi-storied housing developments, dedicated (supposedly) to the living."[7] In a 1962 article called "The Case against Modern Architecture," Mumford tried to uphold his long-held belief that all buildings should be conceived as true homes, dwelling places, in line with an "organic interdependence" that was "based on variety, complexity, and balance," and "continuity through change, stability through adaptation, harmony through finding a place for conflict, chance, and limited disorder, in ever more complex transformations." But what comes through most clearly is his conten- tion that architectural development has "become sterile and frustrated through an excessive effort to conquer nature." In thrall to "mechanical progress" and "new metallic alloys and new plastics," the most "success- ful modern architects" seemed to Mumford to have become more like ad men, "saying, in effect: 'And now! A new taste sensation!' Or, 'You, too, can be *years ahead* with the latest model.'" The new buildings were either dull, blocky homages to The Machine, or flashy, sensational dem- onstrations of "the esthetic audacity of the designer." In short, "the situ- ation in modern architecture" seemed "almost as chaotic and irrational as the political situation of the modern world, in which the heads of state" were almost always on the verge of "mutilating the human race and wiping out civilization."[8]

By 1965, Mumford was starting to embrace the new anti-war move- ment, publishing an "Open Letter to President Lyndon Johnson" in March that aimed "to speak out on behalf of the great body of your countrymen who regard with abhorrence the course to which you are committing the United States in Vietnam."[9] In May, as president of the American Academy of Arts and Letters, Mumford delivered an "Address on the Vietnam Holocaust" that explicitly connected state violence against Vietnamese civilians with state violence against "the oppressed Negroes in Alabama and Mississippi."[10] There was progress that year on the civil rights front, after police came down hard on determined demonstrators and marchers in Selma: President Johnson signed the crucial Voting Rights Act in August. Meanwhile, though, LBJ was also drawing the country deeper into the Vietnam War, and Mumford would continue registering his defiance and disappointment for years to come. In a 1968 speech called "Vietnam—Before and After," he again connected his government's vicious and incompetent militarism overseas with its egregious domestic failures, though in this case he also tried a little harder to be constructive. Like many older intellectuals on the Left, Mumford found the counterculture somewhat distasteful, and worried about chaos on the streets and at universities. But he also expressed his full support for the social and political goals of the up-and-coming generation. "Every new attempt," he said, "to solve the problems of urban congestion, racial conflict, employment opportunity, and housing, must first start from a human premise and aim at a human goal. What our young people are saying to us in every word and gesture is that neither technological gadgets nor financial affluence nor status symbols are an acceptable substitute for a decent life, rooted in friendship, neighborliness, and all those essential facilities for life and growth, urban and rural, that money can never buy, and that technological know-how can never by itself produce."[11]

Here Mumford was riffing on the main theme of *The Myth of the Machine*, whose two volumes bore the same relationship to *Technics and Civilization* as *The City in History* did to *The Culture of Cities*. Again, I have to acknowledge my preference for the 1930s original, especially in its emphasis on radical renewal and biotechnics.[12] But *The Myth of the Machine* is a powerful polemic, full of scathing sarcasm and prophetic pronouncements. Perhaps most importantly, this revision of Mumford's thinking about technics allowed him to insist that even the post-1945 forms of the "modernized megamachine"—the "atomic reactors, the nuclear weapons, the superhighways, the space rockets, the underground control centers, the collective nuclear shelters (tombs)"—were just variations on very old themes, as expressed, for example, by the grandiose "manifestations of power" back in the "Pyramid Age." In parallel fashion, he also acknowledged that his own critique of modern mechanical progress was nothing new but had been around "for well over a century. Whatever Moby Dick may have meant in Melville's unconscious, whether the White Whale was God or Devil, Calvinist predestination or cartesian determinism, the body-denying Superego or the soul-denying Id, *Moby-Dick* the novel admirably symbolized that collocation of institutional and technological forces that were laming the spirit of man and threatening to deprive him of his rightful heritage as a full-bodied being, with all his organs intact, none withered or amputated."[13] The more networked systems we have put in place to assert control and ensure security, the more prone we have become to overwhelming feelings of vulnerability—ever since the Enlightenment. But, for just as long, writers and artists have been voicing warnings and protests, offering the radical possibility of embracing life's uncertainty and vicissitudes.

In 1975, the year Mumford turned eighty, he looked back on his life and published his last significant statement on history and modernity. He called it "Prologue to Our Time: 1895–1975," and it came as a "Postlude" to his book *Findings and Keepings: Analects for an Autobiography*. It is a breathtaking articulation of faith and determination in the face of devastating realities—in the wake of Vietnam, Watergate, and a crippling economic downturn. Lewis was old, broken, furious, disappointed in his society and himself. But he also still believed in "life in all its organic manifestations, and even in its dismaying contradictions, its ultimate tragedies." He still wanted "to do justice to man's central concern, his own humanization," to "sensitiveness, consciousness, responsiveness, expressive intelligence, human-heartedness, and (alas, one cannot use this word now without wincing) creativity. And love! Yes, love above all." Science, he knew, had won the day, with its "blind assurance" in "verifiable knowledge" about "the ultimate boundaries of the material universe." So he would speak a word for "invisible internal activities" and "unfathomable depths," for "self-knowledge" and "discrimination between good and evil." In his acceptance of the tragic world, he would nevertheless uphold the "democratic, egalitarian spirit" that moved some people to "repair the inequities and injustices left over from the past." He would continue to attack the doctrine of mechanical progress, continue to ask: "with a more voluminous productivity, augmented by almost omniscient computers and a wider range of antibiotics and inoculations, with a greater control over our genetic inheritance, with more complex surgical operations and transplants, with an extension of automation to every form of human activity, mankind will achieve— what?" But at the same time he would insist on celebrating *cultural* progress, the "slow accretion, though unsteady and intermittent, of meanings and forms and values," the occasional "upsurge of living ideas," the "realization of life itself flowing through time." He would always embrace that flow of time, never allowing the past or the future to be "swallowed in the void of a meaningless now." He would remain "immersed in the living stream of human history," always looking forward and backward, alert to the possibilities of resonance and connection.[14]

Findings and Keepings was dedicated to Sophia—"The best of my 'Findings,' the most enduring of my 'Keepings.'" By 1975, the Mumfords had been married for more than half a century; together, they had endured pain, grief, ill health, and mutual resentment. Lewis desperately wanted to believe that the final years of their marriage would be calm and affirming, though he knew that it had always been marked by instability. For the most part, through all the social turmoil of the 1960s, through all of his angst and frustration, he and Sophia had managed to deepen their love. In 1963, Lewis wrote that "Sophy and I have fallen into the habit after dinner, and often in spring, after breakfast, of taking a tour of our place, noting what is happening to the vegetation, getting a glimpse of the passing clouds, the setting sun, or the rising mist, and feeling as we do it all sorts of wordless sentiments connected with the place that originally we found here, in all its weedy wildness, and the place that, through a long series of plantings and trimmings, especially during the last dozen years, it has actually become. Last night, after a warm day, there was a cool bank of mist outlining the field toward the river and this tempted us out onto the field, where we are often tempted to get a view of the full vault of the sky. Coming back, Sophy said to me, tenderly, 'You know, this has been a good year: I am very glad that we have had it together.'"[15] Certainly, Lewis's renewed professional success in the early 1960s had helped ease some of the Mumfords' long-simmering tensions. But the years leading up to the publication of *Findings and Keepings* were among the most difficult of their married life.

In 1967, Lewis had started corresponding with a New England painter named Jocelyn Brodie. Lewis's books had helped her feel more grounded: "As a mother, artist, and teacher, I have been encouraged in the values you affirm." Now, in her late thirties (Lewis was in his early seventies), she was hoping to reach beyond her rather isolated life in New Hampshire and Vermont, and she thought that some sort of collaboration with Mumford might benefit both of them. Her first suggestion was that they work on a version of *The City in History* meant for children. Then she thought that Lewis's book on American architecture, *Sticks and Stones*, might be even better in an educational context. Lewis was enthusiastic about both ideas. Then Jocelyn proposed a Lewis Mumford Tour, involving historical markers that she would place in certain locations germane to his life and work, like Sunnyside Gardens, Radburn, Greenbelt, Central Park, and his own garden in Amenia. With Lewis's encouragement, she even imagined writing his biography. Once she met Sophia, she wanted to do a series of paintings capturing the Mumfords' marriage and domestic life together. But meanwhile she and Lewis were falling in love.[16]

Over the course of a few years, Jocelyn and Lewis danced around each other, tracing various intellectual and artistic currents while gradually revealing more of their emotions. Their letters went from formal and cordial to casual and flirtatious to anxious and admonitory to passionate and stormy. Jocelyn sought advice about her stalled career and her troubled marriage, which Lewis readily offered. Lewis, for his part, sought admiration and validation and even affection, as his friends began to die or fade into the background; in 1966, he had written wistfully to Henry Murray: "And may the dry branch of our friendship again bear flowers, as of old!"[17] Jocelyn's insight into Lewis's work clearly meant a great deal to him. In 1969, he thanked her profusely for recognizing that despite his retreat to Amenia he remained as committed to the urban as to the rural: he had grown "pretty tired of hearing that 'Lewis Mumford *hates* the City.'" They even traded ideas about Melville, and Lewis found her "new interpretation of *Moby-Dick*"—she thought it might be Melville's version of *The Rime of the Ancient Mariner*—to be "as startling as my friend Murray's notion that Moby Dick was the Puritan God that Melville wanted to slay." After Lewis edited and published a collection of Emerson's essays and journal entries, he wrote to Jocelyn to acknowledge her appreciation that he had drawn "heavily on those later essays, which show Emerson not as a mealy optimist or too-too etherealized transcendentalist, but one who had faced the terrible realities of life." Of all the fans he had acquired in the 1960s, Jocelyn stood out as the most sensitive, the most lively, the most imaginative, the most compatible. "I have been praying for just such a correspondent as you these last ten years," Lewis wrote in October 1969. He even asked her for comments and suggestions on some of his essay drafts.[18]

When Jocelyn picked up on his cues and started to press more boldly for expressions of intimacy, Lewis simultaneously pushed her away and encouraged her, following his old pattern of wanting it both ways. His letters got longer and more tangled, as he harangued her about honesty and restraint—and also agreed with her that "of course . . . flesh and spirit cannot be separated without doing damage to reality." Toward the end of 1971, he told Sophia what was happening, encouraging her to write to Jocelyn as well (she did), and meanwhile he signed his own letter to her "with a smiling embrace under the mistletoe." By the spring of 1972, Jocelyn was desperate for an actual meeting; after a few unsuccessful queries, she wrangled an invitation to visit Amenia with her husband at the end of July, despite Sophia's misgivings. "I felt very strongly," Sophia wrote in what she called her Day Book, "that I was unwilling to go through an emotional situation with any other woman at this stage of our life. It brought back memories we had given decent burial to, and for once I spoke up to defend our joint life against outside encroachments. Lewis utterly agreed with me." Sophia later enclosed this journal entry with an angry letter to Jocelyn.

From Sophia's perspective, the visit in the summer of 1972 was appropriately formal and halting; most of the long exchanges were between Jocelyn and Alison, who now lived just down the road and was also a painter. Lewis thought it "a strange meeting . . . , as if all five of us had been wrecked in a storm and had somehow been able to make the best of it though the skies remained threatening and unpredictable, with sudden patches of sunlight breaking through." And yes, Jocelyn was correct in sensing some suspicion, or perhaps even jealousy, coming from the Mumfords' daughter: "As for Alison's attitude toward me and my work," Lewis wrote, "that is a long story."

In his letters to Jocelyn that fall, Lewis shared all sorts of intimate details about his previous affairs, but he also drew a sharp, bright line. He had been strictly faithful to his wife for more than three decades. They might be living through a new era of women's liberation and free love, but he was not free. His relationship with Jocelyn, he said, "must not, at this point in my marriage, bring back Sophia's painful memories and make her uneasy. She, too, has been generous and magnanimous, perhaps was too much so back in the thirties: but I have no intention of letting our last years together, in all their mellowness, be disrupted, or even ruffled, by the presence of a rival."[19]

A year later, Lewis and Jocelyn crossed the line. It was October 1973, just before Lewis's seventy-eighth birthday. Jocelyn came to Amenia for a visit. The two of them went for a walk down to the river. They had some sort of sexual moment. And for the rest of the year they wrote love letters to each other—though Lewis's sometimes hit notes of regret and circumspection.

October 15: Jocelyn quoted Baudelaire: "La génie est l'enfance retrouvé" ["Genius is youth rediscovered"].

October 18: Lewis had been savoring "our walk to the river, with its enchanting climax, which made even my wilder fantasies seem tawdry. . . . We shall have to pick our way downward to the foothills of friendship, a more difficult and dangerous path, with sudden precipices, than we encountered on the way up."

October 19 (Lewis's birthday): "But you are: the *most magnificent Man in the modern world*. And I'd rather be miserable over you than mediocre any day."

October 19: "Nothing can take this away. It reconciles me to being seventy-eight, and makes me wonder if I am beginning all over again at 18."

October 23: "Oh Lewis! How you have penetrated my existence!"
October 23: "What has happened between us is irretrievable and
unforgettable; and though the essence of it is tragic, the tragedy
is not of my doing or of your doing. . . . With many other passionate moments of my life behind me I can at least say this: that
at the height of my powers I could not have felt more deeply
within you than I was when we embraced. . . . No other erotic
moment I can remember ever left such a lasting impression upon
me. That we shall never get beyond this point—perhaps?—does
not call for tears or renunciation: so far, if no further, we have
had a glimpse of what love in its fullness might have offered us, if
we could remake the whole scenario of our lives—as neither of
us can actually do. . . . Let us remember that chastity heightens
passion even more than complete fulfillment."[20]

After a few weeks, Lewis told Sophia everything, and for the following two years all three of them were miserable. Sophia began reliving
the torture of the 1930s: Catherine, then Alice—especially Alice—then
Jo. The letters continued, but now they were full of accusations and
pleading and forced rationality and outbursts of agony. "Your letter
touched me," Sophia wrote to Jocelyn, in July 1974. "Alas that the situation was an impossible one for me to submit to. We have all three
wounded and been wounded—and now must pray that in time we will
heal. Sincerely I say I hope you will find your path." Sophia and Lewis
decided together that if Jocelyn could revert to being a friendly correspondent and long-distance collaborator, they might coexist peacefully.
Jocelyn thought that it might help to talk to Sophia in person, and Sophia almost agreed to a meeting but ultimately canceled. In March 1975,
Sophia at last let her story come pouring out:

Until your advent I had assimilated the pain of the early years: I no
longer rehearsed them in my mind: they were part of a life that had
held more joy than sorrow, and I faced the prospect of the final years
of life with glad anticipation, feeling we had together won through to
a deserved peace. For my seventieth birthday Lewis celebrated our
hopes in the most beautiful poem any man could have written to his

wife. And then came the holocaust. I have never known such black despair and anguish as I knew last year. . . .

Bear in mind, Jocelyn, that you are dealing with the lives of two people married to each other for a very very long time. Ours has been a live marriage, never a purely conventional one. I have tried, but I cannot accept as a permanent part of the picture your hopes for a larger share in Lewis's life. I want our life together, his and mine, to matter again as it mattered to both of us before you entered the scene. And it cannot unless you accept the role offered you. If these words are cruel, they are not heartless. I just don't know how else to meet my own turbulent emotions. Faithfully, Sophia.

Jocelyn couldn't blame Sophia, but she did let Lewis know that she felt bullied. "Did you ever ask *me* what I wanted, expected, anticipated? No! You just lectured me on the basis of your past experience."[21]

The severance came in the spring of 1976, despite Lewis's repeated attempts to convince Jocelyn that they could still have a wonderful friendship: "At their worst, our relations had the dignity of tragedy: painful but a blessing. Would you turn your back on all this with a parting curse?" Yes, she would, and she added some hard truths about the way Lewis had treated Sophia, and the way Sophia had failed to develop an independent "sense of self." She saw all too clearly that the Mumfords had not in fact worked through their past trauma. And so Lewis finally withdrew: "To save my marriage with Sophia and to redeem for old love what is left for our remaining years, I must now leave you to find your way alone."

Lewis and Jocelyn did get back in touch a year later and exchange a few more letters, but they were all strained and strange. "As for my painting," Jocelyn wrote, in October 1978, "I am working again on the 'Marriage' series which you and Sophia inspired." Lewis did not reply to that one. When Lewis's second collection of sundry memoirs came out, in 1979, Jocelyn couldn't suppress her disappointment. *My Works and Days: A Personal Chronicle* is more forthcoming and wide-ranging than *Findings and Keepings*, but Jocelyn found it repetitive, and she knew from Lewis's letters that in the book he had covered up the bulk of his infidelity. She typed out a scathing letter, and then scrawled at the top, in brown ink: "*Don't* ever send! *Shut up*! Too late!! The *world*! *Let go*!" I don't think she ever posted it; in any case, after that, there's no more evidence of contact.[22]

Lewis and Sophia did smooth out their relationship, in the end, and recaptured some measure of mellowness. In an admiring mood, early in 1978, Sophia wrote in her private notes that "all the village children loved Lewis—to this day children and animals will go to him first, ignoring other adults in the room. He pays just enough attention to make them feel noticed and wanted, but never concentrates on them in a sticky fashion. He respects them and they him."[23] This was another way in which Mumford was like Thoreau, who often took the children of Concord with him on huckleberrying expeditions, and Sophia genuinely appreciated Lewis's ability to make connections with his heart as well as his head, despite the pain that ability sometimes caused her.

By the late 1970s Lewis felt somewhat depleted, but he was still committed to his role as both a husband and a prophet. "There is one front on which you and I can unite from now on," Sophia had written to Jocelyn: "and that is to respect Lewis's own needs—his need for autonomy and his need for peace and harmony. . . . Let him . . . go back to the writing he so sorely wants to be released to do."[24] Both *Findings and Keepings* and *My Works and Days* are assemblages, miscellanies, experiments in juxtaposition, assortments of mostly old and a few new writings, ranging from letters to journal entries to magazine articles to speeches to personal essays to book excerpts to poems. "There are some enterprises," Ishmael said, "in which a careful disorderliness is the true method."[25] *My Works and Days* is the edgier, more revealing volume, betraying Lewis's cumulative gloom. The last few selections are mostly about "the basic trauma of civilization itself." His general approach in these essays was to trace certain historical trends back to "remote, sometimes prehistoric, events," so as to offset the sloppy, "technocratic" thinking of those who were "bedazzled over our immediate success with nuclear energy, moon-shots, and computers." He hoped that, in the end, his life of writing would be seen as a dedicated attempt "to restore a more life-favoring ecological and cultural equilibrium."[26]

As his "postlude" for this final collection, Mumford chose "Call Me Jonah." He wanted his readers to remember him as at least trying to wrestle with the truth—as similar "to the mythic Jonah in all his ways, not least his temptations"—as someone "who knows that a blessing repeated too often may become a curse, and that a curse faced bravely may become a blessing."[27] To me, he sounds a little like Melville's description of an ideal whaling man, which may also have been a description of himself—a man who had, "by the stillness and seclusion of many long night-watches in the remotest waters, and beneath constellations never seen here at the north, been led to think untraditionally and independently; receiving all nature's sweet or savage impressions fresh from her own virgin, voluntary, and confiding breast. . . . Nor will it at all detract from him, dramatically regarded, if either by birth or other circumstances, he have what seems a half wilful over-ruling morbidness at the bottom of his nature. For all men tragically great are made so through a certain morbidness."[28]

After *My Works and Days*, Mumford turned back to the autobiography he had drafted in the mid-1950s. He found the prose fluid and moving, in need of little revision. But he was still unable to push the story past the mid-1930s—still unable to face his darkest memories. When *Sketches from Life* came out in 1982, its subtitle suggested that there would soon be a follow-up: this was "The Autobiography of Lewis Mumford—The Early Years." But it wound up being the last thing he published. He turned eighty-seven that October, and he was already sliding into the same kind of dementia that had afflicted his mother.

CHAPTER 34

Lizzie (1891–1906)

Melville never would have thought to write an autobiography. But his wife may have wished he had. Almost as soon as Herman died, Lizzie started looking back at his life and ahead to his legacy. It was Lizzie who laid the groundwork for the Melville Revival.

She was assuredly dismayed by her husband's few obituaries. One of the most laudatory was printed as an homage to *Hiram* Melville. In other notices, the emphasis was on the decline of Herman's fame, portrayed as a natural consequence of the fading quality of his books after the gripping *Typee* and *Omoo*. Eventually, the obituaries reported, Melville simply gave up and withdrew. "Even his own generation has long thought him dead," said the New York *Press*, "so quiet have been the later years of his life."[1] And even those who appreciated his work tended to depict him as bitterly antisocial: "his proud and sensitive nature made him a recluse, and led him to bury himself from a world with which he had little in common."[2] Only if you sought out the testaments of a couple of his friendly acquaintances could you get a glimpse of Melville the dedicated poet and charming conversationalist, with his "jovial, let-the-world-go-as-it-will spirit."[3] Lizzie was almost befuddled at times by the strange mischaracterizations she came across: "I do not think my husband's manner ever could be called 'gruff,'" she noted in 1901.[4]

Over the last fifteen years of her life, until she passed away in 1906, Lizzie encouraged everyone in her circle to help her salvage Herman's reputation as both a man and a writer. She clung especially to the rare tributes, as in one western Massachusetts newspaper, claiming Melville as an aesthetic innovator, "original and virile," creator of works "of imagination more powerful and often poetic" than any of his contemporaries.[5] Even more deeply than Herman himself, Lizzie believed in the persistent worth and relevance of his writing. She named the young Arthur Stedman as her husband's literary executor, hoping that he might spend his career promoting Melville (he had just earned a master's degree from Yale with a focus on literary biography). Since 1888, Stedman had been visiting the Melville household regularly and had struck up "a friendly family acquaintance." Now he started publishing biographical appreciations—at least five in the first year after Herman's death. "Mr. Melville," he wrote, "would have been more than mortal if he had been indifferent to his loss of popularity. Yet he seemed contented to preserve an entirely independent attitude, and to trust to the verdict of the future."[6] Most important to that verdict was Stedman's successful effort to bring Melville's novels back into print: in 1892, he edited and published new versions of *Typee, Omoo, White-Jacket,* and *Moby-Dick*.

Those new editions spurred many more in both the United States and Britain over the next decade (there were six additional printings just of *Typee*), ensuring that, at the very least, a number of writers and scholars would continue to discuss Melville's merits. The conversation was especially robust in England, and Lizzie noted the contributions of several British advocates, including the socialist H. S. Salt, who published admiring articles in 1889 and 1892. Indeed, Lizzie kept careful track of the Englishmen who had either written letters to her husband or published something about him, and she may well have reached out to them periodically after Herman died.[7] She was even in touch with a publisher in Dresden about bringing out new German editions of her husband's best-known books.[8] By 1899, a London correspondent for the *New York Times* was sensing among English and European readers a "conspicuous revival of interest in America's sea author."[9] That same year, a Canadian scholar named Archibald MacMechan published an essay about *Moby-Dick* called "The Greatest Sea Story Ever Written," which Salt reprinted in England in 1901. MacMechan was based in Canada, but he frequently taught summer courses at Columbia University, where he grew friendly with Professor W. P. Trent, one of Carl Van Doren's colleagues in the

English department and a coeditor of the *Cambridge History of American Literature*. Van Doren probably saw a 1914 reprint of MacMechan's *Moby-Dick* essay, and it seems to have made an impression.[10]

Arthur Stedman lost interest in his Melville work within a few years, but meanwhile Lizzie started to cultivate another potential biographer, an old friend from Pittsfield named Joe Smith. Between October 1891 and January 1892, Smith published nine installments of a memorial essay about Melville in Pittsfield's *Evening Journal*, which Lizzie saw and endorsed, while also noticing a few mistakes. Smith had known the Melvilles for forty years, ever since they first moved to the Berkshires, where he himself was a popular nature writer, poet, local historian, and guide, often publishing under the name Godfrey Greylock. Herman seems to have been fond of him. In late September 1892, Lizzie met with him in Pittsfield and then wrote to Stedman to let him know that Smith, whom she described as "the most prominent literary man" in the Berkshires, was interested in expanding his newspaper articles into a formal Life of Melville. It's possible that she was even trying to stir up a competition between the two potential biographers—or maybe she just thought that Stedman ought to be informed, given his official status as literary executor. "He spoke to me about it and I approved," she explained to Stedman, "if he would submit the proof to me to correct errors which must necessarily creep in to any such record. . . . He is quite advanced in years and much broken physically, though he does not admit it—and I fear the undertaking will be too much for him (always seeming to have some literary work in hand)—but let him take his own way—as he is so desirous to do it."[11] Lizzie was right to worry about Smith's capacity to take on another project and probably wrong to tell Stedman about Smith's desire. In the end, neither man took up the task.

Smith died in 1896, and the following summer, Lizzie went back to the Berkshires with a plan. During a long vacation in the mountains, she collected all of Smith's memorials, edited them, and published them as a thirty-one-page pamphlet. They had been "scattered in poor type through many numbers of the papers," she observed, "where they would never be read, and I thought they ought to be rescued from oblivion." She also noted that Smith "was Herman's ardent admirer and most faithful friend for these many long years, and I value him for that and regret to lose him from the Pittsfield circle alas now so sadly diminished."[12] Still, Lizzie saw fit not only to correct factual errors but also to excise certain criticisms, as when Smith referred rather casually to "the irrelevant rhapsodies which mar many of Mr. Melville's later works," or claimed that "even in books where he was not avowedly his own hero, he often idealized himself in portions of the story." Lizzie even cut the simple, factual statement that her husband had "often, and sometimes very closely, modelled incidents in his stories upon real ones in his own experience." The books were fiction, after all; she did not want anyone making assumptions about the truth behind the mask.[13]

Surely, though, she herself must have wondered about the relationship between Herman's life and his books—especially his inner life, which he rarely spoke about. "He was not one to display to the common world," Smith wrote, "what should be sacred to his own breast. Perhaps he erred in not always seeking sympathies, even where he could rightfully look for, and was certain to find them. But of that we can only conjecture."[14] Lizzie let those sentences stand, but she never shared her own conjectures about Herman's most intimate thoughts and feelings.

In her own short, unpublished memoir about her husband, which seems to have been intended mostly for her daughters, Lizzie stuck to the basic facts of Herman's life—correcting some common misperceptions, especially about his various voyages—and to descriptions of some of his and the family's possessions. The tone is sometimes solicitous, sometimes proud: "We all felt anxious about the strain on his health," she wrote, but it turned out that "in 13 years he had written 10 books besides much miscellaneous writing." There is nothing about their marriage or their dead sons. She mentioned an old clock and a couple of watches, some vases, some family photographs, some pewter plates and silverware, a snuff box, two ivory miniatures, and some "Whale Pictures."[15] But she seems not to have retained one particular item that had made a strong impression on her granddaughter Frances when Herman was still alive, a "more than life size bust of Antinous," one of her grandfather's "treasures": "It stood on a tall white pedestal in the corner of the front parlor, draped with a long white net veil to keep the city dust from settling on the beautiful features and curly hair of the young Roman. I had to pass the parlor door every time I went to the basement dining room and many was the time I scurried fearfully past the door, glancing hastily in, to see if the still, white figure would raise its inclined head to discover who was going past in such a hurry."[16] Antinous was the emperor Hadrian's male lover, during the Age of the Antonines.

What did Lizzie think, when those beautiful features and that curly hair turned up, again and again, in Herman's writing?[17]

Harry Bolton, in *Redburn*: "He was one of those small, but perfectly formed beings, with curling hair, and silken muscles, who seem to have been born in cocoons. His complexion was a mantling brunette, feminine as a girl's; his feet were small; his hands were white; and his eyes were large, black, and womanly; and, poetry aside, his voice was as the sound of a harp." Young Redburn was thoroughly enchanted with him. Even after Harry had led Redburn through the opulent but "dismal" and "dreadful" nightclubs of England's homosexual Underworld—even after Redburn had recognized him as a lying, gambling drifter—still, he went "arm-in-arm" with him and called him a "dear friend."[18]

Also in *Redburn*: a young immigrant named Carlo, "a rich-cheeked, chestnut-haired Italian boy," whose eye "shone with a soft and spiritual radiance, like a moist star in a tropic sky," and whose head was "heaped with thick clusters of tendril curls, half overhanging the brows and delicate ears." When Carlo played his hand-organ, Redburn melted: "Turn hither your pensive, morning eyes; and while I list to the organs twain— one yours, one mine—let me gaze fathoms down into thy fathomless eye. . . . All this could Carlo do—make, unmake me; build me up; to pieces take me; and join me limb to limb. He is the architect of domes of sound, and bowers of song."[19]

Jack Chase, in *White-Jacket*: "tall and well-knit, with a clear open eye, a fine broad brow, and an abounding nut-brown beard. . . . I thanked my sweet stars, that kind fortune had placed me near him, though under him, in the frigate; and from the outset Jack and I were fast friends. Wherever you may be now rolling over the blue billows, dear Jack! take my best love along with you; and God bless you, wherever you go!"[20]

And in *Billy Budd* (dedicated to Jack Chase): Billy himself, who "looked even younger than he really was, owing to a lingering adolescent expression in the as yet smooth face all but feminine in purity of natural complexion but where, thanks to his seagoing, the lily was quite suppressed and the rose had some ado visibly to flush through the tan." His ear was "small and shapely," and he had "that humane look of reposeful good nature which the Greek sculptor in some instances gave to his heroic strong man, Hercules. But this again was subtly modified by another and pervasive quality . . . , something in the mobile expression, and every chance attitude and movement, something suggestive of a mother eminently favored by Love and the Graces."[21]

What did Lizzie think of the scene in *Moby-Dick* where Ishmael finds himself squeezing spermaceti with his crewmates, "till I myself almost melted into it"—till he begins "squeezing my co-laborers' hands in it, mistaking their hands for the gentle globules"—till he develops "such an abounding, affectionate, friendly, loving feeling . . . that at last I was continually squeezing their hands, and looking up into their eyes sentimentally"?

What did Lizzie think of the way Ishmael fell in love with Queequeg— the way they became "bosom friends" and ultimately imagined themselves as "wedded"? In almost all of Melville's writings, it takes love—the love of male fellowship—to offset society's coldness and alienation, that feeling of having your "warm soul . . . flogged out by adversity." "I felt a melting in me," Ishmael says, once he has spent some time with Queequeg. "No more my splintered heart and maddened hand were turned against the wolfish world. This soothing savage had redeemed it."[22]

What did Lizzie think of her husband's relationship with Nathaniel Hawthorne? The two men did not see each other after 1856, but Hawthorne was never far from the Melvilles' consciousness. In 1884, Nathaniel's son Julian published a memoir about his father in which he reprinted Herman's passionate Berkshire letters of the early 1850s.[23] A few years later, Melville included a poem about Hawthorne in *Timoleon*: "To have known, to have loved him / After loneness long; / And then to be estranged in life, / And neither in the wrong."[24] Melville even compared Billy Budd to a particular "beautiful woman in one of Hawthorne's minor tales."[25] Late in 1903, Julian Hawthorne published another book about Nathaniel, called *Hawthorne and His Circle*, and Lizzie picked it up. "I have been reading your new memorials of your father with great interest," she wrote to the author, "but am much troubled to see such a distressingly poor portrait of Mr. Melville."[26]

I don't think Lizzie was jealous, though. There were a few times when Herman lost control of himself, and she felt the urge to flee. But I don't think she resented him. To me, the evidence of her own writing, combined with the testimony of family members, bespeaks a complicated but ultimately solid marriage. I think Lizzie understood that Herman's time at sea as a young man had made the conventional bonds of society seem thin, ragged, paltry: he would always crave the hearty, outdoor solidarity of the main-top, the embrace of friends with whom he had learned to navigate the "humorously perilous business" of life.[27] I think Lizzie probably appreciated her husband's sense of humor. I think she kept a safe distance at times but was never aloof; on that point, I differ with Mumford, who imagined her as frigid. To me, Lizzie comes across as anxious but steadfast, calmly and confidently caring, always ready to face reality and matter-of-factly make the best of it.

Her granddaughter Eleanor, eventual keeper of the bread box full of manuscripts, summed Lizzie up by asserting that "the strength of her character was a monumental strength—simply kindness."[28] The two became very close in Lizzie's later years. As of 1900, Lizzie was telling a trusted in-law—Herman's cousin Kate, one of several women in the extended family with whom she stayed in touch—that she was already planning to leave certain important items to Eleanor, "who now, by the way, is 18 yrs old with long dresses and her hair up. Can you realise it? I often think what companions these older ones would be now to Herman—for they are extremely bright and intelligent, though it is their grandma who says so."[29] Eleanor's younger sister, Frances, also spoke glowingly of Lizzie: "My grandmother I loved dearly. She never tolerated black hair ribbons on her grandchildren. She had been in mourning so often for members of her family that whenever her grandchildren appeared in black she changed them to bright colors."[30]

FIGURE 16. Lizzie in 1885.

It's true that Lizzie's life had been marked by tragedy, and her letters sometimes took a melancholy turn, though she was also extraordinarily resilient, thanks both to her own fortitude and to a middle-class culture that accepted hardship as part of life.[31] When Stanwix died in 1886, Herman's sister Helen noted that Lizzie "is in great trouble; and seems unable to find solace for her grief—it was *so* hard,—the sickness and death so far away!"[32] There were years, Lizzie admitted, when the holiday season brought "as much sadness as gladness, and the places left vacant by the dear ones who have 'gone up higher' seem more empty still." If it weren't for "the sympathy and interest in the young branches" of the family, who greeted the holidays joyfully, "I for one would almost be glad to let them pass without outward notice."[33] But Lizzie continued holding the requisite celebrations, continued tying brightly colored ribbons in her granddaughters' hair, continued searching doggedly for solace. In the spring and summer of 1872, five years after Malcolm's death, she remembered a photograph of him that Herman had presented to his volunteer regiment, and she launched a letter-writing campaign to retrieve it, which was ultimately successful. It made her "truly thankful" to be able to gaze at the picture of her eldest child, whom Herman had called "the phenomenon."[34] Lizzie was also a stalwart supporter of others when they were in mourning: "I sorrow with all my heart," she wrote to cousin Kate after her husband died in 1899. "All of us who knew him will feel his death as a personal loss, so kind and courteous was his uniform attitude towards us. . . . You are right dear Kate in trying to take up the duties of life again, occupation of mind and body is the surest safeguard from brooding grief."[35]

Lizzie was especially adept at deflecting the grief that her husband sometimes caused her. When Herman was raging about his reviews or struggling to finish a demonic manuscript, Lizzie relied on the sympathy of her female in-laws, some of whom lived with the Melvilles for years at a time, in both the Berkshires and New York. They understood immediately whenever Lizzie asked them to avoid certain topics, or to make an effort to tell Herman he was looking well, or even to refrain from visiting. In the end, Herman and Lizzie were as mutually dependent as Ishmael and Queequeg, when the shipmates were attached by their "monkey-rope," that "elongated Siamese ligature," with the harpooner dangling over the side of the ship and Ishmael holding the cord, which was also fastened "to a strong strip of canvas belted round his waist," so that "should poor Queequeg sink to rise no more," then Ishmael would go tumbling into the sea as well.[36] "When Herman is gone all day," Lizzie wrote, while she was still getting used to his day job, ". . . the house seems utterly desolate—it is quite a new sensation for me to have the days seem *long*." She couldn't wait for him to get time off, so they could take a vacation in the Berkshires: "We are counting the days for going to Pittsfield and think with longing of the refreshing breezes from the hill tops."[37] They shared many deep connections, not least a love for the landscape of western Massachusetts; that was also where they went together immediately after Malcolm died, to help ease their pain. And in the memoir Lizzie wrote about Herman, she made a point of noting that her husband had been responsible for naming one of the local peaks (or renaming it, since it probably already had an Indian name): Melville dubbed it "October Mt., from its brilliant display of foliage in that month," and today you can hike the trails in October Mountain State Forest.[38]

In the last years of Herman's life, he depended on his wife not just for care but for active assistance with his writing. "He has a great deal of unfinished work at his desk which will give him occupation," Lizzie explained to Kate, upon Herman's retirement from the custom house, "which together with his love of books will prevent time from hanging heavy on his hands—and I hope he will get into a more quiet frame of mind, exempt from the daily irritation of overwork."[39] What Lizzie didn't mention is that she herself was already helping to steady his ship, by making clean copies of his manuscripts, and helping to revise and arrange his poems—even when he might have preferred to leave things unfinished. In turn, she was surely touched by the sweet, grateful dedication that Herman wrote to her for *Weeds and Wildings*, with its "melting mood" and its recollection of the times he had brought flowers back to her from the fields and hollows around Arrowhead.[40] And she must have been pleased with the decision to close *Timoleon* with "L'Envoi: The Return of the Sire de Nesle, A.D. 16": "My towers at last! These rovings end, / Their thirst is slaked in larger dearth. . . . / But thou, my stay, thy lasting love / One lonely good, let this but be! / Weary to view the wide world's swarm, / But blest to fold but thee."[41]

When Herman died, and Lizzie set out to promote his work, she was only continuing the labor she had performed, off and on, throughout their marriage. Herman trusted her above all others, and over the years she developed an independence and discernment that were crucial to her identity. You can see her steady confidence even back in 1860, when Herman sailed for San Francisco with his brother and left the manuscript of his first poetry collection with her, asking her to oversee its possible publication, and penning a memo saying that any questions "can be referred to Lizzie" and that she "should by all means see the printed sheets *before* [their] being bound." Lizzie immediately wrote to Herman's well-connected friend Evert Duyckinck in New York, enclosing the memo, and then she sent the full manuscript and offered to consult as necessary. Duyckinck balked, and had trouble finding anyone else who might be interested. But Lizzie persisted: "I am willing to wait patiently for the result," she wrote, "so that the publication is eventually accomplished—and do not consider its rejection by the publishers as any test of its merit in a literary point of view—well knowing, as Herman does also, that *poetry* is a comparatively uncalled for article in the publishing market. I suppose that if John Milton were to offer 'Paradise Lost' to the Harpers tomorrow, it would be promptly rejected as 'unsuitable' not to say, denounced as dull." Her tone let Duyckinck know that she considered herself to be a full member of his circle—that she would keep her own counsel—and that she expected his ongoing help. Tellingly, Lizzie also revealed that the book of poems had been "a profound secret between Herman and myself" for years, and it meant a great deal to both of them, but she thought it was probably better that she was handling these negotiations herself, "for he might be disheartened at the outset by its rejection, and perhaps withhold it altogether, which would be a great disappointment to me."[42]

That collection never made it into print. Lizzie was right: when Herman heard about the manuscript's initial reception, he was so disappointed that he gave up on it. To him, perhaps, it was just another uncompleted work. But, over the years, some of those early poems seem to have been salvaged—first in *Timoleon*, and then, decades later, in *Weeds and Wildings*.[43] It was probably Lizzie's perseverance that enabled their rediscovery.

CHAPTER 35

Sophia (1982-97)

Sophia cared for Lewis until he died in 1990, at the age of ninety four. The final five years, which she referred to as Lewis's "Decline" in her private notes, were particularly trying.[1] But their life together had already changed drastically by 1982, when Lewis lost the ability to write. Throughout their six decades of marriage, Lewis had always spent most of each day sequestered at his desk. Now he was almost entirely dependent on Sophia, and she almost never had time to herself.

Fortunately, the retrospective work they had done together in the 1970s, despite all the pain it caused, left them mostly at peace with each other. As soon as Lewis turned to his autobiographical materials, after publishing *The Pentagon of Power* in 1970, he had enlisted Sophia's help in sorting and arranging them, and especially in deciding what to include and what to leave out. By the time Jocelyn appeared on the scene, then, Sophia was already wrestling with her memories of Lewis's serial infidelity in the 1930s. The affair with Jocelyn made those memories all the more searing, and, for a while, a sense of irremediable trauma hung over the Mumfords' farmhouse. But Sophia was fiercely committed to finding her way through what Lewis called "the maze of marriage."[2] They sometimes took breaks from "the dissection of our own lives," as Sophia put it, but ultimately they considered that labor to be one of their primary responsibilities as life partners. They were even a little bit proud of their efforts. "No psycho-analysis," Sophia wrote, in 1978, ". . . could have dug deeper or more honestly than our probings."[3] To her relief, they had decided that not all of those probings had to be public—that in fact there would be no mention of Alice Decker whatsoever in *My Works and Days*—no mention of the one affair that truly could have severed their bond. And Sophia was also satisfied with the relatively discreet way in which Lewis handled his relationships with Catherine Bauer and Jo Strongin. There was much they could agree on.

In her journal, though, Sophia revealed the depths of her ambivalence. Jocelyn had not been wrong to point out the inequality in their marriage, the way Lewis's all-consuming career had prevented Sophia from developing certain aspects of her selfhood. "Part of Sophia's trauma," Jocelyn had written to Lewis in 1976, ". . . is something else, you—and your marriage—have shielded her from. In a way, the marriage actually took the place of it."[4] In 1978, Sophia herself was coming to a similar conclusion, though she determinedly spun it into a celebration of how her working relationship with Lewis had finally evolved: she wished that from the beginning he had "tried to bring me along with him," rather than "turning to other women for stimulation," for then "he might have brought forth from me some of the qualities he now so welcomes. For the last few years have been quite wonderful in the common responses we have discovered in one another. And it saddens me to think we might much earlier have had at least some measure of it if we *both* had tried. But truly the sadness pales before the delight of these years."[5]

Strange to think that Herman and Lizzie, in the mid-nineteenth century, might have had a slightly stronger intellectual partnership than Lewis and Sophia in the mid-twentieth.[6] But as of the late 1970s, Sophia took on a more significant role in Lewis's work than Lizzie ever did in Herman's. By the time the manuscript of *Sketches from Life* was undergoing copyediting in early 1981, Sophia was the one arguing with the publisher about individual sentences. Her husband, she explained, "firmly believes that a book should express the author's personality and style, even if it is contrary to immediate usage. . . . He *knows* why he uses a word—as a rule."[7] Most of those editorial battles went the Mumfords' way, and *Sketches from Life* was generally acclaimed for its elegant prose.

I would even venture to guess that Sophia had a moderating influence on Lewis's despair in this final book. In February 1980, he was planning

FIGURE 17. Lewis and Sophia in September 1971, after fifty years of marriage.

a new concluding chapter that would offer "my original intuitions of a Dark Age—and carry that theme into the speechless present."[8] But no such Melvillean chapter materialized; chronologically, the book ends in the 1930s, with the Great Depression and the New Deal, and with Mumford's tribute "to the resilience many of our most humble countrymen showed then: to their adaptability, and their wryly comic defenses and comebacks." Once again, with Sophia's support, he was praising persistence and dreaming of renewal. And in the actual concluding chapter, which reads more like an epilogue, he focused on his and Sophia's shared cultivation of the Amenia landscape, "the groundwork" they had laid together "for our entire family life for more than half a century."[9] Though they would always be children of the city, their relationship had become intertwined with their home in the country. For years, walking the valley pathways through the garden and meadows and woods, Lewis had felt the deepest kind of love and connection: there was surely "nothing to equal this intimate experience except a long and close marriage."[10]

Most of the reviews of *Sketches* were excellent. *Time* called the writing "luminous" and dubbed Mumford "an urban Thoreau." The reviewer in *Newsday* especially appreciated the narrative's "leisurely" pace and found that it "summons both a long-gone city and a man who links eras as effortlessly as he does disciplines."[11] But in Mumford's papers I found a clipping that must have infuriated both Lewis and Sophia. It is dated May 16, 1982, and it seems to be among the last items Lewis collected, for this was when his cognitive abilities were starting to fade. It's a review from the *New York Times*, by the newspaper's architecture critic, Paul Goldberger, who approved of Mumford's opinions about architecture but not of his "haughty pronouncements on the ruin of our culture." Moreover, Goldberger saw fit to attack Mumford's brand of urbanism as being too enamored of "order," of top-down efforts to make every city into a simplified, "rational system."[12] In other words, he had completely missed Mumford's emphasis on rediscovery, and community, and contrapuntal collectivism—on what Mumford referred to, in *Sketches*, as the "creative American image of democratic social reconstruction."[13] Well, perhaps the one saving grace of Lewis's dementia was that such radical misconstruals of his worldview were no longer likely to haunt him.

Lewis's voice went silent after *Sketches*, but Sophia spent a lot more time thinking and writing about Lewis's reputation and legacy, spurred, in part, by Donald Miller, the young scholar who had started visiting the Mumfords in 1977 in the hope of writing Lewis's biography. From the beginning, Miller made a good impression, but Lewis actively discouraged him: I'm still writing my own life, he said, and perhaps he added one of his familiar jibes about the perniciousness of PhDs (Miller was a history professor at Lafayette College, thus—like me—"belonging to that low circle in Hell set aside by Dante for academic minds").[14] Once *Sketches* came out, though, and it was clear there would be no sequel, both of the Mumfords became more accommodating. Harry Murray even chimed in, noting that Miller had set up a meeting with him, and the conversation had gone well. "I liked Don Miller immensely," he wrote, in what turned out to be his last letter to Lewis. "I think you can count on a fair deal from him."[15] Lewis and Sophia never agreed to call Miller's book an "authorized" or "official" biography, but they did sit for many interviews, and ultimately they turned over their most private papers for Miller's use—a decision that caused Sophia considerable angst, and even anger, once the biography came out in 1989. During the last few years of Miller's research, Lewis was only intermittently capable of conversation, and only intermittently aware of what Miller was working on. But Sophia had placed her full trust in her husband's biographer, even asking him to be Lewis's literary executor—a request she withdrew after reading his book manuscript.[16]

"I think at the moment I *hate* Don Miller more than I have ever hated before," Sophia wrote, on October 16, 1989. "He combed Lewis's Personalia notes like a creature scratching for grubs (never mind mixed metaphor). . . . In my old age, with Lewis stricken, I had unconsciously suppressed the hurtful days and reveled in my version of our life. Now suddenly I was made to face what Lewis had shielded me from. To what purpose?" Miller had struck through the mask. From my perspective, his work seems trenchant and illuminating—if also, at times, insensitive, and perhaps overwrought. To Sophia, it seemed shockingly invasive and wildly misleading. On the most intimate level, it actually did reveal some new secrets about the extent of Lewis's passion for Alice and Jo: that's what was most hurtful to Sophia. But her distress went much further, because she felt that the overall portrait Miller had drawn of her husband emphasized only his intellect and his libido, and almost entirely excluded the Lewis she knew "as a human being, a husband, a father, a friend."[17] The biography failed to do justice to all their probings, their accommodations, their ultimately cathartic rehearsals of past traumas.

To me, Sophia's eloquent anger helps fill out the picture of the Mumfords' marriage. Miller discovered certain truths, but there were others to which he may never have had access. Lewis had predicted just such a scenario, as early as 1936: "I was remarking to Sophy the other day that my notes would leave an altogether false impression of our marriage. Our good moments have had continuity; the inner rhythm of our life has had a deep harmony and brought an underlying satisfaction. When one is happy one does not talk about it, nor does one note the moments of deep union, or ecstasy, when the partner is one's habitual mate. . . . Even our sensuous and physical experience of each other—like that fine afternoon of rut last summer, which finally culminated on a damp grassy bank by the river, very hasty because the children were around, but also very precious—even this has passed unrecorded up to this moment."[18] Now it was Sophy's turn to look back and try to capture those inner rhythms and harmonies and satisfactions and ecstasies—that continuity of peace so often missed by historians because it defies the definition of history as change over time and the convention of anchoring our chronicles with Wars, Depressions, and Plagues.

She remembered a lot, which is itself remarkable, given the ever-increasing burden of caregiving that she had borne for the previous seven years. I could barely bring myself to read her notes on Lewis's "Decline," because of the resonances with my own parents' last years. Lewis, like my father, had hallucinations, and grew hostile when his spouse could not confirm them. Like my father, he sat in the same chair for hours, staring blankly across the room or out the window. Like my father, he woke up in the middle of the night, got dressed, and asked for breakfast. Lewis fixated on the need to work with "The Group," for the betterment of the world.[19] My father kept insisting that "everyone had to have a say"—in what, we didn't know. After about five years, my mother was so exhausted and resentful that she couldn't even smile at him anymore, and as soon as he died, she plunged into a dementia of her own. Somehow, at a time when even less was understood about dementia care, Sophia kept a more even keel, maintained her hard-earned sense of self and her determination to persevere. She did have the help of a stalwart, companionable man named Dick Coons, who gained Lewis's trust and was strong enough to lift him out of his chair. But mostly Sophia just tried to talk to her husband, reminding him of how he used to read out loud to the children, and play in the fields with them until their bedtime, and turn on classical music, which, for a while, was the only thing that could soothe Alison. Now it soothed Lewis.

"Lewis the egotist," she scribbled, after reading Miller's biography, "Lewis the man ready to sacrifice anyone or anything that might interfere with his work, Lewis the philanderer, the ineffectual parent—all these blot out the Lewis I feel I spent my life with." Sure, Lewis was an egotist, but "what creative person is not an egotist?" In defiance, Sophia remembered "the Lewis who, when he went off to lecture, would leave a good-night message on or under my pillow, or have the florist deliver a lovely potted plant if he was to be gone a week or more." She remembered "the Lewis who invented games to play with his two different children; the Lewis friends in need turned to, the Lewis who never said NO to a young student who wanted to talk. . . . That's the Lewis I hold dear and the Lewis who even now, when life permits it, is gay and teasing and loving and outgoing—and still finds women attractive and welcomes their attention—and is unfailingly courteous—except in those moments when he resents being handled or directed—then, to be honest, he can be quite fierce. But that is the residue of his need for autonomy—a primal need for him."[20] It's astounding, really—her abiding love and her abiding realism. Half a year after she wrote those words, Lewis was dead.

And during this same period, in 1989, Sophia was also writing directly to Don Miller, expressing her anguish and resentment, demanding explanations. She felt not only that some of his writing was malicious and prurient but also that he had broken explicit promises to be discreet about certain topics and to avoid direct quotation from private papers without written permission. Miller replied that he had in fact refrained from using quotations when people outside the family were involved; when it came to the materials that she and Lewis had entrusted to him, though, he thought they had all agreed about how he might use them, and so he hadn't believed it necessary to check every quotation with her. And speaking of what was "necessary," he had tried very hard to use only the details required for him to get his larger points across about Lewis's character. Discretion had been at the very heart of his project. "In this effort," he wrote, "I was guided by one overriding caution: that I would not say anything about the two things you urged me not to write about: Alison's relationship with Lewis and Lewis's relationship with someone we both agreed was not to be even mentioned in the book."[21]

The unmentionable person must have been Jocelyn. But why was Sophia so worried about what Miller might say concerning Alison's view of her father?

As far as I can tell, Sophia never explained. But Miller's reminder that he had honored her two main prohibitions does seem, over time, to have helped her come to grips with the biography. Miller wrote what seems to me a beautiful, gracious condolence letter after Lewis died at the end of January 1990, and though Sophia at first questioned the genuineness of his emotion, she did continue to correspond with him.[22] Over the next few years, she seems to have gone back to the biography again and again, each time with a different set of concerns. On February 19, 1990, shortly after receiving the condolence letter, she noted that she still resented Miller's "intrusion into the intimacies of our marital life," but she was actively revising her opinion of how he had portrayed Lewis: "In all fairness to Don Miller I must recant some of the accusations I have made of his insensibility to Lewis as a human being. . . . He gives more attention to Lewis as a father and a family man than I had realized." Two years later, she was once again convinced that she had to do a page-by-page analysis of the biography's mistakes, exaggerations, and elisions, so as to leave behind "a counterbalance to Donald Miller's belittling account of Lewis's personal life."[23] By the time of her death in 1997, though, she and Miller were once again on friendly terms: this was another relationship she never ceased to work on, even when she was seemingly fed up with it.[24]

Meanwhile, she must have been gratified by the long and glowing obituaries published about her husband. A particularly insightful one, written by Martin Weil for the *Washington Post*, noted that Lewis had been "recognized by his peers as a prophet and sage, a modern Renaissance man and an Olympian figure whose sometimes harsh pronouncements urged America's cities and their builders to return to civilizing principles and humanistic goals." The *New York Times* called him a "visionary social critic" who was also "part poet" and an "innovative thinker of the first rank."[25]

One obituary, though, published by United Press International, struck a somewhat strange tone, in part because it relied on a somewhat strange interview with Alison. Apparently, immediately after his death, she said that Lewis had been in "excellent" health until the end, and that she now felt "very happy for him." Reflecting on his life, she emphasized that his writing had always come first, and "anything that could take away from his peace of mind was not allowed."[26] Sophia surely winced, reading those words: Alison sounded almost like Don Miller. And then, just three and a half years later, Alison herself died, at age fifty-eight, and Sophia was alone again, pondering her family history.

What comes through in the archives is that there were some wonderful periods of closeness when Alison was a child—even, occasionally, in the years after Geddes's death[27]—but that ultimately she and her parents grew distant, and she never shook the feeling that her father's work was more important to him than his family. Lewis seemed to her almost like an Ahab figure, with his "narrow-flowing monomania."[28] As she grew older, she also sensed that her parents had shielded her from certain truths, and it was relatively traumatic when she eventually learned about her father's affairs, and when she finally had her question answered about why she had never met her paternal grandfather: Lewis had been born out of wedlock, and his father was never a part of his life. His shame became her resentment. Alison had initially tolerated Jocelyn, but once Lewis made it clear how attached he was, she exploded: you're paying this much attention to a woman just five years older than me? "Two days ago," Lewis wrote, in June 1973, right after Alison's outburst, "everything changed—as if an atom bomb had dropped on us. I won't analyze how this could have happened: it is still quite incredible—though behind it there is a long history."[29] That history made itself felt again in September 1980, when Lewis had to be hospitalized and refused to let Alison visit him. Sophia tried to mediate: "I don't know if I can help any in the matter of Lewis's having kept himself incommunicado from everyone but myself during the first week in the hospital. I know it seems weird behavior, but for him it was necessary. . . . He could tolerate me—no, he needed me, for I am an extension of his self—but he had nothing to give." Alison, though, was tired of running into her parents' walls: "I didn't know exactly what I could say or what comfort I could give, but I felt sure that once we started talking the right words would come. But we never talked. . . . I have to make clear once and for all that I am not indifferent and never have been—am not cold, am not uncaring. At the same time I'm not frightened any longer of your feelings—whatever they may be—pain, disappointment, anger—whatever—maybe—who knows—I may even have brought you some joy."[30] She had, but the only evidence of it dates back to her childhood. Lewis and Sophia seem never to have reached catharsis with their daughter.

I don't know if Alison considered herself a feminist, but I would be surprised if she didn't read *The Feminine Mystique*; she turned twenty-eight in 1963, the year it was published, and it was a touchstone for many women of her generation. It seems likely to me that Alison resented Lewis for his affairs and Sophia for her long-suffering patience. Perhaps she also noticed how little attention women received in her father's writings: Mumford's neglect was not quite Melvillean (only in *Pierre* do women play any crucial roles), but his perspective was distinctly masculinist. Occasionally, he did acknowledge this narrowness of vision: "there is not a sufficiently detailed reference to woman or the status of the sexes after the 18th century," he noted, while going over the proofs for *The Condition of Man* in 1944.[31] But his vision never got wider. Did Sophia ever object, I wonder? Perhaps, but no doubt less vigorously than Catherine Bauer had.

Sophia lived about four more years after Alison died, and though she had her share of physical ailments, her mind stayed sharp. She seems to have continued going through the family papers, reckoning with the past. Her copious notes on Miller's biography show her undiminished rage at his assertion that she had been so upset about Lewis's affair with Alice in 1935 that she had "regretted" having Alison that April: "p. 347 is unforgivable and re Alison's birth untrue."[32] But had Sophia succeeded in convincing Alison that Miller was wrong? Had they even talked about it?

I hope Sophia also went back over some of the love letters. "My mate!" Lewis wrote, on May 5, 1976. "My dearest!. . . . The reality of your love for me and my love for you is timeless, and will still be there when you and I are gone."[33] Two years later, when Sophia felt as though they had finally put the affair with Jocelyn behind them, she celebrated their renewed sense of togetherness: "Despite all the aches and pains and disabilities that age brings on, we rejoice with and in one another."[34] Once she was alone, though, in her mid-nineties, she also reaffirmed her independence, her ownership over all the decisions she had made. "From very early on," she said, in an interview conducted just months before she died, "I thought I was responsible for my own life, and that has lasted until now, and I still feel it."[35] Despite Lewis's long shadow, she felt that her commitment to their marriage had opened up new worlds to her; in the end, she stood forth her own inexorable self.

I also hope that Sophia occasionally reread the poem Lewis wrote for her on her seventieth birthday:[36]

> My birthday gift for seventy is all our past
> And all our days to come, bound fast
> By love: sharing the storm-tossed raft that was
> And is our life, defying wintry weather
> And wind-whipped waves that slap our creaking planks:
> Our saving hope and final prayer
> To cling together
> Still loving, fiercely one, unto the last.

CHAPTER 36

Rediscovery (2019)

In the summer of 1936, right after the Mumfords moved from Sunnyside Gardens to Amenia, Lewis decided that he wanted to revisit the beaches of Martha's Vineyard, where he had written his Melville biography. He took Geddes with him. Alison was just sixteen months old, so Sophia kept her at home while she got the farmhouse ready for year-round use. But Geddes had turned eleven that summer, and Lewis suspected that he was "a born traveler, ready for whatever the day and the road might bring." Looking back, in *Green Memories*, Lewis painted the trip as one of the most vivid and meaningful experiences of his life. There were "blissful naked hours on the sands under the cliff," where Geddes "had first dabbled in the ocean at two." And Lewis would always remember "Geddes and another lad fishing together, not heeding repeated parental calls to come home to supper, and full of proper indignation and resentment when I ratted him for holding us up." Geddes was becoming independent, making his own connections, defying the clock.

They also spent time in New Bedford, where, Lewis recalled, they bought Geddes's first hunting knife. After pausing for refreshment "in the fragrant interior of a barnlike old tea and coffee shop," they visited "the Whaleman's Chapel and the Whaling Museum, with Geddes more interested in the harpoons than in the half-size model of a whaling ship." On August 27, Lewis made a pencil sketch looking out to sea.[1]

I went to New Bedford in September 2019. It was a quiet, calm, sunny day, a perfect embodiment of the New England shoulder season—after the summer tourists have left, but before the leaf-peepers have turned

FIGURE 18. "New Bedford (with Geddes)," August 27, 1936.

up. Everyone seemed pleasant and considerate: cars kept stopping for me when I crossed streets, something I'm not accustomed to in Massachusetts, where I grew up hearing that "if you step off the curb, you're in play." But the old friend I met for dinner confirmed that, two hundred years after the rise of the Quaker-dominated whaling industry, the whole Southern Shore region is still marked by its religious history. She had recently moved there in part because there were several different Friends meetings to choose from within a few miles.

And the Whaleman's Chapel is still standing, though it is not the original, which was consecrated in 1832 and burned down in 1866. I lingered inside, in the upstairs shrine, reading the cenotaphs, just as Ishmael does in *Moby-Dick* (the marble stones survived the 1866 fire and were built into the walls of the new structure): "In Memory of Capt. Wm. SWAIN, Master of the Christopher Mitchell of Nantucket. This worthy man, after fastning to a whale, was carried overboard by the line, and drowned. . . . Be ye also ready: for in such an hour as ye think not, the Son of man cometh."[2] There's also a plaque supposedly showing which pew Melville used in 1840, before joining the crew of a whaling ship christened with a Wampanoag place-name: the *Acushnet*. Ishmael says simply that "I seated myself near the door"; I don't think there's any reliable documentation suggesting where Melville sat. Nor do we know if Melville had the same emotional reaction to the cenotaphs that Ishmael has. Ishmael feels sure that among his fellow congregants are those "in whose unhealing hearts the sight of those bleak tablets sympathetically caused the old wounds to bleed afresh. Oh! ye whose dead lie buried beneath the green grass; who standing among flowers can say— here, *here* lies my beloved; ye know not the desolation that broods in bosoms like these. What bitter blanks in those black-bordered marbles which cover no ashes! What despair in those immovable inscriptions! What deadly voids and unbidden infidelities in the lines that seem to gnaw upon all Faith." Too much whiteness; too much lingering and looming trauma. And yet Ishmael goes away encouraged, for the marble tablets are inscribed with deep caring, and the chapel, like a cemetery, has become a place of shared, communal loss; the sharing helps offset the grief. "Even from these dead doubts," Ishmael decides, Faith "gathers her most vital hope."[3]

Father Mapple's crow's-nest pulpit, which the preacher approached "as if ascending the main-top of his vessel," derived from Melville's imagination.[4] But when the director John Ford was filming his adaptation of *Moby-Dick* in Ireland in the mid-1950s, shortly after the novel's centenary, he had a ship-themed pulpit built for the set, and those Melvilleans who saw the movie expected to find that same feature when they visited New Bedford. In 1961, the New Bedford Port Society built a replica of Ford's pulpit and installed it in the chapel, where you can still see it today.

You can also still visit the whaling museum, with its harpoons and its ship models. In fact, the museum and the chapel, across the street from each other on Johnny-Cake Hill, are now both part of the New Bedford Whaling National Historical Park. And inside the museum are the archives of the Melville Society, founded by scholars and other revivalists in the mid-1940s.

Digging in those archives, I found a letter from November 1976, in which the society's secretary/treasurer, Donald Yanella, suggested to the chair of the Nominating Committee, a literature professor at the University of Tennessee named Nathalia Wright, that she consider Lewis Mumford as a possible society president. But, Yanella said, be sure to "point out the fact that the position is honorary and he might well choose to serve only as titular head of the Society. I have a suspicion he would not consider a post which demanded time." Indeed, having just turned eighty-one, Mumford was pleased both by the honor and by the lack of responsibility attached to it. Two months later, Professor Wright let Mumford know that he had been elected unanimously, and she thanked him "for allowing us to extend this long overdue honor to you."[5] In *My Works and Days*, Mumford noted with a fair amount of glee that "though I was never included in the ranks of academically accredited Melville scholars, my lifelong interest in Melville was ironically capped in 1977 by my being made an Honorary President of the Melville Society."[6]

Melville was Mumford's constant companion. It was Melville, with all his doubts and traumas, who sustained Mumford's faith, perpetually helping him to reframe his perceptions. "I owe a debt to Melville," Mumford wrote, in July 1944, when Geddes was on the front lines in Italy, "because my wrestling with him, my efforts to plumb his own tragic sense of life, were the best preparations I could have had for facing our present world."[7] That debt only expanded after Geddes's death, and the bombings of 1945, and the dawning of the Cold War, and McCarthyism, and Vietnam, and Jocelyn. Mumford kept turning back to Ishmael and Ahab and Pierre and Israel Potter and Clarel and all of Melville's other flawed, bitter characters who somehow persevere despite the brutality of modernity. *Moby-Dick*, in particular, remained a touchstone, because of its relentless realism, its awareness of both change and continuity, and its perfectly modernist aesthetic, its "double vision which sees with both eyes—the scientific eye of actuality, and the illumined eye of imagination and dream."[8] The story of the doomed *Pequod*, with its amputee captain and its cosmopolitan crew of federated isolatoes, is the story of Americans' shared guilt, and grief, and hope—for survival, solidarity, and renewal.

And Mumford's indebtedness is now mine. In our deeply troubled time, commentators often emphasize how new some of our challenges are, especially the one that I spend the most time thinking about: climate change.[9] It's not just the Covid-19 pandemic that has gotten called "unprecedented." Yes, climate change is a novel threat; but it should also feel familiar, and our paralysis should feel familiar. I imagine that Mumford would react to climate change in the way he reacted to fascism and atomic energy, as a problem demanding immediate, creative, muscular responses—responses adapted to present circumstances but in the same vein as past responses to slavery and industrialization. Climate change is not an abstract threat to the future of the planet; it is a present-day source of vast suffering, often in communities that were already vulnerable.[10] Yes, climate change is a discontinuous problem, touching time scales and planetary systems that are virtually impossible to fathom. But the fundamental causes of the problem, the practices that need to be changed, are precisely the paleotechnic pathologies of colonialism and carboniferous capitalism.[11] The shifts we need to make will require harsh sacrifices and difficult compromises—but we have faced such requirements before, in Wars and Depressions and Plagues and sometimes in everyday life.

I'm grateful to both Melville and Mumford for reminding us that people have been living with the trauma of modernity for a long time. "Our economic activities," Mumford wrote, in *Faith for Living*, "during the era that boasted so loudly of industrial progress," also produced "poverty, secondary starvation, crime, theft, sordid and battered environments, occupied by depressed and battered people: the industrial environment of the larger part of Western civilization."[12] The fantasy of increasing security and comfort—the fantasy of Progress—is pernicious, because it distracts us from the unending misery of others and also inhibits our resilience, undermines our age-old adaptations to hardship. Ralph Waldo Emerson insisted that "society never advances. It recedes as fast on one side as it gains on the other. It undergoes continual changes; it is barbarous, it is civilized, it is christianized, it is rich, it is scientific; but this change is not amelioration. For every thing that is given, something is taken. Society acquires new arts and loses old instincts. . . . The civilized man has built a coach, but has lost the use of his feet."[13] Ishmael put it more succinctly: "there is no steady unretracing progress in this life."[14] To accept backsliding, defeat, frustration, conflict, damage, brokenness, death, as part and parcel of our world, is also to embrace gratitude for all the gifts of our ancestors that somehow, almost impossibly, sustain life.[15] "I believe there is something sleeping beneath the chaos [of American life] that is of extraordinary value," James Baldwin once commented, "if only we have the courage to go down and bring it up."[16]

Once you acknowledge the chaos and admit that every form of "Progress" brings its share of darkness, then it might be easier to rediscover the gifts of the past. As Melville pointed out in *Israel Potter*, men and women did not inevitably become tools in the era of industrialization. Before Israel wound up a miserable brick-maker in London, he had been a farmer in the Berkshires, where "he chose rather to plow, than be ploughed. Farming weans man from his sorrows. . . . In mother earth, you may plant and reap; not, as in other things, plant and see the planting torn up by the roots."[17] History suggests other modes of living and thriving. Of course, as Mumford recognized as soon as he published his first book, about utopias, any modern writer who dares to find the past useful risks being dismissed as a hopelessly nostalgic dreamer. But rediscovery is never about a romantic return to a Golden Age; it is about seeing connections and swimming in time's currents and tides. It is often about recognizing possibilities in the past, as well as recognizing continuity in the face of shocking change.

For Mumford, a full engagement with time depended on a full engagement with place. To walk through any landscape with eyes open to its realities was to begin to understand the relationship between culture and nature, individual and society, the private sphere and the public, and of course the present and the past. Most helpful of all was to revisit old haunts. Mumford knew he was luckier than most to have his Amenia farmhouse, to which he returned again and again, as in April 1942, when he delighted in seeing "the friendly faces of the station master and the grocer and the taxi driver," and then the "dust, misplaced books, dead wasps under the window and live wasps crawling over it, the musty smell of winter and mouldy papers, yet bearing layer upon layer of my past life: full of that sense of time, precisely because of the frayed edges and the battered ends, which Virginia Woolf interpreted so poignantly in 'To The Lighthouse.' (A pang stabs me; for maybe this place, like the Professor's house, will be deserted in the course of the war; and rain and snow and wind will work upon it, too, without even an old scrubwoman to fend them off.)"[18] Eventually, all the rooms and corridors, all the trees and pathways, the garden, the sandpit, were freighted with memories, with the baggage of family history and world history, and in old age, Mumford found that layering effect to be rejuvenating. In 1975, two months before he turned eighty, he took a walk "to what used to be the old peach orchard, dear to my memories of going there with Geddes for a knapsack full of peaches, before the trees were chopt down." He got tired almost immediately, "but the peace of that wilderness settled in my soul, and I kept on walking."[19] Perhaps he patted the remaining trees, winked at the weeds and wildings, shook his head at the river, spoke a word of thanks that the war in Vietnam was finally over.

It is hard, if not impossible, for people to rise up and reabsorb their government, when they are struggling with trauma. And in modern times, those trying to cope with the everyday trauma of poverty, racism, sexism, homophobia, dispossession, and general precarity are probably more representative than exceptional. When it comes to a structural problem like climate change, many people feel simultaneously like victims and perpetrators: we are all affected, and we are all complicit—in different proportions, yes, but perhaps the commonality is what's most important, which would mean that our most urgent strategies might be sharing our grief and building community and cultivating a resilience that doesn't dream of recovery—all of which depend on constantly reinterpreting and reckoning with the past. How did we get here?[20]

Melville turned two hundred in 2019, and to mark the occasion the avant-garde playwright and composer Dave Malloy offered up *Moby-Dick: A Musical Reckoning*. My oldest son and I were lucky enough to get tickets for a performance during the third week of its world-premiere run, in December, in Boston.[21] I try to track any revivals of cultural interest in Melville, but my son, a connoisseur of experimental musicals, knew about this one before I did. The theater was right around the corner from the church where, one year earlier, we had attended a memorial service for my closest friend. Boston is also where my parents died; it is where I grew up and went to college. About a month before the show, I had turned fifty, and my son had turned sixteen—the age Geddes and Alison reached when their father decided to write poems for them. I had not truly enjoyed a musical since I was a kid in Boston. This one made me feel like a kid again.

Honoring the genre-exploding tendencies of his source material, Malloy swerves between vaudeville, jazz, opera, sea chanties, hip-hop, stand-up comedy, and puppetry, as the *Pequod* pursues its prey. He both celebrates Melville and argues with him, emphasizing the ethnic diversity of the crew but also casting women in about half the roles. Ishmael provides commentary throughout, actually holding a copy of the same olive-green edition of *Moby-Dick* I used while writing this book, sometimes addressing the audience, sometimes turning toward a snow-white bust of Melville, expressing a Hamlet-like doubt, and indignation, and curiosity, and wonder. The play is grounded enough in the original text to remind us of the specific social divisions in the United States during the years leading up to the Civil War, but it also reckons with our present-day realities, suggesting how haunted we still are by white supremacy, exploitative labor systems, violent extraction, and environmental degradation.[22] And, just like the original, Malloy's version thrums with the organic energy of the American experiment, with the possibilities, never-yet realized but still hovering on the horizon, of an inclusive collectivism: "If, then, to meanest mariners, and renegades and castaways, I shall hereafter ascribe high qualities, though dark; weave round them tragic graces; if even the most mournful, perchance the most abased, among them all, shall at times lift himself to the exalted mounts; if I shall touch that workman's arm with some ethereal light; if I shall spread a rainbow over his disastrous set of sun; then against all mortal critics bear me out in it, thou just Spirit of Equality, which hast spread one royal mantle of humanity over all my kind! Bear me out in it, thou great democratic God!"[23]

Can democracy offset the looming trauma of climate change, with its inherent threat to our sense of continuity? Only, Mumford would say, if it's a fully inclusive democracy that fosters gratitude and sacrifice.

Only if people rediscover the old rituals that have served to broaden and deepen our humanity in troubled times—that connect us to past generations for the sake of future generations. Only if democratic participation involves embracing all "the small life-promoting occasions for love," as Mumford put it in 1951, after two decades of work on *The Renewal of Life*. "Not a day, then, without nurturing or furthering life: without repairing some deficiency of love in our homes, our villages, our cities: without caring for a child, visiting the sick, tending a garden."[24]

We need to make life-buoys for each other, whether in the form of international treaties, or social welfare programs, or offers of shelter, or poems for our children. We need to reach across every form of difference: only a less traumatized, less divided citizenry will be able to replace carboniferous capitalism. In 1951, Mumford clung to what he thought of as a realist's hope, because some of the unifying and rebuilding efforts of the postwar period seemed to him like rediscoveries of "the most generous dreams of the past." Suddenly, with the rise of the United Nations, it seemed possible to accomplish "an active partnership, as wide and unrestricted as the planet itself." Maybe there could even be "a more just distribution of all the goods of life," if the wealthier countries were willing to sacrifice some of their luxuries.[25] Today, in an age of hurricanes, floods, droughts, fires, epidemics, and refugees, we need to revive the humane tradition of community support. We need to welcome the world's Ishmaels and squeeze each other's hands.

There are no discrete, technical solutions to the problem of climate change—or any other modern problem. There are only continuous, deep relationships with each other and with the world, relationships that demand our committed action and that perpetually need reinventing. There is only a shared faith in the value of human history, with all its catastrophes and renewals, with all its uncertainty.

ACKNOWLEDGMENTS

I didn't start doing the research for this book until 2012, and I didn't start writing it in earnest until 2018. But it started swimming into my consciousness in 2004—at one particular moment, on an October afternoon, when I paused in the biography section at Ithaca's famous Friends of the Library Book Sale. I was in my first semester as a professor, with an eleven-month-old son, and I felt like I hadn't slept in weeks. As I wandered through the warehouse in a daze, I thought I recognized one of my new colleagues from a distance, but I didn't trust my senses, and there was a lot of glare coming off his bald head, which was bent down toward the books—so I approached hesitantly before saying hello. Yes: it was Fred. We chatted for a couple of minutes, and then, as he took his leave, I turned to the shelves, and I came very close to falling over when I immediately saw a book whose spine bore the names of two of my favorite writers. I knew Mumford mostly as the author of *The Culture of Cities*, an incredibly hopeful, constructive book proposing a radical, new urbanism. Why in the world would he be drawn to Melville's ocean-going tragedies?

Now, of course, I recognize Melville and Mumford as sharing a determined realism—an attitude I also associate with my wife, Christine Evans, who has been offsetting my somewhat oversensitive idealism in the most gracious way possible for the last twenty-five years. I owe her pretty much everything, and I'm ever grateful to be moving through life with her, step by step. May we be granted many more years of mutual rediscovery.

Our children, Sam, Abe, and Ozzie, have known some dark times recently. We all have, but the pandemic has been especially hard on teens. I hope they know how much I love them, and how desperately I want them to feel buoyed up by caring and connection. May they always be able to draw on deep currents of resilience and empathy and solidarity. May they always turn back to history, theirs and others'. Every day, I'm grateful for them—for long hugs, for understanding looks, for kind words, for idle chatter and searching conversations, for smiles and laughs—despite all the fighting. They even sat through the 1956 version of *Moby-Dick* with me, and pretended to enjoy it (kind of). Squeezes all around.

Two people read this whole manuscript as it was being composed, and I feel so lucky to have lived it with them. Amy Reading and Rob Vanderlan, you made up the smallest writing group I've ever been a part of, but it may also have been the best. Thank you. Both the support and the criticism were perfect.

Sarah Ensor: do you remember my telling you that I eventually wanted to write this book in Milwaukee, in 2009? Thank you for being such a spectacular interlocutor. And the same goes for Rebecca Hamilton, Amy Kohout, and Daegan Miller. Much of this book arose from conversations with Sarah, Rebecca, Amy, and Daegan about trauma and modernity.

My agent, Zoë Pagnamenta, believed in this project from the beginning, and wound up having to do more heavy lifting than expected in order to see it through. Given how unstable academia and the publishing industry have felt in recent years, I'm especially grateful for Zoë's long-standing sponsorship.

Two research assistants, Daniel Lewis and Joe Giacomelli, did yeoman work in the archives for me. Daniel's resourcefulness in tracking down obscure essays that Mumford published early in his career was matched by the incredible insight of the notes Joe took on some of Mumford's unpublished writings. Many thanks to both, and especially to Joe for teaching me so much about uncertainty, the central theme of his dissertation, which will soon be a published book.

I was fortunate to be able to develop a theoretical framework for this project during a fantastic fellowship year (2013–14) at the Charles Warren Center for Studies in American History at Harvard University. Eternal gratitude to the troika of Larry Buell, Joyce Chaplin, and Robin

Kelsey for selecting me, and also for their generous and astute intellectual leadership. Larry has been supporting my work for thirty years now, and in this case he was an invaluable guide in my explorations of Melvillean ambiguities. What a pleasure and privilege it has been over the decades to soak up the eloquence of his sentences. I'm deeply thankful, too, for the friendship and critical engagement of the whole fellowship group: Cathy Gudis, Nick Howe, Sarah Luria, Neil Maher, Kathy Morse, and Cindy Ott. And hats off to Larissa Kennedy and Arthur Patton-Hock for all their indispensable help.

I learned that I had received the fellowship in March 2013 and was overjoyed at the prospect of moving to Boston, where I anticipated spending a great deal of time with my elderly parents. Then my father died in May. That was devastating, but I'm grateful for the days I had with my mother in what turned out to be her last lucid year. I also relished getting to reconnect with many old friends, including the best teacher I've ever had, David Outerbridge, who read the paper I wrote on Mumford and even came to the talk I gave at Harvard. I can never thank David enough for his generous nurturing, which goes back to 1985, when I was fifteen and in desperate need of moral and intellectual support. Anything I've managed to give to my own students is a tribute to him.

Part of me just wanted to stay in Boston, where I also got to enjoy the company of Midori Evans, Lou Greenberg, Bobbie Hauser, Stephanie Koontz, Chris Malenfant, Naomi Meyer, Suzanne Mosher, Dan Schmidt, Dan Stevens, and Naomi Tokisue. Thank you for the wonderful sense of community you all created.

I'll never forget all the lunches and brunches with Devah Pager over the course of that year. In 2016, she was diagnosed with pancreatic cancer, and she died in 2018, at forty-six. She was the best possible friend a person could have, and I miss her every day.

Almost as soon as I arrived at Harvard, I got an email from my former professor, Nancy Cott, and it has been wonderful to reconnect with her over the last several years, over coffees, a prize committee, and even a conference panel about Mumford and the women in his life. Having read Nancy's work in college and studied with her in graduate school,

I came to think of her as the embodiment of broad-minded profession-alism, and I've always tried to follow her example.

Nancy put me in touch with Ann Braude, whose generosity had a transformative impact on this project. I can never thank Ann enough for telling me about the Jocelyn Brodie Papers at the Schlesinger Library, which Ann herself had collected and was using for her own research on the relationship between Brodie and Mumford. Ann has remained the perfect model of supportive collegiality and unselfish scholarship, and I cannot wait for her book to come out.

Ann organized the panel "Three Loves of Lewis Mumford," which also included Karen Christensen, a thoughtful scholar and publisher who made a huge difference to me during my revising phase. Karen got to know Sophia Mumford in the last years of her life and ever since has been working on a book about her—another publication I'm eager to see.

Karen is based in the Berkshires, not too far from Melville's house, Arrowhead, nor from the beloved home of my long-standing mentor and friend John Demos, who, amazingly, was also a mentor to Nancy Cott. One of the highlights of my year at the Warren Center was a lunch organized by Nancy in honor of John, at which several generations of John's students got to celebrate him and enjoy each other's company. But I could never celebrate John enough. I'll always be grateful for his unstinting warmth and support, and for our sixteen-year streak of going to Fenway Park together to see a Red Sox game. During one of our conversations on the first-base line, John encouraged me to move for-ward with my halting idea of using some inherited money to build a writing studio, and that changed my life. Writing this book in the new studio during a sabbatical was one of the most exhilarating experiences I've ever had. John: thank you.

And thanks to Noah Demarest and Tom Fritz for all their collabora-tive work on the studio's design and construction, which resulted in precisely the sanctuary I had imagined.

The year before my Warren Center fellowship, when I was just start-ing to think through this book's possibilities, Harriet Ritvo invited me to give a talk at MIT on the book I was finishing at the time, and one of the dinner guests after the talk was the Melville scholar Wyn Kelley. I think Wyn actually gasped when I mentioned my inchoate thoughts about Melville and Mumford—because she had once started down a similar path. Where another academic might immediately have become territorial, Wyn chose liberal generosity, sending me what she had written on the topic and encouraging me to move forward. That led to a lovely lunch with her and Harriet in Cambridge during my fellowship year, and ever since then Wyn's Melville writings have brightened my days and helped steer me through all the inevitable shoals and doldrums.

It was not until the Mumford conference panel came together that I finally met (on Zoom) the great Mumford scholar Robert Wotjowicz, who is now serving as Mumford's literary executor. I'm grateful for his wisdom, graciousness, and practical assistance.

On a Mumford research trip to Monmouth University in pre-pandemic times (November 2018), I was lucky enough to meet with the artist Vincent DiMattio, who co-curated an exhibit of Mumford's drawings and watercolors back in 1985. In 2018, the university's main gallery was brimming with DiMattio's own vivid works, in celebration of his fifty years at Monmouth. I walked through the exhibition and then sat with DiMattio in his office; he was incredibly kind, energetic, forthcoming, and funny. I detected his Boston accent, and we each confessed our devotion to the Red Sox. He said that when Sophia brought a small television set into the Mumfords' Amenia farmhouse, Lewis exclaimed: "You have betrayed me!" When I asked him how he would characterize Mumford, he said that one word leapt to mind: "unyielding."

That trip to Monmouth, where I got to peruse the university's Lewis Mumford Collection, including his artworks, was also notable for the amazing hospitality of George Germek and Scott Knauer. Scott also accommodated all of my reproduction and permission requests with great patience and generosity. And what a profound experience it was to see Mumford's annotations of the many Melville volumes he owned. I believe it's thanks to the forthright affability of Vincent DiMattio and his colleague Kenneth Stunkel that so much precious Mumford material wound up at Monmouth.

Most of Lewis and Sophia Mumford's papers—more than two hundred boxes' worth—are at the Kislak Center for Special Collections, Rare Books, and Manuscripts, University of Pennsylvania, a wonderful place to do research. I'm grateful to the whole staff, but especially to John Pollack.

Several other archives and archivists were crucially helpful to me over the course of this project. Huge thanks to all the staff members, from the head curators to the sub-sub-librarians, at Arrowhead and the Berkshire County Historical Society; the Berkshire Athenaeum; the Centre for Research Collections, University of Edinburgh; Cornell University Library; Houghton Library, Harvard University; the Manuscripts, Archives, and Rare Books Division of the New York Public Library; the New Bedford Whaling Museum; and the Schlesinger Library at the Harvard Radcliffe Institute.

If my year at the Warren Center allowed me to launch this project, it was a fellowship provided by the American Council of Learned Societies (ACLS) that allowed me to finish it. I feel deeply honored by that support, and I could not be more grateful for the work that the ACLS does to continue promoting the value of humanistic scholarship. Thanks especially to the anonymous readers who identified my proposal as being worthy of funding.

And where would we academics be without the people who compose our recommendation letters? Eternal gratitude to all who have written on my behalf over the years, but especially to John Demos, Robert Johnston, and Lou Masur, who have always responded enthusiastically to my countless requests and without whose guidance and reassurance I would have jumped ship long ago.

I'm also indebted to my home institution, Cornell University, and to my colleagues there who have supported my work and career, in both obvious and subtle ways. Special thanks to Barb Donnell, Sandra Greene, Katie Kristof, Tamara Loos, Claire Perez, Georgie Saroka, Barry Strauss, Michael Williamson, and Judy Yonkin, for their leadership and administrative roles in the History Department. For direct help with Mumford, thanks especially to Jeremy Foster, George Hutchinson, Whitten Overby, and Josi Ward, plus everyone else who attended my Mumford presentations through the Under Construction working group and the Comparative History Colloquium (and much appreciation to

Josi and to Holly Case for organizing). Cornell's Society for the Humanities gave me a research grant when I was just beginning to do some archival work on Mumford; gratitude to Tim Murray and the Humanities Council. For collegiality and friendship, I'm also grateful to Anindita Banerjee, Ernesto Bassi, Rachel Bezner-Kerr, Lauren Chambliss, Derek Chang, Adrienne Clay, Ray Craib, Oren Falk, Cristina Florea, Jill Frank, Linda Glaser, Larry Glickman, Christy Goodale, Kim Haines-Eitzen, TJ Hinrichs, Colleen Kearns, Lori Leonard, Caroline Levine, Mostafa Minawi, Larry Moore, Nick Mulder, Paul Nadasny, Kelly Presutti, Sara Pritchard, Aziz Rana, Russell Rickford, Noliwe Rooks, Rich Stedman, Claudia Verhoeven, Stephen Vider, Suzanne Wapner, Dave Wolfe, and Wendy Wolford.

Julilly Kohler-Hausmann and Cliff Kraft: you make Cornell feel like home.

It's been an incredible privilege to work closely with Cornell graduate students over the years, many of whom helped me with this project in various ways. I'm ever grateful to Matt Dallos, Sarah Ensor, Heather Furnas, Joe Giacomelli, Amy Kohout, Laura Martin, Daegan Miller, Molly Reed, and Josi Ward. Working with them formed the core of my career, and it pains me every day that changes in the profession and especially the collapse of the academic job market have forced me to step back from advising doctoral students. Still, it's remained a pleasure to work with a few students (mostly outside of my main fields) who have persevered in their studies despite all the challenges. Most recently, I've been grateful to engage with Ellen Abrams, David Miller, Nick Myers, Daniela Samur, Kelsey Utne, and Samantha Wesner. And huge thanks to Benedetta Carnaghi, who poured an incredible amount of energy and enthusiasm into coordinating Historians Are Writers (HAW!), for which I've been privileged to serve as faculty advisor since Daegan Miller founded the group in 2007.

For the past year, I've been delighted to host Charles Petersen as a Klarman postdoctoral fellow at Cornell; he has enlivened my intellectual and writerly community in powerful ways. Many thanks to Cornell's College of Arts and Sciences and Dean Ray Jayawardhana and everyone who read the fellowship applications, as well as donors Seth Klarman and Beth Schultz Klarman.

Beyond Cornell, several colleagues supported me in the work I was doing on Melville and Mumford, in both casual and formal settings. Thank you to Lisa Brady and two anonymous reviewers at *Environmental History*; Shane and Charlotte Brodie; Verena Conley; George Cotkin; Peter Ekman; Nick Lehr and Molly Jackson at *The Conversation*; and Gina Maccoby. I'm especially grateful to Pamela Hartford and Carlo Rotella at Friends of Fairsted and Monique Dufour at Virginia Tech for invitations to present some of my Mumford material. And thanks also to everyone who attended those presentations, as well as the Mumford talks I gave at the World Congress on Environmental History and Kendal at Ithaca. I appreciate the conversations I've had over the years with Lila Corwin Berman, Ben Cohen, Brian Herrera, Jonathan Holloway, Bob Morrissey, Barry Muchnick, Jenny Price, Paul Sabin, Bob Wilson, and Sandy Zipp. I wish I could tell Rob Young how much his friendship meant to me, not to mention his work on Patrick Geddes.

Many other family members and friends have also been powerfully present for me during the long years of this project, and I'm grateful to all. Of course, some are now absent. I can't believe my parents are gone, and I miss them terribly. Same for Auntie Belle and Cousin Ethel.

David Evans: thank you for always being interested and always wanting to talk, and for all the Melville- and Mumford-themed gifts. Daniel Evans: do you *really* want a Melville Society T-shirt? Kirk and Midge Evans: thank you for the cruise, during which I got to stare out at flying fish playing in the waves and write a short article in honor of Melville's two-hundredth birthday. Debbie Sachs Gabor: thank you for all those weeks on Cape Cod, which I like to pretend is Cape Horn. And lots more gratitude, to all the other Evanses and Gabors, and the Cuttlers, Freedmans, Hausers, Levines, and Levmans. Thanks, as well, to Amy Arnett, Wayne Bezner-Kerr, Dorothea Braemer, Mark Chao, Fred Clarke, Jim Goodman, Ari Handel, Karen Harris, Becca Herson, Lisa Hymas, Tom Iurino, Sara Ivry, Mary Lauppe, Carl Lee, Christian Lentz, Adriane Lentz-Smith, Roger Levine, Ben Liebman, Mary Lui, Dan Magaziner, Jenna Mammen, Christian McMillen, Ilona Miko, Shamez Mohamed, Julie Perlman, Geoff Pynn, Ben Ristow, Sarah Rubenstein-Gillis, Payal Sampat, Ruth Schmidt, Carl Schwaber, Michael Smith,

Michael Trotti, Roxanne Willis, and John Young. Even a few words of casual encouragement can sometimes mean everything.

At Princeton University Press, many people contributed to this project, but special thanks to Eric Crahan, Jill Harris, Christie Henry, and Barbara Shi. I'm also grateful to Jenn Backer for excellent and gracious copyediting, and to the four anonymous reviewers, all of whom offered constructive suggestions that immediately helped with my revisions.

As I was responding to the reviewers, who had mixed feelings about my book's unusual structure, I felt a surge of gratitude to the writers who had inspired me to find a form for my project that fit with its exploration of the dialectical relationship between continuity and change. Some of those writers were modernist novelists, like Elizabeth Bowen, Willa Cather, and Virginia Woolf, but others were contemporary authors of nonfiction. For my whole career, I have been trying to argue for the generative compatibility of creative nonfiction and scholarly research, so it can be thrilling when I come across writers who seem to endorse or even embody that conviction. I have long admired nonfiction artists like Robert Pogue Harrison, Daniel Mendelsohn, Hugh Raffles, Lauren Redniss, Rebecca Solnit, and many others, but in the case of this project my single most important influence was Craig Harline, whose book *Conversions* alternates between chapters set in seventeenth-century Holland and twentieth-century California. I had the good fortune to edit Craig's book for the series that John Demos and I co-curate, New Directions in Narrative History, and I've gone back to it repeatedly since it was published. To read Craig's book is to have a constant, visceral experience of the interweaving of past and present, and to feel the urgency of renewing and renegotiating our relationship to history.

Especially in dark times, we need to rediscover the struggles of our forebears—and express our gratitude to them—and honor them with our perseverance.

Aaron Sachs
Ithaca, NY
Fall 2021

NOTES

Preface. Melville, Mumford, Modernity

1. Raymond Weaver's of 1921 was the first: Raymond M. Weaver, *Herman Melville: Mariner and Mystic* (New York: George H. Doran, 1921). Mumford's biography of Melville came out in 1929. There was an additional book sometimes classed as a biography published in 1926 by the Englishman John Freeman, but it is a slight volume and was barely noticed in the United States, though Macmillan did publish a New York edition. Mumford categorized it as a work of literary criticism; he thought of himself as writing the second Melville biography and as responding much more explicitly to Weaver. Freeman, however, somehow knew of Mumford's interest in Melville, for he cited an obscure comment that Mumford had made in 1924: "People have criticized *Moby-Dick* because it is formless and full of irrelevancies; but the truth is that the irrelevancies are an essential part of its form, and had Melville attempted to reduce the bounds of his universe to the scene required for a slick story of the sea, that universe would not have been the multitudinous and terrible thing he sought to create." This comment first appeared in the *American Mercury* of November 1924, as part of an article Mumford published called "Dialogue on Esthetics." But Freeman actually cited a 1925 version that came out as a privately printed pamphlet called *Aesthetics, a Dialogue* (Troutbeck Leaflet Number Three). I have no idea how this pamphlet fell into Freeman's hands, but the fact that it did says something about the unpredictable circulation of ideas. See John Freeman, *Herman Melville* (New York: Macmillan, 1926), 120–21. Mumford himself reprinted the dialogue fifty years later in *Findings and Keepings: Analects for an Autobiography* (New York: Harcourt Brace Jovanovich, 1975), 85–93; Melville comment on 89. Also see Lewis Mumford, *My Works and Days: A Personal Chronicle* (New York: Harcourt Brace Jovanovich, 1979), 164, 505. Mumford also wrote a few pages about Melville in his 1926 book, *The Golden Day: A Study in American Literature and Culture* (Boston: Beacon Press, 1957; orig. 1926), 72–77.

2. Marshall Berman, *All That Is Solid Melts into Air: The Experience of Modernity* (New York: Penguin, 1988; orig. 1982), 15. Clearly, modernity is marked by complexity and paradox. Bob Johnson has argued in *Carbon Nation: Fossil Fuels in the Making of American Culture* that to be modern is to embrace the power of coal and oil to expand our society's material wealth and carrying capacity; *and also* to suppress our creeping anxiety about having become dependent on fossil fuels, whose use entails the permanent scarring of the land, the unleashing of countless toxic substances, and the expansion of some of the most punishingly dangerous and violent industries the world has ever seen. Or, as Ann Cvetkovich has put it, "Trauma and modernity thus can be understood as mutually constitutive categories; trauma is one of the affective

experiences, or to use Raymond Williams's phrase, 'structures of feeling,' that characterize the lived experience of capitalism." See Bob Johnson, *Carbon Nation: Fossil Fuels in the Making of American Culture* (Lawrence: University Press of Kansas, 2014), and Ann Cvetkovich, *An Archive of Feelings: Trauma, Sexuality, and Lesbian Public Cultures* (Durham: Duke University Press, 2003), 17.

Other works on modernity that have been particularly helpful to me include: Liah Greenfeld, *Mind, Modernity, Madness: The Impact of Culture on Human Experience* (Cambridge, Mass.: Harvard University Press, 2013); Jani Scandura, *Down in the Dumps: Place, Modernity, American Depression* (Durham: Duke University Press, 2008); J. Nicholas Entrikin, *The Betweenness of Place: Towards a Geography of Modernity* (Baltimore: Johns Hopkins University Press, 1991); Anthony Giddens, *The Consequences of Modernity* (Stanford: Stanford University Press, 1990); David Harvey, *The Condition of Postmodernity: An Enquiry into the Origins of Social Change* (Cambridge, Mass.: Blackwell, 1990); Stephen Toulmin, *Cosmopolis: The Hidden Agenda of Modernity* (New York: Free Press, 1990); Modris Eksteins, *Rites of Spring: The Great War and the Birth of the Modern Age* (Boston: Houghton Mifflin, 1989); Charles Taylor, *Sources of the Self: The Making of the Modern Identity* (Cambridge, Mass.: Harvard University Press, 1989); and Stephen Kern, *The Culture of Time and Space, 1880–1918* (Cambridge, Mass.: Harvard University Press, 1983).

3. Much of the framing of this book derives from my attempt to grapple with what I've come to think of as the trauma of modernity, through an engagement with modernity studies, trauma theory, and the burgeoning field of affect studies. Over the last two decades or so, scholars in affect theory—especially Lauren Berlant, Ann Cvetkovich, and Kathleen Stewart—have developed the concept of *everyday* trauma to ask whether powerful sociocultural systems might sometimes have the same kind of impact on people as catastrophic events. Cvetkovich, in particular, has argued that scholars may not have paid enough attention to the kind of grinding despair that "resists the melodramatic structure of an easily identifiable origin." And, Cvetkovich goes on, "once the causes of trauma become more diffuse, so too do the cures, opening up the need to change social structures more broadly rather than just fix individual people." See Cvetkovich, *An Archive of Feelings*, 33. Cvetkovich, Stewart, Berlant, and a few others have joined together in a scholarly and artistic collective loosely organized around the theme of Public Feelings. Cathy Caruth's edited volume, *Trauma: Explorations in Memory* (Baltimore: Johns Hopkins University Press, 1995), was especially generative for these scholars (and for me); I would point particularly to Laura S. Brown, "Not Outside the Range: One Feminist Perspective on Psychic Trauma" (100–112), and Kai Erikson, "Notes on Trauma and Community" (183–199). Also see Aaron Sachs, "Our Common Traumas," *American Quarterly* 66 (March 2014): 235–43; Gert Buelens, Sam Durrant, and Robert Eaglestone, eds., *The Future of Trauma Theory: Contemporary Literary and Cultural Criticism* (London: Routledge, 2014); Mark Epstein, *The Trauma of Everyday Life* (New York: Penguin Press, 2013); Ann Cvetkovich, *Depression: A Public Feeling* (Durham: Duke University Press, 2012); Michael S. Roth, *Memory, Trauma, and History: Essays on Living with the Past* (New York: Columbia University Press, 2012); Lauren Berlant, *Cruel Optimism* (Durham: Duke University Press, 2011); Kathleen Stewart, *Ordinary Affects* (Durham: Duke University Press, 2007); Dominick LaCapra, *History in Transit: Experience, Identity, Critical Theory* (Ithaca: Cornell University Press, 2004); LaCapra, *Writing History,*

Writing Trauma (Baltimore: Johns Hopkins University Press, 2001); Ruth Leys, *Trauma: A Genealogy* (Chicago: University of Chicago Press, 2000); Peter Novick, *The Holocaust in American Life* (Boston: Houghton Mifflin, 1999); Cathy Caruth, *Unclaimed Experience: Trauma, Narrative, and History* (Baltimore: Johns Hopkins University Press, 1996); and Shoshana Felman and Dori Laub, *Testimony: Crises of Witnessing in Literature, Psychoanalysis, and History* (New York: Routledge, 1992).

4. On modernity, temporality, and the disconnection from history, see, for instance, Hartmut Rosa (trans. Jonathan Trejo-Mathys), *Social Acceleration: A New Theory of Modernity* (New York: Columbia University Press, 2013); Peter Fritzsche, *Stranded in the Present: Modern Time and the Melancholy of History* (Cambridge, Mass.: Harvard University Press, 2004); and Carl E. Schorske, *Thinking with History: Explorations in the Passage to Modernism* (Princeton: Princeton University Press, 1998).

5. The literature on Melville is of course as vast as the ocean. Among the most crucial sources, for the purposes of this book, have been: Hershel Parker, *Herman Melville: A Biography, Volume 1, 1819–1851* (Baltimore: Johns Hopkins University Press, 1996); Parker, *Herman Melville: A Biography, Volume 2, 1851–1891* (Baltimore: Johns Hopkins University Press, 2002); Cody Marrs, ed., *The New Melville Studies* (New York: Cambridge University Press, 2019); Geoffrey Sanborn, *The Value of Herman Melville* (New York: Cambridge University Press, 2018); K. L. Evans, *One Foot in the Infinite: Melville's Realism Reclaimed* (Evanston: Northwestern University Press, 2018); George Cotkin, *Dive Deeper: Journeys with Moby-Dick* (New York: Oxford University Press, 2012); Andrew Delbanco, *Melville: His World and Work* (New York: Vintage, 2005); Elizabeth Hardwick, *Herman Melville* (New York: Viking, 2000); Robert S. Levine, ed., *The Cambridge Companion to Herman Melville* (New York: Cambridge University Press, 1998); Wyn Kelley, *Melville's City: Literary and Urban Form in Nineteenth-Century New York* (New York: Cambridge University Press, 1996); John Bryant, *Melville and Repose: The Rhetoric of Humor in the American Renaissance* (New York: Oxford University Press, 1993); and Neal L. Tolchin, *Mourning, Gender, and Creativity in the Art of Herman Melville* (New Haven: Yale University Press, 1988).

6. On the Melville Revival, see chapter 32 of this book; meanwhile: Eric Aronoff, "The Melville Revival," in Kevin J. Hayes, ed., *Herman Melville in Context* (New York: Cambridge University Press, 2018), 296–306; Sanford E. Marovitz, "The Melville Revival," in Wyn Kelley, ed., *A Companion to Herman Melville* (Malden, Mass.: Blackwell, 2006), 515–31; and Clare Spark, *Hunting Captain Ahab: Psychological Warfare and the Melville Revival* (Kent, Ohio: Kent State University Press, 2001).

7. Donald L. Miller wrote a thorough, illuminating biography of Mumford that came out just before its subject died: *Lewis Mumford: A Life* (Pittsburgh: University of Pittsburgh Press, 1989). Other significant works on Mumford include Shuxue Li, *Lewis Mumford: Critic of Culture and Civilization* (Bern: Peter Lang, 2009); Kenneth R. Stunkel, *Understanding Lewis Mumford: A Guide for the Perplexed* (Lewiston, N.Y.: Edwin Mellen Press, 2004); Robert Wojtowicz, *Lewis Mumford and American Modernism: Eutopian Theories for Architecture and Urban Planning* (New York: Cambridge University Press, 1996); Thomas P. Hughes and Agatha C. Hughes, eds., *Lewis Mumford: Public Intellectual* (New York: Oxford University Press, 1990); and Casey Nelson Blake, *Beloved Community: The Cultural Criticism of Randolph Bourne, Van Wyck Brooks, Waldo Frank, and Lewis Mumford* (Chapel Hill: University of North Carolina Press, 1990). I found

Blake's perspective particularly helpful. Of course, Mumford also makes significant appearances in a few other works of scholarship, most recently and perhaps most notably in Eugene McCarraher's magisterial book, *The Enchantment of Mammon: How Capitalism Became the Religion of Modernity* (Cambridge, Mass.: Harvard University Press, 2019). Mumford's humanist critiques of capitalism make him something of a hero for McCarraher, who sees Mumford as one of very few American intellectuals on the "Romantic left" who have tried rigorously and consistently to "help their fellow citizens to awaken from the spell of the American Dream" (677)—a goal Mumford shared with Melville, who thought of it as "disenchantment" (see chapter 16 of this book).

8. Christopher Lasch, *The True and Only Heaven: Progress and Its Critics* (New York: Norton, 1991), 81. Also see Eddie S. Glaude Jr., *Begin Again: James Baldwin's America and Its Urgent Lessons for Our Own* (New York: Crown, 2020), and Rebecca Solnit, *Hope in the Dark: Untold Histories, Wild Possibilities* (New York: Nation Books, 2006). And note Adam Hochschild's recent comment that "when times are dark, we need moral ancestors": Adam Hochschild, *Lessons from a Dark Time and Other Essays* (Berkeley: University of California Press, 2018), 2.

9. Most Mumford scholars acknowledge Melville as a significant influence, though only one among many. Perhaps closest to my perspective is Frank G. Novak Jr., *The Autobiographical Writings of Lewis Mumford: A Study in Literary Audacity* (Honolulu: University of Hawaii Press, 1988); furthest is Paul Forman, who asserted in a 2007 article that Mumford's work on Melville "had no great importance for the content or style of his subsequent writings": Paul Forman, "How Lewis Mumford Saw Science, and Art, and Himself," *Historical Studies in the Physical and Biological Sciences* 37, no. 2 (2007): 271–336 (quotation on 283).

10. Herman Melville, *Moby-Dick* (New York: Norton, 1967; orig. 1851), 12–13. This Norton Critical Edition, edited by Harrison Hayford and Hershel Parker, contains the authoritative text of the novel and many other crucial documents and essays. All further references to *Moby-Dick* come from this edition (and there is at least one reference to *Moby-Dick* in every chapter of this book).

11. For an investigation of whether the uncanny might be a distinctively modern experience (I tend to think so), see Jo Collins and John Jervis, eds., *Uncanny Modernity: Cultural Theories, Modern Anxieties* (Houndmills: Palgrave Macmillan, 2008).

12. Lewis Mumford, *Herman Melville* (New York: Harcourt, Brace, 1929), 193.

13. Melville, *Moby-Dick*, 67, 348, 455.

14. Lewis Mumford, *Technics and Civilization* (Chicago: University of Chicago Press, 2010; orig. 1934), 272. Also see Aaron Sachs, "Back to the Neotechnic Future: An Online Interview with the Ghost of Lewis Mumford," *The Appendix* (July 2014), http://theappendix.net/issues/2014/7/back-to-the-neotechnic-future-an-online-chat-with-the-ghost-of-lewis-mumford. On the Lost Generation, see, for instance, Marc Dolan, *Modern Lives: A Cultural Re-reading of "The Lost Generation"* (West Lafayette, Ind.: Purdue University Press, 1996).

15. Kevin Rozario, citing Fredric Jameson, argues that modernity has always had a "catastrophic logic": we ought to perceive it dialectically, as "a quest to make the world more secure (modernity as anti-disaster) through development patterns that move through cycles of ruin and renewal, bust and boom, destruction and construction, producing as their collateral damage myriad social conflicts as well as technological and environmental hazards (modernity as disaster)": Kevin Rozario, *The Culture of Calamity: Disaster and the Making of Modern America* (Chicago: University of Chicago Press, 2007), 10.

16. As the sociologist Jeffrey Alexander has argued, we must "absorb the lessons of failed modernity" while at the same time managing "to eschew the apocalyptic sensibility," acknowledging that "modernity can allow flexibility and adaptation." Jeffrey C. Alexander, *The Dark Side of Modernity* (Cambridge, UK: Polity, 2013), 149–50.

17. Two brilliant histories that had a huge impact on my thinking about continuity are: Jonathan Holloway, *Jim Crow Wisdom: Memory and Identity in Black America since 1940* (Chapel Hill: University of North Carolina Press, 2013), and Craig Harline, *Conversions: Two Family Stories from the Reformation and Modern America* (New Haven: Yale University Press, 2011). *Conversions* is especially notable for the way in which it alternates between chapters about seventeenth-century Holland and twentieth-century California: its structure was a direct inspiration for the structure of my book. I am grateful to both Craig and Jonathan for long conversations about their work and for their intellectual generosity and open-mindedness.

Other books were important to me in showing the possibilities of switching between two different stories, whether separated in time or not: Charles C. Mann, *The Wizard and the Prophet: Two Remarkable Scientists and Their Dueling Visions to Shape Tomorrow's World* (New York: Vintage, 2019; orig. 2018); Sarah Sentilles, *Draw Your Weapons* (New York: Random House, 2017); Alexandria Marzano-Lesnevich, *The Fact of a Body: A Murder and a Memoir* (New York: Flatiron, 2017); Erik Larson, *The Devil in the White City: Murder, Magic, and Madness at the Fair That Changed America* (New York: Vintage, 2004; orig. 2003); and Amitav Ghosh, *In an Antique Land: History in the Guise of a Traveler's Tale* (New York: Vintage, 1994; orig. 1992).

18. See Fritzsche, *Stranded in the Present*, esp. 53–54, and John Demos, *Circles and Lines: The Shape of Life in Early America* (Cambridge, Mass.: Harvard University Press, 2004).

19. See, for instance, John M. Barry, "Pandemics—Then and Now: The Lessons of 1918 Could Have Helped the World in 2020. Why Did We Forget Them?" *Wilson Quarterly* (Spring 2021), https://www.wilsonquarterly.com/quarterly/public-health-in-a-time-of-pandemic/pandemics-then-and-now/; J. Alexander Navarro, "Lessons from the 1918 Pandemic: A U.S. City's Past May Hold Clues," *The Conversation*, July 6, 2020, https://theconversation.com/lessons-from-the-1918-pandemic-a-u-s-citys-past-may-hold-clues-140519; and Richard Hobday, "Coronavirus and the Sun: A Lesson from the 1918 Influenza Pandemic," *Medium*, March 10, 2020, https://medium.com/@ra.hobday/coronavirus-and-the-sun-a-lesson-from-the-1918-influenza-pandemic-509151dc8065.

20. Mumford's letters are peppered with admiring references to Woolf; see, for example, *My Works and Days*, 311. I read several modernist novels as I was developing the form and structure of this book. Among the most inspirational were Woolf's *To the Lighthouse* (1927), Willa Cather's *The Professor's House* (1925), and Elizabeth Bowen's *The House in Paris* (1935). It's no coincidence that all three use a house as a way of marking both the passing and the layering of time; Mumford wound up doing the same thing in his own life. Bowen's novel begins with a long section called, simply, "The Present," setting up a complicated family drama; then comes a long flashback, in part 2, "The Past," which utterly transforms the reader's understanding of what's going on when the scene shifts back to "The Present," in the third and final section of the book.

21. On stories and form in the writing of history, see James Goodman, "For the Love of Stories," in Aaron Sachs and John Demos, eds., *Artful History: A Practical Anthology* (New Haven: Yale University Press, 2020), 189–212.

22. See, for instance, Mumford, *My Works and Days*, 331.

23. Virginia Woolf, *To the Lighthouse* (New York: Harcourt Brace Jovanovich, 1955; orig. 1927), 158.

24. See, especially, Epstein, *Trauma of Everyday Life*; Cvetkovich, *Depression*; LaCapra, *History in Transit*; Caruth, *Trauma*; and Felman and Laub, *Testimony*.

25. Given their determined commitment to confront the world's harshest realities, I'm tempted to see both Melville and Mumford as "American Existentialists before the fact," in George Cotkin's phrase. Cotkin does not mention Mumford in his illuminating study, *Existential America*, but he argues quite aptly that "despair and dauntlessness battle in Melville's pages, not to define truth but to glimpse some inkling of possibility." See George Cotkin, *Existential America* (Baltimore: Johns Hopkins University Press, 2005; orig. 2003), 17.

Chapter 1. Loomings (1927–29)

1. Lewis Mumford, *The Story of Utopias* (New York: Boni and Liveright, 1922), 267–68; Mumford reprinted part of the 1962 preface in Mumford, *My Works and Days: A Personal Chronicle* (New York: Harcourt Brace Jovanovich, 1979), 191. Also see the later section in *My Works and Days* called "What's Wrong with Utopia," esp. 303–4.

2. Lewis Mumford, *Sketches from Life: The Autobiography of Lewis Mumford—The Early Years* (Boston: Beacon Press, 1983; orig. 1982), 452, 454; and Mumford, "Personalia" (a heading he used for many private writings over several decades), July 1929, in the Lewis Mumford Papers, Kislak Center for Special Collections, Rare Books and Manuscripts, University of Pennsylvania, Box 191, Folder 8232. Further references to this archival collection will be shortened to Mumford Papers.

3. See Alan Trachtenberg, "Mumford in the Twenties: The Historian as Artist," *Salmagundi* 49 (Summer 1980): 29–42.

4. Lewis Mumford, *Sticks and Stones: A Study of American Architecture and Civilization* (New York: W. W. Norton, 1924), 29.

5. Lewis Mumford, *The Golden Day: A Study in American Literature and Culture* (Boston: Beacon Press, 1957; orig. 1926). *The Golden Day* had a powerful, long-term impact, not only spurring a slew of studies celebrating antebellum literary culture as the American Renaissance but also helping to launch American Studies as a new field. Mumford's close friend Van Wyck Brooks was especially important in bolstering Mumford's approach, through books like *The Life of Emerson* (1932), *The Flowering of New England: 1815–1865* (1936), and *The Times of Melville and Whitman* (1947). And also see Vernon Louis Parrington, *Main Currents in American Thought, Volume Two: The Romantic Revolution in America, 1800–1860* (New York: Harcourt, Brace, 1927); R. L. Duffus, *The American Renaissance* (New York: Knopf, 1928); and F. O. Matthiessen, *American Renaissance: Art and Expression in the Age of Emerson and Whitman* (New York: Oxford University Press, 1941). For the history of American Studies, see, for instance, Philip J. Deloria and Alexander I. Olson, *American Studies: A User's Guide* (Berkeley: University of California Press, 2017), esp. 25–112: this is a fun and broad-minded book whose only obvious flaw is that it fails to mention Mumford. Sad to say, Mumford's status as a self-taught public intellectual has prevented him from getting as much credit in academic circles as he deserves.

6. Lewis Mumford, *Herman Melville* (New York: Harcourt, Brace, 1929), 5.

7. Ibid., 361.

8. Raymond M. Weaver, *Herman Melville: Mariner and Mystic* (New York: George H. Doran, 1921), 348–49.

9. Mumford, "Melville—Future Work—Notes," October 18, 1927, Mumford Papers, Box 166, Folder 7873.

10. The metaphor of the seldom-flowering aloe was important to Melville his whole life; Mumford's chapter title was meant to acknowledge that importance. Mumford was thinking not only of Melville's late poem, "The American Aloe on Exhibition," but also of an aloe reference in a letter Melville wrote in 1850. See Mumford, *Herman Melville*, 345, and note also that when Mumford published a new edition of the biography in 1962 he used a quotation from "The American Aloe on Exhibition" as the book's epigraph: "But, ah, ye Roses that have passed / Accounting me a weed." For the 1850 letter, and Mumford's marking of the relevant quotation, see his personal copy of Meade Minnigerode, *Some Personal Letters of Herman Melville and a Bibliography* (New York: Edmond Byrne Hackett: The Brick Row Book Shop, 1922), 42—available in the Lewis Mumford Collection at Monmouth University. Many thanks to George Germek for his hospitality in welcoming me to this congenial archive.

11. Mumford, *Herman Melville*, 357, 325.

12. Lewis Mumford, *My Works and Days: A Personal Chronicle* (New York: Harcourt Brace Jovanovich, 1979), 298, 288; Mumford, "Melville—Future Work—Notes," October 12, 1927, Mumford Papers, Box 166, Folder 7873.

13. Mumford, *Sketches*, 453.

14. Mumford, *My Works and Days*, 300; Mumford, *Herman Melville*, 5.

15. Mumford, *Sketches*, 455.

16. Mumford, *My Works and Days*, 288.

17. Ibid., 301.

18. Mumford, *Sketches*, 457.

19. Mumford, *My Works and Days*, 302.

20. Mumford to Josephine Strongin, December 19, 1937, Mumford Papers, Box 91, Folder 6421.

21. Mumford, *Sketches*, 457.

22. Mumford, "Personalia," July 1929, Mumford Papers, Box 191, Folder 8232.

23. Herman Melville, *Moby-Dick* (New York: Norton, 1967; orig. 1851), 12.

24. Lewis Mumford, *Green Memories: The Story of Geddes Mumford* (New York: Harcourt, Brace, 1947), 33–35, quotation on 35.

25. Mumford, "Personalia," July 1929, Mumford Papers, Box 191, Folder 8232.

Chapter 2. The Whiteness of the Page (1856–65)

1. See, for instance, Hershel Parker, *Herman Melville: A Biography, Volume 2, 1851–1891* (Baltimore: Johns Hopkins University Press, 2002), 338–40, 349–50. One reviewer noted that "the book ends where it begins. You might, without sensible inconvenience, read it backwards" (quoted in Parker, 350).

2. Ibid., 282–83, 354.

3. Herman Melville, *Moby-Dick* (New York: Norton, 1967; orig. 1851), 169.

4. Lewis Mumford, *Herman Melville* (New York: Harcourt, Brace, 1929), 306.

5. Ibid., 252.

6. Mumford to Van Wyck Brooks, September 10, 1944, Amenia, N.Y., in Robert E. Spiller, ed., *The Van Wyck Brooks Lewis Mumford Letters: The Record of a Literary Friendship, 1921–1963* (New York: E. P. Dutton, 1970), 258; also see Mumford, *My Works and Days: A Personal Chronicle* (New York: Harcourt Brace Jovanovich, 1979), 290.

7. Mumford, *Herman Melville*, 248.

8. Quoted in Parker, *Herman Melville*, Vol. 2, 289.

9. Quoted in Andrew Delbanco, *Melville: His World and Work* (New York: Vintage, 2005), 245, 250.

10. Ibid., 250–51.

11. Jonathan Franzen, "Why Bother? (The *Harper's* Essay)," in Franzen, *How to Be Alone: Essays* (New York: Picador, 2003), 94.

12. Parker, *Herman Melville*, Vol. 2, 291–94.

13. Delbanco, *Melville*, 253.

14. *The Writings of Herman Melville*, vol. 15, *Journals*, edited by Howard C. Horsford and Lynn Horth (Evanston and Chicago: Northwestern University Press and the Newberry Library, 1989), 52 (subsequently referred to as *Journals*).

15. *Journals*, 80, 83.

16. *Journals*, 51; Hawthorne in Parker, *Herman Melville*, Vol. 2, 300.

17. All these quotations come from the Herman Melville Papers, Houghton Library, Harvard University; they can be found in a series of typescripts of reviews of Melville's lectures, compiled by Merton M. Sealts Jr., for a book that he ultimately published under the title *Melville as Lecturer* (Cambridge, Mass.: Harvard University Press, 1957). The specific reviews I've cited are, in order: Yonkers *Examiner*, December 9, 1858, p. 2, col. 2; Lawrence (Mass.) *Courier*, November 25, 1857; Cincinnati *Enquirer*, February 3, 1858; and Auburn (N.Y.) *Daily Advertiser*, January 6, 1858, p. 5, col. 2.

I find Melville quite funny, as have a number of other scholars, including: John Bryant, *Melville and Repose: The Rhetoric of Humor in the American Renaissance* (New York: Oxford University Press, 1993); Jane Mushabac, *Melville's Humor: A Critical Study* (Hamden, Conn.: Archon Books, 1981); and Edward H. Rosenberry, *Melville and the Comic Spirit* (Cambridge, Mass.: Harvard University Press, 1955).

18. Parker, *Herman Melville*, Vol. 2, 522.

19. Herman Melville, *Clarel: A Poem and Pilgrimage in the Holy Land* (Evanston: Northwestern University Press, 2008; orig. 1876), 387, 5.

20. Herman Melville, *White-Jacket; or, The World in a Man-of-War* (Evanston and Chicago: Northwestern University Press and the Newberry Library, 1970; orig. 1850), 109. Mumford quotes this passage, for example, in *Herman Melville*, 223, and *My Works and Days*, 300–301, but there are many other places, even in his journals and letters.

Chapter 3. Bitter Morning (1918–19)

1. Lewis Mumford, *My Works and Days: A Personal Chronicle* (New York: Harcourt Brace Jovanovich, 1979), 288–89.

2. Ibid., 362.

3. Lewis Mumford, *Sketches from Life: The Autobiography of Lewis Mumford—The Early Years* (Boston: Beacon Press, 1983; orig. 1982), 246.

4. Lewis Mumford, "The Year: 1918," p. 3, typescript, 19 January 1919, Mumford Papers, Box 191, Folder 8225.

5. Mumford, *Sketches*, 196, 209–11. Some of these concerns would come to the fore in Mumford's 1934 book, *Technics and Civilization*.

6. Mumford, *Sketches*, 244; Mumford, *My Works and Days*, 363.

7. See, for instance, Ann Hagedorn, *Savage Peace: Hope and Fear in America, 1919* (New York: Simon and Schuster, 2007), and Jackson Lears, *Rebirth of a Nation: The Making of Modern America, 1877–1920* (New York: Harper, 2009), 327–55.

8. Mumford, *Sketches*, 244, 247–48, 251.

9. Ibid., 250, 248. Also see Mumford, "The Collapse of Tomorrow," *The Freeman*, July 13, 1921, 414–15.

10. Mumford, *Sketches*, 249, 244.

11. Lewis Mumford, *Herman Melville* (New York: Harcourt, Brace, 1929), 364–65.

12. Mumford, *Sketches*, 197, 210, 209.

13. Herman Melville, *Moby-Dick* (New York: Norton, 1967; orig. 1851), 107–8, 52–53.

14. Mumford, *Herman Melville*, 12.

15. Quoted in Robert D. Richardson Jr., *Henry Thoreau: A Life of the Mind* (Berkeley: University of California Press, 1986), 258. Richardson suggests that in this passage Thoreau was "recording his acceptance of some dark, almost Melvillean truths."

16. Mumford, "The Year: 1918," p. 6, typescript, January 19, 1919, Mumford Papers, Box 191, Folder 8225; and see Hagedorn, *Savage Peace*, on 1919.

17. Raymond Weaver, "The Centennial of Herman Melville," *The Nation* 109 (August 2, 1919): 145–46.

18. Mumford, *Sketches*, 245–46, 252; Melville, *Moby-Dick*, 2; and on Sophia, see Karen Christensen, "Jumped-Up Typists: Two Guardians of the Flame," in Juliana Dresvina, ed., *Thanks for Typing: Remembering Forgotten Women in History* (New York: Bloomsbury, 2021), 37–49. Sophia insisted that it had been her decision not to continue with her career, but there were times when she resented Lewis slightly for not having encouraged her on that front, especially when he took up with other accomplished women in the 1930s, and also in old age, after Lewis became incapacitated.

Chapter 4. Fragments of War and Peace (1865–67)

1. Herman Melville, *Moby-Dick* (New York: Norton, 1967; orig. 1851), 391.

2. Quotations of Melville's Civil War poetry will come from Melville, *Battle-Pieces and Aspects of the War: Civil War Poems* (Boston: Da Capo Press, 1995; orig. 1866), which has a useful introduction by Lee Rust Brown. But also see the edition edited by Hennig Cohen: *The Battle-Pieces of Herman Melville* (New York: Thomas Yoseloff, 1963; orig. 1866); as well as Stanton Garner, *The Civil War World of Herman Melville* (Lawrence: University Press of Kansas, 1993); Timothy Sweet, *Traces of War: Poetry, Photography, and the Crisis of the Union* (Baltimore: Johns

Hopkins University Press, 1990), 165–200; and Hershel Parker, *Melville: The Making of the Poet* (Evanston: Northwestern University Press, 2008), esp. 199. Note that Melville refers to some paintings by Ambroise Louis Garneray as "sea battle-pieces" in *Moby-Dick*, 230.

3. See especially Garry Wills, *Lincoln at Gettysburg: The Words That Remade America* (New York: Touchstone, 1992).

4. Lincoln quoted in Louis P. Masur, *Lincoln's Last Speech: Wartime Reconstruction and the Crisis of Reunion* (New York: Oxford University Press, 2015), 173; and Lincoln quoted in Masur, *The Civil War: A Concise History* (New York: Oxford University Press, 2011), 79.

5. Melville, *Battle-Pieces*, 19.

6. Lincoln quoted in Masur, *The Civil War*, 78.

7. Melville, *Battle-Pieces*, 31–32, 247.

8. Ibid., 181. Mumford thought that this poem expressed "Melville's deepest intuition of life": see Lewis Mumford, *Herman Melville* (New York: Harcourt, Brace, 1929), 304.

9. Quoted in Brenda Wineapple, *Hawthorne: A Life* (New York: Knopf, 2003), 367.

10. Hawthorne in Louis P. Masur, *The Real War Will Never Get in the Books: Selections from Writers during the Civil War* (New York: Oxford University Press, 1993), 167, 161.

11. Ibid., 177, 178, 164, 166.

12. Mumford, *Herman Melville*, 234, 298–99. Sebastian Junger has written provocatively about how modernity has made this kind of comradeship almost impossible to come by, except in the military; see his book *Tribe: On Homecoming and Belonging* (New York: Twelve, 2016).

13. Melville, *Battle-Pieces*, 263, 272, 269, 259.

14. Ibid., 259–60, 265–68, 270–71.

15. Ibid., 261, 13, 266–68.

16. Ibid., 268.

17. Melville, *Moby-Dick*, 61.

18. Melville, *Battle-Pieces*, 13.

19. See, for instance, Parker, *Melville: The Making of the Poet*, and Lawrence Buell, "Melville the Poet," in Robert S. Levine, ed., *The Cambridge Companion to Herman Melville* (New York: Cambridge University Press, 1998), 135–56.

20. Isaac Disraeli, a literary historian whom Melville favored, quoted in Parker, *Melville: The Making of the Poet*, 169. As Parker notes, the quotation is a phrase that caught Melville's eye in a book by Disraeli that he purchased in February 1862.

21. Parker, *Melville: The Making of the Poet*, 149.

22. Melville wrote poetry for as long as Whitman and Dickinson did, and for twice as long as he wrote novels.

23. Nathaniel Hawthorne, *The Scarlet Letter* (New York: Modern Library, 2000; orig. 1850), 6.

24. Mumford, *Herman Melville*, 307.

25. Ibid.

26. Lizzie's brother Sam Shaw quoted in Hershel Parker, *Herman Melville: A Biography, Volume 2, 1851–1891* (Baltimore: Johns Hopkins University Press, 2002), 630.

27. Kate Gansevoort quoted in ibid., 627. She actually had not witnessed Herman's recent behavior; she was drawing her own conclusions from a letter written to her by her aunt Maria Melville, Herman's mother. On this time in the family's life, see ibid., 599–600 and 626–35; and Andrew

Delbanco, *Melville: His World and Work* (New York: Vintage, 2005), 275–76. On Melville's role as father and husband see, for instance, Delbanco, *Melville*, 261–65, 277–79; Parker, *Herman Melville, Vol. 2*, 423–25, 465–66, 516–18; and Parker, *Melville: The Making of the Poet*, 127–31.

28. Official correction to the coroner's report quoted in Parker, *Herman Melville, Vol. 2*, 643. On Malcolm's death and life, see 640–50.

Chapter 5. Reconstruction (1930–31)

1. Herman Melville, *Redburn, His First Voyage; Being the Sailor-boy Confessions and Reminiscences of the Son-of-a-Gentleman, in the Merchant Service* (Evanston and Chicago: Northwestern University Press and the Newberry Library, 1969; orig. 1849), 179. There is scattered evidence of Melville's attitude toward the materialism of the Gilded Age, but perhaps it comes across most clearly in some verses of *Clarel*, published in 1876, three years after Mark Twain and Charles Dudley Warner gave the era its notorious nickname. For example: "the march in league avowed / Of Mammon and Democracy" (Part 3, Canto 5); and "Mammonite freebooters" (Part 4, Canto 9); see Melville, *Clarel: A Poem and Pilgrimage in the Holy Land* (Evanston: Northwestern University Press, 2008; orig. 1876), 280, 413.

2. Lewis Mumford, *Sketches from Life: The Autobiography of Lewis Mumford—The Early Years* (Boston: Beacon Press, 1983; orig. 1982), 217–19.

3. For a particularly sensitive unpacking of the culture and psychology of the 1930s, see Jani Scandura, *Down in the Dumps: Place, Modernity, American Depression* (Durham: Duke University Press, 2008).

4. Mumford, *Sketches*, 479.

5. Lewis Mumford, *My Works and Days: A Personal Chronicle* (New York: Harcourt Brace Jovanovich, 1979), 362; the quotation comes from an unpublished essay titled "Our Present Dilemmas: 1930." Also see Mumford, *Sketches*, 441, and 469, where the first paragraph of the essay is reproduced, though with a few slight differences in the wording—reminding us that Mumford did not always quote himself with perfect accuracy. In some cases, it was carelessness; in others, a compulsion to revise.

6. Mumford, *Sketches*, 471–72.

7. Some scholars, in writing about the so-called interwar period, have connected the 1920s and 1930s in useful and thought-provoking ways. See, for instance, Nancy Cott, *Fighting Words: The Bold American Journalists Who Brought the World Home between the Two Wars* (New York: Basic, 2020); Michael E. Parrish, *Anxious Decades: America in Prosperity and Depression, 1920–1941* (New York: Norton, 1994); Glen Jeansonne, *Transformation and Reaction: America, 1921–1945* (New York: Harper Collins, 1994); Lizabeth Cohen, *Making a New Deal: Industrial Workers in Chicago, 1919–1939* (New York: Cambridge University Press, 1990); Roland Marchand, *Advertising the American Dream: Making Way for Modernity, 1920–1940* (Berkeley: University of California Press, 1985); and Ellis W. Hawley, *The Great War and the Search for a Modern Order: A History of the American People and Their Institutions, 1917–1933* (New York: St. Martin's, 1979). Other scholars have linked the two decades by pointing out that the 1920s may have been marked by as much darkness as the 1930s and the 1930s may have been marked by as much light as the 1920s. See David J. Goldberg, *Discontented America: The United States in the 1920s*

(Baltimore: Johns Hopkins University Press, 1999), and Morris Dickstein, *Dancing in the Dark: A Cultural History of the Great Depression* (New York: Norton, 2009).

On the 1920s as the key decade of transformation, the gateway to American modernity, see Paul V. Murphy, *The New Era: American Thought and Culture in the 1920s* (Lanham, Md.: Rowman and Littlefield, 2012); Charles J. Shindo, *1927 and the Rise of Modern America* (Lawrence: University Press of Kansas, 2010); Nathan Miller, *New World Coming: The 1920s and the Making of Modern America* (New York: Scribner, 2003); Lynn Dumenil, *The Modern Temper: American Culture and Society in the 1920s* (New York: Hill and Wang, 1995); Roderick Nash, *The Nervous Generation: American Thought, 1917–1930* (Chicago: Rand McNally, 1970); and Paul A. Carter, *The Twenties in America* (New York: Crowell, 1968).

8. Lewis Mumford, *The Brown Decades: A Study of the Arts in America, 1865–1895* (New York: Dover, 1971; orig. 1931), 2, 23, 3.

9. I make a version of this argument in Aaron Sachs, *Arcadian America: The Death and Life of an Environmental Tradition* (New Haven: Yale University Press, 2013).

10. Mumford, *Brown Decades*, 10.

11. Ibid., 34.

12. Ibid., 22–23. Also see Donald L. Miller, *Lewis Mumford: A Life* (Pittsburgh: University of Pittsburgh Press, 1989), 247–50.

13. Mumford, *Brown Decades*, 4.

14. Mumford to Catherine Bauer, June 27, 1930, Mumford Papers, Box 87, Folder 6337.

15. Lewis Mumford, "The Emergence of a Past," *New Republic*, November 25, 1925, 19. Also see Miller, *Lewis Mumford*, 250–52, and Frank G. Novak Jr., "Lewis Mumford and the Reclamation of Human History," *Clio* 16 (Winter 1987): 159–81.

16. Mumford to Catherine Bauer, April 1, 1930, Mumford Papers, Box 87, Folder 6336.

17. Mumford, "Memories and Anticipations," 1930, long typescript divided into multiple folders, Mumford Papers, Box 166, Folders 7882 ("tragic defiance") and 7879 (longer passage). A slightly edited version of this passage appears in *My Works and Days*, 367.

18. Herman Melville, *Moby-Dick* (New York: Norton, 1967; orig. 1851), 379.

19. Mumford, "Personalia," November 12, 1930, Mumford Papers, Box 193, Folder 8252.

Chapter 6. The Golden Day (1846–50)

1. On Go-Aheadism and rapid modernization, see, for instance, Scott A. Sandage, *Born Losers: A History of Failure in America* (Cambridge, Mass.: Harvard University Press, 2005); Lewis Perry, *Boats against the Current: American Culture between Revolution and Modernity, 1820–1860* (New York: Oxford University Press, 1993); Daniel Walker Howe, *What Hath God Wrought: The Transformation of America, 1815–1848* (New York: Oxford University Press, 2007); and David S. Reynolds, *Waking Giant: America in the Age of Jackson* (New York: Harper, 2008).

2. See especially his letter of February 3, 1847, to his uncle Peter Gansevoort, and note that Herman's mother attested to his effort to catch on at the custom house as early as December 1846: *The Writings of Herman Melville*, vol. 14, *Correspondence*, edited by Lynn Horth (Evanston and Chicago: Northwestern University Press and the Newberry Library, 1993), 81, 69 (subsequently referred to as *Correspondence*).

3. Lewis Mumford, *Herman Melville* (New York: Harcourt, Brace, 1929), 67.

4. Herman Melville, *Typee: A Peep at Polynesian Life* (New York: Penguin, 1996; orig. 1846), 125, 195, 29.

5. Herman Melville, *Redburn, His First Voyage; Being the Sailor-boy Confessions and Reminiscences of the Son-of-a-Gentleman, in the Merchant Service* (Evanston and Chicago: Northwestern University Press and the Newberry Library, 1969; orig. 1849), 100–101.

6. Herman Melville, *Mardi: And a Voyage Thither* (Evanston: Northwestern University Press, 1998; orig. 1849); Brian Higgins and Hershel Parker, eds., *Herman Melville: The Contemporary Reviews* (New York: Cambridge University Press, 1995), 226 (New York *Tribune*, May 10, 1849).

7. *Contemporary Reviews*, 212 (Boston *Post*, April 18, 1849).

8. Letter to Evert A. Duyckinck, February 2, 1850, New York, *Correspondence*, 154.

9. Herman Melville, *Moby-Dick* (New York: Norton, 1967; orig. 1851), 261.

10. Letter to Evert A. Duyckinck, February 2, 1850, New York, *Correspondence*, 154.

11. Melville, *Typee*, 26.

12. Mumford, *Herman Melville*, 68.

13. See Sandage, *Born Losers*; Howe, *What Hath God Wrought*; Reynolds, *Waking Giant*; and John Evelev, *Tolerable Entertainment: Herman Melville and Professionalism in Antebellum New York* (Amherst: University of Massachusetts Press, 2006).

14. Letter to Lemuel Shaw, October 6, 1849, New York, *Correspondence*, 138–39.

15. Melville, *Redburn*, 293, 184, 292.

16. Herman Melville, *White-Jacket; or, The World in a Man-of-War* (Evanston and Chicago: Northwestern University Press and the Newberry Library, 1970; orig. 1850), 390, 374–75; Mumford, *Herman Melville*, 117.

17. Melville, *White-Jacket*, 132, 355, 360.

18. Mumford, *Herman Melville*, 65. Also note Mumford, *The Golden Day: A Study in American Literature and Culture* (Boston: Beacon Press, 1957; orig. 1926), 44: "What is vital in the American writers of the Golden Day grew out of a life which opened up to them every part of their social heritage."

19. Hershel Parker, *Herman Melville: A Biography, Volume 1, 1819–1851* (Baltimore: Johns Hopkins University Press, 1996), 554.

20. Letter to Allan Melville, February 20, 1849, Boston, *Correspondence*, 116.

21. Quoted in Parker, *Herman Melville, Vol. 1*, 743. Herman's cousin Priscilla said that the farm was his "*first love*": quoted in ibid., 733.

22. Ibid., 742–49, 778–79; Andrew Delbanco, *Melville: His World and Work* (New York: Vintage, 2005), 124–27.

23. Parker, *Herman Melville, Vol. 1*, 776.

24. Ibid., 749–77.

25. All the passages quoted in this paragraph are from "Hawthorne and His Mosses," and all of them were marked for emphasis by Lewis Mumford when he read the essay in the 1920s. The edition Mumford owned is Herman Melville, *The Apple-Tree Table and Other Sketches* (Princeton: Princeton University Press, 1922), quotations on 62, 65, 64; it is housed in the Lewis Mumford Collection, Monmouth University.

Chapter 7. Retrospective (1956–82)

1. Herman Melville, *Moby-Dick* (New York: Norton, 1967; orig. 1851), 162–63.

2. For confirmation of the completion of the draft of the autobiography, see Mumford, "Random Notes" (another heading, like "Personalia," that he used for various private scribblings, over several decades), January 21, 1957, Mumford Papers, Box 173, Folder 7933. Also see Lewis Mumford, *Sketches from Life: The Autobiography of Lewis Mumford—The Early Years* (Boston: Beacon Press, 1983; orig. 1982), 422, where he says that he wrote the first draft in autumn 1956.

3. Don Miller to Sophia Wittenberg Mumford, February 6, 1990, in the Sophia Wittenberg Mumford Papers, Kislak Center for Special Collections, Rare Books and Manuscripts, University of Pennsylvania, Box 3, Folder 15. Further references to this archival collection will be shortened to Sophia Wittenberg Mumford Papers.

4. Ellipses in the original. Mumford, "Random Notes," January 21, 1957, Mumford Papers, Box 173, Folder 7933.

5. Mumford, *Sketches*, 3.

6. Ibid., 4.

7. "Offset" printing was an invention of late nineteenth-century England; at first the printing was done on tin, and then a paper-based process was developed in the United States in the first decade of the twentieth century.

8. Mumford, *Sketches*, 6.

9. Lewis Mumford, *Herman Melville* (New York: Harcourt, Brace, 1929), 193.

10. Melville, *Moby-Dick*, 406.

11. Mumford, *Sketches*, 490–92.

12. "Saving opposite" is from Lewis Mumford, *The Culture of Cities* (San Diego: Harcourt Brace Jovanovich, 1970; orig. 1938), 218.

13. Mumford, *Sketches*, 8, 10.

14. Mumford, survey notes (New York), typescript, March 15, 1916, Mumford Papers, Box 180, Folder 8027; "crudely" is crossed out in pencil.

15. Lewis Mumford, *The Story of Utopias* (New York: Boni and Liveright, 1922), 2–3.

16. Mumford, *Culture of Cities*, 142, 74, 293. Also see Mumford, "Random Notes," August 10, 1934, Mumford Papers, Box 192, Folder 8235: "To interpret any given stretch of history as all of one piece seems to me basically false. Every period has its historical dominants, so to say, and its historical recessives. That is why a cross-section of society—such as is implied in contemporary views—is always historically inadequate, because in the nature of things it centers attention upon the dominants."

17. Mumford, notes for a lecture on Melville at Smith College, 1930, Mumford Papers, Box 182, Folder 8070.

Chapter 8. A Bosom Friend (1850–51)

1. *The Writings of Herman Melville*, vol. 14, *Correspondence*, edited by Lynn Horth (Evanston and Chicago: Northwestern University Press and the Newberry Library, 1993), 195–96 (hereafter *Correspondence*).

2. Herman Melville, "Hawthorne and His Mosses," in *The Writings of Herman Melville*, vol. 9, *The Piazza Tales and Other Prose Pieces, 1839–1860*, edited by Harrison Hayford et al. (Evanston and Chicago: Northwestern University Press and the Newberry Library, 1987), 250.

3. Letter to Hawthorne, June 29, 1851, Pittsfield, *Correspondence*, 196.

4. *Correspondence*, 186.

5. Melville, "Mosses," 243.

6. This passage was quoted by Melville in "Mosses," 241–42. Melville did not quote the word "cheerless," but it comes from the first page of "Fire-Worship": Nathaniel Hawthorne, *Mosses from an Old Manse* (Columbus: Ohio State University Press, 1974; orig. 1846), 138.

7. Melville, "Mosses," 244.

8. Herman Melville, *Moby-Dick* (New York: Norton, 1967; orig. 1851), 144.

9. Ibid.

10. Ibid., 399.

11. *Correspondence*, 191–92.

12. Hawthorne to Melville, March 27, 1851, Lenox, *Correspondence*, 608.

13. Lewis Mumford, *Herman Melville* (New York: Harcourt, Brace, 1929), 145.

14. Letter to Hawthorne, July 22, 1851, Pittsfield, *Correspondence*, 199.

15. See Jay Leyda, *The Melville Log: A Documentary Life of Herman Melville, 1819–1891*, vol. 1 (New York: Gordian Press, 1969), 419, 408.

16. Melville, *Moby-Dick*, 52–53.

17. *Correspondence*, 212.

18. Melville, *Moby-Dick*, 348–49.

19. Leyda, *The Melville Log*, 412.

20. Letter to Hawthorne, possibly June 1, 1851, Pittsfield, *Correspondence*, 191.

21. Melville, *Moby-Dick*, 205.

22. Herman Melville, *Israel Potter: His Fifty Years of Exile* (New York: Penguin, 2008; orig. 1855), 5.

23. Letter to Hawthorne, possibly June 1, 1851, Pittsfield, *Correspondence*, 193–94.

24. Letter to Hawthorne, possibly November 17, 1851, Pittsfield, *Correspondence*, 213.

25. Editorial note in *Correspondence*, 211.

26. *Correspondence*, 190–91.

27. Editorial note in ibid., 170.

28. See Andrew Delbanco, *Melville: His World and Work* (New York: Vintage, 2005), 151–57, and Lewis Hyde, "Introduction: Prophetic Excursions," in Hyde, ed., *The Essays of Henry D. Thoreau* (New York: North Point, 2002), xxix–xxxv.

29. Melville, *Moby-Dick*, 29, 36, 54–55.

30. Ibid., 52.

31. Letter to Evert A. Duyckinck, February 12, 1851, Pittsfield, *Correspondence*, 180–81.

32. From letters written by Sophia and quoted in Leyda, *The Melville Log*, 393, and in an editorial note in *Correspondence*, 184.

Chapter 9. Amor Threatening (1930–35)

1. Michael Shelden, *Melville in Love: The Secret Life of Herman Melville and the Muse of Moby-Dick* (New York: Ecco, 2016).

2. See, for instance, Lawrence R. Samuel, *Sexidemic: A Cultural History of Sex in America* (Lanham, Md.: Rowman and Littlefield, 2013), 9–11, 29; John D'Emilio and Estelle B. Freedman, *Intimate Matters: A History of Sexuality in America*, 3rd ed. (Chicago: University of Chicago

Press, 2012), 223–26; and Christina Simmons, "Modern Sexuality and the Myth of Victorian Repression," in Kathy Peiss and Christina Simmons, eds., *Passion and Power: Sexuality in History* (Philadelphia: Temple University Press, 1989), 157–77.

3. Lewis Mumford, *Herman Melville* (New York: Harcourt, Brace, 1929), 274–81; Mumford, *My Works and Days: A Personal Chronicle* (New York: Harcourt Brace Jovanovich, 1979), 294–96, 298–303.

4. See Mumford, *My Works and Days*, 298, where Mumford reproduces the six-line stanza, though with a typo: "Reason's heat" instead of "Reason's seat." For the correct text of the full poem, see Herman Melville, *Poems*, vol. 16 of *The Works of Herman Melville* (London: Constable, 1924), 254–59.

5. Melville, *Poems*, 254–59.

6. Herman Melville, *Moby-Dick* (New York: Norton, 1967; orig. 1851), 15.

7. Mumford, *Herman Melville*, 277.

8. Mumford, "Personalia," March 23, 1930, and "Random Notes," March 22, 1930, Mumford Papers, Box 192, Folder 8235.

9. Mumford, *My Works and Days*, 299.

10. Ibid., 302–3. On Bauer, see H. Peter Oberlander and Eva Newbrun, *Houser: The Life and Work of Catherine Bauer* (Vancouver: University of British Columbia Press, 1999). She later married and became known as Catherine Bauer Wurster.

11. Ibid., 305, 304.

12. Ibid., 301, 299, 298.

13. Quoted in Donald L. Miller, *Lewis Mumford: A Life* (Pittsburgh: University of Pittsburgh Press, 1989), 309–10.

14. Mumford, "Random Notes," April 6, 1930, Mumford Papers, Box 193, Folder 8252.

15. Mumford to Josephine Strongin, December 19, 1937, Mumford Papers, Box 91, Folder 6421.

16. Mumford, "Personalia," April 5, 1930, Mumford Papers, Box 193, Folder 8252.

17. See Mumford, *My Works and Days*, 311, for a letter from Lewis to Catherine Bauer, November 25, 1933: "Sophy was almost as conscious of your charm last night as I was. When we left Clarence's she said: 'Drat your friend Catherine! I hate her—because I really like her so much and I can understand why you do, too.'"

18. Mumford, *My Works and Days*, 315.

19. Catherine Bauer quoted in Miller, *Lewis Mumford*, 334, 331.

20. See, for instance, Robert Vanderlan, *Intellectuals Incorporated: Politics, Art, and Ideas Inside Henry Luce's Media Empire* (Philadelphia: University of Pennsylvania Press, 2010), and Michael Denning, *The Cultural Front: The Laboring of American Culture in the Twentieth Century* (New York: Verso, 1997).

21. Mumford, "Random Notes," October 6, 1934, Mumford Papers, Box 192, Folder 8235.

22. Mumford, *My Works and Days*, 317.

23. Ibid., 318.

24. Mumford, "Random Notes," July 28, 1935, Mumford Papers, Box 192, Folder 8235.

Chapter 10. Cetology (1851–52)

1. See Brian Higgins and Hershel Parker, eds., *Herman Melville: The Contemporary Reviews* (New York: Cambridge University Press, 1995), 353–415. Quotations from 386 (*Parker's Journal*, November 22, 1851) and 410 (*Church Review and Ecclesiastical Register*, January 1852); "strange" appears in almost every review, whether positive or negative.

2. *Contemporary Reviews*, 356 (*Athenaeum*, October 25, 1851). See Hershel Parker, *Herman Melville: A Biography, Volume 2, 1851–1891* (Baltimore: Johns Hopkins University Press, 2002), 17–30, for a discussion of the influence of particular reviews.

3. *Contemporary Reviews*, 359 (*Spectator*, October 25, 1851).

4. Herman Melville, *Moby-Dick* (New York: Norton, 1967; orig. 1851), 185, 374.

5. Ibid., 50–51.

6. Ibid., 118, 117, 121, 128.

7. Ibid., 406.

8. Lewis Mumford, *Herman Melville* (New York: Harcourt, Brace, 1929), 192.

9. Quoted in Aaron Sachs, *The Humboldt Current: Nineteenth-Century Exploration and the Roots of American Environmentalism* (New York: Viking, 2006), 43. Another of Humboldt's followers: J. N. Reynolds, author of "Mocha-Dick" (see ibid., chaps. 4 and 5).

10. It's perhaps also worth noting that, although most of the action in *Moby-Dick* proceeds chronologically, it sometimes does turn back on itself. See, for instance, chapters 62 and 63, which immediately follow the wild action of a whale hunt, when there was so much going on that certain explanations just had to be skipped. Chapter 62 begins: "A word concerning an incident in the last chapter." Chapter 63 begins: "Out of the trunk, the branches grow; out of them, the twigs. So, in productive subjects, grow the chapters." A similar dynamic arises in chapter 72: "In the tumultuous business of cutting-in and attending to a whale, there is much running backwards and forwards among the crew. . . . It is much the same with him who endeavors the description of the scene. We must now retrace our way a little" (245, 246, 270).

11. Ibid., 380, 385.

12. Ibid., 349.

13. Ibid., 433.

14. Mumford, *Herman Melville*, 184–85.

15. Ibid., 186.

16. Melville, *Moby-Dick*, 352, 147, 459.

17. Mumford, *Herman Melville*, 183.

18. Melville, *Moby-Dick*, 184, 147, 454, 438.

19. Mumford, *Herman Melville*, 189.

20. Melville, *Moby-Dick*, 240.

21. Mumford, *Herman Melville*, 187.

22. Ibid., 196.

23. Mumford, *My Works and Days: A Personal Chronicle* (New York: Harcourt Brace Jovanovich, 1979), 300–301.

24. Mumford, *Herman Melville*, 195.

25. Mumford, *My Works and Days*, 270.

26. Melville, *Moby-Dick*, 392.

27. Ibid., 320.

Chapter 11. Neotechnics (1932–34)

1. Lewis Mumford, *Herman Melville* (New York: Harcourt, Brace, 1929), 180.

2. I've written about Mumford's environmental thinking in Aaron Sachs, "Lewis Mumford's Urbanism and the Problem of Environmental Modernity," *Environmental History* 21

(October 2016): 638–59. Other scholars who have focused on Mumford's environmental side include: William J. Cohen, *Ecohumanism and the Ecological Culture: The Educational Legacy of Lewis Mumford and Ian McHarg* (Philadelphia: Temple University Press, 2019); George Hutchinson, *Facing the Abyss: American Literature and Culture in the 1940s* (New York: Columbia University Press, 2018), 334–39; Janet Biehl, *Mumford Gutkind Bookchin: The Emergence of Eco-Decentralism* (Porsgrunn, Norway: New Compass Press, 2011); Ben A. Minteer, *The Landscape of Reform: Civic Pragmatism and Environmental Thought in America* (Cambridge, Mass.: MIT Press, 2006), 51–80; Ramachandra Guha, *How Much Should a Person Consume? Environmentalism in India and the United States* (Berkeley: University of California Press, 2006), 152–74; Mark Luccarelli, *Lewis Mumford and the Ecological Region: The Politics of Planning* (New York: Guilford Press, 1995); Richard White, *The Organic Machine: The Remaking of the Columbia River* (New York: Hill and Wang, 1995), 55–69; Robert L. Dorman, *Revolt of the Provinces: The Regionalist Movement in America, 1920–1945* (Chapel Hill: University of North Carolina Press, 1993); and David R. Conrad, *Education for Transformation: Implications in Lewis Mumford's Ecohumanism* (Palm Springs: ETC Publications, 1976). I'm grateful to Robert Dorman for assigning Mumford in what must have been one of the earliest environmental history seminars in the country, back in spring 1991, when I was a junior in college.

3. Lewis Mumford, *Technics and Civilization* (Chicago: University of Chicago Press, 2010; orig. 1934), 272.

4. Ibid., 157–58.

5. Lewis Mumford, *The Story of Utopias* (New York: Boni and Liveright, 1922), 201. Also note *Technics*, 100: "What went on at court became the criterion of a good life; and the luxurious standards of consumption erected there spread themselves gradually throughout every walk of society."

6. One of Mumford's clear goals was to recapture an older, more positive vision of certain kinds of work. And recent neuroscience research suggests that some forms of modern depression (in the industrial world) are closely linked to the fewer opportunities we have to use our bodies to accomplish necessary tasks: see Kelly G. Lambert, "Rising Rates of Depression in Today's Society: Consideration of the Roles of Effort-Based Rewards and Enhanced Resilience in Day-to-Day Functioning," *Neuroscience and Biobehavioral Reviews* 30 (2006): 497–510.

7. Mumford, *Utopias*, 213, 226, 230.

8. Mumford, *Technics*, 181, 196. The tradition of cultural criticism in the nineteenth century is at the heart of the first two books I wrote, and of course it was absolutely crucial to Mumford. Perhaps the most important critic to consider in this immediate context is Henry George, whose classic work, *Progress and Poverty* (1879), tried to shake Gilded Age Americans out of their whiggish assumptions. George's key policy recommendation was that there should be a hefty tax on large landowners, because they were getting an "unearned increment" through speculation—by sitting on their real estate holdings and allowing them to increase in value. See Aaron Sachs, *Arcadian America: The Death and Life of an Environmental Tradition* (New Haven: Yale University Press, 2013), esp. 225–36, 274–81.

9. Mumford, *Technics*, 5, 183.

10. Ibid., 215, 6, 3.

11. Herman Melville, *Moby-Dick* (New York: Norton, 1967; orig. 1851), 390.

12. Mumford, *Technics*, 69, 13, 43, 13–15.

13. Ibid., 49, 47, 20, 46, 71, 74.

14. See ibid., 109–11.

15. Ibid., 129, 123, 398–99.

16. Ibid., 118, 136, 148–50, 118.

17. Lewis Mumford, *The Brown Decades: A Study of the Arts in America, 1865–1895* (New York: Dover, 1971; orig. 1931), 77.

18. Mumford, *Technics*, 247, 249, 367. Mumford certainly qualifies as one of the constructive critics Marshall Berman celebrated as speaking in "a voice that knows pain and dread, but believes in its power to come through. . . . It is ironic and contradictory, polyphonic and dialectical, denouncing modern life in the name of values that modernity itself has created, hoping—often against hope—that the modernities of tomorrow will heal the wounds that wreck the modern men and women of today." See Marshall Berman, *All That Is Solid Melts into Air: The Experience of Modernity* (New York: Penguin, 1988, orig. 1982), 23.

19. Mumford, *Technics*, 325, 340, 332, 404, 410. Also see Jason Scott Smith, *A Concise History of the New Deal* (New York: Cambridge University Press, 2014), and Neil M. Maher, *Nature's New Deal: The Civilian Conservation Corps and the Roots of the American Environmental Movement* (New York: Oxford University Press, 2009).

20. Mumford, *Technics*, 215, 53. Mumford's analysis of our cultural fascination with technical gadgets is uncannily relevant in the twenty-first century: "One is faced here with a magnified form of a danger common to all inventions: a tendency to use them whether or not the occasion demands" (*Technics*, 240). And one could pull out a dozen more quotations from *Technics and Civilization* that resonate in the age of cell phones and the internet. See Aaron Sachs, "Back to the Neotechnic Future: An Online Interview with the Ghost of Lewis Mumford," *The Appendix* (July 2014), http://theappendix.net/issues/2014/7/back-to-the-neotechnic-future-an-online-chat-with-the-ghost-of-lewis-mumford.

21. Mumford, *Technics*, 104, 368.

Chapter 12. The Ambiguities (1852)

1. Melville to Richard Bentley, April 16, 1852, New York, in *The Writings of Herman Melville*, vol. 14, *Correspondence*, edited by Lynn Horth (Evanston and Chicago: Northwestern University Press and the Newberry Library, 1993), 226.

2. Lewis Mumford, *My Works and Days: A Personal Chronicle* (New York: Harcourt Brace Jovanovich, 1979), 292.

3. Herman Melville, *Pierre; or, The Ambiguities* (New York: Penguin, 1996; orig. 1852), 218.

4. Ibid., 6.

5. Ibid., 11, 69, 341, 89.

6. Ibid., 90, 261, 207, 166, 261–62.

7. Ibid., 4, 142.

8. Ibid., 24, 169; Herman Melville, *Moby-Dick* (New York: Norton, 1967; orig. 1851), 355.

9. Melville, *Pierre*, 137, 139, 128.

10. Ibid., 107, 5, 16, 199.

11. See, for instance, Aaron Sachs, *The Humboldt Current: Nineteenth-Century Exploration and the Roots of American Environmentalism* (New York: Viking, 2006), 65, 196–98, 288–89; Adele Perry, *On the Edge of Empire: Gender, Race, and the Making of British Columbia, 1849–1871* (Toronto: University of Toronto Press, 2001), 20–47, 79–96; Caleb Crain, *American Sympathy: Men, Friendship, and Literature in the New Nation* (New Haven: Yale University Press, 2001); Jonathan Ned Katz, *Love Stories: Sex between Men before Homosexuality* (Chicago: University of Chicago Press, 2001); Susan Lee Johnson, *Roaring Camp: The Social World of the Gold Rush* (New York: W. W. Norton, 2000), 127–30, 159–74, 335–37; Leila J. Rupp, *A Desired Past: A Short History of Same-Sex Love in America* (Chicago: University of Chicago Press, 1999); Steven Maynard, "Making Waves: Gender and Sex in the History of Seafaring," *Acadiensis* 22 (Spring 1993): 144–54; and E. Anthony Rotundo, *American Manhood: Transformations in Masculinity from the Revolution to the Modern Era* (New York: Basic Books, 1993).

12. Melville, *Pierre*, 94, 20, 216.

13. Mumford, *My Works and Days*, 301.

14. Lewis Mumford, *Herman Melville* (New York: Harcourt, Brace, 1929), 218.

15. Melville, *Pierre*, 273, 356, 136.

16. Ibid., 267–69, 266, 271, 141.

17. See Brian Higgins and Hershel Parker, eds., *Herman Melville: The Contemporary Reviews* (New York: Cambridge University Press, 1995), 420, 429, 431, 422, 436 (Boston *Post*, August 4, 1852; *Albion*, August 21, 1852; *Literary World*, August 21, 1852; Boston *Daily Times*, August 5, 1852; New York *Day Book*, September 7, 1852).

18. Melville, *Pierre*, 314.

Chapter 13. Spiritual Freedom (1935–38)

1. Lewis Mumford, "The Recovery of the American Heritage," commencement address at Oberlin College, June 1935, typescript, Mumford Papers, Box 173, Folder 7938; Herman Melville, *Moby-Dick* (New York: Norton, 1967; orig. 1851), 318.

2. Mumford, "The Recovery of the American Heritage." Mumford was tackling one of the biggest and most debated questions in U.S. history. Recent scholarship on the Frontier, shaped by the so-called New Western History of the 1980s and 1990s, quite justifiably emphasizes the colonialist and exploitative aspects of American settlement. At the same time, some scholars have acknowledged an important sense of contingency and possibility and even a robust intellectual radicalism that arose, at times, amid the development of the West. Mumford's perspective, in other words, has aged well. See, for instance, Robert V. Hine, John Mack Faragher, and Jon T. Coleman, *The American West: A New Interpretive History*, 2nd ed. (New Haven: Yale University Press, 2017); William H. Goetzmann, *Beyond the Revolution: A History of American Thought from Paine to Pragmatism* (New York: Basic Books, 2009); Michael L. Johnson, *Hunger for the Wild: America's Obsession with the Untamed West* (Lawrence: University Press of Kansas, 2007); and Lee Clark Mitchell, *Witnesses to a Vanishing America: The Nineteenth-Century Response* (Princeton: Princeton University Press, 1981).

3. Sophia Mumford, journal entry, August 19, 1935, Mumford Papers, Box 193, Folder 8257.

4. See, for instance, John D'Emilio and Estelle B. Freedman, *Intimate Matters: A History of Sexuality in America*, 3rd ed. (Chicago: University of Chicago Press, 2012), 223–26, 229–35, 265–74, and Christina Simmons, "Modern Sexuality and the Myth of Victorian Repression," in Kathy Peiss and Christina Simmons, eds., *Passion and Power: Sexuality in History* (Philadelphia: Temple University Press, 1989), 157–77.

5. Melville references like this one occur in Mumford's correspondence and journals regularly throughout his life. See Herman Melville, *Pierre; or, The Ambiguities* (New York: Penguin, 1996; orig. 1852), 303; but when Mumford referred to this passage he actually paraphrased it: "Well does the drowning man know his danger; willingly would he avoid it; and yet the unfortunate wretch will drown." See Donald L. Miller, *Lewis Mumford: A Life* (Pittsburgh: University of Pittsburgh Press, 1989), 343, citing Lewis's letter to his friend Henry Murray in the Murray papers at Harvard. The letter is now available in the published Mumford-Murray correspondence: Frank G. Novak Jr., ed., *"In Old Friendship": The Correspondence of Lewis Mumford and Henry A. Murray, 1928–1981* (Syracuse: Syracuse University Press, 2007), 98. Murray would have been a sympathetic correspondent, given that he had been having an extramarital affair of his own for a decade already (and it would last three more decades)—with his colleague Christiana Morgan, who would later become one of Mumford's good friends and close correspondents.

6. Quoted in Miller, *Lewis Mumford*, 347.

7. Ibid., 341–53, and for evidence of Sophia's reaction to Miller's inclusion of the affair with Alice, see the correspondence and notes in the Sophia Wittenberg Mumford Papers, Box 3, Folders 13 and 15. One example: "Since Lewis had chosen to eliminate Alice from his account, why not honor his choice during his lifetime? . . . Especially since [Miller] had repeatedly announced to us that the book was to be about Lewis's work, with only enough personal background to bring L.M. to life." Sophia Mumford, typescript documenting her criticisms of Miller's biography, Sophia Wittenberg Mumford Papers, Box 3, Folder 15 (different pages of the typescript have different dates; this one is dated March 9, 1992, and refers to page 342 of Miller's biography).

8. Sophia Mumford, journal entry, August 19, 1935, Mumford Papers, Box 193, Folder 8257.

9. Mumford to Josephine Strongin, December 19, 1937, Mumford Papers, Box 91, Folder 6421.

10. Mumford, "Random Notes/Personalia," April 2, 1936, Mumford Papers, Box 193, Folder 8256.

11. Mumford, "The Recovery of the American Heritage"; "Menace" article in Mumford, *My Works and Days: A Personal Chronicle* (New York: Harcourt Brace Jovanovich, 1979), 377–78. Of course, Mumford had already developed a number of these themes in *Technics and Civilization*: "But comfort and safety are not unconditioned goods; they are capable of defeating life just as thoroughly as hardship and uncertainty; and the notion that every other interest, art, friendship, love, parenthood, must be subordinated to the production of increasing amounts of comforts and luxuries is merely one of the superstitions of a money-bent utilitarian society": *Technics and Civilization* (Chicago: University of Chicago Press, 2010; orig. 1934), 400.

12. Mumford, "The Recovery of the American Heritage."

13. Mumford sometimes referred to Leedsville, but he more commonly said that he lived in Amenia. A postcard from the Toll Gate Inn Restaurant was included in a bundle of Geddes Mumford's possessions, returned to his parents by the U.S. Army after his death: Sophia Wittenberg Mumford Papers, Box 9, Folder 5.

14. See, for instance, Ben A. Minteer, *The Landscape of Reform: Civic Pragmatism and Environmental Thought in America* (Cambridge, Mass.: MIT Press, 2006), 1–50; Kevin C. Armitage, *The Nature Study Movement: The Forgotten Popularizer of America's Conservation Ethic* (Lawrence: University Press of Kansas, 2009), 170–94; Aaron Sachs, *Arcadian America: The Death and Life of an Environmental Tradition* (New Haven: Yale University Press, 2013), 350–59; and Benjamin Heber Johnson, *Escaping the Dark, Gray City: Fear and Hope in Progressive-Era Conservation* (New Haven, Yale University Press, 2017), 75–89.

15. Mumford, "Random Notes/Personalia," November 28, 1936, Mumford Papers, Box 192, Folder 8236; Mumford, "Random Notes," August 31, 1963, Mumford Papers, Box 173, Folder 7933.

16. Robert Wojtowicz, Mumford's literary executor, has emphasized this aspect of Mumford's identity and career. See Robert Wojtowicz, *Lewis Mumford and American Modernism: Eutopian Theories for Architecture and Urban Planning* (New York: Cambridge University Press, 1996); Wojtowicz, ed., *Sidewalk Critic: Lewis Mumford's Writings on New York* (New York: Princeton Architectural Press, 1998); and Wojtowicz, ed., *Mumford on Modern Art in the 1930s* (Berkeley: University of California Press, 2007). Also see Miller, *Lewis Mumford*, 169–91, 486–94, and note Mumford, *From the Ground Up: Observations on Contemporary Architecture, Housing, Highway Building, and Civic Design* (New York: Harcourt Brace Jovanovich, 1956), a collection of pieces from the *New Yorker*; and Jeanne M. Davern, ed., *Lewis Mumford: Architecture as a Home for Man: Essays for Architectural Record* (New York: Architectural Record Books, 1975).

17. Mumford to Josephine Strongin, December 19, 1937, Mumford Papers, Box 91, Folder 6421; Josephine Strongin to LM, December 9, 1937, Mumford Papers, Box 91, Folder 6421; and see Miller, *Lewis Mumford*, 383–87.

18. Mumford, "Random Notes," October 10, 1938, Mumford Papers, Box 192, Folder 8235. Later Mumford misquoted this remark slightly when he used it in *My Works and Days*, 317; he also misdated it to 1936 (the original note he took about what Sophia said is clearly marked 1938).

19. Sophia Mumford, handwritten note, October 20, 1989, Sophia Wittenberg Mumford Papers, Box 3, Folder 15.

20. Mumford, *My Works and Days*, 320–21.

21. Herman Melville, *Mardi: And a Voyage Thither* (Evanston: Northwestern University Press, 1998; orig. 1849), 164, 158, 137, 139, 193.

Chapter 14. The Happy Failure (1853–55)

1. Herman Melville, *Moby-Dick* (New York: Norton, 1967; orig. 1851), 354–55.

2. See Hershel Parker, *Herman Melville: A Biography, Volume 2, 1851–1891* (Baltimore: Johns Hopkins University Press, 2002), 146–60; also note 114–15 for the novel's source material.

3. Ibid., 152.

4. Ibid., 153. Herman's mother, Maria, claimed that he was game to take a consulship, but the evidence is scant, and it seems clear that he did very little to help his own cause. See ibid., 143–56.

5. Brian Higgins and Hershel Parker, eds., *Herman Melville: The Contemporary Reviews* (New York: Cambridge University Press, 1995), 436 (New York *Day Book*, September 7, 1852).

6. Herman Melville, "Cock-A-Doodle-Doo! Or The Crowing of the Noble Cock Beneventano," in Warner Berthoff, ed., *Great Short Works of Herman Melville* (New York: Perennial, 2004), 75. Most quotations from Melville's stories will be from this edition, shortened to *Great Short Works*.

7. Melville, *Moby-Dick*, 12.

8. *Great Short Works*, 75.

9. Kris A. Hansen, *Death Passage on the Hudson: The Wreck of the Henry Clay* (Fleischmanns: Purple Mountain Press, 2004).

10. *Great Short Works*, 75–76, 79, 78.

11. Andrew Delbanco, *Melville: His World and Work* (New York: Vintage, 2005), 208.

12. Lewis Mumford, *Herman Melville* (New York: Harcourt, Brace, 1929), 236.

13. *Great Short Works*, 77.

14. Mumford's markings can be seen in the Lewis Mumford Collection, Monmouth University; Mumford read this story in Melville, *The Apple-Tree Table and Other Sketches* (Princeton: Princeton University Press, 1922), quotation on 214. The resonances with *Walden* (which did not come out until a year later) are uncanny.

15. *Great Short Works*, 77; Parker, *Herman Melville, Vol. 2*, 142.

16. *Great Short Works*, 88–89, 97.

17. *Great Short Works*, 180, 183, 186, 185.

18. *Great Short Works*, 195, 198, 199, 197, 200.

19. Markings in Melville, *The Apple-Tree Table and Other Sketches*, 268.

20. *Great Short Works*, 201.

21. *Great Short Works*, 316–19, 322–24.

22. See Scott A. Sandage, *Born Losers: A History of Failure in America* (Cambridge, Mass.: Harvard University Press, 2005).

23. Melville, *Moby-Dick*, 326.

Chapter 15. Reconnaissance (1899–1925)

1. Lewis Mumford, *Sketches from Life: The Autobiography of Lewis Mumford—The Early Years* (Boston: Beacon Press, 1983; orig. 1982), 14.

2. On Moses and automobility, see, for instance, Roberta Brandes Gratz, *The Battle for Gotham: New York in the Shadow of Robert Moses and Jane Jacobs* (New York: Nation Books, 2010), and Robert Caro, *The Power Broker: Robert Moses and the Fall of New York* (New York: Knopf, 1974).

3. Mumford, survey notes (New York), typescript, March 15, 1916, and "The Jersey River-Front," typescript, Spring 1916, Mumford Papers, Box 180, Folder 8027.

4. A decade earlier, Mumford's exhaustion probably would have been called neurasthenia, but Mumford thought of it as depression. See Ann Cvetkovich, *Depression: A Public Feeling* (Durham: Duke University Press, 2012); David G. Schuster, *Neurasthenic Nation: America's Search for Health, Happiness, and Comfort, 1869–1920* (New Brunswick, N.J.: Rutgers University Press, 2011); Gary Greenberg, *Manufacturing Depression: The Secret History of a Modern Disease* (New York: Simon and Schuster, 2010); Alain Ehrenberg, *The Weariness of the Self: Diagnosing*

the History of Depression in the Contemporary Age (Montreal: McGill-Queen's University Press, 2010); Laura D. Hirshbein, *American Melancholy: Constructions of Depression in the Twentieth Century* (New Brunswick, N.J.: Rutgers University Press, 2009); Dan G. Blazer, *The Age of Melancholy: "Major Depression" and Its Social Origins* (New York: Routledge, 2005); and Stanley W. Jackson, *Melancholia and Depression: From Hippocratic Times to Modern Times* (New Haven: Yale University Press, 1986).

5. Mumford, "At Present," typescript, July 1920, Mumford Papers, Box 191, Folder 8226.

6. For instance, Mumford, *Sketches*, 140. Also note the play he started to write in approximately 1915 called "The Invalids."

7. Herman Melville, *Moby-Dick* (New York: Norton, 1967; orig. 1851), 315.

8. See Mumford, *Sketches*, 144–58, for Mumford's own account of the significance of Geddes in his life; and also note Casey Nelson Blake, *Beloved Community: The Cultural Criticism of Randolph Bourne, Van Wyck Brooks, Waldo Frank, and Lewis Mumford* (Chapel Hill: University of North Carolina Press, 1990), 190–201, and Robert Wojtowicz, *Lewis Mumford and American Modernism: Eutopian Theories for Architecture and Urban Planning* (New York: Cambridge University Press, 1996), 10–42. On Geddes, see Volker M. Welter, *Biopolis: Patrick Geddes and the City of Life* (Cambridge, Mass.: MIT Press, 2002), and Helen Meller, *Patrick Geddes: Social Evolutionist and City Planner* (London: Routledge, 1990). Also note Vincent DiMattio and Kenneth R. Stunkel, *The Drawings and Watercolors of Lewis Mumford*, Studies in Art History, vol. 8 (Lewiston, N.Y.: Edwin Mellen Press, 2004).

9. Mumford, *Sketches*, 147, 151–52.

10. Ibid., 150.

11. Patrick Geddes, preliminary note for the catalogue of the "Cities and Town Planning Exhibit," Dublin, 1911, extract reprinted in Sofia Leonard, *Catalogue of the Archives of the Patrick Geddes Center for Planning Studies*, vol. 1 (Edinburgh: Patrick Geddes Center for Planning Studies, 1998), 37—which I consulted in the Centre for Research Collections at the University of Edinburgh.

12. Mumford, *Sketches*, 155.

13. Mumford, "The Jersey River-Front," typescript, Spring 1916, Mumford Papers, Box 180, Folder 8027; Mumford, "The Pittsburgh District," typescript, August 1917, Mumford Papers, Box 191, Folder 8225.

14. Mumford, survey notes (New York), typescript, August 21, 1916, Mumford Papers, Box 180, Folder 8027.

15. Mumford, "Minding One's Business," typescript, May 6, 1916, Mumford Papers, Box 191, Folder 8225.

16. Geddes quoted in Donald L. Miller, *Lewis Mumford: A Life* (Pittsburgh: University of Pittsburgh Press, 1989), 226. Also note that the marxist geographer Alex Loftus took up a parallel effort, though without citing Mumford, in his book *Everyday Environmentalism: Creating an Urban Political Ecology* (Minneapolis: University of Minnesota Press, 2012); also see Michel de Certeau, *The Practice of Everyday Life*, trans. Steven Rendall (Berkeley: University of California Press, 1988; orig. 1984), esp. 91–110.

17. Mumford, *Sketches*, 145.

18. See, for instance, Welter, *Biopolis*; Meller, *Patrick Geddes*; Kermit C. Parsons and David Schuyler, eds., *From Garden City to Green City: The Legacy of Ebenezer Howard* (Baltimore: Johns

Hopkins University Press, 2002); and Robert F. Young, "'Free Cities and Regions': Patrick Geddes's Theory of Planning," *Landscape and Urban Planning* 116 (May 2017): 27–36.

19. Mumford, *Sketches*, 145.

20. Lewis Mumford, *My Works and Days: A Personal Chronicle* (New York: Harcourt Brace Jovanovich, 1979), 103; Mumford, *Sketches*, 152.

21. Mumford, *Sketches*, 326, 329, 331; Mumford, *My Works and Days*, 98.

22. Mumford, *My Works and Days*, 98.

23. Mumford, *Sketches*, 157.

Chapter 16. Disenchantment (1853–55)

1. Herman Melville, "The Encantadas, or Enchanted Isles," in Warner Berthoff, ed., *Great Short Works of Herman Melville* (New York: Perennial, 2004), 107 (hereafter *Great Short Works*). And see Mumford's Note Card entitled "Melville the Observer," October 13, 1927, Mumford Papers, Box 166, Folder 7875.

2. Andrew Delbanco, *Melville: His World and Work* (New York: Vintage, 2005), 206–43; Hershel Parker, *Herman Melville: A Biography, Volume 2, 1851–1891* (Baltimore: Johns Hopkins University Press, 2002), 151–89.

3. *Great Short Works*, 99–102.

4. Ibid., 101–3.

5. Herman Melville, *Moby-Dick* (New York: Norton, 1967; orig. 1851), 50.

6. *Great Short Works*, 105, 99.

7. Ibid., 40, 45, 40.

8. Ibid., 45–47, 39–40.

9. Ralph Waldo Emerson, "Self-Reliance," in Stephen E. Whicher, ed., *Selections from Ralph Waldo Emerson* (Boston: Houghton Mifflin, 1960), 149.

10. *Great Short Works*, 49, 55, 65, 60, 50, 68.

11. Lewis Mumford, *Herman Melville* (New York: Harcourt, Brace, 1929), 238.

12. *Great Short Works*, 239–40, 242, 245, 295.

13. Mumford, *Herman Melville*, 246.

14. *Great Short Works*, 262. On Melville and Douglass, see Greg Grandin, *The Empire of Necessity: Slavery, Freedom, and Deception in the New World* (New York: Picador, 2014), 197–99; Delbanco, *Melville*, 230; Wyn Kelley, *Herman Melville: An Introduction* (Oxford: Blackwell, 2008), 114; and Robert K. Wallace, *Douglass and Melville: Anchored Together in Neighborly Style* (New Bedford: Spinner Publications, 2005), 101–2, 110–17.

15. *Great Short Works*, 279.

Chapter 17. Counterpoint (1938)

1. Lewis Mumford, *The Culture of Cities* (San Diego: Harcourt Brace Jovanovich, 1970; orig. 1938), 4.

2. Ibid., vii.

3. Ibid., 485–86.

4. Herman Melville, *Moby-Dick* (New York: Norton, 1967; orig. 1851), 118.

5. Mumford, *Culture of Cities*, 486.

6. Ibid., 217, 250–51, 215. Mumford's emphasis on the city and on the challenge of difference is underemphasized in most of the relevant scholarship, as I've argued in Aaron Sachs, "Lewis Mumford's Urbanism and the Problem of Environmental Modernity," *Environmental History* 21 (October 2016): 638–59. Part of the problem is simply that Jane Jacobs (the person iconically associated with the vibrancy of street culture) was so certain that Mumford didn't genuinely like cities: he seemed to her much too fond of green spaces. Also note Mumford's comment about Jacobs's denunciation of the garden city idea, in Mumford's 1970 preface to a new edition of *Culture of Cities*, x. And for direct comparisons of Jacobs and Mumford, see Viviana Andreescu and Karl Bessel, "Lewis Mumford and Jane Jacobs as Precursors of New Urbanism: Residents' Reaction to Different Urban Visions," in Karl Bessel and Viviana Andreescu, eds., *Back to the Future: New Urbanism and the Rise of Neotraditionalism in Urban Planning* (Lanham, Md.: University Press of America, 2013), 15–28, and James G. Mellon, "Visions of the Livable City: Reflections on the Jacobs-Mumford Debate," *Ethics, Place, and Environment* 12 (March 2009): 35–48.

Some critics, like Paul Forman, have gone so far as to call Mumford's politics "authoritarian" and "undemocratic," emphasizing the times when he favored a more technical, orderly, top-down approach to city and regional planning. See Paul Forman, "How Lewis Mumford Saw Science, and Art, and Himself," *Historical Studies in the Physical and Biological Sciences* 37, no. 2 (2007): 305. For a more nuanced perspective, and an appreciation of Mumford's vitalism, see Peter Ekman, "Diagnosing Suburban Ruin: A Prehistory of Mumford's Postwar Jeremiad," *Journal of Planning History* 15 (May 2016): 108–28.

7. Mumford, *Culture of Cities*, 484. Also see Jamin Creed Rowan, *The Sociable City: An American Intellectual Tradition* (Philadelphia: University of Pennsylvania Press, 2017).

8. Note the section on public/communal ownership of land in *Culture of Cities*, 327–31, which resonates with a similar passage at the end of Carey McWilliams's classic work, *Factories in the Field*, which was published one year later. See Aaron Sachs, "Civil Rights in the Field: Carey McWilliams as a Public-Interest Historian and Social Ecologist," *Pacific Historical Review* 73 (May 2004): esp. 241–45.

9. Mumford, *Culture of Cities*, 302–3. In addition to Geddes, Mumford was explicitly invoking the work of Peter Kropotkin, the person most closely associated with the idea of "mutual aid." For recent work on Mumford and ecology, see, for instance, William J. Cohen, *Ecohumanism and the Ecological Culture: The Educational Legacy of Lewis Mumford and Ian McHarg* (Philadelphia: Temple University Press, 2019); George Hutchinson, *Facing the Abyss: American Literature and Culture in the 1940s* (New York: Columbia University Press, 2018), 334–39; Sachs, "Lewis Mumford's Urbanism and the Problem of Environmental Modernity"; and Janet Biehl, *Mumford Gutkind Bookchin: The Emergence of Eco-Decentralism* (Porsgrunn, Norway: New Compass Press, 2011).

10. Mumford, *Culture of Cities*, 220.

11. Ibid., 7, 385.

12. Ibid., 323, 331–32.

13. Ibid., 396. For a solid appreciation of Mumford's regionalist vision (and of regionalism more broadly), see John L. Thomas, "Holding the Middle Ground," in Robert Fishman, ed., *The*

American Planning Tradition: Culture and Policy (Washington, D.C.: Woodrow Wilson Center Press, 2000), 33–63; Robert L. Dorman, *Revolt of the Provinces: The Regionalist Movement in America, 1920–1945* (Chapel Hill: University of North Carolina Press, 1993), esp. 226–78; and John L. Thomas, "Lewis Mumford: Regionalist Historian," *Reviews in American History* 16 (March 1988): 158–72.

14. Mumford, *Culture of Cities*, 471, vii.

15. Ibid., 383, 386, 6, 384.

16. Donald Miller suggests that the book's "weakness is the great weakness of all of Mumford's previous writings about the good society—his failure to offer a political strategy for the achievement of his regionalist republic." See Donald L. Miller, *Lewis Mumford: A Life* (Pittsburgh: University of Pittsburgh Press, 1989), 361. Casey Blake says something similar about Mumford's early work: Casey Nelson Blake, *Beloved Community: The Cultural Criticism of Randolph Bourne, Van Wyck Brooks, Waldo Frank, and Lewis Mumford* (Chapel Hill: University of North Carolina Press, 1990), 205.

17. Urban walkers, as Michel de Certeau has commented, repeatedly lose and find themselves, enjoying "the disquieting familiarity of the city," the haunted and haunting city, unpredictable but recognizable, "prey to contradictory movements that counterbalance and combine themselves outside the reach of panoptic power." See Michel de Certeau, *The Practice of Everyday Life*, trans. Steven Rendall (Berkeley: University of California Press, 1988; orig. 1984), 95–96. Also see Don Mitchell, *The Right to the City: Social Justice and the Fight for Public Space* (New York: Guilford, 2012), and David Harvey, *Rebel Cities: From the Right to the City to the Urban Revolution* (London: Verso, 2012).

18. Mumford, *Culture of Cities*, 5–6.

19. Ibid., 193. When environmental historians have written about Mumford, they have generally focused on his harsh criticism of urban development and his espousal of broad regional planning as a way to conserve green spaces—as if he posited a separation between the built and natural environments. For example, Andrew Isenberg, echoing an argument made by Ari Kelman, dismissed Mumford as having an utter "disregard" for the possibility that nature could even exist in urban areas. See Andrew Isenberg, "Introduction: New Directions in Urban Environmental History," in Andrew C. Isenberg, ed., *The Nature of Cities* (Rochester: University of Rochester Press, 2006), xii, xviii, and Ari Kelman, *A River and Its City: The Nature of Landscape in New Orleans* (Berkeley: University of California Press, 2003), 10, 221. While Isenberg and Kelman see Mumford as a foil for their attempts to bridge the "intellectual divide between city and countryside" (Isenberg, *Nature of Cities*, xii), I see him as a forerunner or model. Many practitioners of urban environmental history don't even take Mumford into consideration; in *The Nature of Cities*, for instance, he doesn't appear outside of Isenberg's introduction. But for a useful consideration of how Mumford managed to be both an urbanist and a regionalist, see Emily Talen, "Beyond the Front Porch: Regionalist Ideals in the New Urbanist Movement," *Journal of Planning History* 7 (February 2008): 20–47. And also note Karl Bessel and Viviana Andreescu, "The City in History: Mumford Revisited," in Karl Bessel and Viviana Andreescu, eds., *Back to the Future: New Urbanism and the Rise of Neotraditionalism in Urban Planning* (Lanham, Md.: University Press of America, 2013), 1–13.

20. Mumford, *Culture of Cities*, 3.

21. Mumford, *Sketches*, 487; Lewis Mumford, *My Works and Days: A Personal Chronicle* (New York: Harcourt Brace Jovanovich, 1979), 504, 311.

22. Mumford, *Sketches*, 486, 484, 488; Alison Mumford to LM, June 1, 1946, Mumford Papers, Box 86, Folder 6333. Also note *My Works and Days*, 334, on Geddes Mumford's attraction to animals.

23. Melville, *Moby-Dick*, 317.

24. Mumford, *Culture of Cities*, 218.

Chapter 18. Redburn (1839–55)

1. Herman Melville, *Redburn, His First Voyage; Being the Sailor-boy Confessions and Reminiscences of the Son-of-a-Gentleman, in the Merchant Service* (Evanston and Chicago: Northwestern University Press and the Newberry Library, 1969; orig. 1849), 5.

2. Warner Berthoff, ed., *Great Short Works of Herman Melville* (New York: Perennial, 2004), 172 (hereafter *Great Short Works*).

3. Melville, *Redburn*, 117.

4. *Great Short Works*, 204, 211, 220–21, 219.

5. Ibid., 158–59, 162, 161, 151, 154, 153, 155. Mesmerism was all the rage in mid-nineteenth-century American culture; it plays an important role in Hawthorne's 1852 novel, *The Blithedale Romance*.

6. Melville, *Redburn*, 200–202, 264.

7. Ibid., 143, 152, 157, 159, 154–55.

8. Ibid., 156, 208, 186.

9. Ibid., 180, 163, 180, 155–56, 144–45, 202.

10. Ibid., 66, 62, 66.

11. Ibid., 61, 274, 58, 112–13.

12. Herman Melville, *Moby-Dick* (New York: Norton, 1967; orig. 1851), 444.

13. Melville, *Redburn*, 105.

14. *The Writings of Herman Melville*, vol. 15, *Journals*, edited by Howard C. Horsford and Lynn Horth (Evanston and Chicago: Northwestern University Press and the Newberry Library, 1989), 7, 42, 41.

15. Melville, *Redburn*, 298, 165, 170–71; also note that Mumford took special notice of Melville's description of the *Irrawaddy*: Mumford, *Herman Melville* (New York: Harcourt, Brace, 1929), 34.

16. Melville, *Redburn*, 169.

Chapter 19. Radburn (1923–39)

1. See Aaron Sachs, "Lewis Mumford's Urbanism and the Problem of Environmental Modernity," *Environmental History* 21 (October 2016): 638–59. Also note: Susannah Hagan, *Ecological Urbanism: The Nature of the City* (London: Routledge, 2014); Peter Hall and Colin Ward, *Sociable Cities: The 21st-Century Reinvention of the Garden City*, 2nd ed. (London: Routledge, 2014); Steffen Lehmann, *The Principles of Green Urbanism* (London: Earthscan, 2010); Howard Gillette Jr.,

Civitas by Design: Building Better Communities, from the Garden City to the New Urbanism (Philadelphia: University of Pennsylvania Press, 2010); and Robert F. Young, "Green Cities and the Urban Future," in Kermit C. Parsons and David Schuyler, eds., *From Garden City to Green City: The Legacy of Ebenezer Howard* (Baltimore: Johns Hopkins University Press, 2002), 201–21.

2. Lewis Mumford, *Herman Melville* (New York: Harcourt, Brace, 1929), 35.

3. This lesson is also evident in Mumford's slightly older contemporary, the painter Edward Hopper, who produced a number of haunting cityscapes, especially early in his career; see, for instance, *New York Corner (Corner Saloon)*, 1913; *Rooftops*, 1926; *Drugstore*, 1927; *The City*, 1927; and *Early Sunday Morning*, 1930. Mumford and Hopper seem to have been neighbors for a time in New York City, and in 1933 Mumford reviewed Hopper's show at the Museum of Modern Art, expressing his admiration for the painter's determination to "find value . . . in the very things people usually turn their eyes from"; indeed, "Hopper, in the work of the last decade, has caught one phase of America, its loneliness *and* its visual exhilaration." See Lewis Mumford, "The Art Galleries: Two Americans," *New Yorker* 9 (November 11, 1933), quotations on 77 and 78.

And note Mumford's eerily similar watercolors in Vincent DiMattio and Kenneth R. Stunkel, *The Drawings and Watercolors of Lewis Mumford*, Studies in Art History, vol. 8 (Lewiston, N.Y.: Edwin Mellen Press, 2004)—especially "View from window of my room" (1916) and "Washington Square" (1918).

Like Mumford, Hopper recognized how atomizing the modern city could be but refused to give up on the possibility of connection. The writer Olivia Laing, in her book *The Lonely City*, spends a long chapter meditating on Hopper, and by the end of it she has begun to see "why his work is not just compelling but also consoling. . . . It's true that he painted, not once but many times, the loneliness of a large city, where the possibilities of connection are repeatedly defeated by the dehumanizing apparatus of urban life. But didn't he also paint loneliness *as* a large city, revealing it as a shared, democratic place, inhabited, whether willingly or not, by many souls?" Olivia Laing, *The Lonely City: Adventures in the Art of Being Alone* (New York: Picador, 2016), 44.

For more on Hopper, see: Carol Troyen, "'The Sacredness of Everyday Fact': Hopper's Pictures of the City," in Troyen et al., *Edward Hopper* (Boston: MFA Publications, 2007), 111–43; Sheena Wagstaff, ed., *Edward Hopper* (London: Tate Publishing, 2004); and Lloyd Goodrich, *Edward Hopper* (New York: Harry N. Abrams, 1989).

4. Lewis Mumford, *The Culture of Cities* (San Diego: Harcourt Brace Jovanovich, 1970; orig. 1938), 4–5.

5. See Lewis Mumford, *Sketches from Life: The Autobiography of Lewis Mumford—The Early Years* (Boston: Beacon Press, 1983; orig. 1982), 341–42.

6. Lewis Mumford, introduction to C. S. Stein, *Toward New Towns for America* (Cambridge, Mass.: MIT Press, 1971; orig. 1957), 14. For more on the RPAA, see Emily Talen, *New Urbanism and American Planning: The Conflict of Cultures* (New York: Routledge, 2005), 213–73; Paul S. Sutter, *Driven Wild: How the Fight against Automobiles Launched the Modern Wilderness Movement* (Seattle: University of Washington Press, 2002), 160–68; Kermit C. Parsons, "Collaborative Genius: The Regional Planning Association of America," *Journal of the American Planning Association* 60 (Autumn 1994): 462–82; Daniel Schaffer, *Garden Cities for America: The Radburn Experience* (Philadelphia: Temple University Press, 1982), 49–77; Carl Sussman, ed., *Planning the Fourth Migration: The Neglected Vision of the Regional Planning Association of America* (Cambridge, Mass.:

MIT Press, 1976); and Roy Lubove, *Community Planning in the 1920s: The Contributions of the Regional Planning Association of America* (Pittsburgh: University of Pittsburgh Press, 1962).

7. Lewis Mumford, *My Works and Days: A Personal Chronicle* (New York: Harcourt Brace Jovanovich, 1979), 107; Stein, *Toward New Towns for America*, 19; Mumford, introduction to Stein, *Toward New Towns for America*, 15.

8. See, for instance, Edward Gale Agran, *Herbert Hoover and the Commodification of Middle-Class America* (Lanham, Md.: Lexington Books, 2016); Phillip G. Payne, *Crash! How the Economic Boom and Bust of the 1920s Worked* (Baltimore: Johns Hopkins University Press, 2015); Michael Brocker, *The 1920s American Real Estate Boom and the Downturn of the Great Depression: Evidence from City Cross Sections* (Cambridge, Mass.: National Bureau of Economic Research, 2013); Julia C. Ott, *When Wall Street Met Main Street: The Quest for an Investor's Democracy* (Cambridge, Mass.: Harvard University Press, 2011); and Jeffrey M. Hornstein, *A Nation of Realtors: A Cultural History of the Twentieth-Century American Middle Class* (Durham: Duke University Press, 2005).

9. Stein, *Toward New Towns for America*, 22, 27, 31–32, and Mumford, introduction to Stein, *Toward New Towns for America*, 16–17.

10. See, for instance, David J. Goldberg, *Discontented America: The United States in the 1920s* (Baltimore: Johns Hopkins University Press, 1999), and David Montgomery, *The Fall of the House of Labor: The Workplace, the State, and American Labor Activism, 1865–1925* (New York: Cambridge University Press, 1987).

11. It had been fairly clear from the beginning that they did not have enough available land to create the kind of green belt they had envisioned; once the Depression hit, and they lost all the remaining land that had not yet been built on, there was no longer even a chance of incorporating either wilderness or industry.

12. Stein, *Toward New Towns for America*, 9.

13. Ibid., 37–73, quotation on 37. For more on Radburn, see Kristin E. Larsen, *Community Architect: The Life and Vision of Clarence S. Stein* (Ithaca: Cornell University Press, 2016), esp. 145–203; Michael David Martin, "Returning to Radburn," *Landscape Journal* 20 (January 2001): 156–75; Eugenie Ladner Birch, "Radburn and the American Planning Movement: The Persistence of an Idea," in Donald A. Krueckeberg, ed., *Introduction to Planning History in the United States* (New Brunswick, N.J.: Center for Urban Policy Research, 1983), 122–51; William H. Wilson, "Moles and Skylarks," in Krueckeberg, ed., *Introduction to Planning History in the United States*, 88–121, esp. 118–19; and Schaffer, *Garden Cities for America*.

14. Mumford, introduction to Stein, *Toward New Towns for America*, 17; and Stein, *Toward New Towns for America*, 41.

15. Stein, *Toward New Towns for America*, 48.

16. On Central Park, see Roy Rosenzweig and Elizabeth Blackmar, *The Park and the People: A History of Central Park* (Ithaca: Cornell University Press, 1992), 78–91, 211–59, and Matthew Gandy, *Concrete and Clay: Reworking Nature in New York City* (Cambridge, Mass.: MIT Press, 2002), 77–113.

17. Stein, *Toward New Towns for America*, 60, 35; Mumford, introduction to Stein, *Toward New Towns for America*, 17.

18. During my time at Radburn, I stopped at the main offices of the Radburn Association (from which the community is governed), where the friendly attendants indulged my questions

and even allowed me to work my way through their bookshelves and file cabinets. Many of the documents I found were incomplete, but I was especially pleased to come across the partial typescript of a speech delivered by Charles Ascher on October 4, 1975, in which he explained how he named the town. The Radburn Association is at 29–20 Fair Lawn Ave, Fair Lawn, NJ, and more information is available on their website, https://www.radburn.org/.

19. Mumford, "Personalia," June 15, 1931, Mumford Papers, Box 193, Folder 8252.

20. Typescript of a speech delivered by Charles Ascher on October 4, 1975, Radburn Association files.

21. Stein, *Toward New Towns for America*, 127. Also see Talen, *New Urbanism and American Planning*, 158–212; Eugenie L. Birch, "Five Generations of the Garden City: Tracing Howard's Legacy in Twentieth-Century Residential Planning," in Parsons and Schuyler, eds., *From Garden City to Green City*, esp. 172–79; Spiro Kostof, *The City Shaped: Urban Patterns and Meanings through History* (Boston: Little, Brown, 1991), 75–82; Kermit C. Parsons, "Clarence Stein and the Greenbelt Towns," *Journal of the American Planning Association* 56 (Spring 1990): 161–83; John Hancock, "The New Deal and American Planning: The 1930s," in Daniel Schaffer, ed., *Two Centuries of American Planning* (Baltimore: Johns Hopkins University Press, 1988), 197–230; and Daniel Schaffer, "Resettling Industrial America: The Controversy over FDR's Greenbelt Town Program," *Urbanism Past and Present* 8 (Winter/Spring 1983): 18–32.

22. Mumford, introduction to Stein, *Toward New Towns for America*, 13, 17. Also see Cathy D. Knepper, *Greenbelt, Maryland: A Living Legacy of the New Deal* (Baltimore: Johns Hopkins University Press, 2001).

23. See Parsons, "Clarence Stein and the Greenbelt Towns"; Hancock, "The New Deal and American Planning"; and Schaffer, "Resettling Industrial America."

24. Mumford, introduction to Benton MacKaye, *The New Exploration: A Philosophy of Regional Planning* (Harpers Ferry and Urbana-Champaign: Appalachian Trail Conference and University of Illinois Press, 1990; orig. 1928), xviii.

25. Stein, *Toward New Towns for America*, 127.

26. My transcription of the voice-over from *The City*, dir. Ralph Steiner and Willard Van Dyke (New York, 1939).

27. On this period in Mumford's life, see Donald L. Miller, *Lewis Mumford: A Life* (Pittsburgh: University of Pittsburgh Press, 1989), 354–73, and for broader historical context, see Morris Dickstein, *Dancing in the Dark: A Cultural History of the Great Depression* (New York: Norton, 2009), and Michael Denning, *The Cultural Front: The Laboring of American Culture in the Twentieth Century* (New York: Verso, 1997).

28. Lewis Mumford, *Regional Planning in the Pacific Northwest: A Memorandum* (Portland, Ore.: Northwest Regional Council, 1939), 1, 3, 20.

29. Lewis Mumford, *Whither Honolulu: A Memorandum Report on Park and City Planning* (Honolulu: City and County of Honolulu Park Board, 1938), 55, 40.

30. Mumford, *My Works and Days*, 340, 325; Mumford, *Sketches*, 420.

31. Sophia Mumford to LM, June 27, 1938, Sophia Wittenberg Mumford Papers, Box 11, Folder 11.

32. Mumford, "Personalia," September 19, 1939, Mumford Papers, Box 192, Folder 8236.

33. Mumford, *My Works and Days*, 325–26.

34. Herman Melville, *Moby-Dick* (New York: Norton, 1967; orig. 1851), 441, 51.

35. See, for instance, Mumford's bleak letter to Henry Murray of August 28, 1938, Honolulu, full of Melville references and the "malignity of the tropics," in Frank G. Novak Jr., ed., *"In Old Friendship": The Correspondence of Lewis Mumford and Henry A. Murray, 1928–1981* (Syracuse: Syracuse University Press, 2007), 141–42.

Chapter 20. Revolutions (1848–55)

1. *The Writings of Herman Melville*, vol. 15, *Journals*, edited by Howard C. Horsford and Lynn Horth (Evanston and Chicago: Northwestern University Press and the Newberry Library, 1989), 43.

2. Quoted in Andrew Delbanco, *Melville: His World and Work* (New York: Vintage, 2005), 103.

3. Quoted in Hershel Parker, *Herman Melville: A Biography, Volume 1, 1819–1851* (Baltimore: Johns Hopkins University Press, 1996), 588.

4. Herman Melville, *Clarel: A Poem and Pilgrimage in the Holy Land* (Evanston: Northwestern University Press, 2008; orig. 1876), 148–49.

5. Herman Melville, *Mardi: And a Voyage Thither* (Evanston: Northwestern University Press, 1998; orig. 1849), 526.

6. Ibid., 520, 512, 514, 521, 523.

7. Ibid., 472, 519, 473, 522, 512–13, 531. Yes: to a careful observer like Melville, Secession was foreseeable in 1849.

8. Ibid., 524–25, 527, 528–29.

9. Ibid., 530.

10. Herman Melville, *Israel Potter: His Fifty Years of Exile* (New York: Penguin, 2008; orig. 1855), 181.

11. *The Writings of Herman Melville*, vol. 14, *Correspondence*, edited by Lynn Horth (Evanston and Chicago: Northwestern University Press and the Newberry Library, 1993), 265.

12. Melville, *Israel Potter*, 7.

13. Ibid., 15, 47, 94–95.

14. Ibid., 144, 192.

15. Warner Berthoff, ed., *Great Short Works of Herman Melville* (New York: Perennial, 2004), 204–5.

16. Melville, *Israel Potter*, 175–78.

17. Herman Melville, *Moby-Dick* (New York: Norton, 1967; orig. 1851), 353.

18. Melville, *Israel Potter*, 180, 185–86, 180–81.

19. Ibid., 186, 157, 25, 176, 188. Also: "He sought to conciliate fortune, not by despondency, but by resolution" (135). Israel is an almost perfect proto-existentialist hero.

20. Ibid., 143, 142, 145, 148, 70.

Chapter 21. Misgivings and Preparatives (1938–39)

1. Herman Melville, *Mardi: And a Voyage Thither* (Evanston: Northwestern University Press, 1998; orig. 1849), 528–29.

2. Lewis Mumford, *Herman Melville* (New York: Harcourt, Brace, 1929), 91. Also note Mumford's 1944 letter to Van Wyck Brooks, where he says of Melville that "the only book of his I regard as a complete failure now is *Mardi*; that was a big intention that didn't come off; but it was the stepping stone from *Typee* to *Moby-Dick* and as such it had a preparatory role; it showed him what he might do." Robert E. Spiller, ed., *The Van Wyck Brooks Lewis Mumford Letters: The Record of a Literary Friendship, 1921–1963* (New York: E. P. Dutton, 1970), 254.

3. Letter to Henry Murray, October 8, 1938, in Frank G. Novak Jr., ed., *"In Old Friendship": The Correspondence of Lewis Mumford and Henry A. Murray, 1928–1981* (Syracuse: Syracuse University Press, 2007), 144.

4. In Donald Miller's generally thorough biography, there is no mention at all of *Men Must Act*, which I find especially strange given how much of a departure the book was for Mumford and how widely it was reviewed (Mumford's clippings folder is bursting with articles about the book: Mumford Papers, Box 111, Folder 6653).

Other scholars have paid a fair amount of attention to *Men Must Act*; see, for instance, Robert Westbrook, "Lewis Mumford, John Dewey, and the 'Pragmatic Acquiescence,'" in Thomas P. Hughes and Agatha C. Hughes, eds., *Lewis Mumford: Public Intellectual* (New York: Oxford University Press, 1990), 301–22; Richard Wightman Fox, "Tragedy, Responsibility, and the American Intellectual, 1925–1950," in Hughes and Hughes, eds., *Lewis Mumford*, 323–37; and Kenneth R. Stunkel, *Understanding Lewis Mumford: A Guide for the Perplexed* (Lewiston, N.Y.: Edwin Mellen Press, 2004), 81–83.

5. Lewis Mumford, *Men Must Act* (New York: Harcourt, Brace, 1939), 6. The copy I got from the Cornell University Library had not been checked out since 1975.

6. Ibid., 117.

7. Wright to Mumford, Taliesin, June 3, 1941, in Bruce Brooks Pfeiffer and Robert Wojtowicz, eds., *Frank Lloyd Wright & Lewis Mumford: Thirty Years of Correspondence* (New York: Princeton Architectural Press, 2001), 184. This letter ended their correspondence for a decade, but they picked it back up again, cautiously, in the 1950s.

8. Mumford, *Men Must Act*, 6–7, 152.

9. Ibid., 8.

10. Ibid., 37–38, 27, 25.

11. Lewis Mumford, *My Works and Days: A Personal Chronicle* (New York: Harcourt Brace Jovanovich, 1979), 377, 385.

12. Lewis Mumford, *Herman Melville* (New York: Harcourt, Brace, 1929), 5.

13. Mumford, *Men Must Act*, 139–40.

14. Mumford, *Herman Melville*, 186.

15. Herman Melville, *Moby-Dick* (New York: Norton, 1967; orig. 1851), 160.

16. Mumford, *Men Must Act*, 28.

17. Mumford started thinking about this parallel in 1935; see his *New Republic* article, "The Menace of Totalitarian Absolutism," reprinted in *My Works and Days*, 377–78.

18. Letter to Henry Murray, October 8, 1938, in Novak, *"In Old Friendship,"* 144.

19. Mumford, *Men Must Act*, 150–51.

20. Ibid., 144, 165, 164, 171.

21. Ibid., 65, 64, 67.

22. Ibid., 119.

23. Mumford, *My Works and Days*, 386, from two different letters, both written in fall 1939.

24. Ibid.

25. Mumford, "Personalia," September 19, 1939, Mumford Papers, Box 192, Folder 8236.

26. Herman Melville, *Pierre; or, The Ambiguities* (New York: Penguin, 1996; orig. 1852), 215.

27. Letter to Van Wyck Brooks, July 25, 1944, Amenia, in Spiller, *Van Wyck Brooks Lewis Mumford Letters*, 254.

28. Mumford, "Chronology," duplicate typescript, 1982, Sophia Wittenberg Mumford Papers, Box 9, Folder 14.

Chapter 22. The Piazza (1856–57)

1. Hershel Parker, *Herman Melville: A Biography, Volume 2, 1851–1891* (Baltimore: Johns Hopkins University Press, 2002), 278.

2. Herman Melville, "The Piazza," in Warner Berthoff, ed., *Great Short Works of Herman Melville* (New York: Perennial, 2004), 383 (hereafter *Great Short Works*). And for a historical and philosophical consideration of the significance of such in-between places, see Charlie Hailey, *The Porch: Meditations on the Edge of Nature* (Chicago: University of Chicago Press, 2021).

3. Quoted in Andrew Delbanco, *Melville: His World and Work* (New York: Vintage, 2005), 245.

4. *Great Short Works*, 328, 353–54, 329. On Mumford and skyscrapers, see Lewis Mumford, "Towers," *American Mercury* 4 (January 1925): 193–96; Mumford, introduction to C. S. Stein, *Toward New Towns for America* (Cambridge, Mass.: MIT Press, 1971; orig. 1957), 16; and Donald L. Miller, *Lewis Mumford: A Life* (Pittsburgh: University of Pittsburgh Press, 1989), 175, 197.

5. *Great Short Works*, 333, 336–37, 345, 338, 332, 353–54, 336, 340. The conflict between wife and husband about modernizing the house is very similar to that in "Jimmy Rose" (see 318).

6. Ibid., 336, 362, 369; Melville also mentions "Spirit Rapping" in "I and My Chimney," 338. On Spiritualism, see, for instance: Molly McGarry, *Ghosts of Futures Past: Spiritualism and the Cultural Politics of Nineteenth-Century America* (Berkeley: University of California Press, 2008); Robert S. Cox, *Body and Soul: A Sympathetic History of American Spiritualism* (Charlottesville: University of Virginia Press, 2003); Ann Braude, *Radical Spirits: Spiritualism and Women's Rights in Nineteenth-Century America* (Bloomington: Indiana University Press, 2001; orig. 1989); and Bret E. Carroll, *Spiritualism in Antebellum America* (Bloomington: Indiana University Press, 1997).

7. *Great Short Works*, 378, 382. Here's Thoreau's version, part of his book's penultimate paragraph: "Every one has heard the story which has gone the rounds of New England, of a strong and beautiful bug which came out of the dry leaf of an old table of apple-tree wood, which had stood in a farmer's kitchen for sixty years, first in Connecticut, and afterwards in Massachusetts,—from an egg deposited in the living tree many years earlier still, as appeared by counting the annual layers beyond it; which was heard gnawing out for several weeks, hatched perchance by the heat of an urn. Who does not feel his faith in resurrection and immortality strengthened by hearing of this? Who knows what beautiful and winged life, whose egg has been buried for ages under many concentric layers of woodenness in the dead dry life of society, deposited at first in the laburnum of the green and living tree, which has been gradually converted into the

semblance of its well-seasoned tomb,—heard perchance gnawing out now for years by the astonished family of man, as they sat round the festive board,—may unexpectedly come forth from amidst society's most trivial and handselled furniture, to enjoy its perfect summer life at last!" Henry David Thoreau, *Walden* (Boston: Beacon Press, 2004; orig. 1854), 311–12.

Also note Frank Davidson, "Melville, Thoreau, and 'The Apple-Tree Table,'" *American Literature* 25 (January 1954): 479–88.

8. Herman Melville, *Moby-Dick* (New York: Norton, 1967; orig. 1851), 406.

9. Markings in Herman Melville, *The Apple-Tree Table and Other Sketches* (Princeton: Princeton University Press, 1922), in the Lewis Mumford Collection, Monmouth University. See the inside front cover and also the "Introductory Note" by the editor, Henry Chapin.

10. Lewis Mumford, *Herman Melville* (New York: Harcourt, Brace, 1929), 243.

11. *Great Short Works*, 368, 385, 387.

12. Ibid., 384–85; Herman Melville, *Pierre; or, The Ambiguities* (New York: Penguin, 1996; orig. 1852), 1.

13. *Great Short Works*, 386, 388.

14. Ibid., 390, 388, 391–92, 394, 395.

15. See Brian Higgins and Hershel Parker, eds., *Herman Melville: The Contemporary Reviews* (New York: Cambridge University Press, 1995), 471, 475, 474 (Berkshire County *Eagle*, May 30, 1856; *National Aegis*, June 4, 1856; New Bedford *Mercury*, June 4, 1856; Philadelphia *Evening Bulletin*, June 4, 1856); and also see Parker, *Herman Melville, Vol. 2*, 284.

16. *The Writings of Herman Melville*, vol. 14, *Correspondence*, edited by Lynn Horth (Evanston and Chicago: Northwestern University Press and the Newberry Library, 1993), 290–95 (two letters).

17. See Parker, *Herman Melville, Vol. 2*, 289, quoting a letter of Shaw to his son, which refers to letters Shaw had received from Lizzie.

18. Mumford, *Herman Melville*, 248.

19. *Great Short Works*, 383. Of course, in *Cymbeline*, Fidele turns out not to be dead; she had just drunk a sleeping potion.

20. *The Writings of Herman Melville*, vol. 15, *Journals*, edited by Howard C. Horsford and Lynn Horth (Evanston and Chicago: Northwestern University Press and the Newberry Library, 1989), 62, 129.

Chapter 23. Faith (1940–43)

1. Herman Melville, *Moby-Dick* (New York: Norton, 1967; orig. 1851), 470.

2. Lewis Mumford, *Faith for Living* (New York: Harcourt, Brace, 1940), v.

3. Lewis Mumford, *My Works and Days: A Personal Chronicle* (New York: Harcourt Brace Jovanovich, 1979), 291. Geoffrey Sanborn, one of the most insightful recent readers of Melville, would agree with Mumford that *Moby-Dick* has a happy ending. To Sanborn, the voice Melville adopted in the novel "was meant to be a stimulant to thought and feeling; it was meant to make your mind a more interesting and enjoyable place. . . . What it wants above all else is to be in a meaningful relationship with you. . . . *Moby-Dick* isn't about the Problem of the Universe, as one of its reviewers derisively suggested; it's about the effort to think about the Problem of the

Universe in the company of another mind, the effort to feel, in the deepest recesses of your consciousness, at least temporarily unalone. Nothing is solved when the *Pequod* goes down, but you and Ishmael are still miraculously afloat." Geoffrey Sanborn, *The Value of Herman Melville* (New York: Cambridge University Press, 2018), 2–3.

4. Mumford, *Faith for Living*, 1, 250, 283.

5. Ibid., 303, 305. The full title of the poem is "OLD COUNSEL of the Young Master of a Wrecked California Clipper": "Come out of the Golden Gate, / Go round the Horn with streamers, / Carry royals early and late; / But, brother, be not over-elate—/ *All hands save ship!* has startled dreamers." Herman Melville, *Poems*, vol. 16 of *The Works of Herman Melville* (London: Constable, 1924), 237.

6. Mumford, *Faith for Living*, 123, 210.

7. Ibid., 85, 136, 138, 141. Note that an earlier version of the passage about the sewer and the garbage pile appears in Lewis Mumford, *Herman Melville* (New York: Harcourt, Brace, 1929), 254–55.

8. Mumford, *Faith for Living*, 136, 139.

9. Ibid., 170–72.

10. Ibid., 189, 313, 220, 223.

11. Ibid., 277.

12. Ibid., 233, 216, 284, 220, 223.

13. Henry Murray to LM, 1939, in Frank G. Novak Jr., ed., *"In Old Friendship": The Correspondence of Lewis Mumford and Henry A. Murray, 1928–1981* (Syracuse: Syracuse University Press, 2007), 149. (Murray was not based in New York City, but he and Mumford were in close touch during this period.)

14. On Frank, see, for instance, Casey Nelson Blake, *Beloved Community: The Cultural Criticism of Randolph Bourne, Van Wyck Brooks, Waldo Frank, and Lewis Mumford* (Chapel Hill: University of North Carolina Press, 1990). There's a great deal of overlap between the writings of Mumford and Frank during this period; note, in particular, Frank's explicit reference to *Men Must Act* near the end of *Chart for Rough Water*; see Frank, *The Re-Discovery of America; and Chart for Rough Water: Our Role in a New World* (two separate books with separate paginations published in one volume) (New York: Duell, Sloan, and Pearce, 1947; orig. 1929 and 1940), 169 (of *Chart*).

15. Donald L. Miller, *Lewis Mumford: A Life* (Pittsburgh: University of Pittsburgh Press, 1989), 394, and Reinhold Niebuhr, *Moral Man and Immoral Society: A Study in Ethics and Politics* (Louisville: Westminster John Knox Press, 2001; orig. 1932), 57. On Niebuhr, see, for instance, Mark Greif, *The Age of the Crisis of Man: Thought and Fiction in America, 1933–1973* (Princeton: Princeton University Press, 2015), 27–37, and Richard Wightman Fox, *Reinhold Niebuhr: A Biography* (Ithaca: Cornell University Press, 1996; orig. 1985).

16. Note, for instance, the direct invocation of Liberty Hyde Bailey, 274.

17. Lewis Mumford, *Sketches from Life: The Autobiography of Lewis Mumford—The Early Years* (Boston: Beacon Press, 1983; orig. 1982), 485–86.

18. Mumford, *Faith for Living*, 276–77, 272–73.

19. Miller, *Lewis Mumford*, 404–5. The slogan "Keep Calm and Carry On" was first used by the British government on posters in the summer of 1939.

20. Mumford, *Faith for Living*, 312, 248.

21. Miller, *Lewis Mumford*, 400. Other reviewers, like the one for *Time*, dismissed Mumford as an alarmist, suffering from various "apocalyptic afflictions": "Intellectuals, Arise," *Time* 36 (2 September 1940): 65.

22. Mumford, *Faith for Living*, 144, and see Miller, *Lewis Mumford*, 407–8.

23. See, for instance, Aaron Sachs, "Virtual Ecology: A Brief Environmental History of Silicon Valley," *World Watch* 12 (January–February 1999): 12–21; Rebecca S. Lowen, *Creating the Cold War University: The Transformation of Stanford* (Berkeley: University of California Press, 1997); and Stuart W. Leslie, *The Cold War and American Science: The Military-Industrial-Academic Complex at MIT and Stanford* (New York: Columbia University Press, 1993).

24. Mumford, *Faith for Living*, 144, 212.

25. Mumford, *My Works and Days*, 396–97.

26. Lewis Mumford, *Green Memories: The Story of Geddes Mumford* (New York: Harcourt, Brace, 1947), 267.

27. Stanford University to Professor Mumford, February 19, 1943, Sophia Wittenberg Mumford Papers, Box 9, Folder 1.

28. Mumford to Geddes, February 9, 1942, New York, in Sophia Wittenberg Mumford Papers, Box 9, Folder 1.

29. Mumford, *Green Memories*, 230.

30. See the essays by "Jack Mumford" in Sophia Wittenberg Mumford Papers, Box 9, Folder 1. Lewis was painfully aware that his son felt "burdened" by his own name, because it was unusual, and many people mispronounced it—so Geddes sometimes went by Jack or Bill: see *Green Memories*, 125–26.

31. Mumford to Geddes, November 11, 1943, Amenia, Mumford Papers, Box 86, Folder 6334.

Chapter 24. The Metaphysics of Indian-Hating (1856–57)

1. *The Writings of Herman Melville*, vol. 15, *Journals*, edited by Howard C. Horsford and Lynn Horth (Evanston and Chicago: Northwestern University Press and the Newberry Library, 1989), 50 (hereafter *Journals*).

2. Herman Melville, *Redburn, His First Voyage; Being the Sailor-boy Confessions and Reminiscences of the Son-of-a-Gentleman, in the Merchant Service* (Evanston and Chicago: Northwestern University Press and the Newberry Library, 1969; orig. 1849), 155.

3. Herman Melville, *Moby-Dick* (New York: Norton, 1967; orig. 1851), 101, 37.

4. Warner Berthoff, ed., *Great Short Works of Herman Melville* (New York: Perennial, 2004), 355–56, 359–60.

5. Letter to Van Wyck Brooks, September 10, 1944, Amenia, in Robert E. Spiller, ed., *The Van Wyck Brooks Lewis Mumford Letters: The Record of a Literary Friendship, 1921–1963* (New York: E. P. Dutton, 1970), 258; also see Mumford, *My Works and Days: A Personal Chronicle* (New York: Harcourt Brace Jovanovich, 1979), 290.

6. See, for instance, Adam Arenson, *The Great Heart of the Republic: St. Louis and the Cultural Civil War* (Cambridge, Mass.: Harvard University Press, 2011); Michael F. Holt, *The Fate of Their Country: Politicians, Slavery Extension, and the Coming of the Civil War* (New York: Hill and

Wang, 2004); Michael A. Morrison, *Slavery and the American West: The Eclipse of Manifest Destiny and the Coming of the Civil War* (Chapel Hill: University of North Carolina Press, 1997); Helen Trimpi, *Melville's Confidence Men and American Politics in the 1850s* (Hamden, Conn.: Archon Books, 1987); and Robert M. Utley, *The Indian Frontier of the American West, 1846–1890* (Albuquerque: University of New Mexico Press, 1984).

7. Herman Melville, *The Confidence-Man: His Masquerade* (Indianapolis: Bobbs-Merrill, 1967; orig. 1857), 203, 206, 212.

8. Ibid., 155. The "moderate man" is practicing a version of what Jean-Paul Sartre would later call "bad faith"; see, for instance, Sarah Bakewell, *At the Existentialist Café: Freedom, Being, and Apricot Cocktails* (New York: Other Press, 2016), 156–7.

9. Hershel Parker, *Herman Melville: A Biography, Volume 2, 1851–1891* (Baltimore: Johns Hopkins University Press, 2002), 255.

10. See, for instance, Amy Reading, *The Mark Inside: A Perfect Swindle, a Cunning Revenge, and a Small History of the Big Con* (New York: Knopf, 2012), 24–27.

11. Melville, *Confidence-Man*, 342, and see, for instance, Lewis Perry, *Boats against the Current: American Culture between Revolution and Modernity, 1820–1860* (New York: Oxford University Press, 1993), and Karen Halttunen, *Confidence Men and Painted Women: A Study of Middle-Class Culture in America, 1830–1870* (New Haven: Yale University Press, 1986; orig. 1982).

12. Herman Melville, *Israel Potter: His Fifty Years of Exile* (New York: Penguin, 2008; orig. 1855), 170, 164.

13. *Confidence-Man*, 198–99; also see 216–20 for the description of Moredock.

14. Herman Melville, *Typee: A Peep at Polynesian Life* (New York: Penguin, 1996; orig. 1846), 21, 25–27, 203.

15. See Brian Higgins and Hershel Parker, eds., *Herman Melville: The Contemporary Reviews* (New York: Cambridge University Press, 1995), 35 and 46 (*American Whig Review*, April 1846, and New York *Evangelist*, April 9, 1846).

16. Herman Melville, *Omoo: A Narrative of Adventures in the South Seas* (New York: Penguin, 2007; orig. 1847), 29.

17. *Contemporary Reviews*, 130 (New York *Weekly Tribune*, June 26, 1847).

18. Melville, *Moby-Dick*, 312.

19. Melville, *Omoo*, 185, 202, 196–97.

20. Henry David Thoreau, *A Week on the Concord and Merrimack Rivers* (New York: Penguin, 1998; orig. 1849), 78.

21. *Contemporary Reviews*, 487, 495, 500, 501 (Albany *Evening Journal*, April 2, 1857; New York *Dispatch*, April 5, 1857; Philadelphia *Evening Bulletin*, April 11, 1857; Burlington *Free Press*, April 25, 1857; New York *Independent*, May 14, 1857).

22. Quoted in Parker, *Herman Melville, Vol. 2*, 343; the words actually belong to Herman's uncle Peter, who was paraphrasing Herman's mother, Maria, who was paraphrasing Herman himself.

23. *Journals*, 104.

24. Lewis Mumford, *Herman Melville* (New York: Harcourt, Brace, 1929), 255.

25. Ibid., 279; *Journals*, 82, 111–12, 65.

26. *Journals*, 66, 73, 75, 78, 112, 114, 119.

27. Ibid., 128–29.

Chapter 25. The Darkness of the Present Day (1944)

1. Lewis Mumford, *Green Memories: The Story of Geddes Mumford* (New York: Harcourt, Brace, 1947), 287, 285.

2. Ibid., 283–88, quotation on 288.

3. Ibid., 286, 289.

4. Ibid., 290, 287, 292.

5. Ibid., 234, 304, 302.

6. Ibid., 309, 311.

7. Donald L. Miller, *Lewis Mumford: A Life* (Pittsburgh: University of Pittsburgh Press, 1989), 412.

8. Lewis Mumford, *The Condition of Man* (London: Martin Secker & Warburg, 1944), v. Mark Greif sees *Condition* as part of the broader midcentury project of "re-enlightenment" and notes how Mumford embodies "a certain, irrepressible optimism, which never left the American discourse of man": see Mark Greif, *The Age of the Crisis of Man: Thought and Fiction in America, 1933–1973* (Princeton: Princeton University Press, 2015), 57–60.

9. Mumford, "Random Notes/Personalia," December 17, 1942, Mumford Papers, Box 192, Folder 8239.

10. Mumford, *Condition*, v, 423, 422, 407, 397. On revolution, Mumford quoted in Miller, *Lewis Mumford*, 422.

11. Mumford, *Condition*, 419.

12. It has become clearer in recent years that trauma can be passed between generations; the children of Holocaust survivors, for instance, sometimes share a particular psychological profile, as do children of returned veterans. See Elizabeth Rosner, *Survivor Café: The Legacy of Trauma and the Labyrinth of Memory* (Berkeley: Counterpoint, 2017), and Sarah Sentilles, *Draw Your Weapons* (New York: Random House, 2017).

13. Mumford, *Condition*, 12.

14. Ibid., 12–14; Herman Melville, *Moby-Dick* (New York: Norton, 1967; orig. 1851), 385.

15. Mumford, *Condition*, 39, 43, 125, 119, 99, 278.

16. Ibid., 246, 240, 254, 235, 172.

17. Ibid., 51, 147, 399, 416; Mumford, *Green Memories*, 286.

18. "Vacation" is from a letter to Henry Murray of July 29, 1944, Amenia, in Frank G. Novak Jr., ed., *"In Old Friendship": The Correspondence of Lewis Mumford and Henry A. Murray, 1928–1981* (Syracuse: Syracuse University Press, 2007), 209; but there are several other letters to Murray during this period that capture Mumford's mindset (200–209), and see also the letters of this summer to Van Wyck Brooks, in Robert E. Spiller, ed., *The Van Wyck Brooks Lewis Mumford Letters: The Record of a Literary Friendship, 1921–1963* (New York: E. P. Dutton, 1970), 244–63.

19. Mumford, *Green Memories*, 332–33, 315–16.

20. Ibid., 318–22, 325.

21. Ibid., 326–27.

22. Ibid, 327–28.

23. Ibid., 333–36, 339.

Chapter 26. More Gloom, and the Light of That Gloom (1856–76)

1. Herman Melville, *Pierre; or, The Ambiguities* (New York: Penguin, 1996; orig. 1852), 165–72.

2. Hershel Parker, *Herman Melville: A Biography, Volume 2, 1851–1891* (Baltimore: Johns Hopkins University Press, 2002), 351.

3. Elizabeth Shaw Melville, "Memoranda," in Merton M. Sealts Jr., *The Early Lives of Melville: Nineteenth-Century Biographical Sketches and Their Authors* (Madison: University of Wisconsin Press, 1974), 169.

4. Melville to Malcolm, September 1, 1860 (Item 176), Herman Melville Papers, Houghton Library, Harvard University. Also see *The Writings of Herman Melville*, vol. 14, *Correspondence*, edited by Lynn Horth (Evanston and Chicago: Northwestern University Press and the Newberry Library, 1993), 347–54 (hereafter *Correspondence*).

5. *Correspondence*, 364–67.

6. See Parker, *Herman Melville, Vol.* 2, 686–89, and the scholarly edition of *Clarel*: vol. 12 of *The Writings of Herman Melville*, edited by Harrison Hayford, Alma A. MacDougall, Hershel Parker, and G. Thomas Tanselle (Evanston and Chicago: Northwestern University Press and the Newberry Library, 1991), 531–40, 651–55.

7. See Aaron Sachs, *Arcadian America: The Death and Life of an Environmental Tradition* (New Haven: Yale University Press, 2013), 187–94.

8. Herman Melville, *Clarel: A Poem and Pilgrimage in the Holy Land* (Evanston: Northwestern University Press, 2008; orig. 1876), 14, 23.

9. Ibid., 25, 5, 8.

10. Ibid., 489; for Mumford's markings, see the copy in the Lewis Mumford Collection, Monmouth University: *Clarel* (New York: G. P. Putnam's Sons, 1876), 2:559.

11. *Clarel* (2008 ed.), 491, 499.

12. Ibid., 117, 308; Herman Melville, *Moby-Dick* (New York: Norton, 1967; orig. 1851), 424.

13. *Clarel* (2008 ed.), 383.

14. Ibid., 158, 279, 222, 148.

15. Ibid., 401–2, 413, 452.

16. Ibid., 31.

17. Lewis Mumford, *Herman Melville* (New York: Harcourt, Brace, 1929), 320–21.

18. *Correspondence*, 483.

19. Quoted in Parker, *Herman Melville, Vol.* 2, 792.

20. Mumford, *Herman Melville*, 323.

21. *Clarel* (2008 ed.), 102, 380, 128, 126, 300–301, 317.

22. Ibid., 384, 203, 397–98.

23. See the scholarly (1991) edition of *Clarel* (Hayford et al., eds.), 659.

24. See the inside front cover of volume 1 of the edition in the Lewis Mumford Collection at Monmouth University, and Mumford, *Sketches from Life: The Autobiography of Lewis Mumford—The Early Years* (Boston: Beacon Press, 1983; orig. 1982), 456.

25. Letter to Brooks of September 10, 1944, Amenia, in Robert E. Spiller, ed., *The Van Wyck Brooks Lewis Mumford Letters: The Record of a Literary Friendship, 1921–1963* (New York: E. P. Dutton, 1970), 259; also see Mumford, *My Works and Days: A Personal Chronicle* (New York:

Harcourt Brace Jovanovich, 1979), 290. Mumford and Brooks had a brief falling out over Mumford's interventionism (and Brooks's isolationism) in February 1940, but within a year they had reestablished a congenial, if not totally forthcoming, correspondence. For the disagreement, see Spiller, *Van Wyck Brooks Lewis Mumford Letters*, 176–86.

26. Mumford, *Herman Melville*, 260, 322, 272, 325.

Chapter 27. Survival (1944–47)

1. Letter to Van Wyck Brooks, July 25, 1944, Amenia, in Robert E. Spiller, ed., *The Van Wyck Brooks Lewis Mumford Letters: The Record of a Literary Friendship, 1921–1963* (New York: E. P. Dutton, 1970), 251; Mumford actually says "colored crayons," but I think he meant what we would call pencils or possibly pastels.

2. I'm not sure if the date ("Oct. 19, 1944") can be trusted, because there is also a note on the back of the picture that says, in quotation marks, "Shortly before news of Geddes's death," but other strong evidence indicates that the news came on the evening of October 17. See, for instance, Lewis Mumford, *Green Memories: The Story of Geddes Mumford* (New York: Harcourt, Brace, 1947), 335. There is also a one-sentence letter from Lewis to Henry Murray dated October 18 that passes along the sad news; see Frank G. Novak Jr., ed., *"In Old Friendship": The Correspondence of Lewis Mumford and Henry A. Murray, 1928–1981* (Syracuse: Syracuse University Press, 2007), 209.

3. Mumford, *Green Memories*, 91–92.

4. Mumford, "Personalia," December 14, 1944, Mumford Papers, Box 192, Folder 8240. Sophia was already feeling guilty back in 1941, at the height of their joint efforts (in Lewis's words) "to rouse our friends, our neighbors, and where possible a wider public." "Children and world crises don't mix!" Sophia had written, in June of that year. "I never dreamed I would find myself almost resenting the time I must give to listening to Geddes's confidences or assuring Alison her dolly is beautiful." It is clear that Sophia gave much more time of this sort to the children than Lewis did. See *Green Memories*, 256.

5. Mumford, "Personalia," July 24, 1945, Mumford Papers, Box 192, Folder 8240.

6. Herman Melville, *Moby-Dick* (New York: Norton, 1967; orig. 1851), 39.

7. Lewis Mumford, *My Works and Days: A Personal Chronicle* (New York: Harcourt Brace Jovanovich, 1979), 400.

8. Ibid., 406–8.

9. Mumford, "Random Notes/Personalia," December 15, 1944, Mumford Papers, Box 192, Folder 8240.

10. Mumford, "Random Notes/Personalia," February 13, 1945, Mumford Papers, Box 192, Folder 8240.

11. Mumford, *My Works and Days*, 402; also Mumford, "Random Notes/Personalia," December 18, 1944, Mumford Papers, Box 192, Folder 8240.

12. Letter of November 30, 1944, Amenia, in Novak, *"In Old Friendship,"* 216.

13. Mumford, "Personalia," January 1, 1946, Mumford Papers, Box 192, Folder 8240.

14. Mumford, "Random Notes/Personalia," December 15, 1944, Mumford Papers, Box 192, Folder 8240.

15. Lewis Mumford, *Values for Survival: Essays, Addresses, and Letters on Politics and Education* (New York: Harcourt, Brace, 1946), 229.

16. Ibid., 82, 85–86, 98, 96, 86.

17. Ibid., 249, 247, 259, 274, 311–13. *Values for Survival* demonstrates how certain forms of universalism and humanism survived World War II, as George Hutchinson argues in *Facing the Abyss: American Literature and Culture in the 1940s* (New York: Columbia University Press, 2018). For a powerful and poignant meditation on German identity in the long aftermath of the war, see Nora Krug, *Belonging: A German Reckons with History and Home* (New York: Scribner, 2018).

18. Mumford, *Green Memories*, 125.

19. Ibid., 36.

20. Mumford, *My Works and Days*, 403.

21. Mumford, *Green Memories*, 3–4.

22. Ibid., 147, 149, 3, 152–53; Herman Melville, *Typee: A Peep at Polynesian Life* (New York: Penguin, 1996; orig. 1846), 126.

23. Mumford, *Green Memories*, 150–51, 75.

24. Miller, *Lewis Mumford*, 442.

25. Mumford, *Green Memories*, 164–65, 78.

26. Ibid., 115.

27. Mumford, *My Works and Days*, 349.

28. Letter of October 20, 1944, Amenia, in Novak, *"In Old Friendship,"* 210.

29. Mumford, *Green Memories*, 183.

30. Letter of November 25, 1946, Topsfield, Mass., in Novak, *"In Old Friendship,"* 247.

31. Note that here my interpretation differs pretty markedly from Miller's; he thought there was a permanent rupture between the two men, but I don't see that in the surviving correspondence. Of course, it's possible that Miller's position on this issue derived from private conversations with Mumford in the 1980s, in which case the real question would concern the accuracy of Mumford's memory. See Miller, *Lewis Mumford*, 442–43. Novak has a more balanced view: see his introduction to the collected letters, 21–22. Also note that Mumford and Murray had actually known each other since August 1928, when Mumford reached out to Murray to ask about some Melville materials.

32. Mumford, *Green Memories*, 5, 4.

33. Ibid., 329–30.

34. Ibid., 316.

35. Letters of November 16, 1947, Hanover, N.H., and August 12, 1947, Amenia, in Novak, *"In Old Friendship,"* 269–70, 262.

36. Mumford, "Personalia," June 9, 1944, Mumford Papers, Box 192, Folder 8239.

37. Mumford, *My Works and Days*, 403. I've used the quotation exactly as it appears in *My Works and Days*, though it should be noted that for the sake of that publication Mumford made a couple of slight revisions to the original text, for which see his letter of November 16, 1947, Hanover, N.H., in Novak, *"In Old Friendship,"* 269.

38. Mumford to Murray, July 28, 1947, Amenia, in Novak, *"In Old Friendship,"* 259.

39. See Mumford, *My Works and Days*, 404.

40. Letters of November 16, 1947, Hanover, N.H., and August 12, 1947, Amenia, in Novak, *"In Old Friendship,"* 271, 263.

Chapter 28. The Warmth and Chill of Wedded Life and Death (1876–91)

1. See Brian Higgins and Hershel Parker, eds., *Herman Melville: The Contemporary Reviews* (New York: Cambridge University Press, 1995), 536–37 (Springfield *Republican*, July 18, 1876).

2. *Contemporary Reviews*, 538 (*Saturday Review*, August 26, 1876).

3. Lizzie quoted in Hershel Parker, *Herman Melville: A Biography, Volume 2, 1851–1891* (Baltimore: Johns Hopkins University Press, 2002), 820.

4. Letter to John C. Hoadley, March 31, 1877, New York, in *The Writings of Herman Melville*, vol. 14, *Correspondence*, edited by Lynn Horth (Evanston and Chicago: Northwestern University Press and the Newberry Library, 1993), 452–54 (hereafter *Correspondence*).

5. Herman Melville, *Moby-Dick* (New York: Norton, 1967; orig. 1851), 143.

6. *Correspondence*, 452.

7. Ibid., 453–54. Technically there were only two "Antonines"—Titus Antoninus Pius and Marcus Aurelius Antoninus—but Gibbon included the reigns of Nerva, Trajan, and Hadrian in what he called "The Age of the Antonines." Melville explicitly referred his brother-in-law to Gibbon, suggesting that he "turn to '*Antonine*' &c" in the index of *The Decline and Fall of the Roman Empire* (*Correspondence*, 452). But in fact one could simply read the first three chapters, which argue that "The Age of the Antonines" was pretty clearly "the period in the history of the world during which the condition of the human race was most happy and prosperous." Gibbon was not known for understatement. See Edward Gibbon, *The Decline and Fall of the Roman Empire*, vol. 1 (New York: Knopf, 1993; orig. 1776), 90.

8. Gibbon, *Decline and Fall of the Roman Empire*, 90.

9. *Correspondence*, 454.

10. See ibid., 450–51, for Melville's comment on Hayes.

11. See *Contemporary Reviews*, 545 (New York *Mail and Express*, November 20, 1888).

12. Lewis Mumford, *Herman Melville* (New York: Harcourt, Brace, 1929), 326, 331.

13. Eleanor Melville Thomas Metcalf, "Recollections," in Merton M. Sealts Jr., *The Early Lives of Melville: Nineteenth-Century Biographical Sketches and Their Authors* (Madison: University of Wisconsin Press, 1974), 179.

14. Frances Cuthbert Thomas Osborne, "Recollections," in Sealts, *Early Lives of Melville*, 180.

15. Lewis Mumford, *Sketches from Life: The Autobiography of Lewis Mumford—The Early Years* (Boston: Beacon Press, 1983; orig. 1982), 456.

16. Eleanor Melville Thomas Metcalf, in Sealts, *Early Lives of Melville*, 178.

17. Frances Cuthbert Thomas Osborne, in Sealts, *Early Lives of Melville*, 182–83.

18. Mumford, *Herman Melville*, 331.

19. Elizabeth Melville to Kate Gansevoort, July 29, 1885, New York, Gansevoort-Lansing Collection, New York Public Library, Box 311 (Melville Family Papers), Folder 3. Further references to this archival collection will be shortened to G-L Collection.

20. Elizabeth Melville to Kate Gansevoort, January 10, 1886, New York, G-L Collection, Box 311, Folder 3.

21. Frances Cuthbert Thomas Osborne, in Sealts, *Early Lives of Melville*, 183–84.

22. Oscar Wegelin, "Herman Melville as I Recall Him," in Steven Olsen-Smith, *Melville in His Own Time: A Biographical Chronicle of His Life, Drawn from Recollections, Interviews, and Memoirs by Family, Friends, and Associates* (Iowa City: University of Iowa Press, 2015), 150.

Wegelin was by no means the only person to report that Melville did not live up to his reputation as a misanthrope. Joseph Smith, of Pittsfield, used very similar language in describing his impression of Melville's last visit to the Berkshires, in 1885: "Mr. Melville bore nothing of the appearance of a man disappointed in life, but rather had an air of perfect contentment." See Joseph Edward Adams Smith, "Herman Melville," in Sealts, *Early Lives of Melville*, 139.

23. Herman Melville, *Poems*, vol. 16 of *The Works of Herman Melville* (London: Constable, 1924), 197–204.

24. Ibid., 224–31.

25. Ibid., 232–33.

26. Ibid., 243–44.

27. Ibid., 284, 270.

28. Ibid., 361.

29. *The Philosophy of Disenchantment* was an important 1885 book on Pessimism by Edgar Saltus; early in that same year, an admirer of Melville's (James Billson) sent him the volume *The City of Dreadful Night and Other Poems*, by James Thomson. See William B. Dillingham, *Melville and His Circle: The Last Years* (Athens: University of Georgia Press, 1996), 32–86.

30. Frances Cuthbert Thomas Osborne, in Sealts, *Early Lives of Melville*, 184.

31. Letter to James Billson of January 22, 1885, New York, in *Correspondence*, 486.

32. Melville, *Poems*, 303–4, 321. The dedication actually says "To Winnefred," but as Raymond Weaver explained (he was the first editor to publish *Weeds and Wildings*), Melville himself had made the annotation "Lizzie" in pencil in the manuscript. In any case, the substance of the dedication could not be addressed to anyone but Melville's wife. Also, as previously noted, Mumford was especially taken with "The American Aloe on Exhibition."

33. Ibid., 304.

34. Mumford, *Herman Melville*, 351. I'm guessing that Mumford was thinking both of Freud's "oceanic feeling" here and of Melville's desire to lie on the grass with Hawthorne and experience the interconnectedness of life.

35. Ibid., 349–50. Note that Melville's first title for the poem was "Pontoosuc," which is still the local name used for the lake in the twenty-first century. Then he started using "The Lake" as his title. But his final choice was "Pontoosuce," with the final "e," which he seems to have added on his own initiative, perhaps to soften the sound of the name. Both Mumford and Robert Penn Warren (who edited a collection of Melville's poems) believed that Melville improved as a poet, technically, as he aged and gained experience. In Melville's final three collections, Penn Warren thought, "he often managed to purge his language of many of the stale poeticisms and the fillers used to patch out meter. Now, at best, he had learned to sustain a rhythmical and syntactical movement through a series of lines with more freedom than had before been possible for him except in his happiest moments." See Robert Penn Warren, ed., *Selected Poems of Herman Melville* (New York: Barnes and Noble, 1998; orig. 1970), 446 (on Pontoosuce) and 50 (on Melville's improvement as a poet).

36. Melville, *Poems*, 431–34. Both this poem and Mumford's gloss on it are perfect embodiments of what I've interpreted as the Arcadian tradition in American culture: see Aaron Sachs, *Arcadian America: The Death and Life of an Environmental Tradition* (New Haven: Yale University Press, 2013).

Chapter 29. Chronometricals and Horologicals (1944–51)

1. Mumford, "Personalia," December 14, 1944, Mumford Papers, Box 192, Folder 8240.

2. Mumford, "Random Notes," August 8, 1945, Mumford Papers, Box 192, Folder 8240.

3. Lewis Mumford, *My Works and Days: A Personal Chronicle* (New York: Harcourt Brace Jovanovich, 1979), 402.

4. Mumford, "Chronology," duplicate typescript, 1982, Sophia Wittenberg Mumford Papers, Box 9, Folder 14.

5. Mumford, *My Works and Days*, 403.

6. Ibid., 404–5.

7. Mumford, "Random Notes," March 29, 1948, Mumford Papers, Box 192, Folder 8241.

8. Sophia and Lewis Mumford to Alison, October 21, 1945, Hanover, N.H., Mumford Papers, Box 86, Folder 6332.

9. Mumford, "Chronology," duplicate typescript, 1982, Sophia Wittenberg Mumford Papers, Box 9, Folder 14.

10. Mumford, "Personalia: 1947," December 29, 1947, Mumford Papers, Box 192, Folder 8241.

11. Mumford, *My Works and Days*, 405.

12. Mumford, "Random Notes," January 21, 1948, Mumford Papers, Box 192, Folder 8241.

13. Mumford, "Chronology," duplicate typescript, 1982, Sophia Wittenberg Mumford Papers, Box 9, Folder 14; Mumford, "Personalia," January 1, 1946, Mumford Papers, Box 192, Folder 8240.

14. Mumford, "Chronology," duplicate typescript, 1982, Sophia Wittenberg Mumford Papers, Box 9, Folder 14.

15. Mumford, "Personalia," January 1, 1949, Mumford Papers, Box 192, Folder 8241.

16. Quotation from "Random Notes," October 3, 1944, Mumford Papers, Box 173, Folder 7936. Also see Mumford, *My Works and Days*, 344–52; "Personalia," December 8, 1945, Mumford Papers, Box 192, Folder 8240; and "Random Notes," April 20, 1950, Mumford Papers, Box 192, Folder 8243.

17. Mumford to Alison, 1945, Mumford Papers, Box 86, Folder 6332.

18. "The negative pole of existence, just as real as the positive one . . . , must be faced and embraced too: an arduous discipline." Lewis Mumford, *The Conduct of Life* (New York: Harcourt, Brace, 1951), 81.

19. Mumford, "Personalia: 1947," December 29, 1947, Mumford Papers, Box 192, Folder 8241.

20. Sophia was still thinking about Lewis's Rorschach test fifteen years later, in 1962: "I find him very difficult to pin down," she wrote, "for every facet of his being seems to be balanced by some other." He was almost impossible to argue with, because, as the test results suggested, "he had no anxiety about himself, his inner man." Sophia Mumford, "Random Notes," April 1, 1962, Mumford Papers, Box 193, Folder 8258.

21. Mumford, *My Works and Days*, 438–39.

22. Donald L. Miller, *Lewis Mumford: A Life* (Pittsburgh: University of Pittsburgh Press, 1989), 431–32.

23. Mumford, *My Works and Days*, 438.

24. See Everett Mendelsohn, "Prophet of Our Discontent: Lewis Mumford Confronts the Bomb," in Thomas P. Hughes and Agatha C. Hughes, eds., *Lewis Mumford: Public Intellectual* (New York: Oxford University Press, 1990), 343–60.

25. Lewis Mumford, *In the Name of Sanity* (Westport, Conn.: Greenwood Press, 1973; orig. 1954), 30, 22; this book is a collection of Mumford's anti-nuclear writings, and both of these quotations come from an article originally published in 1946.

26. On the late-nineteenth-century obsession with Atlantis, see Aaron Sachs, *Arcadian America: The Death and Life of an Environmental Tradition* (New Haven: Yale University Press, 2013), 300–346.

27. Mumford, "Random Notes," August 20, 1947, Mumford Papers, Box 192, Folder 8240.

28. Quoted in Miller, *Lewis Mumford*, 434. On this complicated period in U.S. history, still sometimes mistaken for a time of happy stability, see, for instance: Peter J. Kuznick and James Gilbert, eds., *Rethinking Cold War Culture* (Washington, D.C.: Smithsonian Books, 2010); Elaine Tyler May, *Homeward Bound: American Families in the Cold War Era* (New York: Basic Books, 2008; orig. 1988); Lisle A. Rose, *The Cold War Comes to Main Street: America in 1950* (Lawrence: University Press of Kansas, 1999); Ellen Schrecker, *Many Are the Crimes: McCarthyism in America* (Boston: Little, Brown, 1998); and Stephen J. Whitfield, *The Culture of the Cold War* (Baltimore: Johns Hopkins University Press, 1996; orig. 1991).

29. Mumford, "Random Notes," February 2, 1950, Mumford Papers, Box 192, Folder 8243. For Mumford's take on Emerson, see his introduction to the volume of Emerson's selected works that he published: Lewis Mumford, ed., *Ralph Waldo Emerson: Essays and Journals* (New York: Nelson Doubleday, 1968), 9–30.

30. Mumford, *The Conduct of Life*, 81.

31. Ibid., v.

32. Ralph Waldo Emerson, "Fate," in Stephen E. Whicher, ed., *Selections from Ralph Waldo Emerson* (Boston: Houghton Mifflin, 1960), 352.

33. See, for instance, Paul S. Boyer, *By the Bomb's Early Light: American Thought and Culture at the Dawn of the Atomic Age* (Chapel Hill: University of North Carolina Press, 1994; orig. 1985), for affirmation that the bomb "bisected history" (133). But there's also a strong argument to be made for the ways in which the Cold War represented continuity: see, for instance, Mary L. Dudziak, *War Time: An Idea, Its History, Its Consequences* (New York: Oxford University Press, 2012), esp. 63–94.

34. Mumford, *The Conduct of Life*, 228.

35. Ibid., 165–66.

36. Ibid., 251, 254.

37. Ibid., 254, 253.

38. For instance, Malcolm Cowley, in his review in the *New Republic*, November 19, 1951, 17–18; and Mumford's biographer Donald Miller, *Lewis Mumford*, 446–51.

39. Mumford, *The Conduct of Life*, 254, 152–53, 124.

40. Ibid., 156; this is from the same letter Mumford quotes in *Green Memories* (327), and I've quoted it in chapter 25. "It's hard for men, who live only because they co-operate, to explain things to people who live only as semi-isolated individuals. A front line soldier will almost always *give* you half of his last dollar or one of his last two cigarettes. An American civilian finds it hard to lend you half of his surplus."

41. Mumford, *The Conduct of Life*, 141, 79.

42. Ibid., 16.

43. Herman Melville, *Moby-Dick* (New York: Norton, 1967; orig. 1851), 399.

44. Mumford, *The Conduct of Life*, 56, 251.

45. Ibid., 290.

Chapter 30. The Life-Buoy (1891; 1924–29)

1. Herman Melville, "Billy Budd, Sailor (An Inside Narrative)," in Warner Berthoff, ed., *Great Short Works of Herman Melville* (New York: Perennial, 2004), 504–5 (hereafter *Great Short Works*).

2. Lewis Mumford, *The Conduct of Life* (New York: Harcourt, Brace, 1951), 263.

3. Herman Melville, *Moby-Dick* (New York: Norton, 1967; orig. 1851), 429–33.

4. See the scholarly introduction to the edition of *Billy Budd, Sailor* published by Harrison Hayford and Merton M. Sealts Jr. (Chicago: University of Chicago Press, 1962), 3–4.

5. Letter to Archibald MacMechan, December 5, 1889, New York, in *The Writings of Herman Melville*, vol. 14, *Correspondence*, edited by Lynn Horth (Evanston and Chicago: Northwestern University Press and the Newberry Library, 1993), 519. Also note Melville's comment in "Billy Budd" (*Great Short Works*, 501): "Truth uncompromisingly told will always have its ragged edges; hence the conclusion of such a narration is apt to be less finished than an architectural finial."

6. See Hayford and Sealts, introduction to *Billy Budd, Sailor*, 1–20, and Hershel Parker, *Herman Melville: A Biography, Volume 2, 1851–1891* (Baltimore: Johns Hopkins University Press, 2002), 883–85.

7. Hayford and Sealts, introduction to *Billy Budd, Sailor*, 1–12, and Parker, *Herman Melville, Vol. 2*, 880–902.

8. Joseph Edward Adams Smith, "Herman Melville," in Merton M. Sealts, Jr., *The Early Lives of Melville: Nineteenth-Century Biographical Sketches and Their Authors* (Madison: University of Wisconsin Press, 1974), 148.

9. See Hershel Parker, *Reading Billy Budd* (Evanston: Northwestern University Press, 1990), 42–48, and Parker, *Herman Melville, Vol. 2*, 887–88.

10. Eleanor Melville Metcalf, *Herman Melville: Cycle and Epicycle* (Cambridge, Mass.: Harvard University Press, 1953), 288–89, 292–94.

11. Melville, *Moby-Dick*, 187, 410–11, 464, 468, 470. Ishmael's survival is explained in a one-page epilogue, which Melville's chowder-headed British publisher excised—leading to reviews in England that condemned the entire text as a logical fallacy, since the story's narrator seemed to have died in the final scene. Melville could count many publishing frustrations in his career, but this was probably the one that left him the most bitter, since he thought of *Moby-Dick* as his masterwork. See Parker, *Herman Melville, Vol. 2*, 17–30, 99–106.

12. *Great Short Works*, 494–95.

13. Melville, *Moby-Dick*, 397, 53, 271.

14. *Great Short Works*, 439, 434, 433, 448, 459, 476–78, 485, 502, 497, 500. Melville originally called Vere's ship the *Indomitable* but changed its name to the more ominous and political *Bellipotent*. See Hayford and Sealts, introduction to *Billy Budd, Sailor*, 5–8.

15. Melville, *Moby-Dick*, 17–18, 31–32, 51, 43, 20–21.

16. The volume put out by Hayford and Sealts is absolutely crucial for any study of *Billy Budd*. But also see Parker, *Reading Billy Budd*; Parker, *Herman Melville, Vol. 2*, 886–88; Paul Hurh, "*Billy Budd*: Pessimism for Post-Critique," in Cody Marrs, ed., *The New Melville Studies* (New York: Cambridge University Press, 2019), 151–68; William V. Spanos, *The Exceptionalist State and the State of Exception: Herman Melville's Billy Budd* (Baltimore: Johns Hopkins University Press, 2011); and William T. Stafford, ed., *Melville's Billy Budd and the Critics* (Belmont, Calif.: Wadsworth, 1961).

17. Brian Higgins and Hershel Parker, eds., *Herman Melville: The Contemporary Reviews* (New York: Cambridge University Press, 1995), 550 (*Times Literary Supplement*, July 10, 1924).

18. *Great Short Works*, 503.

19. Ibid., 467. Also note Eve Kosofsky Sedgwick, *Epistemology of the Closet* (Berkeley: University of California Press, 1990), 91–130.

20. *Great Short Works*, 464.

21. See Weaver's introduction to the 1928 edition, which was the first American edition of the story (Weaver's 1924 version was British); part of the 1928 introduction is reprinted in Stafford, ed., *Melville's Billy Budd and the Critics*, 72, from which I've drawn this quotation. Also see Parker, *Reading Billy Budd*, 65, and for Weaver's first impression, see Raymond M. Weaver, *Herman Melville: Mariner and Mystic* (New York: George H. Doran, 1921), 381.

22. Lewis Mumford, *Herman Melville* (New York: Harcourt, Brace, 1929), 356–57. In using the word "incongruous" here, Mumford thought that he was directly echoing a note that Melville had made in the original "Billy Budd" manuscript (and later crossed out). Mumford had been led to this belief by Weaver's transcription of the note—which turns out not to have been entirely reliable. Weaver read it as "Here ends a story not unwarranted by what happens in this incongruous world of ours—innocence and infirmity, spiritual depravity and fair respite." More thorough examination of the manuscript has offered a couple of corrections, though the word Weaver interpreted as "incongruous" has never received a "satisfactory reading," according to Hayford and Sealts (plate VIII). The currently accepted transcription is: "Here ends a story not unwarranted by what sometimes happens in this [one undeciphered word] world of ours— Innocence and infamy, spiritual depravity and fair repute" (Hayford and Sealts, introduction to *Billy Budd, Sailor*, 8); also see Parker, *Reading Billy Budd*, 66–67.

23. Herman Melville, *White-Jacket; or, The World in a Man-of-War* (Evanston and Chicago: Northwestern University Press and the Newberry Library, 1970; orig. 1850), 14–15.

24. *Great Short Works*, 497, 500.

Chapter 31. Man's Role in Changing the Face of the Earth (1951–62)

1. Lewis Mumford, *The Conduct of Life* (New York: Harcourt, Brace, 1951), 286.

2. Mumford, "Random Notes," December 22, 1953, Mumford Papers, Box 173, Folder 7941.

3. Quoted in Donald L. Miller, *Lewis Mumford: A Life* (Pittsburgh: University of Pittsburgh Press, 1989), 454.

4. Mumford to Henry Murray, January 3, 1953, Amenia, in Frank G. Novak Jr., ed., "*In Old Friendship*": *The Correspondence of Lewis Mumford and Henry A. Murray, 1928–1981* (Syracuse: Syracuse University Press, 2007), 317–18.

5. See Miller, *Lewis Mumford*, 434, and Mumford's letter to Van Wyck Brooks of July 17, 1952, Amenia, in Robert E. Spiller, ed., *The Van Wyck Brooks Lewis Mumford Letters: The Record of a Literary Friendship, 1921–1963* (New York: E. P. Dutton, 1970), 378.

6. Letter to Frederic J. Osborn of February 22, 1953, Amenia, in Michael Hughes, ed., *The Letters of Lewis Mumford and Frederic J. Osborn: A Transatlantic Dialogue, 1938–70* (New York: Praeger, 1972), 210.

7. Mumford, "Personalia," January 2, 1952, Mumford Papers, Box 192, Folder 8243.

8. Letter to Van Wyck Brooks of June 7, 1953, Paris, in Spiller, *Van Wyck Brooks Lewis Mumford Letters*, 385.

9. Letter of August 7, 1954, Amenia, in Novak, *"In Old Friendship, "* 321.

10. See, for instance, Laura J. Martin, "Proving Grounds: Ecological Fieldwork in the Pacific and the Materialization of Ecosystems," *Environmental History* 23 (July 2018): 567–92.

11. Lewis Mumford, "Anticipations and Social Consequences of Atomic Energy," *Proceedings of the American Philosophical Society* 98 (April 1954): 151 (read before the society on November 12, 1953).

12. Sophia Mumford, "Personalia," November 1, 1955, Mumford Papers, Box 193, Folder 8258.

13. Quoted in Miller, *Lewis Mumford*, 455.

14. Lewis Mumford, "Prospect," in William L. Thomas Jr., ed., *Man's Role in Changing the Face of the Earth* (Chicago: University of Chicago Press, 1956), 1146–47. On the symposium, and on the guiding influence of one of the other key organizers, the geographer Carl Sauer, see, for instance, Robert M. Wilson, "Retrospective Review of *Man's Role in Changing the Face of the Earth*," *Environmental History* 10 (July 2005): 564–66; David Lowenthal, *George Perkins Marsh: Prophet of Conservation* (Seattle: University of Washington Press, 2000), 409–12; Michael Williams, "Sauer and 'Man's Role in Changing the Face of the Earth,'" *Geographical Review* 77 (April 1987): 218–31. On environmental thinking in the 1950s, see, for instance, Michael G. Barbour, "Ecological Fragmentation in the Fifties," in William Cronon, ed., *Uncommon Ground: Toward Reinventing Nature* (New York: Norton, 1995), 233–55.

15. Herman Melville, *Moby-Dick* (New York: Norton, 1967; orig. 1851), 161, 155.

16. Mumford, "Prospect," 1152.

17. Ibid.

18. Lewis Mumford, *The Transformations of Man* (New York: Harper & Brothers, 1956), 5–6, 9, 11, 185, 195. Mumford started working through these ideas while writing *The Conduct of Life*, and many of them are also to be found in the early 1950s lectures published as: Mumford, "From Revolt to Renewal," in Sculley Bradley, ed., *The Arts in Renewal* (Philadelphia: University of Pennsylvania Press, 1951), 1–31, and Mumford, *Art and Technics* (New York: Columbia University Press, 2000; orig. 1952).

In invoking "One World culture," Mumford was referring to Wendell Willkie's best-selling book, *One World*: see Samuel Zipp, *The Idealist: Wendell Willkie's Wartime Quest to Build One World* (Cambridge, Mass.: Harvard University Press, 2020).

19. Quoted in Miller, *Lewis Mumford*, 457.

20. "Bartleby, the Scrivener," in Warner Berthoff, ed., *Great Short Works of Herman Melville* (New York: Perennial, 2004), 73–74.

21. Melville, *Moby-Dick*, 268–69.

22. See, for instance, Peter J. Kuznick and James Gilbert, eds., *Rethinking Cold War Culture* (Washington, D.C.: Smithsonian Books, 2010); Elaine Tyler May, *Homeward Bound: American Families in the Cold War Era* (New York: Basic Books, 2008; orig. 1988); and Stephen J. Whitfield, *The Culture of the Cold War* (Baltimore: Johns Hopkins University Press, 1996; orig. 1991).

23. Sophia Mumford, "Random Notes," April 1, 1962, Mumford Papers, Box 193, Folder 8258; also see Miller, *Lewis Mumford*, 459–63.

24. Donald Miller called *The City in History* Mumford's "masterwork" (Miller, *Lewis Mumford*, 463). It's also worth noting that Mumford had started tweaking his perspective on urbanism back in the 1940s, especially in his wartime volume, *City Development: Studies in Disintegration and Renewal* (New York: Harcourt, Brace, 1945). This collection of essays resonated especially well with the British, after what they had endured during the Blitz, and its publication spurred Mumford's friend Frederic J. Osborn to invite Mumford to England for the summer of 1946, where he received an award and consulted with government planners about their new Garden City initiative.

25. Lewis Mumford, *The City in History: Its Origins, Its Transformations, and Its Prospects* (San Diego: Harcourt Brace, 1989; orig. 1961), xi, 39, 42.

26. Ibid., 510, 573. And see James G. Mellon, "Visions of the Livable City: Reflections on the Jacobs-Mumford Debate," *Ethics, Place, and Environment* 12 (March 2009): 35–48. On Jacobs, Carson, and Friedan, see Rebecca Solnit, "Other Daughters, Other American Revolutions," in Solnit, *Storming the Gates of Paradise: Landscapes for Politics* (Berkeley: University of California Press, 2007), 297–303.

27. Mumford, *The City in History*, 576.

Chapter 32. Revival (1919–62)

1. On the Melville Revival, see Aronoff, "The Melville Revival"; Sanford E. Marovitz, "The Melville Revival," in Wyn Kelley, ed., *A Companion to Herman Melville* (Malden, Mass.: Blackwell, 2006), 515–31; and Clare Spark, *Hunting Captain Ahab: Psychological Warfare and the Melville Revival* (Kent, Ohio: Kent State University Press, 2001).

2. Hershel Parker, ed., *The Recognition of Herman Melville: Selected Criticism since 1846* (Ann Arbor: University of Michigan Press, 1967), vii.

3. Carl Van Doren, "Contemporaries of Cooper," reprinted in Parker, ed., *Recognition*, 154.

4. Weaver quoted in Parker, ed., *Recognition*, vii–viii.

5. Raymond M. Weaver, *Herman Melville: Mariner and Mystic* (New York: George H. Doran, 1921), 331–2.

6. Woolf didn't like Melville as much she liked Thoreau, whose centenary she had marked just two years earlier and who seemed to her the more disciplined and constructive thinker: he "defined his own position to the world not only with unflinching honesty, but with a glow of rapture at his heart." See Virginia Woolf, *Books and Portraits: Some Further Selections from the Literary and Biographical Writings of Virginia Woolf*, ed. Mary Lyon (New York: Harcourt Brace Jovanovich, 1977), 72–89, for the essays on Thoreau, Brooke, and Melville, in 1917, 1918, and 1919. Quotations from 82, 76, 84, and 81. Also see Sean Brawley and Chris Dixon, *The South Seas: A Reception History from Daniel Defoe to Dorothy Lamour* (Lanham, Md.: Lexington Books, 2015), esp. chapter 8, "The Great War and the Lost Generation," 115–33.

7. See, for instance, Charles King, *Gods of the Upper Air: How a Circle of Renegade Anthropologists Reinvented Race, Sex, and Gender in the Twentieth Century* (New York: Doubleday, 2019).

8. It was actually published in September 1919, but it stayed popular for a long time: Frederick O'Brien, *White Shadows in the South Seas* (New York: The Century, 1919), quotations from 123. Also see Brawley and Dixon, *The South Seas*, 119–20. The best-selling work of nonfiction in 1920 was H. G. Wells's *The Outline of History*, an ambitious, Mumfordian chronicle encompassing all of "Life and Mankind," as one of the book's subtitles put it. Unsurprisingly, Mumford identified Wells as one of his "earliest patron saints": see Lewis Mumford, *My Works and Days: A Personal Chronicle* (New York: Harcourt Brace Jovanovich, 1979), 10.

9. Note this theme in D. H. Lawrence's chapter on *Moby-Dick* in his *Studies in Classic American Literature* (New York: Viking, 1923), 145–61.

10. On the revival of the KKK, see Linda Gordon, *The Second Coming of the KKK: The Ku Klux Klan of the 1920s and the American Political Tradition* (New York: Liveright, 2017), and on the general divides of the 1920s, see David J. Goldberg, *Discontented America: The United States in the 1920s* (Baltimore: Johns Hopkins University Press, 1999).

11. Margaret Mead, *Coming of Age in Samoa* (New York: Perennial, 2001; orig. 1928), 160.

12. Lewis Mumford, *The Golden Day: A Study in American Literature and Culture* (Boston: Beacon Press, 1957; orig. 1926), 73.

13. Mumford, notes for a lecture on Melville at Smith College, 1930, Mumford Papers, Box 182, Folder 8070.

14. On modernist literature, art, and culture, see, for instance: Janis P. Stout, *Cather among the Moderns* (Tuscaloosa: University of Alabama Press, 2019); Eric Aronoff, *Composing Cultures: Modernism, American Literary Studies, and the Problem of Culture* (Charlottesville: University of Virginia Press, 2013); Paul V. Murphy, *The New Era: American Thought and Culture in the 1920s* (Lanham, Md.: Rowman and Littlefield, 2012), esp. 73–108; Robert M. Crunden, *Body and Soul: The Making of American Modernism* (New York: Basic, 2000); Christine Stansell, *American Moderns: Bohemian New York and the Creation of a New Century* (New York: Henry Holt, 2000); and Roderick Nash, *The Nervous Generation: American Thought, 1917–1930* (Chicago: Rand McNally, 1970), esp. 90–103.

15. Lewis Mumford, *Findings and Keepings: Analects for an Autobiography* (New York: Harcourt Brace Jovanovich, 1975), 89.

16. Lawrence, *Studies in Classic American Literature*, 159; William Faulkner, "Confessions," *Chicago Daily Tribune*, July 16, 1927, 12; E. M. Forster, *Aspects of the Novel* (New York: Harcourt, Brace, 1927), 203; also see David M. Ball, "Modernism," in Kevin J. Hayes, ed., *Herman Melville in Context* (New York: Cambridge University Press, 2018), 307–16.

17. Herman Melville, *Moby-Dick* (New York: Norton, 1967; orig. 1851), 18; Ralph Ellison, *Invisible Man* (New York: Vintage, 1982; orig. 1952), 1, 6–12, 69–95. On Ellison and Mumford, see Jennifer L. Lieberman, *Power Lines: Electricity in American Life and Letters, 1882–1952* (Cambridge, Mass.: MIT Press, 2017), 167–209, and Ball, "Modernism," 313–14.

18. See Aronoff, "The Melville Revival"; Ball, "Modernism"; and Marovitz, "The Melville Revival."

19. Van Doren's article appears in a publication of the Literary Guild of America called *Wings* 3, no. 3 (March 1929): 4: "Why the Editorial Board Selected *Herman Melville*." I read a copy

in the Melville Collection, Box 2, Folder 8, at the Berkshire County Historical Society at Arrowhead.

20. Lewis Mumford, *Herman Melville* (New York: Harcourt, Brace, 1929), 346.

21. Ibid., 281, 208, 238, 252.

22. Ibid., 292, 319, 295.

23. Ibid., 193.

24. See, for instance, Marovitz, "The Melville Revival"; Spark, *Hunting Captain Ahab*; Alfred J. Drake, Rick Armstrong, and Shep Steiner, eds., *The New Criticism: Formalist Literary Theory in America* (Newcastle upon Tyne: Cambridge Scholars Publishing, 2013); and Mark Jancovich, *The Cultural Politics of the New Criticism* (New York: Cambridge University Press, 1993).

25. Letters to Henry Murray of August 12, 1947, Amenia, and August 14, 1928, Amenia, in Frank G. Novak Jr., ed., *"In Old Friendship": The Correspondence of Lewis Mumford and Henry A. Murray, 1928–1981* (Syracuse: Syracuse University Press, 2007), 263, 30–31. The current dean of Melville biographers, Hershel Parker, knew Murray fairly well and said that "the brilliant, covetous, manipulative, generous, secretive psychologist Henry Murray liked to hoard Melville documents, and he lived long enough to hoard some of them for more than half a century." See Hershel Parker, *Melville Biography: An Inside Narrative* (Evanston: Northwestern University Press, 2012), 143.

26. Mumford to Murray, February 5, 1952, New York; Murray to Mumford, 1939; and Mumford to Murray, October 20, 1944, Amenia, all in Novak, *"In Old Friendship,"* 310, 149, 209.

27. Mumford to Murray, February 25, 1952, New York, in Novak, *"In Old Friendship,"* 312.

28. Melville, *Moby-Dick*, 404.

29. Henry A. Murray, "In Nomine Diaboli," reprinted in Richard Chase, ed., *Melville: A Collection of Critical Essays* (Englewood Cliffs, N.J.: Prentice-Hall, 1962), 66, 68, 70. The essay originally appeared in December 1951, in the *New England Quarterly*—the same journal in which Murray published his review of Mumford's Melville biography in July 1929, in the second year of the journal's existence (it is still alive today).

30. Mumford to Murray, February 25, 1952, New York, in Novak, *"In Old Friendship,"* 313.

31. Lewis Mumford, *My Works and Days: A Personal Chronicle* (New York: Harcourt Brace Jovanovich, 1979), 291; also note Mumford's letter to Murray of June 22, 1947, Amenia, in Novak, *"In Old Friendship,"* 257.

32. Mumford, "Preface to the New Edition," 1962 reprinting of *Herman Melville* (New York: Harcourt, Brace, and World), xii, ix.

33. Quoted in Lieberman, *Power Lines*, 173.

34. Lewis Mumford, *Herman Melville* (New York: Harcourt, Brace, 1929), 5; H. A. Murray Jr., review of Lewis Mumford, *Herman Melville*, *New England Quarterly* 2 (July 1929): 523–26. Murray was hoping for more of a "sojourn in darkness and chaos" (526).

35. Mumford to Murray, July 28, 1947, Amenia, in Novak, *"In Old Friendship,"* 259.

36. Mumford, "Preface to the New Edition," xi–xiii.

37. Mumford, *My Works and Days*, 292–93, but note that Mumford changed "analysis" to "dissection": see the letter of June 29, 1949, Amenia, in Novak, *"In Old Friendship,"* 288. And see Melville, "Hawthorne and His Mosses," in *The Writings of Herman Melville*, vol. 9, *The Piazza*

Tales and Other Prose Pieces, 1839–1860, edited by Harrison Hayford et al. (Evanston and Chicago: Northwestern University Press and the Newberry Library, 1987), 249.

38. Mumford, *My Works and Days*, 296–97.

Chapter 33. Call Me Jonah (1962–82)

1. Lewis Mumford, *Technics and Human Development: The Myth of the Machine, Volume One* (New York: Harcourt Brace Jovanovich, 1967), 13.

2. Mumford, "Personalia," February 27, 1967, Amenia, Mumford Papers, Box 173, Folder 7933.

3. Lewis Mumford, *My Works and Days: A Personal Chronicle* (New York: Harcourt Brace Jovanovich, 1979), 527–31. As Geoffrey Sanborn has commented, in reference to reading Melville: "No one knows what is coming next or how to bear it. Everyone needs a sense of the value of what has come before." Geoffrey Sanborn, *The Value of Herman Melville* (New York: Cambridge University Press, 2018), 8.

4. See especially Michael Zuckerman, "Faith, Hope, Not Much Charity: The Optimistic Epistemology of Lewis Mumford," in Thomas P. Hughes and Agatha C. Hughes, eds., *Lewis Mumford: Public Intellectual* (New York: Oxford University Press, 1990), 361–76.

5. Mumford, *My Works and Days*, 493.

6. Ibid., 408–12.

7. Ibid., 408.

8. Lewis Mumford, "The Case against 'Modern Architecture,'" in Jeanne M. Davern, ed., *Lewis Mumford: Architecture as a Home for Man: Essays for Architectural Record* (New York: Architectural Record Books, 1975), 179–87.

9. Mumford, *My Works and Days*, 461–62.

10. Ibid., 462–67.

11. Lewis Mumford, "Vietnam—Before and After" (extracts from a speech delivered by Lewis Mumford at the Ethical Culture Society, May 3, 1968), Mumford Papers, Box 173, Folder 7933.

12. Here I'm in pretty direct disagreement with Gale H. Carrithers Jr., who understands the later Mumford as more confident, astute, and impactful; see his intriguing book, *Mumford, Tate, Eiseley: Watchers in the Night* (Baton Rouge: Louisiana State University, Press, 1991), esp. 1–106.

13. Lewis Mumford, *The Pentagon of Power: The Myth of the Machine, Volume Two* (New York: Harcourt Brace Jovanovich, 1970), 300, 376.

14. Lewis Mumford, *Findings and Keepings: Analects for an Autobiography* (New York: Harcourt Brace Jovanovich, 1975), 369–89.

15. Mumford, "Random Notes," Amenia, August 31, 1963, Mumford Papers, Box 173, Folder 7933.

16. I would have had no knowledge of Mumford's relationship with Jocelyn Brodie were it not for the generosity of Ann Braude, who told me about it in the fall of 2013 and to whom I am deeply grateful. Braude knew Brodie and rescued her personal papers after Brodie's death in 2009, depositing many of them at the Arthur and Elizabeth Schlesinger Library on the History of Women in America, part of the Radcliffe Institute, at Harvard University. Interested readers should look for Braude's forthcoming book on the relationship between Brodie and Mumford.

I've drawn my account of the relationship from the Papers of Jocelyn Brodie, 1967–1984, available at the Schlesinger Library. It's a collection of two boxes, holding about seven hundred letters, mostly written by Lewis and Jocelyn, plus a few by Sophia. The letters are organized in folders marked with the correspondents' names and date ranges. Further references to this archival collection will be shortened to Brodie Papers.

The quotation here comes from Brodie's first letter to Mumford, dated March 8, 1967, West Townshend, Vt.

17. Letter of December 29, 1966 [Cambridge], in Frank G. Novak Jr., ed., *"In Old Friendship": The Correspondence of Lewis Mumford and Henry A. Murray, 1928–1981* (Syracuse: Syracuse University Press, 2007), 397.

18. Brodie Papers, JB to LM, April 28, 1969, West Townshend, Vt.; LM to JB, February 4, 1973; LM to JB, September 21, 1971, Amenia; LM to JB, October 23, 1969. Also note Lewis Mumford, ed., *Ralph Waldo Emerson: Essays and Journals* (New York: Nelson Doubleday, 1968).

19. Brodie Papers, LM to JB, December 18, 1971, Amenia; Sophia Mumford to JB, July 18, 1974; LM to JB, August 5, 1972, Amenia; LM to JB, November 3, 1972. On feminism and sexuality in the early 1970s, see, for instance, Lawrence R. Samuel, *Sexidemic: A Cultural History of Sex in America* (Lanham, Md.: Rowman and Littlefield, 2013), 47–106, and John D'Emilio and Estelle B. Freedman, *Intimate Matters: A History of Sexuality in America*, 3rd ed. (Chicago: University of Chicago Press, 2012), 301–18.

20. Brodie Papers, JB to LM, October 15, 1973; LM to JB, October 18, 1973, Amenia; JB to LM, October 19, 1973, "A Birthday Greeting"; LM to JB, October 19, 1973, Amenia; JB to LM, October 23, 1973; LM to JB, October 23, 1973, Amenia.

21. Brodie Papers, Sophia Mumford to JB, July 10, 1974; Sophia Mumford to JB, March 4, 1975, Cambridge, MA; JB to LM, March 4, 1976.

22. Brodie Papers, LM to JB, March 7, 1976, Amenia; JB to LM, February 21, 1976; LM to JB, March 15, 1976, Amenia; JB to LM, October 25, 1978, West Townshend, Vt.; JB to LM (unsent?), May 11, 1979.

23. Sophia Mumford, "Random Notes/Personalia," March 10, 1978, Mumford Papers, Box 193, Folder 8260.

24. Brodie Papers, Sophia Mumford to JB, July 18, 1974.

25. Herman Melville, *Moby-Dick* (New York: Norton, 1967; orig. 1851), 304.

26. Mumford, *My Works and Days*, 477, 468–69.

27. Ibid., 531.

28. Melville, *Moby-Dick*, 71.

Chapter 34. Lizzie (1891–1906)

1. Hershel Parker, *Herman Melville: A Biography, Volume 2, 1851–1891* (Baltimore: Johns Hopkins University Press, 2002), 921–92 (quotation on 921).

2. Oliver G. Hillard, quoted in Steven Olsen-Smith, *Melville in His Own Time: A Biographical Chronicle of His Life, Drawn from Recollections, Interviews, and Memoirs by Family, Friends, and Associates* (Iowa City: University of Iowa Press, 2015), 183.

3. Joseph Edward Adams Smith, "Herman Melville," in Merton M. Sealts Jr., *The Early Lives of Melville: Nineteenth-Century Biographical Sketches and Their Authors* (Madison: University of Wisconsin Press, 1974), 139.

4. Quoted in Parker, *Herman Melville, Vol. 2*, 820.

5. Quoted in ibid., 921.

6. Arthur Stedman, "Introduction to the 1892 Edition of *Typee*," in Sealts, *Early Lives of Melville*, 163, 166.

7. See Elizabeth Shaw Melville, "Memoranda," in Sealts, *Early Lives of Melville*, 171–72.

8. Elizabeth Shaw Melville to Kate Gansevoort, April 14, 1897, New York, G-L Collection, Box 311, Folder 4.

9. Quoted in Sanford E. Marovitz, "The Melville Revival," in Wyn Kelley, ed., *A Companion to Herman Melville* (Malden, Mass.: Blackwell, 2006), 516.

10. See Aronoff, "The Melville Revival," 297.

11. See Sealts, *Early Lives of Melville*, 29–41, quotations on 39.

12. Elizabeth Shaw Melville to Kate Gansevoort, September 5, 1897, Pittsfield, Mass., G-L Collection, Box 311, Folder 4.

13. Quoted in Sealts, *Early Lives of Melville*, 40, 146.

14. Joseph Smith, "Herman Melville," in Sealts, *Early Lives of Melville*, 140.

15. Elizabeth Shaw Melville, "Memoranda," in Sealts, *Early Lives of Melville*, 167–77.

16. Frances Cuthbert Thomas Osborne, "Recollections," in Sealts, *Early Lives of Melville*, 183–84. Note that Frances remembered the bust being donated to the public library in South Orange, New Jersey, where she grew up, though it is unclear when the donation happened, and as of the 1960s the bust's location was unknown: Sealts, *Early Lives of Melville*, 253.

17. I'm following a long line of Melville scholars in raising questions about the homoeroticism of Melville's writing and about his own sexual inclinations. But see especially Elizabeth Hardwick, *Herman Melville* (New York: Viking, 2000), and Eve Kosofsky Sedgwick, *Epistemology of the Closet* (Berkeley: University of California Press, 1990), 91–130.

18. Herman Melville, *Redburn, His First Voyage; Being the Sailor-boy Confessions and Reminiscences of the Son-of-a-Gentleman, in the Merchant Service* (Evanston and Chicago: Northwestern University Press and the Newberry Library, 1969; orig. 1849), 216, 231, 234, 302, 310.

19. Ibid., 247, 250.

20. Herman Melville, *White-Jacket; or, The World in a Man-of-War* (Evanston and Chicago: Northwestern University Press and the Newberry Library, 1970; orig. 1850), 13–14.

21. Warner Berthoff, ed., *Great Short Works of Herman Melville* (New York: Perennial, 2004), 436–37 (hereafter *Great Short Works*).

22. Herman Melville, *Moby-Dick* (New York: Norton, 1967; orig. 1851), 348, 53, 271; Melville, *Redburn*, 10.

23. Julian Hawthorne, *Nathaniel Hawthorne and His Wife: A Biography* (Boston: Houghton, Mifflin, 1893; orig. 1884).

24. Herman Melville, *Poems*, vol. 16 of *The Works of Herman Melville* (London: Constable, 1924), 267 ("Monody"). Also in *Timoleon*, of course, is the poem "After the Pleasure Party" (discussed in chapter 9), in which the main character is named Urania—a name frequently

plucked by Victorian poets from Plato's *Symposium* to signify idealized homoerotic desire. See, for instance, Wyn Kelley, *Herman Melville: An Introduction* (Oxford: Blackwell, 2008), 168.

25. *Great Short Works*, 438.

26. Elizabeth Shaw Melville to Julian Hawthorne, December 23, 1903, G-L Collection, Box 311, Folder 6. Lizzie was actually talking about a visual portrait, and offered to send a better photograph to him. See the illustration facing p. 32 of Julian Hawthorne, *Hawthorne and His Circle* (New York: Harper and Brothers, 1903).

27. Melville, *Moby-Dick*, 270.

28. Eleanor Melville Metcalf, *Herman Melville: Cycle and Epicycle* (Cambridge, Mass.: Harvard University Press, 1953), 55.

29. Elizabeth Shaw Melville to Kate Gansevoort, April 27, 1900, New York, G-L Collection, Box 311, Folder 5.

30. Frances Cuthbert Thomas Osborne, "Recollections," in Sealts, *Early Lives of Melville*, 180.

31. This theme of resilience earned through engagement with hardship (especially death) in the nineteenth century is central to my book, *Arcadian America: The Death and Life of an Environmental Tradition* (New Haven: Yale University Press, 2013).

32. Quoted in Parker, *Herman Melville, Vol. 2*, 889.

33. Elizabeth Shaw Melville to Kate Gansevoort, January 9, 1872, New York, G-L Collection, Box 311, Folder 1.

34. Elizabeth Shaw Melville to Kate Gansevoort, July 17, 1872, Sailors Snug Harbor, G-L Collection, Box 311, Folder 1 (and see several other letters from Lizzie to Kate between May and July of that year); and HM to Allan Melville, February 20, 1849, Boston, in *The Writings of Herman Melville*, vol. 14, *Correspondence*, edited by Lynn Horth (Evanston and Chicago: Northwestern University Press and the Newberry Library, 1993), 116.

35. Elizabeth Shaw Melville to Kate Gansevoort, November 19, 1899, New York, G-L Collection, Box 311, Folder 4.

36. Melville, *Moby-Dick*, 270–71.

37. Elizabeth Shaw Melville to Kate Gansevoort, July 2, 1873, New York, G-L Collection, Box 311, Folder 1.

38. Elizabeth Shaw Melville, "Memoranda," in Sealts, *Early Lives of Melville*, 174. On the trip to the Berkshires after Malcolm's death, see Parker, *Herman Melville, Vol. 2*, 646–49.

39. Elizabeth Shaw Melville to Kate Gansevoort, January 10, 1886, New York, G-L Collection, Box 311, Folder 3.

40. Melville, *Poems*, 304.

41. Ibid., 295.

42. Elizabeth Shaw Melville to Evert Duyckinck, June 1 and 4 (Pittsfield, Mass.), and June 23 (Arrowhead), 1860, Duyckinck Family Papers, New York Public Library, Box 12, Folder 15.

43. See the discussion in Hershel Parker, *Melville: The Making of the Poet* (Evanston: Northwestern University Press, 2008), esp. 135–43.

Chapter 35. Sophia (1982–97)

1. Sophia Mumford, "LM, Notes on Decline, 1986–90," Sophia Wittenberg Mumford Papers, Box 10, Folder 7.

2. Lewis Mumford, *My Works and Days: A Personal Chronicle* (New York: Harcourt Brace Jovanovich, 1979), 82.

3. Donald L. Miller, *Lewis Mumford: A Life* (Pittsburgh: University of Pittsburgh Press, 1989), 553.

4. Brodie Papers, JB to LM, February 21, 1976.

5. Quoted in Miller, *Lewis Mumford*, 553. Both Lewis and Sophia occasionally felt some regret about her abandonment of her career, though both of them usually repressed such feelings. They spill out just a bit in this passage from *Green Memories*: "Being 'there' was part of Sophy's compact as a parent; it was for the sake of being there that Sophy had dropped all thought of resuming her editorial work once Geddes was born. . . . [She] put motherhood first, by instinct, even though the fashion of the moment was set against it, and even though, being human, she shared some of that fashion and was tormented occasionally by the thought of more public goals and less grubby triumphs than those of keeping a child secure and healthy or a husband serene and concentrated on his work." Lewis Mumford, *Green Memories: The Story of Geddes Mumford* (New York: Harcourt, Brace, 1947), 30.

6. Lewis could never have agreed with such a proposition. There is evidence in his biography of Melville that he did try to see things from Lizzie's perspective, but his writing about her comes across as (unsurprisingly) condescending: see Lewis Mumford, *Herman Melville* (New York: Harcourt, Brace, 1929), 86–90.

7. Quoted in Miller, *Lewis Mumford*, 557.

8. Mumford, "Random Notes/Personalia," February 20, 1980, Mumford Papers, Box 192, Folder 8250.

9. Lewis Mumford, *Sketches from Life: The Autobiography of Lewis Mumford—The Early Years* (Boston: Beacon Press, 1983; orig. 1982), 477, 482.

10. Quoted in Miller, *Lewis Mumford*, 561.

11. These quotations come from blurbs on the back of the paperback edition.

12. Paul Goldberger, "Seduced and Abandoned by N.Y.C.," *New York Times Book Review*, May 16, 1982, 13–14, included in Mumford Papers, Box 191, Folder 8218. Goldberger's opinion is echoed in Paul Forman, "How Lewis Mumford Saw Science, and Art, and Himself," *Historical Studies in the Physical and Biological Sciences* 37, no. 2 (2007): 271–336, esp. 305.

13. Mumford, *Sketches*, 479.

14. Miller, *Lewis Mumford*, vii, xvii; Mumford, *My Works and Days*, 178. I could have chosen a dozen other such comments about academics (but who's counting). For instance: "Up to now I've written nothing, except perhaps *Green Memories*, paradoxically enough, that is likely to be read by anyone except a PhD fifty years from now; and to be read by PhD's is nothing short of a second burial": letter of May 6, 1948, Hanover, N.H., in Michael Hughes, ed., *The Letters of Lewis Mumford and Frederic J. Osborn: A Transatlantic Dialogue, 1938–70* (New York: Praeger, 1972), 161.

15. Letter of August 8, 1979, Cambridge, Mass., in Frank G. Novak Jr., ed., *"In Old Friendship": The Correspondence of Lewis Mumford and Henry A. Murray, 1928–1981* (Syracuse: Syracuse University Press, 2007), 441.

16. See Sophia Wittenberg Mumford Papers, Box 3, Folder 13; also Miller, *Lewis Mumford*, xvii. Miller discusses Mumford's mental decline very briefly at the end of the biography, but not at all in the preface, where he describes gaining Mumford's trust and being granted permission to see all the personal papers. Part of Sophia's anger may have stemmed from the sense that

Miller took advantage of Lewis's decline to gain favors that Lewis probably would not have granted had he been in full possession of his mind.

In 1990, after Lewis's death, Sophia asked the scholar Robert Wojtowicz to become Lewis's literary executor, and he accepted the invitation. He and Sophia became good friends in the last years of her life. See Robert Wojtowicz, ed., *Mumford on Modern Art in the 1930s* (Berkeley: University of California Press, 2007), xi.

17. Sophia Mumford, reactions to Miller's biography of Lewis, notes from October 16, 1989, and March 9, 1992, Sophia Wittenberg Mumford Papers, Box 3, Folder 15. Sophia recorded many different reactions to the book, over the course of several years. Some comments are typed, some handwritten on yellow pads.

18. Mumford, "Random Notes/Personalia," April 2, 1936, Mumford Papers, Box 193, Folder 8256.

19. Sophia Mumford, "LM, Notes on Decline, 1986–90," Sophia Wittenberg Mumford Papers, Box 10, Folder 7.

20. Sophia Mumford, reactions to Miller's biography of Lewis, notes from September 13, 1989, October 17, 1989, and July 25, 1989, Sophia Wittenberg Mumford Papers, Box 3, Folder 15. On Alison and classical music, see the note Lewis jotted down on February 13, 1946, explaining that they had just played Mozart for Alison for the first time (she was about to turn eleven): "she positively wriggled with pleasure and said to Sophy: Oh, I didn't know that anything in the world could be so beautiful." Mumford Papers, Box 192, Folder 8240.

21. Don Miller, undated letter to Sophia Mumford, in response to her letter of July 21, 1989, Sophia Wittenberg Mumford Papers, Box 3, Folder 13.

22. Don Miller to SM, February 6, 1990, Sophia Wittenberg Mumford Papers, Box 3, Folder 13. The letter is typed, and signed "With love and warm wishes." Sophia added her own handwritten gloss sometime in the following month: "Don was doing his best to cover the points he knew I had objected to. If I thought he was truly repentant I would relent. But it strikes me as merely another one of Don's maneuvers to keep on top."

23. Sophia Mumford, reactions to Miller's biography of Lewis, notes from February 19, 1990, and March 9, 1992, Sophia Wittenberg Mumford Papers, Box 3, Folder 15.

24. See the correspondence in Sophia Wittenberg Mumford Papers, Box 3, Folder 13.

25. Martin Weil, "Social Critic Lewis Mumford Is Dead at 94," *Washington Post*, January 28, 1990, https://www.washingtonpost.com/archive/local/1990/01/28/social-critic-lewis-mumford-is-dead-at-94/ba8f2809-17fd-410b-8e34-499baa6e8b7c/; "Lewis Mumford, a Visionary Social Critic, Dies at 94," *New York Times*, January 28, 1990, section 1, 30.

26. "Historian-Philosopher Lewis Mumford Dies at 94," UPI Archives, January 27, 1990, https://www.upi.com/Archives/1990/01/27/Historian-philosopher-Lewis-Mumford-dies-at-94/1645633416400/.

27. See, for instance, Alison's letter of June 1, 1946: "Dear Dad, The last walk we took together was really wonderful, wasn't it? I will always remember it as one of the nicest things we did." Mumford Papers, Box 86, Folder 6333.

28. Herman Melville, *Moby-Dick* (New York: Norton, 1967; orig. 1851), 161.

29. Brodie Papers, LM to JB, June 25, 1973. Lewis told Jocelyn about what had happened, and it was an issue they wrestled with together over the next several months. "The darkness

thickens," Lewis wrote to Jocelyn on June 30, "and a damp drizzle, one of Melville's phrases, penetrates my soul. . . . But this letter has become all too Melvillian and I must stop long enough to recover my sense of humor, without which neither of us could so long have survived." On November 20, Jocelyn wrote to him to tell him what he ought to say to Alison: "'I want you to know that I have only *one* daughter. And no one can ever replace my own child.'" Jocelyn continued: "Why, it's better for her to know 'the worst' about me than to imagine any 'sibling rivalry.' She must be assured that 'Jocelyn is *not* my daughter!'"

30. Sophia Mumford to Alison, September 12, 1980, and Alison Mumford to her parents ("Dear Lewis and Soph"), September 11, 1980, Mumford Papers, Box 86, Folders 6332 and 6333.

31. Mumford, "Random Notes," March 12, 1944, Mumford Papers, Box 192, Folder 8239.

32. Sophia Mumford, note written in pencil in the margins of the undated letter Don Miller sent to her in response to her letter of July 21, 1989, Sophia Wittenberg Mumford Papers, Box 3, Folder 13.

33. Mumford, note to Sophia of May 5, 1976, Mumford Papers, Box 86, Folder 6329.

34. Sophia Mumford, "Random Notes/Personalia," March 21, 1978, Mumford Papers, Box 193, Folder 8260.

35. The interviewer, Karen Christensen, is working on a book partly about Sophia; see her podcast for the interview: https://www.berkshirepublishing.com/2016/06/17/sophia -mumford-talks-about-working-at-the-dial-in-the-1920s/. Also note Karen Christensen, "Jumped-Up Typists: Two Guardians of the Flame," in Juliana Dresvina, ed., *Thanks for Typing: Remembering Forgotten Women in History* (New York: Bloomsbury, 2021), 37–49.

36. Mumford, *My Works and Days*, 502.

Chapter 36. Rediscovery (2019)

1. Lewis Mumford, *Green Memories: The Story of Geddes Mumford* (New York: Harcourt, Brace, 1947), 105; pencil sketch from Monmouth collection.

2. My personal notes from September 20, 2019. The cenotaph I quote is from 1844, so Melville could not have seen it in 1840, but it suggests that the accident of getting snarled in your own whale line was probably not uncommon. On the history of the chapel, see Hershel Parker, *Herman Melville: A Biography, Volume 1, 1819–1851* (Baltimore: Johns Hopkins University Press, 1996), 184–85. Note that it's officially known as the Seamen's Bethel. The text from some of the cenotaphs is actually included in *Moby-Dick*: Herman Melville, *Moby-Dick* (New York: Norton, 1967; orig. 1851), 39–40.

3. Melville, *Moby-Dick*, 39–41.

4. Ibid., 42.

5. Donald Yanella to Nathalia Wright, November 10, 1976, and Nathalia Wright to Lewis Mumford, January 5, 1977, Archive of the Melville Society, New Bedford Whaling Museum, Box 3.

6. Lewis Mumford, *My Works and Days: A Personal Chronicle* (New York: Harcourt Brace Jovanovich, 1979), 289.

7. Letter of July 25, 1944, to Van Wyck Brooks, in Robert E. Spiller, ed., *The Van Wyck Brooks Lewis Mumford Letters: The Record of a Literary Friendship, 1921–1963* (New York: E. P. Dutton, 1970), 254.

8. Lewis Mumford, *Herman Melville* (New York: Harcourt, Brace, 1929), 194.

9. For example: Dipesh Chakrabarty, "The Climate of History: Four Theses," *Critical Inquiry* 35 (Winter 2009): 197–222, and Chakrabarty, "Climate and Capital: On Conjoined Histories," *Critical Inquiry* 41 (Autumn 2014): 1–23.

10. See, for instance, Tracey Skillington, *Climate Justice and Human Rights* (New York: Palgrave Macmillan, 2017); Michael Renner, "Climate Change and Displacements," in Worldwatch Institute, *State of the World 2013: Is Sustainability Still Possible?* (Washington: Island Press, 2013), 343–52; Christian Parenti, *Tropic of Chaos: Climate Change and the New Geography of Violence* (New York: Nation Books, 2011); Robin Mearns and Andrew Norton, eds., *Social Dimensions of Climate Change: Equity and Vulnerability in a Warming World* (Washington, D.C.: World Bank, 2010); and Rafael Reuveny, "Climate Change–Induced Migration and Violent Conflict," *Political Geography* 26 (2007): 656–73.

11. See, for example, Slavoj Žižek, *Living in the End Times* (London: Verso, 2010), 327–36.

12. Lewis Mumford, *Faith for Living* (New York: Harcourt, Brace, 1940), 214.

13. Ralph Waldo Emerson, "Self-Reliance," in Stephen E. Whicher, ed., *Selections from Ralph Waldo Emerson* (Boston: Houghton Mifflin, 1960), 165.

14. Melville, *Moby-Dick*, 406.

15. See, for instance, Anna Lowenhaupt Tsing et al., eds., *Arts of Living on a Damaged Planet: Ghosts and Monsters of the Anthropocene* (Minneapolis: University of Minnesota Press, 2017); Donna Haraway, *Staying with the Trouble: Making Kin in the Chthulucene* (Durham: Duke University Press, 2016); Tsing, *The Mushroom at the End of the World: On the Possibility of Life in Capitalist Ruins* (Princeton: Princeton University Press, 2015); and Oliver Burkeman, *The Antidote: Happiness for People Who Can't Stand Positive Thinking* (New York: Faber and Faber, 2012).

16. Baldwin quoted in Geoffrey Sanborn, *The Value of Herman Melville* (New York: Cambridge University Press, 2018), 121.

17. Herman Melville, *Israel Potter: His Fifty Years of Exile* (New York: Penguin, 2008; orig. 1855), 13.

18. Mumford, *My Works and Days*, 331.

19. Mumford, "Random Notes," August 27, 1975, Mumford Papers, Box 192, Folder 8249.

20. Michael Rothberg aptly describes the traumatized modern person as an "implicated subject," and, in a very clear-headed and careful way, he opens up the question of whether trauma theory could be applied to climate change: see Michael Rothberg, "Preface: Beyond Tancred and Clorinda—Trauma Studies for Implicated Subjects," in Gert Buelens, Sam Durrant, and Robert Eaglestone, eds., *The Future of Trauma Theory: Contemporary Literary and Cultural Criticism* (London: Routledge, 2014), xvi–xvii. Also see Rothberg, "Multidirectional Memory and the Implicated Subject: On Sebald and Kentridge," in Liedeke Plate and Anneke Smelik, eds., *Performing Memory in Art and Popular Culture* (New York: Routledge, 2013), 39–58.

On the psychology of climate change in particular, see, for example, Kari Marie Norgaard, *Living in Denial: Climate Change, Emotions, and Everyday Life* (Cambridge, Mass.: MIT Press, 2011), and Per Espen Stoknes, *What We Think About When We Try Not to Think About Global Warming: Toward a New Psychology of Climate Action* (White River Junction, Vt.: Chelsea Green Publishing, 2015), esp. 3–84.

For a pandemic-inflected take on the significance of a historical perspective to the fight against climate change, see David Roberts, "The Scariest Thing about Global Warming (and COVID-19)," *Vox*, July 7, 2020, https://www.vox.com/energy-and-environment/2020/7/7/21311027/covid-19-climate-change-global-warming-shifting-baselines.

Roberts writes suggestively about how "shifting baselines syndrome" makes it especially hard for modern cultures to have a full appreciation of the tides of time, which in turn means that it is incumbent on "journalism and the arts to pull the lens back and try to recenter a richer historical perspective." Mumford would have approved.

21. I'm using "Boston" as shorthand to mean the Greater Boston area. The play was at the American Repertory Theater in Cambridge, and I grew up in Newton.

22. The show's program includes a "Note" from the Puppet Designer that is quite explicit about the production's environmental values: "We are situated in a society that normalizes, even glamorizes, overconsumption. We are in a climate/capitalist crisis. . . . This production is concerned with the most pressing themes of our time, and it is my sincere hope that the images you see in this production haunt you. The puppetry in Moby-Dick is designed to remind you of your own complicity in the problems we face as a society, especially those connected to our changing climate and environmental justice" (Program, 15). Malloy's *Pequod* also runs into the Great Pacific Garbage Patch.

23. Melville, *Moby-Dick*, 104–5. One of my favorite interpretations of Melville's democratic spirit is C.L.R. James, *Mariners, Renegades, and Castaways: The Story of Herman Melville and the World We Live in* (Detroit: BEWICK/ED, 1978; orig. 1953).

24. Lewis Mumford, *The Conduct of Life* (New York: Harcourt, Brace, 1951), 287.

25. Ibid., 3.

ILLUSTRATION CREDITS

FIGURE 1. Lewis and Geddes Mumford, 1926 or 1927. Photograph. Lewis Mumford Collection, Monmouth University Library, used with permission. The annotation on the back of this photo says that it's 1926 and that Geddes is two years old, but he was born in 1925, so if he was actually two, then the year had to be 1927.

FIGURE 2. Herman Melville, 1860. Photograph by Rodney H. Dewey. Berkshire Athenaeum, Pittsfield, Massachusetts, used with permission.

FIGURE 3. Lewis Mumford, "Self-Portrait (in Navy Costume)," 1918. Pencil on paper, 7 × 8 ¼ in. Lewis Mumford Collection, Monmouth University Library, used with permission.

FIGURE 4. Elizabeth Shaw Melville, c. 1847. Daguerreotype. Berkshire Athenaeum, Pittsfield, Massachusetts, used with permission.

FIGURE 5. Lewis Mumford, "Our House on the Other Side of the Road," October 17, 1944. Color pencil on paper, 6 × 9 in. Lewis Mumford Collection, Monmouth University Library, used with permission.

FIGURE 6. Lewis Mumford, "Mills from Bluff St., Pittsburgh," 1917. Pen and ink on paper, 4 × 6 in. Lewis Mumford Collection, Monmouth University Library, used with permission.

FIGURE 7. Clarence Stein, "Plan of a Typical Lane at Radburn," 1929. Clarence S. Stein Papers, #3600. Division of Rare and Manuscript Collections, Cornell University Library, courtesy of Cornell University, Ithaca, New York.

FIGURE 8. Lewis Mumford, 1940. Photograph. Lewis Mumford Collection, Monmouth University Library, used with permission.

FIGURE 9. Lewis, Sophia, and Geddes Mumford at Stanford, January 1944. Photograph. Lewis Mumford Collection, Monmouth University Library, used with permission.

FIGURE 10. Melville children, c. 1860. Daguerreotype. Berkshire Athenaeum, Pittsfield, Massachusetts, used with permission.

FIGURE 11. Herman Melville, c. 1861. Photograph by Rodney H. Dewey. Berkshire Athenaeum, Pittsfield, Massachusetts, used with permission.

FIGURE 12. Herman Melville, 1868. Copy from tintype. Berkshire Athenaeum, Pittsfield, Massachusetts, used with permission.

FIGURE 13. Lewis Mumford, "Pasture at Foot of Old Mitchell Place," October 1944. Color pencil on paper. Lewis Mumford Collection, Monmouth University Library, used with permission. The marking on the back says, "October 19, 1944, (shortly before news of Geddes's death)," but the news about Geddes came on October 17, so either the date of creation is wrong or the piece was done shortly *after* the news about Geddes arrived.

FIGURE 14. Herman Melville, 1885 or 1886. Photograph by Rockwood. Berkshire Athenaeum, Pittsfield, Massachusetts, used with permission.

FIGURE 15. Lewis Mumford, autumn 1973. Photograph by Nancy Crampton. Lewis Mumford Collection, Monmouth University Library, used with permission.

FIGURE 16. Elizabeth Shaw Melville, 1885. Photograph by Rockwood. Berkshire Athenaeum, Pittsfield, Massachusetts, used with permission.

FIGURE 17. Lewis and Sophia Mumford, September 1971. Photograph by Jill Krementz, in possession of Ann Braude, owned by Shane Brodie, used with permission. Scan courtesy of Ann Braude. Lewis sent this photograph to Jocelyn Brodie, with a note saying that it was taken on his and Sophia's fiftieth anniversary.

FIGURE 18. Lewis Mumford, "New Bedford (with Geddes)," August 27, 1936. Pencil on paper, 4 × 6 in. Lewis Mumford Collection, Monmouth University Library, used with permission.

INDEX

Note: "HM" refers to Herman Melville and "LM" refers to Lewis Mumford. Page numbers in *italic* type indicate illustrations.

Adams, John, 172

affect theory, 372n3

affordable housing, 156, 160, 162, 164

African Americans: in early twentieth century, 32; injustices committed against, 99, 182, 222, 274–75, 319; in *Moby-Dick*, 60; Reconstruction's outcome for, 29. *See also* black Englishmen; race and racism; slavery

Agricola, 85

Ahab (literary character): and death, 77, 279–80, 282; LM's understanding of, 181, 276, 312; as modern figure, 312; persons (actual or fictional) compared to, 6, 84, 92, 130, 246, 248, 253, 276, 311, 349; power sought and wielded by, 76–77, 84, 181, 295–96; single-mindedness of, 276; and the tragedy/darkness in life, 54, 75–76, 94; trauma of, 20, 75, 151, 312; various significances of, 76–77, 311–12

Albany *Evening Journal* (newspaper), 209–10, 213

Alexander, Jeffrey, 375n16

Alien Act (1918), 16

Allen, Ethan, 210

aloe, 4, 39, 261–62, 377n10

ambiguity, 67, 71, 90–91, 101, 108, 274, 278, 285, 288–89, 306, 314, 316–17. *See also* openness; uncertainty

Amenia, New York, 48–49, 51, 103–4, 142, 163, 183–84, 200, 203–4, 219, 225, 240–43, 250, 264, 268, 292, 322–25, 343, 357–58

American Academy of Arts and Letters, 319

American Aloe, 261–62, 377n10

American literature, 3, 41, 144, 302, 309

American Mercury (magazine), 371n1

American Philosophical Society, 293

American Renaissance, 3, 376n5

American Revolution, xvii–xviii, 24, 91–92, 144, 166–68, 170–73, 175–76, 207, 209

American Studies, 376n5

Antinous, 333–34, 425n16

Appalachian Trail, 155

architecture: Bauer and, 68, 162; change and continuity in, 97, 319; HM and, 215, 260; LM and, 3, 33, 65, 104, 119, 138, 299, 319, 323; suited to contemporary needs, 160

Ardeatine Cave memorial, 318–19

Arendt, Hannah, 288

Arvin, Newton, 310

Ascher, Charles S., 161

Ascher, Helen, 5–6

atomic bomb, 243–44, 273, 308, 312. *See also* nuclear testing

Auden, W. H., 288

Augustine, 185

automobiles, 117, 154, 158–59, 300

avant-garde, 136, 358